TACKLING SOCIAL EXCLUSION IN EUROPE

Tackling Social Exclusion in Europe

The contribution of the social economy

Edited by

ROGER SPEAR
Open University, Milton Keynes, United Kingdom

JACQUES DEFOURNY
University of Liege, Belguim

LOUIS FAVREAU
University of Québec, Canada

JEAN-LOUIS LAVILLE
CRIDA-LSCI, CNRS, Paris, France

Routledge
Taylor & Francis Group

LONDON AND NEW YORK

First published 2001 by Ashgate Publishing

Reissued 2018 by Routledge
2 Park Square, Milton Park, Abingdon, Oxon OX14 4RN
711 Third Avenue, New York, NY 10017, USA

Routledge is an imprint of the Taylor & Francis Group, an informa business

Notice:
Product or corporate names may be trademarks or registered trademarks, and are
used only for identification and explanation without intent to infringe.

Publisher's Note
The publisher has gone to great lengths to ensure the quality of this reprint but
points out that some imperfections in the original copies may be apparent.

Disclaimer
The publisher has made every effort to trace copyright holders and welcomes
correspondence from those they have been unable to contact.

A Library of Congress record exists under LC control number: 00111536

ISBN 13: 978-1-138-63514-2 (hbk)
ISBN 13: 978-1-138-63515-9 (pbk)
ISBN 13: 978-1-315-20468-0 (ebk)

Contents

List of Contributors

Karl BIRKHÖLZER is a Doctor, social scientist and member of the scientific staff of the Berlin University of Technology (Institute for Vocational Training, University Education and Further Training Research). Since 1985 he has headed the Interdisciplinary Research Group (IFG) on Local Economy at the same University. Since 1994 he has been Chairman of the European Network for Economic Self-Help and Local Development. He has also participated in numerous transnational projects and publications on local economic strategies, social economy and third sector, social enterprises and local social capital. His recent articles are: 'Local economic development: a European-wide movement towards more economic democracy and social justice', in *Local Economy 1* (1999); 'A philosophical rationale for the promotion of local economic initiatives: development dilemmas in Berlin and the eastern part of Germany', in *Community Economic Development: Rhetoric or reality?*, Twelvetrees (ed.) (1999); *The Contribution of Social Enterprises to Community Economic Development. Country reports from Britain, Germany, France, Italy, Sweden and Spain* (1997); 'Intermediate labour market initiatives in Germany', in *Local Economy 2* (with G. Lorenz, 1997); *Social Enterprises and New Employment in Europe* (with G. Lorenz, 1998).

Carlo BORZAGA is Associate Professor of Comparative Economic Systems in Financial and Political Economy, Labour Economics and Co-operative Firm Economics at the Faculty of Economics. He is also President of the Istituto Sviluppo Aziende Nonprofit (ISSAN) at the University of Trento. He is researching the economic role of non-profit organisations with particular reference to social enterprises and their employment potential. He has participated and co-ordinated numerous research projects for the European Community, the Italian Government and local authorities. He has served on many scientific committees of journals, institutional and public bodies. He is also the author and collaborator of a number of Italian and international books and publications. Some of the most recent include: *The Multi-stakeholders versus the Nonprofit Organisation* (1997); *Social Enterprises and New Employment in Europe* (1998); *Insertion et nouvelle économie sociale* (1998).

Jacques DEFOURNY is Professor of Economics at the University of Liege where he also acts as a director of the 'Centre d'Économie Sociale'. He holds a PhD in Economics and a Master's degree in Public Administration. His main fields of interest include quantitative and conceptual approaches of the third sector as well as the economic analysis of co-operative, mutual and non-profit organisations. He worked as a co-ordinator of several international research projects and presently coordinates the European EMES Network (on the emergence of social enterprises) as well as an ILO international research project on social economy in developing countries. In addition to many articles in various journals, he has published several books including *Démocratie coopérative et efficacité économique* (1990), *Économie Sociale – The Third Sector* (with J.-L. Monzon, eds, 1992), *Vie associative et fonctions collectives* (with M.-J. Laloi, eds, 1992), *Développer l'entreprise sociale* (ed., 1994), *Avec quelle croissance devons-nous apprendre à vivre?* (with J.-Ch. Jacquemin, eds, 1996), *Insertion et nouvelle économie sociale* (with L. Favreau and J.-L. Laville, eds, 1998) and *L'Économie sociale au Nord et au Sud* (with P. Develtere and B. Fonteneau, eds, 1999).

Danièle DEMOUSTIER is a Professor at the Institut d'Études Politiques of Grenoble in the Economics group. She is responsible for the 'Politics and Social Economy' section of the 'second cycle' degree as well as for the Activities development Policy and Social Economy Enterprises for the third cycle Degree. She is also in charge of the Socio-Economic Associative and Co-operative Team (SCACT/ESSEAC), within which she develops researches on the socio-economic logic and these of Social Economy, and on the economic activity of associations, in relation with the different movements. On the top of several articles, she has published several papers on the production co-operatives. Her research is at present centered on employment in Social Economy in France and in Europe.

Bernard EME is assistant Professor at the Institut d'Études Politiques in Paris and researcher at the CRIDA in Paris. The subject of his research is mainly the transformation of economic relations through social economy instruments.

Louis FAVREAU is Professor of Sociology and Social Work at the University of Québec (Hull) Canada, where he has the Chair of Research on Community Development. He is been a researcher for the last ten years at CRISES (Research Centre on Social Innovations within the Social

Economy), leads the Team for 'Économie Sociale'. He is also Chief Editor of the review *Économie et solidarités* (journal for CIRIEC-Canada). His research is mainly on the new social movements, the new social economy and community economic development. He has published several books including: *Développement économique communautaire, economie sociale et intervention* (with B. Lévesque, 1996); *Théorie et pratiques en organisation communautaire* (with L. Doucet, 1991); *Mouvement populaire et intervention communautaire* (1989).

Benedetto GUI is Professor of Economics at the University of Padova (Italy). His research activity has ranged from labour economics (employment subsidies, employment effects of profit sharing, and team human capital) to the economics of self-managed firms (property rights, financing, pay scales and workers' mobility, comparative efficiency) and non-profit organisations (economic rationale, classification, and policy recommendation) and, more recently, to the economics of interpersonal relations (relational goods). He is the author of numerous chapters of edited books, of articles published in international journals including *I sussidi marginali all'occupazione* (1990); *The Nonprofit Sector in the Mixed Economy* (with Avner Ben-Ner, eds, 1993); *Il Terzo Settore tra economicità e valori* (ed., 1997). He is editing a special issue of the journal *Annals of Public and Cooperative Economics* on *The Economics of Interpersonal Relations*.

Harri KOSTILAINEN is doing post graduate studies in the University of Tampere focusing on evaluation methodologies suitable for the social economy organisations. He has studied social sciences at the University of Helsinki and worked there at the Institute of Co-operative studies as an research assistant for two years. He is also qualified co-operative advisor in Finland and associated in the consulting enterprise Idekoop co-operative. He has an article in a book that deals with the new co-operatives in Finland and he has done surveys and evaluations for social economy organisations.

Jean-Louis LAVILLE is a social scientist and researcher in a laboratory of the National Centre for Scientific Research – Centre of Research and Information for Scientific Research about Democracy and Autonomy (CRIDA) in Paris, France. In a general approach of economic sociology, examining what the relations are between economy and society in the contemporary period, he led different international projects specially in the fields of workers' participation in enterprises and local initiatives in

Europe. His most recent publications are: *Vers un nouveau contrat social* (Collaboration, 1996), *Le travail, quel avenir?* (Collaboration, 1997), *Vers une économie plurielle* (Collaboration, 1997), *Sociologie de l'association* (with R. Sainsanlieu, 1997).

Peter Ulrich LEHNER as an autodidact he deals with basic research and history of the insurance industry as employee of a common interest insurance society. He is co-founder and managing editor of the magazine *Mitbestimmung – Zeitschrift für Demokratisierung der Arbeitswelt*. He is a member of the managing committee of *Institute für Wissenschaft und Kunst*, where he heads a seminar concerning studies of labour movement. He is also a member of *the International Scientific Commission on the Social and Cooperative Economy of CIRIEC*. His publications have contributed to the history of the Austrian Trade Union of the employees of insurance industry (1983), to the five volumes of *Versicherungsgeschichte Österreichs* (*History of the Austrian Insurance Industry*) and to other books and magazines concerning similar subjects.

Günther LORENZ has degrees in the teaching of commerce and in economics. Since 1986 he has been member of the Interdisciplinary Research Group (IFG) on Local Economy at the Berlin University of Technology. Since 1992 he has been the project co-ordinator for research and development with the European Network for Economic Self-Help and Local Development. He has participated in numerous transnational projects and publications on local economic strategies, social economy and third sector, social enterprises and alternative financing. His recent publications include: 'Intermediate labour market initiatives in Germany', in *Local Economy 2* (1997); *Social Enterprises and New Employment in Europe* (1998) (both with K. Birkhölzer).

Marianne NYLUND is a researcher at the University of Helsinki, Department of Social Policy. She has a master's degree in Social Policy (University of Helsinki) and in Sociology (University of Alberta, Canada). Presently, she is preparing her doctoral thesis about mutual support and voluntary action in Finland. She is the Finnish contact person for the Nordic Third Sector Research Network, and for the European Experts on Self-Help Groups Network. She has published several Finnish articles about self-help groups and volunteer activities, and has presented about the same themes in international seminars.

Marthe NYSSENS is a Professor at CERISIS (Centre de recherches interdisciplinaires pour la solidarité et l'innovation sociale) and IRES (Institut de recherches économiques et sociales), Department of Economics, Université Catholique de Louvain. She teaches several courses in the area of third sector and social policies. Among her recent publications, a first set is focused on the role and the dynamics of third sector organisations besides the State and for-profit enterprises in the field of social services. A special interest is the interaction between third sector and social policies. Interactions between informal sector and third sector dynamics in the less developed countries constitute the second set of analyses. Some of her recent publications are 'Embeddedness, cooperation and popular-economy firms in the informal sector', with B. Van der Linden, *Journal of Development Economics*, 2000; 'L'Économie sociale dans les services de proximité: pionnière et partenaire dans un champ en développement', with B. Gilain, *Revue des études coopératives, mutualistes et associatives*, July, 1999; 'Économie populaire: creuset de pratiques d'économie solidaire?', with B. Fonteneau and A. Fall in *L'Économie sociale au Nord et au Sud* (co-ordinated by J. Defourny, P. Develtere and B. Fonteneau, 1999).

Pekka PÄTTINIEMI is Development Manager for The Institute for Co-operative Studies at the Universty of Helsinki since 1994. He is a member of board of the Finnish scientific association Kooperatiiviry and of the Swedish scientific association Föreningen Kooperativa Studier. He has written several articles and chapters on worker co-operatives, social enterprises and social economy published both in Finland and abroad as well as articles and books on social history in Finland.

Fabrizio POVINELLI graduated in Economics at the University of Trento in 1996, collaborates with the Department of Economics of the University of Trento. His main scientific interests are in Labour Economics.

Michel SIMON is an historian and economist who works as a researcher at the Centre d'Économie Sociale of the University of Liège. His research and publications focus mainly on work integration, but also on volunteering, non-profit organisations, services to people and the new technologies within the sphere of the social economy. He is the co-author of *L'Entreprise d'insertion en Wallonie. Premières leçons de sept projets-pilotes* (Work-integration enterprises in Wallonia. First lessons of seven pilot-projects, 1996), and he is the author of a synthesis report on all pilot-projects of work-integration enterprises in Wallonia, *L'Entreprise d'insertion à l'épreuve de la réalité économique* (The work-integration enterprise put to the test of economic reality, 1998).

Roger SPEAR is Chair of the Co-operatives Research Unit and teaches Systems in the Centre for Complexity and Change, the Open University, and is Chair of the International Co-operative Alliance Research Committee. He has been active in research on co-operatives and employee-owned Enterprises for many years. Studies have included a three-year research project on co-operatives in the UK, a training pack for UK co-operatives and community businesses, a six-country study of worker buy-outs in Europe; a study of social co-ops in the UK; a comparative study of employee ownership in the Netherlands and the UK; a four-country study of social audit in the social economy funded by DG23; a study of labour market integration in several European countries; a comparative study of social enterprises in Europe (EMES project FW4). He is one of the co-ordinators of a major CIRIEC project on unemployment and the third system (funded by DG12). His publications include several books and numerous papers.

Yohanan STRYJAN is a social scientist, Associated Professor (Docent) in sociology (Uppsala 1994) and, since 1997, Lecturer in Business Administration at Södertörns Högskola, a newly established state university in Southern Stockholm. He has led research projects on planning and organisation in new worker co-operatives, organisational change and adaptation in farmer co-operation, transformation in Central and Eastern Europe and on co-operative enterprises in the transformation of the Swedish welfare sector. Visiting Professor and ACE/Phare Fellow at CZU, Prague in 1996. Currently Program Director for the research program Entrepreneurship in the Baltic Sea Region, and for the research project Local Society, Local Government and Local Economy. He is a vice-chairman of ICAs Research Committee and a member of the board of the Swedish Society for Co-operative. Author of *Impossible Organizations* (1989), numerous articles and book-chapters.

Isabel VIDAL is Professor of the Department of Economics at the University of Barcelona and Director of the Centre d'Iniciatives de l'Economia Social (CIES). Her fields of specialisation are the economics of the third sector, especially employee owned companies, co-operative and non-profit organisations. She has contributed numerous analyses of the sector in Spain and internationally. Her main publications include: *Delivering Welfare: Repositioning Non-profit and Cooperative Action in Western European Welfare state* (with Perri 6, eds, 1994); *Social Enterprises and New Employment in Europe* (with Borzaga and Santuari, eds, 1998); and

Perspectivas empresariales de las sociedades laborales en la Union Europea (with A. Vilaplana, 1999).

Filip WIJKSTRÖM has an MBA from the Stockholm School of Economics (SSE), and received his PhD in Business Administration in May 1998. At present, Dr. Wijkström is Assistant Professor at SSE on a research scholarship in the field of economics, leadership and organization in the nonprofit sector, granted jointly by the Swedish Red Cross and the Swedish Cancer Society. Publications: 'The nonprofit sector in Sweden' (with L. Lundström, 1997); *Different Faces of Civil Society* (EFI, 1998); 'Cooperatives and nonprofit organizations in swedish social welfare' in *Annals of Public and Cooperative Economics* (with Y. Stryjan, 1996); and *The Swedish Nonprofit Sector in International Comparison* (1997).

Foreword

This book is the result of a research that was first carried out under the auspices of the International Centre of Information and Research on the Public and Cooperative Economy (CIRIEC). That work ended with the publication of a book in French (*Insertion et nouvelle économie sociale*, Desclée de Brouwer, Paris, 1998). Most of the authors then extended their collaboration within the 'European EMES Network', a research network sponsored by the European Commission and working on the emergence of 'social enterprises' in Europe. On the basis of an agreement with CIRIEC, the EMES Network has now published, in English, an updated and revised edition of the CIRIEC book realised with the contribution of the European Commission - DG research.

Although this book is the result of the collective effort of many people, we would like to show our gratitude in particular to: Christine Dussart (CIRIEC) who provided administrative support to the research group with great skill and friendliness, Enzo Pezzini, CECOP (European Confederation of worker co-ops, social co-ops and participative enterprises) for organising translations, Angela Walters (Open University) for excellent secretarial support for the several edited drafts, Andrew Bury for providing professional editorial support for the final copy, and Isobel McLean for work on the index.

ROGER SPEAR, JACQUES DEFOURNY,
LOUIS FAVREAU AND JEAN-LOUIS LAVILLE

INTRODUCTION

1 Introduction to an International Evaluation

JACQUES DEFOURNY, LOUIS FAVREAU AND
JEAN-LOUIS LAVILLE

Since the second half of the 1970s, researchers from a number of disciplines have expressed a growing interest in voluntary sector and co-operative economic initiatives that belong neither in the sphere of classic private enterprise nor to the public economy. In fields such as economics, sociology, political science, management, law and history, more and more research into the social and economic realities of this 'third sector' is appearing.

For most researchers throughout the world the idea of a third sector is certainly the most satisfactory approach to an overall understanding of this area. The association established by researchers in 1995 was not called the 'International Society for Third Sector Research' by chance. However, this title conceals a wide diversity of approaches in different countries. In the United States these organisations are most often referred to as *non-profit organisations* (NPO) or as the *independent sector*, whereas in the United Kingdom the idea of *voluntary organisations* predominates. French-speaking countries have increasingly adopted the concept of the *social economy* to cover not only voluntary organisations but co-operative and mutual bodies too. This three- or even four-pronged approach (if we include charitable foundations) is also being used increasingly worldwide, although this does not mean that all national approaches are modelled on the French pattern.[1]

---

[1] The appearance of several new international scientific journals, and the relaunch of existing journals with a view to improved coverage of this field, are evidence of the growth of research in the area. In the French-speaking world, attention may be drawn to the new dynamism displayed by the *Revue des études co-opératives, mutualistes et associatives* (formerly the *Revue des études co-opératives*, Paris). In English, the journal *Voluntas* founded in 1990, and the revived *Non-profit and Voluntary Sector Quarterly* (previously the *Journal of Voluntary Action Research*) are certainly the best examples.

In recent years, several major research projects on an international scale have attempted to define the limits and the extent of this third sector.[2] Although there remains much to do in this field, the main questions for the future relate to the contribution made by these types of organisations and businesses in the context of the crisis that has hit developed countries. Such a perspective has also given rise to the collective research which has brought about the present work.

The main purpose of this work, undertaken by around 15 researchers over a four-year period, was to record on a comparative, international basis (using a sample of nine countries) the new responses of the voluntary organisations and the co-operative movement to the crisis in employment and the welfare state, starting from an approach to employability in which voluntary sector and co-operative projects have multiplied over the last two decades: the social and occupational integration of people excluded from the traditional routes into employment.

However, our approach has not been governed by the question of integration through work[3] alone. This area was chosen, on the contrary, as illustrative of the new generation of voluntary organisations and co-operatives, an area that would expose the problems faced by society as a whole and raise questions regarding enterprises within the social economy as a whole. This is why, after outlining the challenges posed by unemployment and the increase of exclusion, and sketching the main public policies aimed at people who have the greatest difficulties in integrating into society, we will set these circumstances in the context of the social economy. In this way we intend not merely to set the scene but to present the whole framework of considerations which form the context of our analysis.

---

[2] This was the chief objective of an international research project under the auspices of CIRIEC coordinated by J. Defourny and J.L. Monzon Campos (1992) covering nine European countries and North America. Another example is the *Comparative Nonprofit Sector Project* established by the American Johns Hopkins University, which has covered the Third Sector in a dozen countries in its first stage (Salamon and Anheier, 1996 and 1998).

[3] In French-speaking countries, the expressions 'integration through work' and 'integration through economic activity' both sometimes predominate. In this text they are both used and assumed to be equivalent terms.

1. Unemployment and the Rise of Exclusion

Since the 1970s, western societies have been faced with serious structural unemployment. The countries of the European Union and certain others, such as Canada, have been especially severely hit by this phenomenon: most of these countries experienced a dramatic rise of their unemployment rate, from 3 or 4% 30 years ago to more than 10% through the 1980s and the 1990s. Although a declining trend may be observed for the very last years, unemployment was still above 11% for countries like France and Italy and above 9% for Germany in mid-1999. In the whole European Union, there were still more than 15-million people who were officially registered as unemployed,[4] without counting all those people who would like to work but are excluded from unemployment statistics for various reasons.

A great deal has already been written in analysis of the causes of this massive unemployment in Europe. The hypotheses most often advanced to explain the situation suggest slow growth accompanied by a weak increase in jobs, and very high salary costs particularly for low-skill work. Others, on the other hand, draw attention to inadequate public measures for the regulation of the labour market. However most researchers agree, whatever the causes advanced, in emphasising the need to address exclusion and persistent long-term unemployment. Without entering into this debate, let us stress at once the extent of this fact: for the European Union as a whole, the proportion of long-term unemployed (without work for more than a year) has consistently remained above 40% throughout the last ten years. Today the figure has passed 50%, while it has barely reached 12% in the United States and 15% in Japan. Of the European jobless, 30% have been without work for over two years.

However, the destabilisation of paid employment is not a peculiarly European phenomenon. The United States, for example, is also extensively affected by the growing insecurity of many jobs that is a feature of our economies in the context of the globalisation of trade and increasingly keen international competition. This insecurity is characterised by the widespread use of fixed-term contracts, the increase in non-typical kinds of work, the rise of non-voluntary part-time working, a progressive deterioration in working conditions, etc. We can observe at the same time a reduction in the social conditions of an increasingly large part of the

---

[4] Variations between countries may be considerable. For example, in July 1999 Spain had 16% unemployment as against less than 5% in the Netherlands, Austria and Denmark.

population and the swelling numbers of those social groups that are progressively excluded from the traditional routes into work.

The development of public policy in response to exclusion and the increased risk of exclusion is revealed in somewhat symptomatic terms that refer increasingly to the unemployed who are 'hard to place'.[5] This kind of approach is not really new; since the Second World War, many industrialised countries have targeted the physically or mentally disabled in a similar way and have developed policies organising them into work in more or less 'sheltered' or adapted environments. Today's excluded workers are rather implicitly defined by a kind of social and occupational handicap that keeps them below the 'employability threshold'. To make matters worse, this failure to meet the demands of the labour market is self-sustaining: the longer people are out of work, the more their professional abilities deteriorate (the 'human capital' in economists' terms) and the weaker their motivation to seek work becomes. In the same way we may fear that applying the institutionalising label of 'people in difficulties' may itself be a source of stigma and confirm potential employers in the idea that some parts of the active population are in objective terms unemployable.[6]

According to Erhel *et al.*,[7] the statistics show that the hard core of unemployed people fall into three major categories. The easiest group to identify is that of the long-term unemployed (over one or two years according to the classification system adopted). A second category lumps together various heterogeneous groups of individuals who experience recurrent unemployment punctuated by brief spells in work and who have at the same time other particular problems (drug addiction, especially poor educational levels, serious family problems, etc.). The third group consists of those covered by social security or minimum income schemes although they are fit for work.

The existence of such groups of citizens, and in particular the increase in these groups, presents society with the challenge of employability, because in a society in which social integration is primarily achieved through paid work, unemployment is not solely an economic problem but also a socio-political issue.[8] Certainly various analyses have diagnosed a

---

[5] Erhel *et al.* (1996).

[6] Elbaum (1994).

[7] Erhel *et al.* (1996).

[8] The massive experience of unemployment has led us to realise once more that a job is not just a way to 'earn a living', an income from labour, but also confers status and with it social recognition. From this point of view integration seeks as far as possible to restore work, income, status and recognition.

downgrading of the position of paid work and its importance in society, stressing the reduction of the amount of time devoted to economic activity in human life.[9] It has also been possible to identify the different ways in which people distance themselves from work, including a new involvement in the realm of private life and an increasing emphasis on leisure activities.[10] However, having a job remains no less an essential condition for independence and social identity. Conversely, the massive long-term exclusion of individuals brings into focus the issue of employability and the working of society as a whole: not only is it a very difficult situation for those concerned, but the macro-economic and macro-social consequences may be very heavy in terms of the wastage of human resources and social cohesion with increasing poverty and the erosion of social bonds.

For some, the waged society is crumbling to an extent which calls into question the very foundations of social organisation.[11] This is because the decline in regular, full time, permanent work is accompanied by a decentralisation of professional contacts and a rise in the importance of small businesses, breaking with the centralisation and the dominant position of large businesses characteristic of collective bargaining during the period of expansion.[12] The crisis in public regulation, both as regards mode of operation and financial means, has led in turn to the shrinking or commercialisation of public services. Finally, many companies are relocating to take advantage of investment opportunities. These, among others, are the strategic causes of a double crisis, in employment and in the social state, each directly impinging on the other.

How can public authorities tackle the problems of employment, which, as the central factor in exclusion and insecurity, now also involves social policy, within its shrinking scope for manoeuvre at the institutional and financial level?

2. The Development of Public Employment Policy

Over the last two decades, compensation measures for the unemployed have taken on an growing importance in public employment policy.[13] But the worsening problems have forced these policies to move far beyond

---

[9] Perret and Roustang (1995); De Foucauld and Piveteau (1995).
[10] Perret (1995).
[11] Castel (1995).
[12] Lallement (1996).
[13] For an overall view, see Barbier (1997).

compensation. As the groups of people affected by unemployment were increasingly observed to be young, and as those receiving social security included more and more people who were employable, the view spread that it was not possible simply to pay people for remaining inactive. Hence the hypothesis, and subsequently the conviction, that some of this expense must be transferred from 'passive' to 'active' expenditure.

Side-by-side with a general trend to an increased quantitative flexibility, European governments, which were aware of the limits of measures supporting growth and were improving unemployment benefit and supporting retirements from the labour market, turned to 'active labour and employment policies'.

More specifically, during the 1980s, 'the system of unemployment benefit was gradually drawn into a new framework of active policies for employment, becoming a tool for active policy and structural adjustment'. The system of benefits was altered to provide incentives to occupational integration. In the United Kingdom, the 16 and 17-year-old unemployed ceased to qualify for benefit payments; but all the unemployed in this age group were entitled to a place on a young people's training programme, and in this case an allowance could be made. 'Compensation could also be linked with keeping in work staff threatened with dismissal and with the victims of industrial restructuring. In this case compensation could be paid even before dismissal came into force, if the employer took the appropriate measures to classify the worker as redundant.'[14]

The marked 'qualification deficit' in the labour market has made it essential to co-ordinate employment and training policies for improving employability. The link between training and employment is evident in the widespread use of day-release schemes, which combine theoretical, academic training with the acquisition of a qualification in the work place. The success of this formula is clear from the fact that youth unemployment is less high in countries which have vocational training schemes combining apprenticeship in a firm with compulsory attendance at a vocational training institution, and the acquisition of a final qualification. Because of the high number of young people leaving the education system without any vocational training – over 30% of 16 and 17-year-olds in Great Britain and Italy – day release programmes have been introduced in an attempt to match the effectiveness of the German programmes: 90% succeed in qualifying there under the dual system with 9% remaining unemployed, as

---

[14] These quotations are taken from Garonna (1990).

compared with 50% and 30% respectively in France.[15] The various work-training contracts in France, the *contratti formazione lavoro* in Italy, and the content of the Youth Training Schemes in the United Kingdom have been designed in these three countries as elements in a necessary shake-up of the vocational training system. Schemes involving immersion in the work place before the training element are preferred to those in which the course precedes employment. The usual educational logic is reversed: the work situation provides the incentive for undertaking training, instead of training being considered as a preparation for work.

Overall, these active employment policies assume a wide variety of forms which can be classified as follows:[16]

(a) *Training support programmes*. These programmes generally seek to take account of both the aptitudes and training needs of their target public, and the demands of possible and existing openings in the labour market. Most of the time these training programmes concentrate on bringing basic skills up to scratch and vocational training. In practice, there are many approaches, ranging from face-to-face teaching to work experience in the strict sense, with many mixed systems in between. In favour of on-the-job training, some studies have shown that these schemes give better results for people experiencing grave difficulties in integrating. However, the evaluation of measures of this kind can only be properly carried out by following the individuals concerned over a long period. It must also be recognised that the drop-out rates along the way are rather high.[17]

(b) *Remotivation programmes and job search assistance*. This is a matter of providing the unemployed with more effective techniques in their search for work, and increasing their dynamism and self-confidence. Measures of this kind often combine short intensive sessions with interviews and individual follow-up aimed at working out personal reintegration plans. They can give good results at the local level. However, at a macro-economic level the effects may primarily be those of relocation.[18] This kind of monitoring may also be very inadequate to the needs of some people.

---

[15] According to Dalle and Bounine (1987).
[16] See, among others, Demazière (1995); Erhel *et al.* (1996); or Van der Linden (1997).
[17] See, for example, Disney (1992).
[18] See Björklund and Regnér (1996).

(c) *Subsidies for recruiting people with serious integrational difficulties.* This direct or indirect support aims to make up for the lack of appeal these people have in the eyes of employers, particularly in the private sector. It often consists of a one-off or recurring subsidy, or takes the form of complete or partial exemption from social security charges. These techniques are very widely used but appear to be rather ineffective since they are generally insufficient to overcome the reluctance of employers.[19]

Overall, as Gazier says,[20] these employment policies are characterised by two features: activism, and a wait-and-see approach, activism initially, since these voluntaristic initiatives on the part of public authorities have multiplied everywhere to check the rise in long-term unemployment; then wait-and-see, because many of these measures have proved disappointing, often with rather hazy results. Hopes have thus been pinned on a medium-term improvement in business competitiveness and the revival of the economy.

However useful they may have been, active employment policies have not ultimately been without their ambiguities. The chief of these lies in the conjunction between the German-style 'qualification offensive' and the drop in labour costs that has allowed doubts over the priorities held to persist. No country has escaped the 'substitution effect': young people have replaced older workers, or have been preferred to the adult unemployed. To this must be added the effects of anticipation and selection: recruitment has been brought forward to profit from economic advantages, the rejection of people in difficulties has persisted. To sum up, these policies have benefited unemployed people with some resources, but have not really offered any opportunities to the most vulnerable groups. This is why – according to Gazier – they have also moved in the direction of selectivity, because the persistence of high rates of long-term unemployment and financial constraints have made it necessary to target the priority groups: the long term unemployed, and those people experiencing serious difficulties in integrating, including young people lacking their first experience of work.

---

[19] See, for instance, Gautié *et al.* (1994).

[20] Gazier (1992).

3. Temporary Employment in the Public and Non-profit Sectors[21]

This selective approach is expressed in particular through a raft of measures based on new forms of work linking productive work with social integration, in this case through the creation of temporary jobs in the public and non-profit sectors. The jobs thus created are intended to satisfy unmet needs in the social, cultural, environmental or other spheres. Wage costs are generally born directly, either wholly or in part, by the public authorities.

These measures draw inspiration from a simple observation. On the one hand we have a number of unsatisfied needs; on the other, a significant number of people without work. It thus seems logical to encourage the creation of jobs in the areas meeting these new requirements.

In France, 'relief work' programmes, TUCs (*Travaux d'utilité collective*), were set up in 1984 to carry out activities aimed at meeting public needs without competing with existing businesses, recruiting young people aged from 16 to 21 for a period of between three and twelve months. This measure, and its sister programmes (the local integration programme, PIL for adults, the AIG programme for people receiving the minimum integration income (RMI), etc.) reached a growing number of people until its replacement in 1989 by the CES, the employment solidarity contracts. These are contracts for work (unlike TUC contracts that lent vocational trainee status) intended to encourage the occupational integration or re-integration of jobless people through 'developing activities in response to unmet public needs'. The state provides a contribution of between 85% and 100% of the wage costs.

In Germany, the ABM work creation programme (*Arbeits Beschaffung Massnahmen*), which involved almost 400,000 people in 1993, falls into this category of measures for limiting the unemployment rate. As for the CES in France, the German State (via the federal labour office) finances around 80% of wage costs for these workers for one or two year period, on the assumption that at the end of this time, thanks to this help, employers will be able to assume the cost of these jobs entirely.

In Great Britain, the Community Programme of 1982 was a continuation of an earlier programme established in 1975. Positions were for a maximum of one year, paid at the normal hourly rates for the job, with the reimbursement of employers' social security charges and wage costs up

---

[21] By the 'non-profit sector' we mean here all those non-profit organisations that belong neither to the public sector nor to the traditional, profit-oriented private sector.

to a guaranteed minimum. Up to 25,000 places were offered under this scheme.

In Belgium, there were programmes such as one for setting the unemployed to work (CMT) from 1963 to 1989, and the special temporary management programme (CST) which ran from 1977 to 1989. In Québec too, 'employability bodies' specialised in setting up public programmes along similar lines.

The extent of unemployment thus led countries with a strong welfare state tradition to explore previously unexplored social responses to unemployment. This social approach to unemployment exposes an important change: on the one hand, it attempts to bring together social policy and economic activity, out of a conviction that participation in the economic sphere is a principle source of social integration,[22] on the other, it introduces terms of employment which are positioned between work and welfare.

All the programmes described above represent a break with the norm of full-time, permanent employment. Access to temporary work is considered worthwhile in itself, and is made possible by introducing an intermediate status allowing employers' staff costs to be reduced through public financing. The short cut between new methods of redistribution and an increase in available jobs is achieved at the cost of certain restrictions. The target public is narrowly defined, with jobs being reserved for particularly disadvantaged categories; the field is limited to tasks of public concern that are not fulfilled by private initiatives; the bodies appointed are public-sector establishments, local authorities or voluntary organisations. Without questioning the value of this social approach to unemployment, which has saved many from permanent exclusion, its limitations have become obvious with time.

The first limitation is that the availability of jobs takes precedence over personal career choice, just as too often happens in training. Regardless of an initial concern with quality, the pressure exercised by the volume of unemployment is such that it produces a slide towards quantitative objectives. It is a matter of 'running at a profit'. Though strong initial guarantees are given to prevent programmes from replacing regular jobs in the public or private sectors and to ensure that they will lead to genuine occupational integration, they nevertheless find themselves steadily eroded. 'In local authorities particularly, where staff numbers are steadily falling, it is hard to prevent certain jobs being taken over by people

---

[22] Barbier and Gautié (1998).

working in these programmes. This pursuit of public services by other means has led to the birth of a distinctive labour market on the margins of the official services in which low-skill jobs are filled on the basis of poorly paid short-term contracts.'[23]

Furthermore, since the effects of unemployment are far-reaching, these programmes often seem to benefit qualified workers more than others through the effects of substitution. At the worst, they can drive the poorly qualified even further from traditional labour markets, trapping them in a secondary market where they run the risk of alternating between insecure jobs and unemployment.[24] In any case, even though these measures may perform a useful function in terms of reintroducing people to work and providing services, many of them have no significant impact on the likelihood that the least qualified individuals concerned will reintegrate into the traditional labour markets.[25]

Unable to play an effective transitional role between unemployment and permanent employment, they may actually lay the foundations for a second permanent labour market in which the unemployed continue to be work on a temporary basis. There is some evidence for this development in Germany: six months after leaving, 43% of people working on such schemes have begun another ABM while 23% are unemployed, in training or otherwise not working. In Great Britain 69% were either undergoing training or not working after passing through the Community Programme. In France 'at the end of 1991, the 1989 school-leavers were more likely to be unemployed if they had held a CES place than if they had followed another training route; this held true for all levels of qualification'.[26] The adult unemployed fare better from their time under the CES scheme, 'but they are most likely to find work in the form of a second CES contract, particularly if they are older, and their chances of finding a job remain low'.[27] In total, of the 611,200 people who completed a CES in 1994, more than one third were immediately unemployed once more.[28] These evaluations coincide with those carried out in Belgium, which shows that the likelihood of finding traditional employment was lower for those

---

[23] Auer (1990).
[24] See Nicaise *et al.* (1995).
[25] See for example Mahy (1994), for Belgium.
[26] According to Elbaum (1994).
[27] Elbaum (1994).
[28] See 'Les contrats emploi-solidarité débouchent rarement sur un travail' in *Le Monde*, 27 March 1995.

leaving an unemployment reduction programme than for the jobless who had not had this advantage.[29]

This state of affairs leads to another limitation, the confusion between integration and new occupations. The measures relating to the social approach to unemployment tend to devalue those activities designed more for the benefit of the people in need of occupational integration than for that of users and clients. This uncertainty over the nature of the objective, reinforced by the incompatibility of temporary jobs and permanent needs, gives rise to recurrent failures in the functioning of these schemes. Mutual frustration results: the representatives of district authorities and administrations who encourage this kind of measure are disappointed with the results they get, while the programme promoters feel that they are being poorly supported. Overall, the increase in low-cost temporary contracts has discouraged a number of activities which everyone regards as 'casual work'.[30]

Temporary work programmes, because they rely heavily on non-profit organisations, cause other difficulties, such as contributing to disquiet in the voluntary sector. During the 1980s, the State admitted that it could not act alone in the fight against unemployment. The role of voluntary bodies was therefore recognised.[31] Heavily engaged in the social approach to unemployment, which matched a more professional management approach on their part, the voluntary organisations have now found themselves caught up in the establishment of programmes and other measures to the extent that many are questioning the direction and control of their work.

4.   A Society in Reaction Against Unemployment

Occupational integration through economic activity has relied on temporary employment programmes, but it cannot be restricted to the context of public measures. Whether in conflict or in dialogue with these programmes, it also bears witness to different way of tackling the issue, which instead of resulting from a top-down movement has emerged from a bottom-up approach. A number of local schemes have succeeded in establishing themselves in the area of integration through economic activity. These experiences have emerged from civic projects which have gradually come

---

[29] Mahy (1994), quoted in the contribution on Belgium.

[30] See, for example, the special report on 'Emplois stérilisés' in *Le Monde initiatives*, 14 June 1995.

[31] Baron *et al.* (1998).

together to create a vehicle for change in public policy, although this has all taken place under difficult conditions.

Confronted by the limitations of public policy, particularly in social approaches to unemployment, an economic militancy has emerged looking for new ways of integrating people in difficulty. These structures were set up outside the law, but as their role was recognised they were granted a legal framework.

In Belgium, vocational training companies, EAPs, (recognised in 1987) followed by on-the-job training companies, EFTs, (1995) developed in this way. In France, following various innovations, the circular known as 'Circular 44' of the Ministry for social affairs established a fund to provide work experience for the 'socially disabled' in 1979. The Minister of Labour, in 1985, set up an experimental support programme for enterprises for work-integration through economic activity. In 1987, following the development of voluntary organisations to help the unemployed, a series of laws set out the legal and regulatory framework for intermediate voluntary organisations. These aimed to encourage services corresponding to the hidden needs of individuals, local authorities or businesses while at the same time contributing to the occupational integration of unemployed people who could be offered occasional work. While, in Italy, the 1991 law on social co-operation, prompted by the growth in 'social solidarity co-operatives', acknowledged that such co-operation was not restricted to fostering the interests of members and could make a contribution to the interests of society at large. As a result it was accepted that their voluntary members (up to a maximum of 50%) and users made up a part of their membership alongside workers in the fight against exclusion. And in Québec, as well as production enterprises and mutual aid groups, consultative bodies work to bring community organisations together and to give a stimulus to their projects: these are known as 'community development corporations' (CDC). Other community organisations, known as 'societies for aid for local development' (SADC) or 'community economic development corporations' (CDEC) are expanding their membership to include partners from the public and private sectors to strengthen local development.

The process whereby public authorities have legitimised grass-roots initiatives clearly shows that integration through economic activity, unlike the social approach to unemployment, relies on an entrepreneurial dimension that helps avoid the pitfalls of occupational work schemes. Nevertheless, such a process, by its innovative nature, is a long and complex one. It comes into constant conflict with the boundaries between social, labour and training policies resulting in a selective approach to these initiatives. In Spain, the 300 social integration initiatives have so far received neither legal protection nor public assistance. In Belgium, limiting access to vocational training companies to young people not qualifying for benefit and aged between 18 and 25 has led to the founding of other voluntary organisations aimed at the long-term unemployed, for example the integrated development actions (AID). The evidence thereby provided was necessary for their inclusion in a joint framework combining them with the vocational training enterprises in new the on-the-job training companies which can now take on both young people and the long-term unemployed aged over 25.

In France, help for intermediate enterprises was withdrawn in 1986 before being restored in 1989; the reasons behind this were at once political (opposition from employers' representative who complained of unfair competition) and administrative (resistance to the multi-dimensional approach). Furthermore, alongside the community enterprises for occupational integration, initiatives arising from social work have been supported but those put forward by people out of work, or aiming at the creation of lasting jobs have not received the same attention.[32] The wide range of voluntary organisations set up for and by the unemployed have been reduced to a single model, the intermediate voluntary organisation. On the admission of one of those responsible for this law, this was a mistake that has led to 'a certain lack of esteem for new skilled activities, described pityingly as 'casual work', and for those who work in them who are too quickly dismissed as 'unemployable' in the normal labour market'.[33] Nor is the damaging effect limited to a single country, since the intermediate voluntary organisation model has been imported into Québec in the form of temporary job creation programmes (CIT), adopting this instrument without questioning its effectiveness. We find a similar direction elsewhere, in the setting up of neighbourhood management associations (RQs) in Belgium, where they are regarded as measures appropriate to deprived areas, whereas the National Committee for RQs in France has always insisted on the importance of a close knit residents' association, rejecting the setting up of such voluntary organisations by means of simple measures superimposed on a complex reality.

---

[32] See Laville (1991); Chopart *et al.* (1998).
[33] Malgorn (1995).

Nevertheless, despite all these ups and downs, occupational integration through economic activity has made it possible to begin to introduce a new link between public authorities and civic society with the aim of realigning the relationship between economic and social needs.[34]

5. Co-operative and Voluntary Initiatives

In many countries, occupational integration through economic activity has developed out of the sometimes conflictual interactions between public programmes and local initiatives which are able to bring to bear an essential but often missing ingredient: the experience and energies of a 'social enterprise sector'[35] closely linked to the needs and routines of day to day life. Sometimes these local initiatives have actually preceded and played a part in establishing public policies. In other cases they have multiplied in response to public programmes which make available the resources to organise occupational integration projects.

In a general way, local initiatives play an important role in the implementation of public policies, very often through 'negotiated involvement', i.e. participation under certain conditions which the authorities try to impose through negotiation. The various measures used are often founded on different principles that are at times in direct contradiction:

(a) consultation and association with public authorities in the context of partnership, or an instrumental approach through sub-contracting;

(b) a decentralised policy in which voluntary organisations and local authorities take on responsibilities which they share with a central government that tries to dictate criteria;

(c) an experimental approach which emphasises the fact the public assistance is not by nature definitive, as against the recognition of the relevance of the voluntary organisations over the long-term.

During the last two decades, occupational integration has thus become the arena for a crucial challenge for both public authorities and people acting through the community (movements, local authorities, etc.): that is finding new modes of intervention which are capable of improving

---

[34] Lallement (1999).
[35] EMES Network (1999); Borzaga and Santuari (1998).

employability and fighting effectively against exclusion and insecurity. Social mobilisation for occupational integration has been particularly strong since the beginning of the 1980s. It has come about through a variety of kinds of initiatives, including:

(a) employment training initiatives through educational voluntary organisations to foster various apprenticeships linked to the labour market;

(b) sectoral initiatives for social integration through economic activity, within which people generally get some work experience – of variable length – which should in time enable them to find a job in the traditional labour market;

(c) local initiatives for economic and social renewal involving the integration of sections of disadvantaged local communities by bringing together all those involved in integration in a particular location through a multi-activity programme.

Despite their variety, these initiatives have common features due to their co-operative or voluntary sector legal status. In this respect they belong with the post-1968 movement of voluntary bodies and co-operatives. The 1970s and 1980s in particular saw a growth in attempts by qualified manual and white collar workers to use the co-operative structure to create their own employment. In Great Britain, Italy, France and Québec these new co-operatives opened up the co-operative movement to the intellectual and cultural services sectors, among others. In the mid-1980s, co-operatives appearing in the service sector represented 45% of workers' co-operatives in Great Britain, 13.5% in Québec, and 18.1% in France. To these collectives, voluntarily set up, must be added 'forced' co-operatives arising from the wave of employee buy-outs of businesses threatened with closure. In Italy there were more than a thousand of these between the mid-1970s and mid-1980s, most of them in the north of the country. In France, the years 1982 and 1983 saw a peak, with 109 and 95 buy-outs respectively, but this surge was checked from 1984 onwards, the average size and number of business buy-outs dropping considerably. As in Germany where there were about 30 attempts during the 1980s, or in Great Britain during the 1970s with co-operatives that received a very artificial level of support,[36] the dangers faced by buy-outs which were prompted

---

[36] By the Minister for labour at the time, Tony Benn, after whom these were known as 'Benn co-operatives'.

more by political imperatives than by an objective assessment of economic factors, soon materialised. After this tide had ebbed, successes were concentrated in businesses which reflected the historic strengths of the co-operative movement – organisations of limited size whose principle asset is the know-how of their members.

In Spain, besides co-operatives, buy-outs also took the form of public companies that – according to incomplete statistics – accounted for 1300 buy-outs with a minimum of 50,000 workers before 1985.[37] These were defensive operations designed to maintain existing jobs, but with the persistence of mass unemployment there were other initiatives aimed rather at the occupational integration of people excluded from the labour markets or at creating employment in disadvantaged regions. Many adopted the constitution of non-profit organisations, whether as community enterprises in the United Kingdom, employment and training organisations in Germany, on-the-job training companies in Belgium, intermediate voluntary organisations, neighbourhood management associations, and work-integration enterprises in France. However, a generation of co-operatives also appeared, with the social co-operatives and social solidarity co-operatives in Italy, Sweden and the United Kingdom.

In other words, the experiences of work integration through economic activity are the product of the confluence of the voluntary and co-operative movements.[38] This is why they take their place within the general framework of the social economy or third sector, giving rise to the hypothesis that a *new social economy* is emerging, corresponding more or less closely, according to the circumstances, to the 'historical' composition of the social economy[39] being made up essentially from the same major distinctive elements:

(a) the *aims*, which are not to serve the interests of capital but to fulfil social functions, in the sense that the activity is intended to ensure economic viability and social usefulness (in the service of individuals and groups in difficulty);

---

[37] Among many works devoted to initiatives of this kind, see Defourny, 1988, and, for a summary, Laville (1994b), and Paton (1989).

[38] Perry 6 and Vidal (1994).

[39] Defourny and Monzon Campos (1992); Vienney (1994); EMES Network (1999); Laville (1994a); Favreau and Levesque (1996).

(b) the *people involved* and beneficiaries, from or associated with working-class people experiencing problems in the labour market or in responding to their basic needs;

(c) *structures and regulations* designed to promote participation, and which do not allocate power on the basis of capital held;

(d) *business activities*, in the sense that the production of goods and services develops through conquering markets to ensure a certain degree of self-financing for the business, whilst simultaneously relying on public authority support.

The problem that arises is one of continuity as much as that of differences with earlier versions of the social economy. In order to respond, we should first recall some key elements in the development of the original social economy.

6.   The Social Economy – A Historical Perspective

The first salient point which emerges from a century and a half of history of the social economy is as follows: the social economy, and notably its co-operative branch, sprang up amongst the exploited working classes who were struggling to improve their highly insecure living conditions. In other words, as H. Desroche has often stressed, co-operation was initially the 'daughter of necessity', a response to the pressure of needs strongly felt by various populations.[40] This *condition of need* is a first dimension, socio-economic in character, that needs to be incorporated in our overview in order to understand the 'new social economy'. Thus we may also identify one of the traditional roles played by the social economy that is heavily stressed in the economic theories of the non-profit organisations: the social economy is born and develops as a response to the failings of the dominant economy, and particularly to those needs that the markets fail to address.[41]

Thus consumer co-operatives, for example, were initially the expression of collective efforts to find solutions to certain basic needs: to obtain food, clothing and other basic products at the best possible price, since the means of subsistence were very limited at the time. For their part, workers' manufacturing co-operatives initially represented the response by workers (particularly in the crafts sector) who wished to save their

---

[40] See, for example, Desroche (1976).
[41] The concept of 'market failure' has notably been expounded by Hansmann (1980).

occupations from the threats posed by industrial capitalism and remain masters of their own work rather than letting themselves become locked into wage-earning status, at that time practically a synonym for dispossession. A further element was those who were just thrown out of work by the changing face of capitalism and whose reaction was to try and create their own businesses. The history of the mutual sector can be evoked along the same lines. Mutual aid societies multiplied from the beginning of the 19th century because the state welfare systems were inadequate while the risks of accidents at work and illness were very high. Having very little in the way of financial means to pay the costs of medical treatment and to cover the temporary of permanent loss of income caused by illness or invalidity, a growing number of families came together to set up hardship funds which would aid them in time of need, paid for by modest but regular subscriptions.

However, this explanation is not in itself adequate. A second socio-political or socio-cultural dimension needs to be taken into account in order to describe the motivations for the social economy. Indeed, need is an insufficient explanation for the social mobilisation that lay behind its manifestations. The *collective identity*, the belonging to a group whose members were aware that they shared a common destiny, is a second rung of the explanation already developed by De Tocqueville,[42] who considered the voluntary organisation to be a condition for democracy through the public engagement that it revealed and maintained. In this sense the dynamism shown by the social economy in the working-class world of the 19th and early 20th centuries was the expression of a craft culture which was threatened by and linked to the requirements of democracy,[43] and the expression of a class culture which was certainly dispossessed but also largely mutually supportive. It is from this associative world that various types of organisation emerged: trade unions, workers' political parties, mutual societies, co-operatives and voluntary organisations.[44] Their members were bound together by work, by a shared popular culture, and by struggles that meant that they lived through what has been termed 'integration through conflict'.[45] There were thus many collective identities

---

[42] De Tocqueville (1991).

[43] See the analyses in Sewel (1983).

[44] Thus contributing to the transformation of the 'proletariat' of the last century (characterised by social marginalisation, insecurity of employment and the absence of rights) through the struggle of the labour movement to the status of 'workers' and finally to fully salaried status with full citizens' rights (Dubet and Lapeyronnie, 1992; Castel, 1995).

[45] Touraine (1973).

– or at least a *shared destiny* – which tended to generate new institutions representing the roots of the social economy. As such, the social economy was born out of the movements that saw themselves as mechanisms for social change and as affirmations of the possibility of bringing social solidarity to life through economic activities.[46]

A similar analysis can be made for the rural social economy. Thus in Belgium, for example, more than a century ago Flemish smallholders established a co-operative movement of remarkable dynamism, with numerous highly effective rural funds and with co-operatives that today market a large proportion of agricultural production. This co-operative movement was built on the strong but largely unrecognised socio-cultural identity of a population that spoke only Flemish while French was the official language imposed by the nobility and middle classes. By using all available means to market its products and getting its supplies cheaper than the prices imposed by major wholesalers, this rural world was aiming for autonomous economic development whilst at the same time affirming its identity. The same factors can be found in the history of the co-operatives in francophone Canada at the turn of the century. The condition of collective identity is also present in this case: was there not a francophone Catholic identity to be defended against Protestant Anglo-Saxon domination?[47] As for the condition of need, this was as valid for francophone Canada as for Flanders a century ago.[48]

The history of the Mondragon co-operative complex shows that this reading is not only valid for the older forms of social economy. Indeed, the extent to which the affirmation of Basque identity has played a major role in the birth and development of Mondragon can be seen, even though it is combined with other factors likely to promote the emergence of co-operation. Fundamentally, the two conditions are adequately fulfilled: need in terms of the requirement for reconstruction in the aftermath of the Civil War and the Second World War, and collective identity in terms of the

---

[46] This dimension can weaken with time, as can be seen from the evolution of certain traditional co-operatives and mutual societies that, by developing and/or adopting more traditional economic strategies, have become more or less distanced from the social movements that lie at their roots.

[47] Religion as a motivating factor in a collective identity that supports a social economy is well covered in the works of E. James (1989). James holds that private non-profit provision of social and educational services is more developed in countries where strong religious groups are present and where they compete among themselves.

[48] The articulation of these two conditions, need and collective identity (or shared destiny) was initially presented by Defourny (1995).

reaction of an entire culture – an entire people – to the threat of Castilian domination. These two factors go a long way to explaining the dynamism and the lasting vitality of this co-operative movement.

The same parameters can be found in many Southern countries where a solidarity-based economy[49] is developing in a way that to some extent recalls the development of the social economy in industrialised countries. As just one example amongst many, Villa el Salvador in Peru is a kind of Latin American Mondragon: 300,000 inhabitants of suburban Lima have arranged for spatial layout which combines block by block organisation of neighbourhoods and the organisation of community services clustered around 120 public open spaces and a network of small businesses with connections to the solidarity economy.[50] In this case the shared destiny is undoubtedly founded less on specific cultural identity than on broadly common social conditions and on a precise territorial affiliation, which is also the case for Mondragon.[51] To sum up, co-operation, and indeed the whole of the social economy, springs from necessity and from a collective identity. Made up of economic initiatives set up to respond to vital needs, the social economy is also carried forward by a collective identity or a shared destiny forged by cultural factors (language, religion, shared territory, etc.) or even, in certain cases, by social movements.

7. A New Social Economy

If we are to accept this reading, or at the very least if we feel that it throws some light on the subject, the conditions for the renewal of the social economy seem to be an updating of the socio-economic and socio-political dimensions which characterised the initial emergence of the social economy. In the industrialised countries, given the structural crisis of our societies and our economies, the condition of need is far more clearly in evidence than it was in during the post-war economic boom. New fields are

---

[49] Larrachea and Nyssens (1994); Defourny *et al.* (1999).

[50] On this issue see Favreau and Fréchette (1993); and Rodrigo (1990).

[51] Here we are summarising the work of several researchers who explain the launching of social economy initiatives by membership of sectoral or territorial collectives. On this topic see particularly the Canadian (Fairbain, 1991), American (Christenson and Robinson, 1989, Perry and Steward, 1987) and European (Jacquier, 1992) studies. This work has shown that where there is strong social and cultural identity within an enterprise or a collectivity, it is far more likely to protect its specific characteristics, its independence and its ability to act on its own account.

thus opening up for social economy initiatives. In particular, the retreat of the welfare state in many areas and the loss of millions of jobs is leading to the emergence of new needs for more and more people who were previously protected. New social demand is appearing, a manifestation of needs which can no longer be properly satisfied by the market or by public intervention. If the social economy of the 19th century was both a reaction and a functional adaptation to the market economy, then at the end of the 20th century the new social economy is a reaction against the inability of either the market or the State to provide full employment as they had been able to during the period of expansion.

In our societies the condition of collective identity, the stirring up of a community to produce a positive dynamic, is undoubtedly a greater problem than the condition of need. A number of factors are pitted against this collective identity: a prevailing climate of individualism, the breaking of social ties and the weakening of the forces which have traditionally cemented society together (religion, schools, stable neighbourhood communities, trade unionism, the labour movement, etc.). Unemployment too is clearly a force working against the maintenance of the fabric of society, work being a fundamental vehicle for social integration. However, it seems to us that there is still fertile ground where genuine collective dynamics can take root and where many social economy initiatives can spring up. This fertile ground is the voluntary sector that is seething with ideas and comes in many forms throughout western society.[52] It is admittedly rare that the current proliferation of voluntary organisations is the expression of a united collective identity. However, it testifies to growing collective awareness of the challenges that face us. One of the most striking examples is undoubtedly the growth of civic commitment to the social integration process by social workers, trade unionists and economic decision-makers. It has been said that this rising awareness leads in part to increasing demands put on public authorities. However, it also leads citizens to group together and to develop projects themselves, locally at first and sometimes on a larger scale. In this respect it is a factor in the growth of a shared identity felt by its members with a certain degree of intensity for a certain length of time.

In any case, one of the central hypotheses that pervades the national studies assembled here is that since the voluntary sector sometimes extends into co-operative development, it is the melting pot from which a renewal

---

[52] Lewis (1999); Mertens (1999); Leduc Browne (1996).

of the social economy may emerge. The comparative study of nine countries demonstrates some facets of this.

As the experience in these countries over ten or fifteen years shows, local integration initiatives seem to be on the way to becoming a socio-economic network combining market and non-market dimensions within productive activities with an embracing perspective of the social and solidarity economy. These initiatives seek to reinforce social membership of a community, employability, and the creation of jobs, going against the tendency to take 'adaptation to the market economy' as the sole factor.[53]

In other words, while taking on board some of the constraints imposed by the market economy, these economic activities try to set themselves apart in qualitative terms by bringing together those excluded from the labour market, pursuing both social and economic goals, putting primary emphasis on a voluntary sector form of management, and by using the available capital through social or collective entrepreneurship.

What is the exact scale of this phenomenon in each national context? Is it an expression of neo-philanthropy or a potential source of development of new forms of identity and social utility? Does it bear witness to an instrumentalisation of local projects within the framework of a social approach to unemployment, or to an unprecedented response to local needs and to a contribution to democratic life?

It is these questions which the case studies have attempted to tackle, taking as a starting point the exposition of data (often gathered with some difficulty) in order to enable a comparative assessment in economic and sociological terms of the original contribution made by integration through work, and to reach a conclusion based on an investigation of the social economy in general and the potential scope of these initiatives.

References

Auer, P. (1990), 'Emploi, marché du travail et stratégies de lutte contre le chômage', in *Chroniques internationales du marché da travail et des politiques de l'emploi 1986–1989*, La Documentation Française, Paris.

Barbier, J.-C. (1997), *Les Politiques de l'emploi en Europe*, Flammarion, Paris.

Barbier, J.-C. and J.Gautié, J. (1998), *Les Politiques de l'emploi en Europe et aux États-Unis*, PUF, Paris.

Baron, C., Bureau, M.-C., Leymarie, C. and Nivolle, P. (1998), *Insertion: les feux follets de la démocratie*, Desclée de Brouwer/Éditions Charles Léopold Mayer, Paris.

---

[53] Laville (1994a).

Bjorklund A. and Regner, H. (1996), 'Experimental Evaluation of European Labour Market Policy', in G. Schmid *et al.* (eds), *International Handbook of Labour Market Policy and Evaluation*, Edward Elgar, Cheltenham.

Borzaga, C. and Santuari, A. (eds) (1998), *Social Enterprises and New Employment in Europe*, Regione Autonoma Trentino Alto Adige and Consorzio Nazionale della Cooperazione Sociale, Trento.

Castel, R. (1995), *Les Métamorphoses de la question sociale*, Fayard, Paris.

Chopart, J.-N., Eme, B., Laville, J.-L. and Mouriaux, R. (1998), 'The welfare recipients collective action in Europe: the situation in France', in R. Van Berkel, H. Coenen and R. Vlek (eds), *Beyond Marginality? Movements of Social Security Claimants in the European Union*, Perspectives in Europe Contemporary Interdisciplinary Research, Ashgate, Aldershot.

Christenson, J.A. and Robinson, J.W. (1989), *Community Development in Perspective*, Iowa State University Press, Iowa.

Coenen, H. and Van Berkel, R. (eds) (1997), *The Collective Action of Welfare Recipients in Europe*, University of Utrecht.

Dalle, F. and Bounine, J. (1987), *Pour développer l'emploi*, Masson, Paris.

De Foucauld, J.-B. and Piveteau, D. (1995), *Une société en quête de sens*, Odile Jacob, Paris.

Defourny, J. (1995), 'L'Avenir des pratiques co-opérantes dans un monde en mutation', in M.-Th. Seguin (ed.), *Pratiques co-opératives et mutations sociales*, L'Harmattan, Paris.

Defourny, J. (1988), *Démocratie co-operative et efficacité économique*, De Boeck, Brussels.

Defourny, J. (ed.) (1995), *Développer l'entreprise sociale*, Fondation Roi Baudouin, Brussels.

Defourny, J. and Develtere, P. (1999), 'Origines et contours de l'économie sociale au Nord et au Sud', in J. Defourny, P. Develtere and B. Fonteneau (eds), *L'Économie sociale au Nord et au Sud*, De Boeck Université, Paris/Brussels, pp. 25–58.

Defourny J. and Monzon Campos, J.-L. (eds) (1992), *Économie sociale – The Third Sector*, De Boeck Université, Paris/ Brussels.

Defourny, J., Develtere, P and Fonteneau, B. (eds) (1999), *L'Économie sociale au Nord et au Sud*, De Boeck Université, Paris/Brussels.

Demazière, D. (1995), 'Le Chômage de longue durée', *Que sais-je?*, no. 2939, PUF, Paris.

Demoustier, D. and Pezzini, E. (1999), 'Économie sociale et création d'emplois dans les pays occidentaux', in J. Defourny, P. Develtere and B. Fonteneau (eds), *L'Économie sociale au Nord et au Sud*, Paris/Brussels, De Boeck Université, Paris/Brussels, pp. 123–141.

Desroche, H. (1976), *Le Projet co-opératif*, Éditions ouvrières, Paris.

De Tocqueville, A. (1991), *De la démocratie en Amérique*, Gallimard, Paris.

Disney, R. (ed.) (1992), *Helping the Unemployed. Active Labour Marker Policy in Britain and Germany*, Anglo-German Foundation, London.

Dubet, F. and Lapeyronnie, D. (1992), *Les Quartiers d'exil*, Seuil, Paris.

Elbaum, M. (1994), 'Les Activités intermédiaires: une sphère d'insertion autonome et un mode de partage du travail par défaut', *Travail et emploi*, October.

EMES Network (1999), *The Emergence of Social Enterprises in Europe*, Report to the European Commission, Brussels.

Erhel, C., Gautier, S., Gazier, B. and Morel, S. (1996), 'Job opportunities for the hard to place', in G. Schmid *et al.* (eds), *International Handbook of Labour Market Policy and Evaluation*, Edward Elgar, Cheltenham.

Fairbain, B. (1991), *Co-operatives and Community Development*, Centre for the Study of Co-operatives, University of Saskatchewan, Saskatoon.

Favreau, L. and Frechette, L. (1993), 'Du bidonville à la municipalité autogérée: acquis et tensions à Villa el Salvador', *Économie et humanisme*, no. 326, October.

Favreau, L. and Levesque, B. (1996), *Développement économique communautaire, économie sociale et intervention*, Presses de l'Université du Québec, Sainte-Foy.

Garonna, P. (1990), 'Indemnisation du chômage et politiques de l'emploi', *Revue française des affaires sociales*, no. 8.

Gautié, J., Gazier, B. and Silvera, R. (eds) (1994), *Les Subventions a l'emploi: analyse et expériences européennes*, La Documentation Française, Paris.

Gui, B. (1991), 'The economic rationale for the third sector', *Annals of Public and Co-operative Economics*, vol. 4.

Hansmann, H. (1980), 'The role of nonprofit enterprise', *Yale Law Journal*, vol. 89.

Jacquier, C. (1992), *Voyage dans dix quartiers européens en crise*, L'Harmattan, Paris.

James, E. (ed.) (1989), *The Nonprofit Organizations in International Perspective, Studies in Comparative Culture and Policy*, Oxford University Press, New York.

Lallement, M. (1996), 'Du gouvernement à la gouvernance de l'emploi', SET-METIS-CNRS, Université de Paris X, Paris.

Lallement, M. (1999), *Les Gouvernances de l'emploi*, Desclée de Brouwer, Paris.

Larrachea, I. and Nyssens, M. (1994), 'Les Défis de l'économie populaire en Chili', *Revue des études co-opératives, mutualistes et associatives*, vol.49, no. 252.

Laville, J.-L. (1991), 'L'Insertion par l'économique, évolution d'une problématique', *Problèmes économiques*, La Documentation Française, Paris, no. 2211.

Laville, J.-L. (ed.) (1994a), *L'Économie solidaire, une perspective internationale*, Desclée de Brouwer, Paris.

Laville, J.-L. (1994b), *Collectifs et co-opératives de travail en Europe. Éléments pour un bilan 1970-1980*, CRIDA-LSCI, CNRS, Paris.

Leduc Browne, P. (1996), *The Voluntary Sector in an Age of Cuts*, Canadian Centre for Policy Alternatives, Ottawa.

Lewis, D. (ed.) (1999), *International Perspectives on Voluntary Action. Reshaping the Third Sector*, Earthscan, London.

Lipietz, A. (1996), *La Société en sablier (le partage du travail contre la déchirure sociale)*, La Découverte, Paris.

Mahy, B. (1994), 'Politiques et recherche d'emploi: Évaluation microéconometrique', in *Reflets et perspectives de la vie économique*, vol. 33, no. 1–2.

Malgorn, B. (1995), *Pleine emploi ou pleine activité?*, Roneo.

Mertens, S. (1999), 'Nonprofit organizations and social economy: two ways of understanding the third sector', *Annals of Public and Cooperative Economics*, in press.

Muller, J.-L. (1994), *Les Politiques publiques*, Presses universitaires de France, Paris.

Nicaise, I. Bollens, J., Dawes, L., Laghaei, S., Thaulow, I., Verdié, M. and Wagner, A. (1995), *Labour Market Policies for the Poor in Europe: Pitfalls and Dilemmas – and How to Avoid Them*, Avebury, Aldershot.

Paton, R. (ed.) (1989), *Reluctant Entrepreneurs. The Extent, Achievements and Significance of Workers Takeovers in Europe*, Open University Press, Milton Keynes.

Perret, B. (1995), *L'Avenir da travail: les démocraties face au chômage*, Seuil, Paris.

Perret, B. and Roustang, G. (1995), *L'Économie contre la société*, Collection Esprit/Seuil, Paris.

Perri 6 and Vidal, I. (eds) (1994), *Delivering Welfare*, CIES, Barcelona.

Perry, L.F. and Stewart, E. (1987), *Communities on the Way (Rebuilding Local Economies in the United States and Canada)*, State University of New York Press, Albany.

Rifkin, J. (1995), *The End of Work The Decline of the Global Labor Force and the Dawn of the Post-Market Era*, Putnam's Son, New York.

Rocard, M. (1996), *Les Moyens d'en sortir*, Seuil-essais, Paris.

Rodrigo, J.-M. (1990), *Le Sentier de l'audace. Les Organisations populaires a la conquête de Pérou*, L'Hannattan, Paris.

Roustang, G., Laville, J.-L., Eme, B., Mothé, D. and Ferret, B. (1996), *Vers un nouveau contrat social*, Desclée de Brouwer, Paris.

Salamon, L.M. and Anheier, H.K. (1996), *The Emerging Nonprofit Sector, an Overview*, Manchester University Press, Manchester and New York.

Salamon, L.M., Anheier, H.K. (and Associates) (1998), *The Emerging Sector Revisited, a Summary, Initial Estimates*, Johns Hopkins University, Baltimore.

Séchet, R. (1996), *Espaces et pauvretés*, L'Harmattan, Paris.

Sewell, H. (1983), *Gens de métier et révolution*, Aubier, Paris.

Touraine, A. (1973) *Production de la société*, Seuil, Paris.

Van Der Linden, B. (ed.) (1997), *Chômage. Réduire la fracture*, De Boeck, Brussels.

Vienney, C. (1994), *L'Économie sociale*, La Découverte, Paris.

PART I: WORK INTEGRATION AND THE NEW SOCIAL ECONOMY IN TEN INDUSTRIALISED COUNTRIES

2 Austria: Recent Employment Initiatives within a Strong Tradition of Public Action

PETER ULRICH LEHNER

1. Employment Policies and the *Aktion 8000* Programme

Before the First World War the public authorities in Austria were not responsible for regulating the labour market and intervening to foster employment. However, this situation changed in 1917 with the creation of the Ministry of Social Affairs, which began work the following year.[1] This new ministry was responsible in particular for recruitment agencies and providing assistance for the unemployed.

In the aftermath of the First World War the new Austrian republic implemented the directives of the International Labour Organisation[2] and laid the foundations of a social policy that has remained virtually unchanged to this day. A law of March 1920 replaced temporary unemployment benefit with compulsory legal insurance against unemployment. This means that the social problem of unemployment is basically a matter for the government's social policy,[3] and the public institutions are responsible for taking steps to combat unemployment.

After 1945, given the political situation in Austria and its impact on economic development, it proved necessary to wait several years before achieving a satisfactory employment situation. The government was forced to adopt measures to assist certain groups of the population who found it difficult to gain access to employment. Hence immediately after the war two successive laws were passed, one in July 1946 and the second in July 1953; the first obliged companies to employ disabled people and the second to recruit young people. This latter law was intended to respond to the

---

[1] Klenner (1951); Tálos (1981).
[2] Lehner (1995b).
[3] Tálos (1981).

31

arrival on the labour market of young people who had experienced the war and had completed their education.

However, the main instrument used to create and maintain employment was the nationalisation of the heavy industries in 1946 and 1947. The trade unions called for this measure with a view to improving the employment situation and reducing unemployment.

It is true to say that in Austria, the nationalised heavy industry was for a long time the cornerstone of a satisfactory labour market,[4] achieving full employment for many years. What is more, in the 1970s, when there was a slowdown in economic growth, heavy industry made it possible to maintain a high level of employment.[5] From a macroeconomics point of view, this nationalisation also brought about a redistribution in favour of earned income.[6]

The measures intended to improve the economic structures in Austria included, among others, the adoption in 1968 of a law aimed at promoting the labour market. This made it possible, for the first time, to entrust job-seeking activities to charitable organisations, professional commercial associations or legal bodies defending the interest of specific groups that, like the trade unions, were authorised to negotiate collective agreements under certain conditions.

In 1998, the level of unemployment in Austria (4.4%) was slightly more than two-thirds that of the OECD (6.8%) and half of that of the European Union (9.9%). However, unemployment, which has just risen back to its 1953 level, has become a major political problem. Currently, companies are no longer prepared to keep their staff on until the economy recovers. In addition, even when demand rises, this does not necessarily bring with it new jobs or investments, since companies are worried about fluctuations in orders.[7]

The measures adopted over the past 15 years for the economy and employment are in some respects contradictory. On the one hand, since the end of the 1980s, the Austrian government has followed the general trend towards deregulation and privatisation, thereby worsening the unemployment problem in the short term. In addition, the public employment policy has been undermined by the need to achieve a balanced budget, with the resultant social costs.[8] On the other hand, further efforts

---

[4] Langer (1966).
[5] Goldmann (1993); Grünwald (1993).
[6] Hwaletz (1990).
[7] Lechner *et al.* (1988).
[8] Althaler and Dimmel (1993).

have been made to improve the effectiveness of job seeking, in which voluntary organisations are directly involved. These efforts are in line with the OECD recommendations in favour of local employment initiatives aimed at avoiding regional underdevelopment.[9]

In 1983, the adoption of an amendment to the law on the promotion of the labour market enabled the Ministry of Social Affairs to reach agreements with 'institutions with a general purpose' whose mission is to create and safeguard jobs. On the basis of such agreements, the Ministry granted these voluntary organisations aid that could go as far as covering all their personnel and equipment costs. Thanks to this amendment, the 'experimental labour market policy', as it has come to be known, came into being. However, it should be noted that this concept has not been systematically developed in Austria. Its main feature is adapting to circumstances by adopting innovative measures.[10]

A year later, the Ministry of Social Affairs launched a special programme aimed at creating 8000 new jobs ('*Aktion 8000*') for the long-term unemployed.[11] This programme has been implemented in the 'non-profit' sector in the context of the 'experimental labour market policy'. It has become the main instrument in the fight against long-term unemployment.[12]

For the first time in the history of post-war Austrian labour market policy, private companies have been excluded from employment promotion measures. In fact, the jobs must be created exclusively in the public services or sectors of general interest (generating public benefit or utility including those activities with a non-profit-making character). Focusing this programme on non-profit organisations has lent it an experimental aspect. Apart from its job creation measures, *Aktion 8000* also has to play a role as regards the supply policy. Hence it could fill gaps in social security networks, promote cultural activities, improve housing and living conditions or participate in environmental protection schemes.

To improve the possibilities of reintegration for those receiving assistance, *Aktion 8000* aims to consolidate and improve existing knowledge and abilities. The programme also has to ensure adequate remuneration to avoid the risk of poverty or social decline among the beneficiaries. This is why the implementing regulation for *Aktion 8000*

---

[9] Feiler (1991).
[10] Klien (1995).
[11] Feiler (1991).
[12] Klien (1995).

stipulates that revenue must be granted in line with the pay levels in the region concerned or on the basis of the relevant collective agreements.[13]

In order to ensure that this measure does not lead to the development of a 'second class' labour market, the programme has defined preconditions: participation must be voluntary; the remuneration must be in line with all the standards prevailing in industrial or social law and with common practices in the area; the job must last at least one year; the job must be enriching, offering the opportunity for self-improvement; the work must be as interesting as possible; finally, it must be accessible to the unemployed who are not entitled to unemployment benefit, so that they can recover this entitlement once they have fulfilled the condition of having worked for a minimum of 12 months.[14]

The *Aktion 8000* programme is not based exclusively on co-operation with voluntary organisations, but the latter do play a leading role in it. Without *Aktion 8000,* which is still underway, voluntary organisations would not make such a major contribution to reintegration through work.

2.   The Organisations Involved in Integration

Unfortunately there is no detailed description of all the organisations involved in employment and reintegration. The 1983 amendment only refers to 'institutions of general interest' that can benefit from the support of the Ministry of Social Affairs. A law of 1994 instituting a labour market service simply refers to 'appropriate institutions'. These are based on the principle of mutual assistance and create jobs for people who do not have work or who face redundancy, such as employment or reintegration initiatives and associations offering social services, training and care activities. The institutions develop significant participation for the workers on the basis of equality and consultation.

These 'institutions of general interest' do not have to have any specific legal form. However, apart from mutual societies, which do not work in the fields of employment and reintegration, co-operatives and autonomous enterprises – the latter two rarely taking initiatives in the field of employment – the most appropriate legal form in terms of 'general interest' is that of a voluntary organisation.

---

[13] Lechner *et al.* (1988).
[14] Klien (1995).

2.1. *Voluntary Organisations*

Voluntary organisations with responsibilities in terms of labour market policy can be divided into three categories: umbrella organisations, voluntary organisations linked to established organisations, and autonomous voluntary organisations.

Umbrella organisations When the *Aktion 8000* programme was launched, umbrella organisations were created in several Austrian provinces. These organisations have very close links either with the provincial government, or with a group of supervisory institutions such as the social partners or public organisations. They may be responsible for all the *Aktion 8000* target groups, or for more specific groups. Working relations are established between the members and the umbrella organisation and not between the member and the voluntary organisation or the project for which he works. The umbrella organisation enables a municipal service or a voluntary organisation to find positions for its members, thereby constituting a form of labour force contracting.

This procedure relieves the labour market service of some of its duties to the extent that the administrative tasks are undertaken by the umbrella organisation. Consequently this is welcomed by the agencies of the labour market service working on the ground, but on the other hand the municipalities are increasingly abandoning their responsibilities as regards finding jobs for those who have reached the end of the programme.

Such umbrella organisations exist, for example, in the provinces of Carinthia and Tyrol. They were set up to ensure intra- and inter-regional harmonisation of the implementation of *Aktion 8000*, to reduce bureaucracy or to focus the employment promotion measures on certain target groups.[15]

Voluntary organisations linked to established organisations This second type of voluntary organisation usually has links with political parties or other institutions such as Churches. Generally speaking, these voluntary organisations provide social services or act within the framework of the social security policy. They serve a general purpose and, as such, are taken into consideration by the labour market service when implementing the *Aktion 8000* programme. Examples of this include the *Caritas* humanitarian organisations linked to the Catholic Church, or *Volkshilfe*, which is linked

---

[15] Lechner *et al.* (1988).

to the Social Democrat Party.[16] However, all the voluntary organisations of this type existed well before the launch of the *Aktion 8000* programme.

Autonomous voluntary organisations   The main characteristic of the autonomous voluntary organisations is the fact that they are not linked to established institutions. Apart from that, they operate in exactly the same way. Many of them were set up in the wake of the development of the public policy for the fight against unemployment. Unfortunately no national survey of these voluntary organisations is available, mainly because there are too many of them and they are too specific to local contexts. All that exists is an overall survey of social projects in the province of Upper Austria, but this merely consists of case studies and not a standardised and systematic analysis.

The only data available concern 63 voluntary organisations that belong mainly to the category of autonomous voluntary organisations and that develop projects in various sectors of activity. There are 95 projects most of which operate in the following areas: 28 in the education sector (30%), 20 in the field of employment (21%) and 45 in social welfare and well-being (47%). Of the 63 voluntary organisations, 53, or 84%, have been set up since 1983. The impact of the 1983 amendment referred to above is clearly visible here. Hence between 1963 and 1982 only ten such voluntary organisations were created. These figures clearly illustrate the influence of the development of the legal frameworks of the employment policy on voluntary organisations at the regional level.[17]

These different types of voluntary organisation are among the 'external assistance and services institutions' that assist the labour market service through activities requiring special experience and know-how. They specialise in supporting certain problem groups, such as drug addicts, young people with social difficulties, former prisoners, those with psychological problems, those overburdened with debt, immigrants, the long-term unemployed, those on social security benefit or women with specific employment problems.[18]

---

[16] Lehner (1995a).
[17] 'Neubeginn' (1994); personal evaluations by the author.
[18] Fast and Schopf (1994).

2.2. Job Promotion or Job Protection Projects

Two main types of project have been set up in conjunction with the labour market service.[19]

Autonomous enterprises These emerged from the context of commercial enterprises threatened with closure and taken over by the workers.

A 'Socio-economic Employment' Policy: P.S.I.–Freizeitanlagenbau

P.S.I.-Freizeitanlagenbau is a leisure infrastructure construction company located in Friedburg in the province of Salzburg, whose support organisation is an autonomous voluntary organisation of the same name.

P.S.I.-Freizeitanlagenbau was born from the desire to develop project activities aimed at reintegrating the long-term unemployed in a peripheral region. Its activities, which focus on wood processing, consist of the production, assembly and installation of products for play areas and gardens.

The projects offers disadvantaged individuals one-year contracts with a standard employer–employee relationship and socio-pedagogic support. Every year, three months are devoted to woodwork training. The project is aimed mainly at certain groups of people: the long-term unemployed, young people with social integration problems, who either have attended a school for pupils with psychological or mental problems or do not have a learning certificate, disadvantaged older unemployed people, immigrants, former prisoners or those who are on probation.

Candidates belonging to these groups can be recruited, provided the placement agency agrees. Once they have been taken on, workers are supported by a director, two workshop heads, a social assistant and a secretary.

The public authorities only provide the share of the costs not covered by the sale of the goods and services produced by the project. The project is not normally expected to generate a surplus, except possibly to pay for promotional measures and subsidy.[20]

They benefit from support from the labour market service upon start-up in the form of a subsidy or a loan to establish, take over or save the enterprise. Subsequently, the enterprise has to become profitable and ensure its own

---

[19] Klien (1995).
[20] 'Neubeginn' (1994).

survival. This type of enterprise has the legal status of a private limited liability company or more rarely a co-operative.

The subsidy granted amounts to around 150,000 Austrian schillings per job.[21] This is a relatively small sum compared with the assistance granted by the public authorities to establish or develop profit-oriented businesses, which varies from 300,000 to 1 million schillings per job.[22]

The 'socio-economic employment projects' These projects, which aim to integrate disadvantaged people into the labour market, draw much of their revenue from the production and sale of goods and services.[23] However, unlike autonomous enterprises, profitability is not a prerequisite for their launch. Their main aim is to reintegrate the long-term unemployed who currently find it impossible to integrate into ordinary working life.

Socio-economic employment projects have a role to play both in terms of the employment policy and the social policy. They offer the beneficiaries jobs with financial support for a limited period, as a transition to the conventional labour market. Integration into the labour market is also seen as a vehicle for social integration. In most cases, alongside vocational training socio-pedagogic support is provided to ensure the transition towards the conventional labour market the greatest possible chance of success.[24]

Since the productivity of those placed in such jobs is usually limited, it is impossible for these projects to achieve economic autonomy. Consequently, permanent financial aid from the support organisation and/or the public authorities is essential.

3.   An Evaluation of the *Aktion 8000* Programme

The results of research covering two periods provides a relatively complete picture of the programme. The first of these periods runs from 1984 to 1986,[25] while the second covers the years 1988 to 1990.[26] The year 1987 and more recent years have not yet been analysed in depth.

---

[21] Around 13.8 Austrian schillings to 1 euro (August 1997).

[22] *Betriebliche*, s.d.; Paulesich (1996); Klien (1995).

[23] Fast and Schopf (1994).

[24] Klien (1995).

[25] Lechner *et al.* (1988).

[26] *Anforderungsgerecht* (1995).

3.1. *The Profile of the Beneficiaries*

Between the beginning of the *Aktion 8000* programme in 1984 and 1994, around 45,000 people benefited from these measures.[27] Between 1984 and 1986, the annual average was 2191 people and from 1988 to 1990, this figure was 2962. Given that these figures are considerably lower than the average of 4500 people a year during the programme as a whole, it may be concluded that the strongest growth has been recorded in more recent years which have not yet been analysed.

The breakdown according to age between the two periods shows that the number of beneficiaries aged over 25 has risen from 42% to 68%. As for the breakdown by gender, it is striking to note that the number of women rose substantially between the first and second period. Men only account for a significantly higher percentage in the over-45 age group during the second period, and this phenomenon disappears when this group is included in the over-25s. This trend in favour of women has also continued since 1990: by the first half of 1994 the proportion of women beneficiaries reached two-thirds.[28]

During the first period, a substantial proportion of the beneficiaries (48%), were unemployed people aged under 25, who had been without work for between three and six months, while 44% of those aged over 25 had been without work for between six and 12 months. These figures show that these are basically people whose period of unemployment meets the criterion for assistance.[29] During the second period, around 80% of all age groups were classified as long-term unemployed.[30]

There are no data on training levels in the first period. For the second period, most of the beneficiaries simply had the compulsory school attendance certificate, while almost one-third (31.4%) of the beneficiaries did not have any qualifications at all. These unskilled people worked on village enhancement projects, renovation, marketable goods and services, or environmental protection. It should be added that these activities were undertaken mainly by men, while a considerable proportion of unskilled women (42%) worked in the field of personal services.

---

[27] *Anforderungsgerecht* (1995); Klien (1995).
[28] *Anforderungsgerecht* (1995).
[29] Lechner *et al.* (1988).
[30] *Anforderungsgerecht* (1995).

3.2. *The Institutions and the Sectors of Activity*

A comparison of the two periods reveals that the role of the public institutions has declined relative to that of the voluntary organisations, and the autonomous voluntary organisations sector has expanded substantially.

During the first period, the number of jobs with municipalities fell from 47% in 1984 to 29% in 1986, while jobs with the autonomous voluntary organisations rose from 9% to 25%, due to the decline in the availability of jobs with municipalities.[31] This trend continued during the second period. Overall, the results of the survey show that the public authorities are increasingly withdrawing from the promotion of employment.[32] Assisted jobs are concentrated in sectors of activity where needs are great, but inadequately covered by the market. Consequently, the risks of competition are limited.[33]

During these two periods, social services played a major role. However, the increasing share of income from marketable goods and services in the second period is a sign of the performance of socio-economic employment projects, which sell their products and services in the market. Compared with the initial phase of *Aktion 8000*, the employment sectors expanded during the second period. However, it is important to note that social services continue to play a leading role, even if they no longer hold the pre-eminent position they had from 1984 to 1986.[34]

3.3. *The Results of* Aktion 8000 *in Terms of Integration*

In all, 50.8% of the beneficiaries in the first period were still in work at the end of the project, either with the same employer or with someone else. The remainder include those who found work in another province and who therefore no longer appear in the social security database of the original province.

Around two-thirds (63.5%) of those who continued to work (1388) remained with the initial organisation. When the organisation in question is a municipality, the possibility for the beneficiary to retain his or her position obviously depends on the budgetary situation. When cutbacks have to be made, the municipal officials very often try to find work for this

---

[31] Lechner *et al.* (1988).
[32] *Anforderungsgerecht* (1995).
[33] Lechner *et al.* (1988).
[34] *Anforderungsgerecht* (1995).

person in a private company. However, the extent to which a job is maintained varies from one sector of activities to another.[35]

The trends observed during the first period continued during the second, although a larger number of jobs (57%) were retained, particularly with the original organisation.[36] However, the possibilities for reintegration vary depending on the category of the beneficiaries. The degree of reintegration is far higher among women than among men: 56% of women in such situations have a regular job, as against just 36% for men. Compared with other obstacles to employment, a period of unemployment lasting over six months constitutes a very serious handicap to integration.[37]

3.4. The Budgetary Impact of the Programme

Participation in the *Aktion 8000* programme provides the beneficiary with a regular income, which is higher than unemployment benefit. Very often during the integration period, the beneficiary improves his or her qualifications, thus holding out the prospect of ultimate integration into the labour market with a higher salary. As regards public finances, additional revenue, or higher revenue arises from an increase in the amount collected in taxes and duties. If the person concerned had remained among the ranks of the unemployed, the public authorities would not have been able to benefit from these additional taxes. However, it should be noted that if, after the period of assistance, it has not proved possible to reintegrate a person who was previously not eligible for unemployment benefit and who therefore remains without a job, this person will be able to claim this benefit and consequently the public authorities will have to pay an amount which was not due before the assistance was received, resulting a further charge to be borne by the budget.[38]

The cost of unemployment for society as a whole includes the direct costs (benefits paid to the unemployed) and the indirect costs (loss of tax revenue and social security contributions). In 1993 the cost of unemployment per individual amounted to an average of 250,000 schillings. The average cost of the promotion measures per person is far lower: between 70,000 and 150,000 schillings. This means that if the programmes succeed, the state benefits substantially in financial terms.

---

[35] Lechner *et al.* (1988).

[36] *Anforderungsgerecht* (1995).

[37] *Anforderungsgerecht* (1995).

[38] Lechner *et al.* (1988).

Consequently it is difficult to understand why there is so much hesitation and reluctance to implement these programmes in Austria.[39]

An evaluation for 1990 confirms that the *Aktion 8000* programme had a positive outcome for the public authorities. In fact, the additional receipts that came into the social security coffers thanks to the new jobs created amounted to around 119 million schillings, while the additional tax receipts were estimated at 90.5 million schillings. Overall, receipts therefore totalled around 209.5 million schillings. On the opposite side of the calculation, additional expenditure amounted to some 25.4 million schillings. This gives a balance of 184.1 million schillings, exceeding the 155.8 million schillings paid out in unemployment benefit. Consequently, the profits generated by these assistance measures in 1990 totalled around 28.3 million schillings.

4.   The Results of Autonomous Enterprises and Socio-economic Employment Projects

We have noted that one group of integration initiatives not based on the *Aktion 8000* programme are known as autonomous enterprises. A survey has been conducted on 29 of these enterprises during the period 1990 to 1992. Some of the results, when compared with data on profit-oriented businesses,[40] give rise to the following observations:

(a) The economic performance of most of the enterprises considered is very stable, and in some cases improving. As the average personnel costs are higher than those of industry as a whole, it may be concluded that these structures offer a higher salary level.

(b) An average of 1.3 jobs were created per business in conventional small and medium-sized enterprises, while this figure is 3.5 times higher for autonomous enterprises. Of all the enterprises surveyed, those involved in small-scale industry integrate the largest number of workers. The trade sector has the highest growth rate and offers the longest period of employment. The 'gastronomy and culture' sector has the highest level of fluctuation, probably due to the qualifications required. The 'gastronomy and culture' and 'trade and services' sectors also have the highest proportion of part-time jobs.

---

[39] Klien (1995).
[40] Paulesich (1996).

(c) As regards to training, the results obtained by the enterprises considered were not very convincing; nor were those relating to the creation of jobs for women.

(d) The application of co-operative principles, which is one of the conditions to be fulfilled in order to receive the subsidies, was not satisfactory. The identity principle whereby 'all proprietors are also members of staff' is undermined by external shareholders. The principle of solidarity is weakened by the differentiation of functions and a tendency towards hierarchical organisation. And the democratic principle of 'one person, one vote' was only applied in the creation phase, but was subsequently limited to shareholders and not applied to other workers.[41]

(e) The results of the research show that autonomous enterprises are heavily dependent on external financial resources granted mainly by ministries, provincial governments or municipalities.

Finally, as regards the socio-economic employment projects, no precise conclusions can be drawn from the available data. However, all the employment indicators have clearly risen, even though the number of projects has remained stable. A slight increase may also be observed in the level of self-financing thanks to own revenue generated by the sale of goods and services, although the share of costs borne by the public authorities is around 60%.

5. Conclusions and Outlook

The implementation of social projects aimed at integration was initially viewed with suspicion and reservation by the established institutions, particularly the employers' organisations and the trade unions – even though the minister who launched these measures was a staunch trade unionist. It was impossible to convince the politicians that social projects were the only way of providing an opening into the labour market for the long-term unemployed or other groups in difficulties. The financial resources therefore remained inadequate and people only gradually came to understand that such efforts required the services of professionals who needed to be paid an adequate salary.[42]

---

[41] Paulesich (1996).
[42] Klien (1995).

It is now generally agreed that the *Aktion 8000* programme has been and still is a success, as can be seen from the two surveys we have reviewed.[43] Although this success has gradually become clear, it is surprising to note that year after year not all the financial resources earmarked for the labour market policy have been used and that in Austria the budget allocated to active labour market policy has remained below the European average.[44] Given the lack of political will to fight unemployment, there is reason to fear that the unsatisfactory development of the labour market will not only continue but could even worsen. Consequently, 'technical' measures alone will not be sufficient to solve the problem.

The *Aktion 8000* programme could be expanded and used to increase the involvement of institutions of general interest. For this, the following requirements would have to be satisfied: an extension of the period covered by the assistance, the compulsory involvement of a growing number of labour market players, the intensification of the advice and assistance services provided by the support bodies, the preparation of specific programmes for groups with particular difficulties, such as women or immigrants, improved public relations, the intensification of research and evaluation, and finally a better combination of measures relating to education and employment.[45]

References

Althaler, K.S. and Dimmel N. (1993), 'Sozialpolitische Handlungsfelder der experimentellen Arbeitsmarktpolitik', *Österreichische Zeitschrift für Politikwissenschaft*, no. 3, pp. 343–360.

Anforderungsgerecht (1995), *Aktion 8000. Arbeitsplätze fördern statt Arbeitslosengeld bezahlen. Die Wirkung des Beschäftigungsprogramms Aktion 8000*, L&R Sozialforschung, Vienna.

Betriebliche Selbstverwaltung in Österreich, (vol. 3 of *Schriftenreihe Forschungsberichte aus Sozial-und Arbeitsmarktpolitik*), Bundesministerium für Arbeit und Soziales (Hrsg.), s.d., Vienna.

Bichler, H. (1996), 'Auf die Zielsetzung kommt es an', *Mitbestimmung*, 4/1996, pp. 5–8.

Biffl, G. (Randgruppen) (1995), 'Innovative Arbeitsmarktpolitik für Randgruppen', in *Kurswechsel*, Vienna, pp. 91–100.

Eberl, K. and Nagel, R., 'Maldek–Malerei und Dekoration, registrierte Genossenschaft m. b. H., Wien', in *Betriebliche Selbstverwaltung in Österreich* (vol. 3 of *Schriftenreihe Forschungsberichte aus Sozial-und Arbeitsmarktpolitik*), Bundesministerium für Arbeit und Soziales (Hrsg.), s.d., Vienna, pp. 105–141.

---

[43] Lechner *et al.* (1988); *Anforderungsgerecht* (1995).

[44] Klien (1995); Biffl (1995).

[45] Lechner *et al.* (1988); Klien (1995).

Fast, R. and Schopf, R. (1994), *Die österreichische Arbeitsmarktpolitik, Ziele, Instrumente und Organisation,* Bundesministerium für Arbeit und Soziales (Hrsg.), Vienna.

Feiler, L. (1991), 'Zehn Jahre ÖSB', *ÖSB-Informationen,* no. 2, p. 4.

Goldmann, W. (1993), 'Verstaatlichten-Politik in der Ära Kreisky', in F. Weber and T. Venus (eds), *Austro-Keynesianismus in Theorie und Praxis,* Jugend & Volk Verlag und Dachs Verlag, Vienna, pp. 129–134.

Grünwald, O. (1993), 'Verstaatlichte Industrie in der Ära Kreisky', in F. Weber and T. Venus (eds), *Austro-Keynesianismus in Theorie und Praxis,* Jugend & Volk Verlag und Dachs Verlag, Vienna, pp. 118–128.

Hwaletz, O. (1990), *Über den Prozeß von Akkumulation und Kapitalverwertung in Österreich,* Böhlau Verlag, Cologne, Vienna.

Kischko, I. (1990), 'Acht Jahre Maldek Genossenschaft', *ÖSB-Informationen,* no. 2, p. 8.

Klenner, F. (1951), *Die österreichischen Gewerkschaften. Vergangenheit und Gegenwartsprobleme,* vol. 1, Verlag des Österreichischen Gewerkschaftsbundes, Vienna.

Klien, R. (1995), 'Sozialprojekte im Kampf gegen die Langzeitarbeitslosigkeit', in *Stellenwert der Sozialprojekte im Kampf gegen die Langzeitarbeitslosigkeit,* Pungor János and the Verein zur Verbreitung Wissenschaftlicher Kenntnisse, Szombathely, pp. 36–57.

Langer, E. (1966), *Die Verstaatlichungen in Österreich,* Verlag der Wiener Volksbuchhandlung, Vienna.

Lechner, F., Reiter, W. and Fehr-Duda, H. (1988), 'Evaluation der *Aktion 8000.* Die Wirkungsanalyse eines arbeitsmarktpolitischen Förderprogramms' (vol. 23 der *Schriftenreihe Forschungsberichte aus Sozial-und Arbeitsmarktpolitik*), Bundesministerium für Arbeit und Soziales (Hrsg.), Vienna.

Lehner, P.U. (1995a), 'Care for the elderly. An example from Austria. The Viennese model', paper for the 'associations' working group of the CIRIEC, Vienna.

Lehner, P.U. (1995b), 'Die Internationale Arbeitsorganisation. Zur Geschichte einer mühevollen Beharrlichkeit', *Gemeinwirtschaft,* no. 1, pp. 49–70.

'Neubeginn' (1994), 'Für viele ein Neubeginn', *80 Oberösterreichische Sozialprojekte in Selbstdarstellungen,* Plattform der Oberösterreichischen Sozialprojekte (Hrsg.), Linz.

Paulesich, R. (1996), 'Kooperative Unternehmensgründungen', in *AMS-info 2,* Wissenschaftsverlag, Vienna.

Tálos, E. (1981), *Staatliche Sozialpolitik in Österreich. Rekonstruktion und Analyse,* Verlag für Gesellschaftskritik, Vienna.

3 Belgium: Voluntary Organisations and Integration through Work in Francophone Belgium

JACQUES DEFOURNY, MARTHE NYSSENS AND MICHEL SIMON

1. Public Policy and Voluntary Organisations Confront Unemployment

Despite a spectacular rise in employment between 1984 and 1991 Belgium has been characterised by an indifferent performance in the area of job creation. Unemployment, particularly among the poorly qualified, dogs the Belgian labour market.[1]

The Belgian system of unemployment insurance is conspicuous by its lack of time limits. A growing number of unemployed people are seeing their benefits challenged due to progressively restrictive regulations. But essentially, there is no time limit to the system of public assistance when it takes over from unemployment insurance. This insurance system seems to have a negative overall impact on the rate at which people move in and out of employment:[2] it slows the rate at which they move into employment, and discourages them from the option of taking retirement. For this reason a wide range of active policies have been introduced to encourage a more positive approach to job seeking and job creation. The development of vocational training, programmes to reduce unemployment, and help for recruitment are the main planks of these active policies. These initiatives work closely with the growth of associative (voluntary sector) initiatives, we must first stress the importance of the unemployment reduction programmes (*Programmes de résorption du chômage*, PCR). They provide a varied range of measures.

---

[1] De Villé and Van der Linden (1994).
[2] Dor *et al.* (1995).

In 1975, the public authorities launched a programme for getting the unemployed back to work (*Chômeurs mis au travail*, CMT), which lasted until 1989. The special temporary management programme (*Cadres spéciaux temporaires*, CST) ran from 1977 to 1989; the *Troisieme Circuit de travail* (TCT), set up in 1982, operated until 1990 in Wallonie and still exists elsewhere; the inter-departmental fund for job promotion *(Fonds budgétaire interdépartemental de promotion de l'emploi*, FBI) was also founded in 1982; the subsidised contract scheme (*Agents contractuels subventionnés*, ACS) was set up in 1986; and from 1990, regional work-integration projects (*Projets régionaux d'insertion dans le marché d'emploi*, PRIME) replaced the TCT programme in Wallonie. Finally, 1997 saw the establishment of vocational transition programmes (*Programmes de transition professionelle*, PTP). In all these programmes, the public authorities assume responsibility for a high proportion, and sometimes almost all, of the wage costs of taking on unemployed people to work on projects for the general interest, be it for long or short periods of time.

For a long time these unemployment reduction programmes were a federal responsibility, but since 1989 they have been managed by the regions. They now employ almost 100,000 people. Around 40,000 of these posts are in the voluntary sector. Many voluntary organisations working on the ground have developed socially useful projects in many areas of activity, organising and managing the return to work of thousands of unemployed people. Designed to function as 'bridging or intermediary jobs' leading to reintegration into the labour market, these placements, in spite of their low status, have in fact become long-term jobs, though with some more and some less secure than others. Furthermore, evaluation studies indicate that those who have had the advantage of these placements are less likely than other unemployed people to move on to a 'real' job.[3] The promoters of projects receiving regional grants towards such placements point out that, apart from the problems of insecurity, it is difficult to find people who simultaneously satisfy the condition that they be unemployed and are right for the job.

But the voluntary sector, and the social economy sector more generally, are not recent arrivals in the fight against unemployment. On the more commercial side of the social economy, we can look back as far as the second half of the 19th century, when voluntary organisations and workers' co-operatives brought together workers trying to create their own jobs or get together to save a business threatened with closure. After a very

---

[3] Mahy (1994).

long period of eclipse, a new wave of workers' co-operatives appeared in the second half of the 1970s and the beginning of the 1980s. However, co-operation along these lines remained very weak compared with the vast users' co-operatives (consumers, savers, farmers, etc.) that dominated the history of the Belgian co-operative movement.

The voluntary organisations, embodying an essentially non-commercial social economy, have undergone an astonishing development since the Second World War. Whether constituted as non-profit voluntary organisations (*Associations sans but lucratif*, ASBL) a legal structure introduced in 1921, or simply as *de facto* voluntary organisations, they have multiplied over a growing range of activities bearing witness to the vitality of civil society.[4] Besides this, various factors more or less specific to Belgium, have contributed to give voluntary organisations a position and growing role in the provision of many services, even within public service missions (teaching, health, socio-cultural matters, etc.):

(a) the organisation of Belgian society by very separate Christian and secular branches, each controlling its own organisations and services;

(b) the continued presence in government of Christian social parties that have traditionally defended the intermediate associative bodies;

(c) the exceptional flexibility of the ASBL constitution that allows, among other things, significant commercial activities in pursuit of a voluntary organisation's social objectives;

(d) and the proliferation of dynamic voluntary organisations following closely on the events of May 1968, etc.

Today the Belgian voluntary sector is like a vast nebula made up of a huge number of small and medium sized voluntary organisations as well as ASBL, which have become large employers: without counting the *de facto* voluntary organisations, recent studies have shown that there are around 50,000 ASBL active in Belgium today, and as well as involving a considerable number of voluntary workers the ASBL employ about 297,000 workers.[5]

---

[4] Whereas during the 1950s around 500 ASBL were set up annually.

[5] Defourny *et al.* (1997). This figure includes the 70,440 jobs in hospitals set up as ASBL but does not include the very special case of schools in the 'free network' (essentially Catholic) which are generally constituted as ASBL and employ more than 132,000 workers.

2. Initiatives for Integration through Economic Measures: the Main Forms

Starting at the end of the 1970s, in response to the failure or limited success of traditional policies for integration, the voluntary organisations developed fresh initiatives which were better suited to the most disadvantaged among the unemployed, especially the least qualified. Two major types of scheme can be distinguished: those offering trainee opportunities for occupational training, and those which aimed to create stable jobs for unqualified workers.

2.1. Occupational Training

During the 1980s a series of small companies were set up with ASBL legal structure to offer people, who had broken with the traditional education system, the opportunity to work while receiving training through the supervision of specialised instructors. However, these companies operated on the margins of the law: their promoters were not in a position to respect the whole range of legal constraints which applied to them. Until 1986, they even completely flouted some legal requirements (regarding fraudulent work, wage protection, the guaranteed minimum wage, opportunities to pursue a career, and compulsory education).

For this reason, in 1987, the French Community in Belgium recognised vocational training companies, *Entreprises d'apprentissage professionel* (EAP). The conditions for approval and method of subsidy were set out in 1991 and revised in 1995 by the regional authorities in Wallonie when they assumed administrative responsibility for the scheme. At this stage the EAP were included in a somewhat wider framework, to be known in future as on-the-job training companies, *Entreprise de formation par le travail* (EFT). The conditions for EFT recognition include the following main points. The EFT must be designed to give their trainees training based on education through productive work; they are authorised to produce and market goods or services as far as necessary to realise their objectives; and trainees cannot remain on the scheme for more than 18 months. For their part, trainees must fulfil three main conditions: they must be aged over 18, they must not be enrolled full-time in an educational establishment, and they must not hold a lower secondary school certificate. Note that the EFT are open to people over the age of 25 and to people on unemployment benefit, which was seen as a considerable advance on the position that predated the 1995 legislation.

In the Brussels region, the terminology is slightly different, using the term *Ateliers* (workshops) *de formation par le travail* (AFT). A general law relating to the various bodies for social and professional integration, which was adopted in 1995 only requires people entering an AFT to be residents of the Brussels region, in search of work, and without the lower secondary school certificate. Other aspects of legislation for the AFT are still being studied.

There are now about 60 EFT in francophone Belgium, which offer more than 1000 training posts at any time.

Very similar schemes also exist in Flanders, where they are known as *leerwerkbedrijven, leerwerkplaatsen,* or *werkervaringsprojecten.* These projects aim to reintegrate disadvantaged people into the labour market by providing them with work. The length of this 'on-the-job' training may not exceed one year. These bodies work in much the same spirit as the EFT, however, there are two important differences: the absence of strict criteria for admission, and the existence of a legal structure very close to an employment contract for people undergoing training.

2.2. Job Creation Initiatives

Other initiatives aim to provide unqualified people with a secure job rather than vocational training.

Sheltered workshops Beginning in the 1960s, initiatives for providing lasting jobs for the least qualified increased, being principally aimed at people with physical or mental disabilities. Today there are 150 sheltered workshops in Belgium, offering secure paid work to about 20,000 disabled people through the production of goods and services sold in the market, which enables these particular firms to be partly self-financing (about 50% on average). The sheltered workshops have the legal form of an ASBL and receive public subsidies according to very precise rules, in order to finance the supervision of the disabled workers and compensate for their lower productivity.

Social workshops In Flanders, the idea of sheltered employment, for so long mainly aimed at helping people with physical or mental disabilities into work, has now found another practical expression. Since the beginning of the 1980s, severely disadvantaged people with serious social and professional difficulties (few qualifications, illiteracy, a criminal record, difficult family situations, etc.) have been welcomed into the social workshops, *sociale werkplaatsen* (SWP).

The approach developed by these bodies is closely related to the idea of on-the-job training, but there is no time limit. They provide a lasting job, generally in activities, which are useful to the community enabling them to generate some income of their own, but which also need a high level of subsidy.

The *sociale werkplaatsen* operated for a long time under precarious conditions without any formal recognition. However, in 1994, the Flemish region established an experimental legal and financial framework for these initiatives. In time it expects to produce a general law on sheltered employment that will regulate both social and sheltered workshops.

At present, there are at least 60 *sociale werkplaatsen* in Flanders, providing work for almost 900 people who have severe difficulties in social and work integration, and providing about 150 supervisory posts. According to a study of 46 *sociale werkplaatsen* carried out by the SWP federation[6] the people involved have an average age of about 35. There are equal numbers of men and women. More than 40% have got no further than primary school, and others have at most a lower secondary school certificate.

Work-integration enterprises During the last three or four years we appear to have reached a new phase with the appearance of enterprises with a social purpose but within an entirely commercial context. Although these businesses need a certain amount of public finance, particularly during the early years, their purpose is to operate in conventional commercial markets and to find the majority of their required resources there.

In francophone Belgium, the *Fondation Roi Baudouin* has been the driving force behind the development of these schemes. Following a study published by the Foundation in 1994,[7] which set out a possible model for a work-integration enterprise, the *Fondation Roi Baudouin* launched a call for projects encouraging the creation of work-integration enterprises (capable of recruiting at least three people into work-integration posts in the first year). From about 50 projects the Foundation selected seven pilot projects in Wallonie and five in Brussels for financial support, supplemented by contributions from the European Social Fund and Regional authorities. Continuous monitoring, and regular discussions concerning problems within these pilot projects, made it possible to learn several lessons that provided a basis for future policies.[8]

---

[6] Van de Velde (1995).

[7] FRB (1994).

[8] Defourny *et al.* (1996).

In Flanders too, a dozen work-integration enterprises, *invoegbedrijven,* have appeared during the last three years, seeking to create permanent jobs for the poorly qualified long-term unemployed. Set up with a commercial legal structure (compared to Wallonie where they are frequently ASBL) these enterprise receive significant public financial support during their first three years. However, this support is on a sliding scale and the firms are required to become self-financing by the end of this period. It must be stressed, however, that as in Wallonie the scheme is in an experimental phase, and its subsequent evaluation will influence future policy with regard to initiatives of this type.

3. Choosing the Practices to Achieve Results

Given the variety of schemes existing throughout the country, the present analysis will concentrate on some, to the detriment of others. In particular, we shall focus on the most innovative initiatives paying special attention to the francophone part of the country where recent work makes it possible to carry out a synthetic analysis.

3.1. Evaluating Occupational Training Enterprises[9]

The 1000 or so training posts offered by the EFT are filled, each year, by more than 2000 trainees, young, unqualified, and made vulnerable by problematic social experiences. On average, the trainees stay in an EFT for nine months. The range of activities covered by the EFT is wide, but the construction sector and service industries (catering, sales, personal services) predominate.

With regard to the training provided by the EFT, Fusulier and Mertens' analysis emphasises the wide variety of objectives pursued. Some stress the 'apprenticeship' aspect, that is training in technical expertise which will be an asset in the labour market. Others put the emphasis on 'vocational socialisation', i.e. inculcating the standards of social behaviour that are needed in the labour market. Finally, some voluntary organisations give priority to education, to encourage the personal development of each individual in his or her socio-cultural environment.

To finance their activities, the EFT make use of both commercial (through the sale of goods and services on the market) and non-commercial resources (through public subsidy). Voluntary contributions (through

---

[9] Drawn from the results of a study by Fusilier and Mertens (1996).

volunteers, donations, etc.) remain only a minor source of income. Only 20% of EFT make use of volunteer workers. On average, commercial activities meet 27% of business costs.[10] The cost of training is around 360 BF per hour, which seems generally lower than more traditional training costs. The special feature of the EFT is that they have a double product: goods or services for sale on the market, and a non-commercial training activity. A breakdown of the added value makes this double function clear: 54% of added value is commercial, and 46% generated by training activities.

Financing training personnel and supervisors relies largely on programmes for reducing unemployment, since 86% of posts are covered by these measures. Unemployed people returning to work become supervisors of trainees. The public authorities have gone some way to recognising this paradox, insofar as the conditions for admission to unemployment reduction programmes have been made much more flexible for the EFT, thereby making it possible to recruit qualified staff. Of the permanent staff, 38% have had the benefit of higher education.

Generally, the EFT are heavily involved in the networks for training and social and vocational integration. Many local partnerships have been formed, some with organisations offering psycho-social support, others with bodies which aim to find people work. The emphasis is on a 'route into integration', which allows the development of a number of interlinked schemes.

What is the success rate of on-the-job training companies? If we take this to mean the percentage of trainees who get a job or leave to undergo further training, the average rate of integration of trainees in 1994 for EFT in francophone Belgium was 49%, 27% found a lasting job, a little over half of them on a permanent contract, and 22% began training leading to a qualification.[11] Given the overall economic situation, this result is in itself quite good, but it does not alter the fact that the other half of the trainees failed to find any immediate career avenue. This situation, and the structural impasse in which trainees are caught, are explained by the saturation of the labour market, especially for low qualified workers; the absence of structures suited to their needs; more fundamental personal

---

[10] This ratio is equivalent to the relationship between the gross margin and the difference between total charges and raw materials. It thus reflects the capacity of the EFT to cover its other charges through commercial activities once the raw materials have been paid for.

[11] OTC officials have no information about the subsequent experiences of 26% of trainees.

problems (prison, treatment for drug abuse, etc.); or, in quite another scenario, by their employment in the black economy.

As a general rule, it is difficult to achieve long-term integration into social and working life. This makes it the more necessary to develop complementary measures for the assessment of EFT performance as well as looking at reintegration rates.

3.2. Evaluating Work-integration Enterprises

First, let us remember that the work-integration enterprise scheme is still at an experimental stage and except for a few older organisations it only involves a very small number of workers in both Wallonie and Flanders.

In spite of being at an early stage of development, the work-integration enterprises have excited much interest. In particular, they embody a social economy that simultaneously attacks the hard core of unemployment, and through its commercial resources weighs much less heavily on the public finances than most voluntary organisations providing social, cultural and other services.

In comparison with the average profile of EFT trainees, workers in work-integration enterprises are further down the road to social integration. Hence they display greater reliability, an essential quality in businesses that must court customer satisfaction. However, it remains true that achieving the habit of work, professional conduct and the necessary technical skills always presents a challenge. Supervising these individuals is thus crucially important. According to the evaluation of the seven pilot projects in Wallonie, one supervisor is needed for every 1.5–3 workers in integration posts, at least during their first year.[12]

The same study also reveals the wide range of activities chosen. Work-integration enterprises exploit traditional activities (such as joinery) and new ones (electronic document archives), with several engaged in activities linked to environmental problems (rehabilitation of disused industrial sites, recycling of paper or cars, etc.). In this last case, getting public contracts is often the essential condition for the viability of the enterprise. In this respect the ASBL legal structure, chosen by most work-integration enterprises in Wallonie, can be a handicap, as the tender procedures for many public contracts impose conditions that cannot be met by an ASBL.

On the basis of a financial analysis of the first year of operation, it would appear that on average, work-integration enterprise turnover covers

---

[12] Defourny *et al.* (1996).

about 60% of total costs. The remaining 40% must be met by non-commercial resources, which indicates the importance of public subsidy in launching these initiatives.

Analysis of the seven pilot projects shows that a determining factor in the creation, development and survival of work-integration enterprises, is the existence of a support structure. All the pilot projects have developed under the umbrella of a well established organisation, whether this be an EFT, a sheltered workshop, or some other form of social enterprise. In such cases the work-integration enterprise benefits from the very start from a general infrastructure that is already in place – buildings, administrative services, accountants, etc. – and, where the activities involved are similar, from the equipment, know-how, and order book of the support structure. Such a situation enables the enterprise to become productive rapidly, whilst postponing certain investments that would be impossible at the beginning. Furthermore, if the support structure is an EFT or a sheltered workshop, the enterprise can engage staff who have been trained there in the relevant skills or trade. Finally, the support structure is even more important at the financial level. Work-integration enterprises suffer from a chronic lack of liquidity, and a support structure offers an indispensable financial cushion, guaranteeing cash advances, capital contributions, and sometimes donations.

However, it must be stressed that it is often difficult to develop two such parallel structures without damaging one of them. In particular, to rise to the challenge inherent in commercial activities, the work-integration enterprise may be led to draw heavily, perhaps for a long time, on the better part of the order book and/or the management capacity of the support structure. During the early years there is a constant search to strike a balance between the necessary help from the support structure and the need for growing autonomy. This may be achieved by setting up a separate working organisation and moving into separate premises, so that the work-integration enterprise can develop its own style.

4.   Public Policies in a Time of Change

How have the public authorities acted with regard to these associative initiatives for integration? To what extent have they supported and supervised them while respecting their dynamic? Is the legal structure available to this kind of enterprise appropriate? These are some of the questions that we will try to answer, focusing on some of the major types of public intervention in the field of integration.

4.1. Public Financial Support

In Belgium, integration schemes can benefit from financial support from various administrative levels: federal government, the regions, language-based authorities, provinces, local authorities. Very often, too, the European Commission supplies much appreciated aid through the European Social Fund.

The Belgian authorities provide support mainly through grants for supervisory personnel for posts on the various unemployment reduction programmes: such as TCT, FBI, ACS and PRIME, under regional impetus. As we have seen, for the public authorities such posts represent the assumption of responsibility for a large part of the wages bill. However, because they are closely linked to active policies in the labour market, this support is at risk of being challenged, at the mercy of changes in these same labour policies. Hence the importance of approval procedures that are likely to stabilise and give a proper structural form to the necessary subsidies.

The support of the European Social Fund is often vital for the EFTs because it represents 35% of their total subsidies. In fact ESF subsidies provide, almost single-handedly, the liquidity that enables the EFTs to cover their running costs (rent, charges, educational materials, wages, which remain the responsibility of the promoters, etc.). Nevertheless, the delay with which these payments are often dispensed, regularly causes serious cash-flow problems.

There is, however, an interesting and new development concerning finance. At the request of the Walloon region, the regional investment company (the *Société régionale d'investissement de Wallonie*, SRIW), the holding company for public industrial policy, set up a subsidiary in 1995 with the aim of financing the 'commercial social economy'. The *Société wallonne d'économie sociale marchande*, SOWECSOM, was founded with an initial budget of 300 million Belgian Francs. A guarantee fund with capital of 150 million BF was also established. These new mechanisms aim to provide support for enterprises in the social economy, which meet at least 50% of their financial needs through their own turnover. Work-integration enterprises are thus much more likely to benefit under this scheme than the EFTs.

There are still other original sources of public financial support, but they are not yet well established. For example, the government of Flanders has provisionally decided to subsidise the wages of workers in the *invoegbedrijven* up to a limit of 100% in the first year, 70% in the second, and 30% in the third. But since making this subsidy heavily dependent on a requirement for self-financing could be fatal to many of the projects that are underway, there is considerable uncertainty as to the future of this provisional framework. On the other hand, significant federal exemptions on employers' contributions (on a sliding scale from 100% to 25% over four years) will be available to all work-integration enterprises in both the north and south of the country, but at present, they are linked to a scheme for regional approval, which is not yet in place.[13]

4.2. The Legal Framework

At present, initiatives for integration through economic measures generally choose the ASBL structure for their legal framework. This legal structure is very flexible and undemanding: founding an ASBL requires no initial capital and is much simpler, from the administrative point of view, than a commercial company. Besides, this legal structure is needed to qualify for various public subsidies meant for activities with a strong social dimension, which are not available to commercial companies. In particular, approval as an EFT (or previously as an EAP) is dependent on ASBL legal structure. Last but by no means least an ASBL can carry out a supplementary industrial or commercial activity without paying company taxes.

Nevertheless, for initiatives operating under a clear commercial dynamic ASBL legal structure has drawbacks and limitations. An innovative way of overcoming these limitations was opened up by a recent law, passed in April 1995, allowing the creation of commercial companies with a social purpose (*'à finalité social'*). This federal law concerns all kinds of commercial enterprises (co-operative societies, public companies, companies with limited liability, etc.); from 1 July 1996, these companies may be called *'Sociétés à finalité social'* (SFS), provided their purpose is 'not to increase the wealth of their partners' and their articles of association comply with a number of conditions.[14] The wording of some of these show

---

[13] In 1996, however, provisional approval was granted to about 40 initiatives so they could take advantage of these exemptions.

[14] The company with a social purpose is not a new form of company to be set beside the existing forms, SA, SPRL, SC, etc. Rather it offers the possibility, for commercial companies, of calling themselves *'SA à finalité social*, *'SC à finalité social'*, etc.

the main advances of this legislation, which will play a crucial role for work-integration enterprises.

The articles of association of a company with a social purpose, SFS, must stipulate that 'the members seek only a limited return on assets or no return at all' (where the company does pay out a return to its members, this must not exceed a certain rate of interest). The articles must also set out a policy for the allocation of profits which complies with the internal and external purposes of the company. Should the company go into liquidation, it must be provided that 'once all debts have been cleared and the partners have recovered their initial investment, any surplus will be distributed in a way which reflects as closely as possible the social purpose of the company'. If the company surrenders its SFS legal structure 'any existing reserves may not be distributed in any form'. These last two articles aim at protecting the company against attempts to generate substantial capital gains. SFS legal structure also introduces a democratic element into companies, since the articles of association must provide the means for every employee to acquire partner status within a year of his or her engagement. Furthermore the articles also state that 'no-one may, in the General Assembly, cast a number of votes greater than one-tenth of the voting rights of the shares represented; this percentage will be reduced to one-twentieth in the event that one or several partners have the status of staff member hired by the company'.

Two essential points must be made about the SFS. First, qualifying as a company with a social purpose imposes demands in addition to the requirements of traditional company legal structure; this will never be really attractive to those involved in the social economy unless other measures provide fiscal or social advantages to the SFS in return for services rendered to the community and/or to compensate for the particular expenses which handicap them.

Next, though this legal structure imposes a certain number of conditions relating to the social economy, it is not possible to distinguish those SFSs that are solely involved in integration schemes, and still less to come to an exact definition of a 'work-integration enterprise'. Only a set of conditions, possibly including SFS legal structure, could guarantee a definition of, or better still formal approval for, work-integration enterprises.

4.3. Policies for Recognition and Approval

Experience shows that the various kinds of public support for integration initiatives can be neither reliable nor properly co-ordinated without a system of recognition, generally based on some kind of formal approval procedures. Since the 1960s, sheltered workshops have had the advantage of a whole series of beneficial measures on the condition that they comply exactly with a set of criteria and undergo checks by a specialised agency.[15] Similarly, help for the EAP, and subsequently for the EFTs, and progressively a structured system for granting approval was introduced. In Flanders, approval procedures for *invoegbedrijven* and the *sociale werkplaatsen* have also recently been introduced, leading to entitlement to subsidies, but this is still at an experimental stage. However, work-integration enterprises in Wallonie and Brussels are still waiting for a legal and financial framework that would put their subsidies on a secure footing.

Beyond these important differences, the current development of public policy comes up against one persistent problem: the increasing dichotomy between fundamentally non-commercial integration initiatives and those that are expected to some considerable extent to be at least self-financing. The attitude of the government of Wallonie to the EFT and work-integration enterprises, illustrates this differential approach, although work-integration pilot projects often emerge from EFT.

New conditions for granting approval to EFTs set out in 1995 aim to place strict limits on their commercial and productive activities. EFTs will in future be considered as non-commercial organisations providing training services and expected to combine training and production activities less than before. Accusations of unfair competition against some EFTs, the ability of a number of them to generate substantial resources, the distrust and even traditional hostility displayed towards voluntary organisations in some circles, and a lack of transparency in the accounts of some EFTs, have all contributed to these changes.

No conditions and procedures for recognising work-integration enterprises have yet been established regionally, but the intentions of government and, to an even greater extent, the social partners (employers and trade unions) are very clear: since they claim access to public and private markets, work-integration enterprises should adopt the articles of association appropriate to a commercial company (with a social purpose) and renounce the hand out of subsidies, which should be available only to

---

[15] The agency for the integration of disabled people (*L'Agence wallonne pour l'integration des personnes handicapées*, AWIPH).

the ASBL. In the same way, public financial subsidies should only be justified during an initial period or to help the most severely disadvantaged workers into employment.[16] Finally, whereas subsidising EFTs is mostly a matter of social policy, work-integration enterprises can already apply for loans and possibly even capital contributions from the *Société wallonne d'économie sociale marchande*.

5.   Work-integration Enterprises: The Conditions for Success

Given the wide variety of initiatives operating, it is not easy to bring out the factors, which seem to be really critical for their success or failure. Besides, expectations of the degree of success in the schemes is itself a delicate matter, given their combination of social purposes and economic objectives. However, based principally on observations collected in the south of the country, we think it may be possible to indicate, on the one hand, certain conditions for the success of projects for integration through training aimed at disadvantaged people, and on the other, key elements in the entrepreneurial dynamic driving these projects.

5.1. Reintegration through Training

The special feature of these associative initiatives is their training and reintegration programmes based on commercial production. Both enterprises for occupation training and work-integration enterprises combine training activities with production. Projects of this kind are able to act as a strong force for integration for low-qualified people, who have often been left vulnerable by their problematic social experiences. Rather than providing real technical training, the function of associative integration initiatives is most often to provide a psycho-social framework for their users. The success of these initiatives thus depends on the co-ordination of this dual production, of training and commercial goods or services. The educational function cannot be divorced from the economic activity.

Another increasingly important factor in the success of these initiatives is their integration within a wider partnership. The schemes are successful when they form part of a true 'path to integration' rooted in a regional development plan involving local authorities, training professionals and

---

[16] The same or even stricter conditions apply to the experimental approval procedures for *invoegbedrijven* in Flanders.

traditional businesses. This still-tentative approach through local development is very gradually beginning to assert itself, and opens up possibilities for influencing the environment in which reintegration must take place.

5.2. Key Factors in Entrepreneurial Projects

Without making any claim to construct a model, it can certainly be said that the emergence and development of associative integration schemes, results from a combination of at least four key elements: an entrepreneur, a product, a market, and supplementary finance. These elements can be imagined symbolically as the foundations of a square – but not a magic square.[17]

Even though it is often a group of people who carry out the project, integration initiatives are always headed by a single individual, who provides the creative force and whose personality plays a vital role. Bringing natural leadership qualities and real entrepreneurial ability, allied to a fundamental concern for society, these entrepreneurs throw themselves heart and soul into the business. They generally have a sharp awareness of social needs and the desire to contribute to establishing a socially useful project.

Integration through work also involves the production of goods and services. The very wide range of activities bears witness to the creativity which drives the sector, but it must be said that their choice is often the result of chance circumstances and opportunities rather than strategic decisions. However, the very nature of these enterprises forces them to choose labour intensive activities, in which unqualified labour plays an important part.

These products are placed on the market but, at least at first, their outlets are mostly provided by a network of sympathisers. Later they expand and according to the circumstances this may lead to a captive market or to a situation of strong competition. In the latter case, the co-existence of EFT or work-integration enterprises and traditional SME can present certain problems. However, several studies have shown that the presence of these businesses, and their active support from public finance, does not contravene national or European competition law.[18]

Public aid to supplement market income represents the fourth side of our square, and is one of the most characteristic features of integration

---

[17] This account is mainly inspired by the work *Développer l'entreprise sociale*, FRB (1994).
[18] *Développer l'entreprise sociale*, FRB (1994), ch. 4.

through economic measures. In comparison with other businesses, social enterprises have no chance of becoming viable or competitive if they themselves have to absorb the excess costs of low productivity from workers in integration posts and the very significant amount of extra supervision that such workers require. This is why supplementary finance is indispensable, though the forms this take may be very varied: taking over a part of the wages costs, paying for the supervisory staff, help with investment, etc. Through such public support, it is a little as if the community, via its elected leaders and management bodies, were 'buying' the second product (in reality the first product) of the EFT and work-integration enterprises – namely their reintegration and training product. This transaction and this manner of providing finance are not in themselves exceptional since they apply throughout the non-commercial sector. What is original, though some find it hard to grasp, is the combination of commercial and non-commercial elements within a single organisation. However, is this not fundamentally the same reasoning as that behind the sometimes massive public intervention to prop up businesses in danger of failing? In any case it is obvious that this kind of combination may well claim to be the most economical solution for society as a whole: calculations have shown that in many hypothetical instances the development of appropriately subsidised work-insertion enterprises, would have a positive impact on public finance given the costs avoided and loss of revenue of getting the unemployed into work.[19]

Alongside these four fundamental elements, we must remember the importance of a support structure, especially for launching work-integration enterprises, and more generally, the part played by what we might call sponsorship – all the support, financial or otherwise, which frequently provide founders of such enterprises with the guarantees and extra boost they need to pull a project off. This sponsorship is of varying types and origins. It comes from well established schemes, local authorities, or charities, and can take the form of technical or financial collaboration. These are external forms of sponsorship, from organisations that are separate from the sponsored company. However, there are also internal forms of sponsorship. These arise when internal growth leads to the

---

[19] Defourny *et al.* (1994).

creation of a new group working in the social economy born out of a parent structure, most often set up as an ASBL.[20]

6.   Passing Beyond the Experimental Stage

The factors we have discussed belong to a 'micro' dimension and are generally independent of the number of integration schemes. The question is now how far such enterprises can multiply on a wider scale in Belgium. In other words, let us consider from the 'macro' perspective, the question of the conditions under which they can develop, and pass beyond the present stage, which remains in many respects experimental.

In a general way, it is clear that public policies may be more or less encouraging to initiatives of this kind, and that this is an important determining factor. In the light of recent changes the situation seems rather paradoxical. On the one hand, federal and regional governments have never been more favourable to the social economy, particularly where the reintegration of unqualified people is concerned. Furthermore, a number of financial and legal measures are already in place, and several others are in preparation: approval procedures for work-integration enterprises, and the advantages arising from them, the new legal structure of 'company with a social purpose', and the opening up of certain public markets, etc. On the other hand, financial constraints and restrictions have never been more severe, and these have an enormously limiting effect on the realisation of governmental good intentions.[21]

Public budgetary constraints are obviously the main 'limiting factor' for all essentially non-commercial enterprises, particularly for the occupational training enterprises in Wallonie and the *sociale werkplaatsen* in Flanders. In this field, projects continue to be set up, following the example of the very flourishing and dynamic associative movement (voluntary sector) in Belgium. But they inevitably come up against the limits of financial allocations that in recent years have not increased and may even have been reduced. In Wallonie, for example, the number of

---

[20] The *Terre* group is the most obvious example of this technique: starting from the ASBL *Terre*, the group now comprises three non-profit associations, two public companies and a co-operative society (see Appendix).

[21] Almost all European Union governments are making huge efforts to reduce their budget deficits, but in Belgium, the exceptional burden of the national debt (130% of GDP) has for some time left very little room for manoeuvre.

approved EFTs has been effectively frozen since 1987, at a time when it could certainly have doubled if not more.

The general position is not fundamentally any different for schemes that are predominantly commercial, but governments are much more inclined to favour an increase in their numbers and support for such businesses can be designed to taper off at the same time as they bring about a structural reduction in public authorities' costs. The establishment of an organisation like SOWECSOM in Wallonie, and the experimental plan for the *invoegbedrijven* in Flanders provide good illustrations of this eagerness to support projects that aim at a high level of self-financing. Consequently, the most significant 'limiting factor' is instead the difficulty of founding and running commercial enterprises capable of coping with the challenges of the market, while at the same time giving priority to the employment of people excluded by the same market reasoning.

An analysis of existing initiatives shows that this simply cannot be achieved except with the help of a support structure. The most natural source of such support is obviously the EFTs, for which work-integration enterprises are the ideal development. But the rather small number of EFTs and the weak commercial involvement of many of them, clearly show the limitations of this approach. In other words, the development of work-integration enterprises will necessarily take place through other enterprises or organisations that will have to take on the supporting role in these projects.

Within the social economy, sheltered workshops are perhaps likely to provide the most rapid response. They represent an additional stage in the social and vocational integration of disabled people. It is realistic to expect a degree of support from the traditional co-operative movements, but their energies are entirely, or almost entirely, absorbed by the 'classic' challenges of their respective sectors. The friendly societies would provide a reliable springboard, but the exploitation of new sources of jobs in the service sector does not sit easily with the task of employing people who have serious problems of integration. The rest of the voluntary sector undoubtedly includes a certain number of potential support organisations. Even though the distance between essentially non-commercial activities and projects with a strong commercial component is often great, it is probably through the development of groups working in the social economy, based on well-established ASBL, that work-integration enterprises have the most future.

Another route is through middle-sized and, in particular, large businesses, insofar as they divert a (very small) part of their resources to the support of integration initiatives. During recent years, companies such as Petrofina and Tractebel have directed some of their sponsorship funds into such schemes. Furthermore, even more recently the Cockerill-Sambre group, the backbone of industry in Wallonie, has provided not only financial support but has seconded executive staff to set up integration initiatives. This has come about as a result of internal discussions and mobilisation involving workers, executives and management representatives. This example may remain an isolated case, or be no more than an inexpensive gesture towards 'citizenship' on the part of the company. However, it suggests in principle a possible way of freeing more significant resources, including management expertise. Much will depend on the attitude of the trade unions, which are particularly important in Belgium. When we consider the snowball effect made possible by agreements between the social partners, for example the allocation of resources for the training of 'groups at risk', it is clear that the possible mobilisation of the trade union movement may well be a key factor in the future of integration through economic measures.

However, at present trade union organisations seem to be torn between a number of possible positions. On the one hand they are increasingly aware of the need to open up new innovative approaches, which are inevitably more difficult to organise within traditional rules. On the other hand, their fears of the effects of substitution or the weakening of existing jobs sometimes lead them to reject opportunities and consequently to reinforce the opposition of some employers' bodies that are concerned mainly with preventing the appearance of new kinds of competition. Between these two extremes, there is certainly scope for gradual, controlled moves forward. However, experience seems to suggest that such advances mostly come about when the social partners, and indeed public decision-makers generally, have a better understanding of integration initiatives. It is often a grasp of the concrete realities and the efforts that are being made in the field of integration, rather than ideological debates, which can change the mentalities and views of traditional players.

Finally, in the same perspective, we cannot avoid stressing the absolutely vital need to overcome the tension between the commercial and non-commercial aspects of integration, or at least to reduce its consequences. We have referred to this aspect several times in our analysis, because it more or less explicitly underpins most attitudes and policies towards integration schemes. However, in reality one of their main characteristics is the ability to combine inseparably commercial and non-commercial added value. If we could succeed in grasping this in a more coherent fashion, many of the challenges of integration, including financial challenges, would be posed in more open terms.

Appendix – Two Case Studies

The Terre *Group*

Terre was founded in 1949. Initially its aim was to fight the poverty resulting from the war years without recourse to charity. Later it developed socially useful projects both in developing countries and in Belgium. Between 1961 and 1980, *Terre's* activities focused principally on Third World development projects. In 1980, in view of increasingly acute social problems caused by the economic crisis, *Terre* launched the 'Wallonie project', with the hope of proving that it was possible to set up a business, 70% of whose workforce came from marginalised people. It wanted to show that a business could have a social purpose as its principal aim, and that this can work on the condition that any profits are put towards the benefit of the greater number. Today the *Terre* group comprises the following entities: *Terre* ASBL, the ASBL *Emmäus Contravis* (an EFT that takes on marginalised people initially before they are definitively employed in another arm of the group), the ASBL *Terre Tiers-Monde et Information*, *Pan-Terre SA* (manufacture of insulation panels), Terre Engineering SA (a research consultancy) and *Co-Terre SCRL* (acoustic insulation, metal joinery, finishing work).

Terre began by rehabilitating slums and distributing coal, foodstuffs, toys and sometimes even money to severely deprived people. The ASBL *Terre* has widened its scope a good deal since its inception and the group now operates in ten fields of activity: selective collections (paper – 1500 tonnes a month, old clothes – 500 tonnes a month, and non-ferrous metals); the reuse of textiles (sorting, reconditioning, packaging and marketing); reuse of old paper (in making cardboard, recycled newsprint, corrugated iron and *Pan-Terre* panels); the manufacture of *Pan-Terre* thermal and acoustic insulating panels; work linked to the application of *Pan-Terre* panels (floor and ceiling thermal and acoustic partitions, insulating caissons, etc.); a mechanical welding workshop (manufacture of seaside pedal cars); research, maintenance, and administration; and last, Third World development projects. Over a little more than a decade the *Terre* group has grown spectacularly. Turnover increased from 26 million BF in

1981 to 157 million in 1986 and 296 million today. The budget is substantially based on its own resources.

Employment in the *Terre* group has grown very significantly in the last ten years. It now employs about 280 people, all of whom had experienced one kind of exclusion or another (CPAS, long-term unemployment, former prisoners, disability, etc.). After a probationary period, the group offers them a permanent contract. Vocational training provided by *Terre* is organised on the ground so as to put workers in direct contact with the realities of work.

Le Germoir

Unqualified and without work experience, many poorly educated women need stable employment in order to become independent. This is difficult enough under favourable circumstances, but almost impossible in the economic environment of the Hainault region. The ASBL *Le Germoir* was set up in Charleroi in 1982 to help women in this position. *Le Germoir* was organised as an EFT, offering a period of training leading to a permanent contract. This provided the women with an opportunity to distance themselves from the black economy, which cuts them off from social security as well as social recognition.

Since it was founded, *Le Germoir* has developed three areas of activity so as to enable workers to choose their vocation: sewing, industrial cleaning, and the catering trade (a vegetarian restaurant). Subsequently two co-operative societies, *R-Net* and *Le Préambule* were established to offer work to women at the end of their training period at *Le Germoir*, but also to give them the opportunity to manage their own businesses. *Le Germoir's* turnover has grown steadily, from 2 million BF in 1985 to 7.2 BF in 1994.

Le Germoir focuses on helping women with little education and no work experience, living on the bread line as single parents of one or several children. The ASBL employs nine people, with an average of 23 trainees working in the business. The aim is to bring their education up to a basic level and to give them the skills required in working life: respect for time keeping, learning to work in a team, etc. It also gives training in modern industrial cleaning techniques and sewing. *Le Germoir* aims at reintegration into work through employment within the ASBL initially, and ultimately with the co-operative societies.

References

Community fund for the social and professional integration of disabled people (FCISPPH) (1993), *Les Ateliers protégés en communauté Française*, FCISPPH, Brussels.

Defourny, J. (ed.) (1994), *Développer l'entreprise sociale*, Fondation Roi Baudouin, Brussels.

Defourny, J., Simon, M. and Van Pachterbeke, I. (1996), *L'Entreprise d'insertion en Wallonie. Premières leçons de sept projets-pilotes*, Fondation Roi Baudouin and the Region of Wallonie, Brussels.

Defourny, J., Dubois, P. and Perrone, B. (1997), *La Démographie et l'emploi rémunéré des ASBL employeurs en Belgique*, Centre for social economy, University of Liège.

De Villé, P. and Van der Linden, B. (1994), 'Emploi et chômage en Belgique: dérive actuelle et tendances longues', in *Reflets et perspectives de la vie économique. L'emploi sous perfusion*, vol. 33, no. 1/2, de Boeck, Brussels, pp. 7–21.

Dor, E., Van der Linden, B. and Lopez-Novela, M. (1995), *On Labour Market Policies and Aggregate Unemployment Outflows*, discussion paper no. 9515, IRES, Catholic University of Louvain.

Fondation Roi Baudouin (1992), *Werken aan werk. Flexible arbeidsmodellen voor de armsten* (1992), Fondation Roi Baudouin, Brussels.

Fondation Roi Baudouin (1994), *Développer l'entreprise sociale*, FRB, Brussels.

Fusulier, B. and Mertens, S. (1996), *L'Intervalle formateur*, Fondation Roi Baudouin, Brussels.

Mahy, B. (1994), 'Politiques et recherche d'emploi: évaluation microéconométrique', in *Reflets et perspectives de la vie économique. L'Emploi sous perfusion*, vol. 33, no. 1/2, pp. 87–102.

Van de Velde, I. (1995), *Tussen droom en werkelijkheid. Doelgroepanalyse Sociale Werkplaatsen*, Samenwerkingsverband Sociale Werkplaatser, Berchem.

Vermasse, G. (1993), *Kansen voor Kanslozen? De Sociale Werkplaats als uitkomst voor wie door alle mazen van het net valt*, Persconferentie, Vlaamse Raad, 7 January.

4   Canada: Social Mobilisation, Insertion and Local Development in Canada (Québec)

LOUIS FAVREAU

1.   Historical Overview: Development of The Labour Market and Public Unemployment Policy[1]

1.1.   The Labour Market and Dualisation

Canada, and Québec in particular, has suffered from unemployment rates of over 10% for a number of years.[2] In certain cities unemployment rates can be over 15%. Young people are the hardest hit (18–20%). Furthermore, since 1990 the level of employment has been dropping: in 1998 it was only 65.7% for Canada as a whole, 62.5% in Québec.

However, the overwhelming feature is that the nature of unemployment is changing. At the beginning of the 1990s there were three times more unemployed people than 30 years ago (4.6% in 1966 against 11.5% in 1998), staying unemployed for three times as long (an average six

---

[1] Most of the statistics given in this document deal with Québec, without, however, losing view of its position in Canada as a whole. To reiterate the salient features of the economy of Québec as a region of Canada and as a society: Québec's GDP of $CDN 173.6 billion accounts for 23.2% of that of Canada, and its 7.2 million inhabitants are 24.8% of the Canadian population. Its main areas of economic activity are production of manufacturing goods, telecommunications equipment, transport equipment and metals, forestry and paper-making.

[2] After reaching a maximum of 13.9% in 1983, up to 1998 the rate of unemployment in Québec has varied between 10% and 13% (8% and 10% for Canada as a whole). Unlike the USA and Japan, Canada shares the European pattern of structural unemployment, which has been growing since the 1970s.

months now as opposed to two months then).[3] Three in ten of them are young people. In contrast with the 1960s there is a complete reversal in the relationship between working ability and age. Even though manufacturing industry's share of GNP remains around 20%, there is an increasing trend towards loss of jobs in the manufacturing sector and big business in general, while job creation occurs most often in the service sector and as part-time work in small businesses.[4]

At the same time, the ever-decreasing room for manoeuvre of the two levels of government (federal and provincial) has put public social measures (health, social services, education, etc.) at risk, in such a way that social and geographical dualisation is tending to grow.[5]

1.2. Changes in Public Policy in the Face of Unemployment: Introduction of Active Measures

The response of public authorities to unemployment and the dualisation it brings with it has been hesitant and contradictory. The first response was the great about-turn that challenged the precepts of the 'passive' policies of the '30 glorious years' (1945–75). In the 1970s adult education, compensation for the unemployed and aid for providers of income support, started to be targeted more directly on active employment policies.

Carried along by the growth rate, employment policies prior to 1975 were established on the basis that unemployment was short-term, and operated through adjustments in the labour market to encourage a stable relationship between businesses and the workforce. Imbalances in the labour market gradually made it necessary to take measures regarding increasingly specific groups of the unemployed, including measures for younger and younger able to work groups. Thus, by the mid-1980s new vocational training programmes were coming into operation: vocational training centres were being resurrected; vocational training was taken under the wing of the Ministry of Employment rather than the Ministry of

---

[3] Since 1990, around 400,000 Québécois workers have been receiving benefits annually from the Canadian Federal unemployment insurance programme (369,000 in 1998, 448,000 in 1999); 483,000 others were in receipt of income support under the Québécois programme, mainly the long-term unemployed. This represents 22% of the working population.

[4] Between 1976 and 1995, 670,000 jobs were created in Québec, of which 73% can be considered atypical (Matte *et al.*, 1998). The same study notes that this growth in Québec has not been able to create sufficient activity to replace the jobs lost during the recessions of 1981–2, and 1991–2.

[5] *Conseil des affaires sociales* (CAS) (1989); *Conseil de la santé et du bien-être* (CSBE) (1996).

Education; programmes of aid for employment and the improvement of the employability of those capable of work and receiving welfare, following a reform of the welfare system (short-term traineeships); and the creation of the *Société Québécois de développement de la main-d'oeuvre* (SQDM – Québec Society for Manpower Development) in 1993, which marked a turning point in vocational training.

The mid-1980s thus saw the arrival of the first public measures for employment and social insertion. In 1990, as part of the reform of the unemployment insurance scheme, the Canadian federal government moved with the trend by making up to 15% of the balance of the unemployment insurance fund for 'productive' purposes. Since 1990 $CDN 1.3 billion has been made available, more than $CDN 800 million of which has gone to fund activities in training, integration into the labour market, and aid to employment.[6] In 1997–8 the Québec government reinforced public efforts towards active measures, negotiating an agreement with the federal government for the repatriation of measures targeted on the unemployed. It proposed reforming the entire system, integrating unemployment insurance, training of the labour force, aid and insertion for income support claimants within the framework of local employment centres.[7]

The main stumbling block to these policies and measures is that, despite everything, unemployment is not falling; instead, it has changed in volume and nature. In this new situation that, for a little over a decade, we have been witnessing a remobilisation of civil society and increasing numbers of social experiments (insertion through economic activity and local development), which is pointing the way to a new developmental model.

---

[6] Before their modification in 1996, in Québec passive measures (compensation) and active measures (vocational training and employment promotion) accounted for nearly $10 billion in 1995, including $5.18 billion from the Canadian federal government (for the unemployed) and $4.45 billion from the Québec government (for those in receipt of income support). Out of this total, only $1.6 billion go towards active measures: $835 million from Québec and $790 million from the federal government. See *L'Emploi, travaillons-y ensemble*, Government of Québec (1995).

[7] MSR (1996).

2.   The Voluntary Sector Movement and the Fight Against Unemployment

2.1. Portrait of the Voluntary Sector Movement

The voluntary sector in Québec consists of 90,600 voluntary organisations.[8] Publicly available data makes it possible to obtain information on a little over 24,500 of these voluntary organisations. These can be categorised along the lines of their area of action: 56.6% of the voluntary organisations fall within three divisions of the 'social' sector (social and community links, social and cultural leisure activities, social action). The other main area for action is sport (21.6%). Although these data are highly useful, they fail to enlighten us on the voluntary organisations' economic activities. It can, however, be estimated that around 20,000 voluntary organisations in Québec carry out some form of economic activity.[9] Furthermore, the 'community organisations' – which generally serve as our best indicator as they constitute the most active kernel of the voluntary sector movement[10] – carry out an economic activity in the vast majority of cases, i.e. they employ staff and produce goods or provide services. Thus, today, in the health and social services sector alone, around 2500 community bodies had nearly 10,000 regular employees, 15,000 casual staff and 340,000 volunteers.[11]

There are three generations of these organisations. The first, which dates back to the mid-1960s, has close ties with occupational trade unionism. It consists of groupings of citizens calling for the public authorities to provide public amenities and services to meet the requirements of local communities. The second generation, which sprang up at the beginning of the 1970s, brings together citizens and professionals offering services as an alternative to those provided publicly. The third and

---

[8] Lévesque and Malo (1992).

[9] Of the 71,500 voluntary organisations registered as charitable bodies in Canada, 85% – 60,775 – employ staff (five or fewer in two-thirds of cases). *Pro rata*, Québec should thus have 20,000 voluntary organisations employing staff (Leduc Browne, 1996).

[10] Bélanger *et al.* (1994).

[11] Bélanger (1995). There are several thousand organisations operating in other fields: more than 1000 involved in popular education, 800 non-profit crèches, 100 or so community leisure centres, 100 or so community media organisations, more than 1000 housing co-operatives, 100 food distribution co-operatives, more than 150 labour co-operatives, 500 community kitchens, some 200 community employment training bodies, around 100 community or insertion undertakings targeted on the service sector (home helps, domestic maintenance, catering, paper recycling, housing renovation, etc.).

final generation started to emerge from the mid-1980s onwards, in the fields of insertion, local development and community economic development. Community organisations belonging to this generation are more explicit in categorising their work as part of the 'social solidarity economy',[12] as these wide-ranging experiments satisfied the two criteria defining the solidarity economy, namely the mutual creation of supply and demand by end-users and those working in the organisations (both paid staff and volunteers), and crossovers between the market, non-market (i.e. public) and non-monetary (voluntary and local contract-based) economies. The jobs created along the way by these organisations are usually dependent on the services on offer and on the emphasis given to them by both workers and end-users.[13]

2.2. Voluntary Sector (and Co-operative) Integration Initiatives

The last decade has seen the emergence of a new activism, economic in nature, among the social movements (trade unions, voluntary organisations, etc.). This activism is focusing on creating new organisational forms and finding new areas for intervention.

Alongside the voluntary sector movement and the base-level co-operatives (housing, labour, etc.), the mobilisation that has taken place in the field of integration by economic means has been centred on three types of initiative: territorial initiatives for economic and social regeneration, such as the regional committees for the relaunch of employment and the economy (CRÉE), the community economic development corporations (CDEC), the community development corporations (CDC) and societies for aid for local development (SADC); sectoral initiatives for socio-professional integration (bodies working in training for employment, community enterprises, integration enterprises), and funding initiatives (development funds and loan associations).

---

[12] A concept that distinguishes them from the powerful and historic co-operative bodies operating in the financial and agricultural sectors. On this topic, see Aubry and Charest (1995); Favreau (1999).

[13] Laville (1992).

A Community Economic Development Corporation in Montréal

Launched in 1985, the CDEST is part of a movement formed in three declining working class districts of Montréal. In 1984 ten or so voluntary organisations in one of these districts put pressure on the Québec welfare ministry and obtained a subsidy to encourage new measures for employment and the revitalisation of the area. Thus the first Québecois community economic development corporation (CDEC) was born. Two others, including that in the east (CDEST) followed closely on its heels. Ten years on, these three first generation CDECs do not merely cover the original neighbourhoods, but have expanded to cover three times the area. Furthermore, other 'second generation' CDECs now cover the whole Montréal area. They operate in the following spheres:

(a)   Development of the abilities of the resident population through various measures: reference and follow-up services, assistance to job-seekers, and training activities for those excluded from the labour market (raising the educational level, specific apprenticeships).

(b)   Active intervention in the labour pool by improving the position of local businesses: support for management and financing of existing businesses and support for start-ups from a community development fund.

(c)   Support for the reconstruction of the fabric of society: tackling the distancing of schools from society, and preventing the isolation of families on welfare, etc.

The CDECs benefit from five-year agreements with the public authorities. They exercise certain powers with governmental authority over their area to encourage the birth of local production systems. For this purpose, the first CDECs set up an employment development fund, the *Fonds de développement Emploi-Montréal*, in conjunction with the Québecois workers' solidarity fund (FTQ) and the City of Montréal. Additionally, projects for insertion through economic means have access to other sources of funding such as the Montréal Community Loan Association and the lending circles.

The CDEST has a general operating budget of around $1 million, drawn from five different public sources. It employs 25 regular staff, mainly as development agents. A few of the most well-known insertion initiatives which have sprung up in the CDEST area are the *Chic Resto Pop*, a community catering enterprise, *Boulot Vers*, a social insertion enterprise for young people aged between 16 and 25, *La Puce Communautaire*, an microcomputer training business whose priority is the returning women to the labour market, and the *Hochelaga-Maisonneuve* network of community kitchens.

From the trade union aspect, there has been a clear convergence with voluntary organisations in the fields of integration and local development. Indeed, since the 1980s there have been moves towards buyouts of enterprises in difficulty, a number of social innovations at the level of organisation of labour within traditional businesses, and more generally a change of direction towards what can be termed 'co-operation in conflict'.[14] At a local level, unions – with the support of their regional and national leaderships – have become little by little more involved in public and voluntary sector structures for integration and social development. We have even witnessed joint efforts by trade unions, voluntary organisations and major co-operatives alongside part of the private sector for action on the thorny topic of employment. Two experiments have proved particularly revealing in this area: the National Employment Forum[15] and the regional and sectoral development funds created by the social economy institutions (the *Mouvement desjardins*[16] and the venture capital funds of the major trade union organisations).

3. The Experience of Social Integration through Economic Activity

3.1. General Scope of these Initiatives

Voluntary organisations' initiatives in the sphere of integration have often been modelled on co-operative enterprises (although not in general taking on that formal status), and those dealing with local development on the experience of development co-operatives in peripheral regions such as the JAL in eastern Québec, or on the more urban experience of the American CDECs.[17] Carried out on a province-wide scale (not just the most isolated

---

[14] Boucher and Favreau (1994).

[15] The National Employment Forum has been in existence since 1989. After having held forums in the various regions of Québec and subsequently bringing together 1600 participants in a national meeting (500 trade union delegates, 250 delegates from voluntary organisations, 200 representatives of co-operatives, 135 delegates from the private sector and 175 delegates from the two wings of central government), a national secretariat and regional co-ordinating bodies were set up. Since 1990 the National Forum has regularly hosted, co-ordinated and organised promotional activities in support of employment and the revival of local communities.

[16] It should be recalled that the *Mouvement desjardins*, the most major financial institution in Québec, is principally based on a network of 1300 savings and loan co-operatives, operating in 625 local communities.

[17] Favreau (1994a).

regions), these moves are triply innovative. First, they bring together parties that represent the whole spectrum of society – trade unions, employers, citizens, voluntary organisations and public sector bodies; secondly, they are aiming less at calling for state intervention and more for solving economic and social problems through the action of the bodies mobilised; and finally, they are among the actions searching for new models of development, with a new balance between the 'social' and the 'economic'.

What, in the end, can be said of each of the main elements of this type of initiative? First, the experience of territorially based intervention demonstrates that it is possible to work simultaneously on several problems as a partnership, to encourage the integration of the most disadvantaged members of local communities. Furthermore, sectoral economic initiatives for social integration show evidence of a trend towards responsibility being taken locally to meet the social demand for the provision of local and personal services, which can become both sources of employment and instruments for reconstructing social solidarity: child care, domestic maintenance (gardening, decorating, various repairs, etc.), upkeep of river banks, lakesides and beauty spots, repair workshops (for household goods, bicycles, etc.), catering for neighbourhood schools, home help services, etc. Third, trade unions and voluntary organisations are setting up their own development funds since the traditional financial institutions are reluctant to support these initiatives, which are considered too high-risk and low-yield. This funding can in some cases be on a national scale, as in the instance of the trade union funds,[18] or otherwise be funds created by local communities using local personal savings.

Taking the examples presented in this text, it will be seen that for a given geographical area these initiatives are succeeding in setting up a genuine socio-economic network, combining market and non-market aspects within productive initiatives. Furthermore, the prospects for a solidarity-based economy rest, at least in part, on a number of these initiatives. These seek in effect to strengthen both the social ties of a community and job creation, thus refusing to have their conduct dictated purely by market principles.

---

[18] Fournier (1993).

Hochelaga-Maisonneuve *Community Kitchens*

Launched in 1997, the *Hochelaga-Maisonneuve* community kitchens consist of ten groups, each of eight to ten people. Since 1990 the groups have formed into a network bringing together women – often heads of one-parent families. The community kitchens help their members to pool money for food, to negotiate good prices with local suppliers, and to get together several times a month to cook a number of meals for the freezer, with on average two to three hundred meals being prepared each month. The kitchens of this locality were also the initiators of a plan to follow the model of Québec city by bringing together a hundred of the five hundred or so catalogued to date. The organisers of these groups are hoping to set up purchasing co-operatives. All of these community kitchens have close ties with their local voluntary sectors. The majority of them are or have been supported by the local CLSC or by a local church.

Other kitchens in Montréal have already launched projects that go beyond mutual aid to create real businesses. This is the case of the *Cuisine des parents*, who chose to launch a small business in 1991, currently seven women hold a regular job preparing hot meals for 680 children attending three local schools. This community enterprise also provides part-time work for 23 people.

In this last instance, intervention by the CDEC encouraged this group of women to move on into the commercial sphere. It provided the assistance needed in the start-up phase, basic vocational training including practical literacy, financial support and lastly but not least backing for the management of the business. After six years operation the business has reached a steady state with an annual budget of around $325,000 to $300,000, of which 60–65% is for work with local schools.

Although they allow themselves in some measure to be constrained by market forces, these economic activities – project promotion, occupational training, real manufacturing activity and the funding of projects – seek to introduce a qualitative distinction. This is primarily evident in their origins in initiatives seeking to bring together those excluded from the labour market. Subsequently, distinctions can be drawn because of objectives primarily linked with realising the economic and social capacities of a group or a community in difficulties. They can also be distinguished by their management practices, which are primarily those of a voluntary organisation. A final distinction can be drawn from their reliance on capital, which has a double nature, being simultaneously entrepreneurial and associative. However, the economic fragility of these initiatives often leads to their being set up in a stronger partnership with local economic and social institutions, the latter serving as a form of fallback position. These initiatives thus establish links with co-operative financial bodies (savings banks and credit unions), charitable institutions and voluntary organisations (foundations, religious communities) and certain local and regional public bodies such as local community service centres (CLSC),[19] city councils and regional manpower training centres, etc.

3.2. Areas Covered by these Initiatives

Territorial programmes for integration and local development The CDEC, the CDC and the SADC have shown themselves to be vital tools in the economic and social revitalisation of communities in difficulties through multiple activities, co-ordinating the forces available to a community and implementing a policy for local development. Such measures to assist integration do however run a risk: local communities can have their development priorities taken over by public authorities attempting to pursue their own agendas. Here there is a clash between two different approaches: the administrative rationale behind public programmes with their own targets and the approach taken by voluntary organisations within these local bodies, tending to put greater value behind the social structures of a community, small-scale operation, etc. Further tension exists between businesses involved in these initiatives, primarily interested in commercial development in certain sectors identified as the most profitable, and voluntary organisations who put more value on employment in connection with local development. There are thus two different approaches: social and economic revitalisation of local areas themselves or development of businesses within these areas.

Sectoral integration initiatives This sub-category includes three types of initiative: insertion enterprises, community enterprises and vocational training bodies. These integration initiatives are mainly positioned downstream from the social and economic revitalisation of communities. There is an awareness that their work all too often finishes at the factory gate, and they are therefore developing an 'on the hoof' internal approach to employment, in which they are forced to operate within the ever tighter

---

[19] The CLSCs, set up in the 1970s, are front-line public organisations providing health care and social services for local communities of on average 50,000 population. They generally employ between 100 and 150 health care and social service professionals (nurses, nutritionists, social workers, home helps, community organisers, etc.).

Chic Resto Pop, *a Community Catering Enterprise*

Launched in 1984, this community catering business currently prepares over a thousand low-price meals on its premises daily, largely from recovered foodstuffs, and caters for seven local schools. It is a non-profit making body (OSBL) that provides work for 18 permanent staff and 105 others in the process of reinsertion. Its clientele consists in the main of welfare recipients, the unemployed and the low-paid. Its annual budget is close to the million dollar mark: in 1996 it was $930,000, including $448,000 in proceeds from its services, more than $150,000 from sources in the voluntary sector (Centraide and donations) and $328,000 from various public sources (Health and social services, the income support service, the education council, etc.).

This business is also a venue for mutual aid, social work and training for employment (taking on trainees, literacy training, alternative French language teaching, community psychiatric care and cultural promotion of young local musical talent). It has special ties with the whole voluntary network in the district, including sending a representative to a local development round table. In its early days it was supported by the local CDEC, the CDEST as a community-based enterprise (assistance in the launch, funding and management support), and by the district's local community service centre which provided expert advice on community organisation and nutrition. Additionally the Pop-mobile (a mobile catering service directly linked to *Chic Resto Pop*) employs three permanent staff and takes on around 20 trainees. The *Chic Resto Pop* was also active in the launch of a local music festival (250 volunteers, four days of entertainment and 20,000 admission in its first year, 1992). This led to the creation of a new enterprise operating in the cultural field.

---

rules of the public programmes, which were set up to deal with social emergencies. Depending on the area and the type of business, between 30% and 50% of the unemployed and welfare recipients registered with these enterprises end up back where they started, although there have been a number of successes.[20]

Thus, in a period when the problem is not merely unemployment, but also rising job insecurity,[21] successes are becoming ever rarer. Like a breath of fresh air in a stifling atmosphere of unemployment and insecure jobs,

---

[20] In a recent study of 26 insertion enterprises considered to be innovative and dynamic, researchers found that the rate of placement in jobs or further education or training was 70%, and that 78% of trainees were still employed or in education six months later (Valadou, 1995).
[21] Castel (1995).

those running projects within these bodies are restricted in their scope for work; they often have to struggle with the need to plan their projects with no support from the public programmes, or to manage public programmes having continually to find compromises in order to reach a minimum of social effectiveness. In short, for this category of initiative, there are three essential keys to meeting the newest challenge: not merely to rely on the capacity of existing enterprises to handle initiatives; for public programmes, not to limit themselves to local solutions, and to take a more direct blanket approach to the revitalisation of local communities (in this instance community economic development).

Initiatives for the financing of integration   This new provision of funding comes in large measure through non-traditional financial channels and results from the pressure of local demand. It aims at meeting the demands of the SME and microenterprise sector, which includes a number of social economy enterprises (voluntary organisation-based or co-operative). These development funds thus seem to be precious tools for local, regional and community development.[22] Some of these funds are basically market-oriented, while others aim to combine economic viability and social utility.

4.   The Interface between Voluntary Sector Insertion Initiatives and the Public Authorities

Since the mid-1980s the various social actors in Québec have become increasingly aware that the development model which has been taken as the norm since the Second World War is now going into reverse. This awareness is based on a number of observations, the two most important of which are the inability of the Fordian production model to find a solution to the problem of unemployment and, in parallel with it, the inability of the consumption model and the welfare state in particular to respond to new needs as it has to those already taken on.

In this new climate, how have public authorities tended to react? Do they support those who are running projects? Two trends have come to light: on the one hand public authorities react mainly to emergencies and hardly at all to development; however, in the current atmosphere of institutional uncertainty, gaps have started to appear: the various initiatives for integration through labour and local development have started to gain a certain degree of recognition.

---

[22] Lévesque *et al.* (1995, 1999).

Montréal Community Loan Association

The *Montréal Community Loan Association* (MCLA) was set up in 1990, inspired by the American model of community loan funds. It was established on the initiative of a Montréal CDEC. Projects for insertion through economic activity therefore have a locally-based source of funding on hand. With a current capital of $376 000, the MCLA provides loans over two years to small businesses of between $2000 and $15,000. Twenty three loans have been made in four years, to a total value of $220,000. Two people work for the fund, one – a social worker by training – as a co-ordinator, while the other has training in business administration. Two or three people from various employment programmes monitor the various cases and provide assistance for projects. The MCLA has three accounts: a loan capital account of around $200,000, a reserve fund of $70,000 and an operating budget that enables the employment of two staff.

The MCLA defines itself as a coalition of lenders, borrowers and technical advisors, whose aim is to provide loans to business projects which will create jobs in the community, particularly for single mothers, immigrants, and refugees as well as those receiving welfare. The capital comes from a wide range of sources including churches, the City of Montréal, businesses, foundations and individuals. Its loans are repayable at lower than market rates. It is also able to serve as a guarantor to banks and savings and loans during the start-up of a business. The MCLA is autonomous and receives no state funding. Its loan capital comes from various institutions and businesses which have recognised the value of this initiative. Some people are already calling it 'the community bank'.

4.1. Public Policy and Integration Initiatives: The Programmes for Target Group

The majority of public policies for aid to employment are tightly targeted on particular populations and intervene on the basis of urgent need. The primary effect has been to stack up a range of measures designed to shore up the damage caused by 'progress', for all sorts of specific categories of the unemployed and welfare claimants.[23] In this context the public authorities' social insertion initiatives have been considered as social palliatives.

---

[23] Up until 1996 there had been 102 programmes, 73 coming under the Québec government and 29 coming under the Canadian federal government. Since the reforms of 1997–8, public employment services are provided through local development services, which support five large programmes and integrate more specific measures.

The criticism emanating from those working in the field and analysts centres on the following points: these policies and the practices that accompany them are compartmentalised; the sums invested in short-term measures are considerably more than those committed to development projects in communities in difficulty; the programmes are generally too inflexible and involve keeping the beneficiaries under surveillance; and finally, if their initial impact is to respond to immediate needs, their secondary effects tend rather to lend validity to the current process of social dualisation.

Within this framework the interface between voluntary sector initiatives and the public authorities is increasing the risk of a drift towards subcontracting and service provision, due to the low levels of support given to project managers, whose leadership is vital to the programmes' success. In the long run, for every programme that is launched successfully, another fails to gel or ends up reducing its work to mere substitution.

4.2. The Emergence of Horizontal Public Policies

Alongside this very strong tendency, under pressure from local communities and social movements, a local development policy did however, emerge. This second trend gave much greater credit and autonomy to voluntary organisation experience in insertion and to the accompanying development measures such as CDECs, CDCs and SADCs. Rather than simple damage limitation, these programmes were able to encourage the economic and social revitalisation of communities in difficulty. Consider a few examples: in the field of social affairs, *Centres locaux de services communautaires* (CLSCs, community local service centres) are implementing an intervention policy for neighbourhood teams taking an area-based approach, rather than targeting a particular population; in the domain of vocational training and regional development, public programmes in support of local authorities are providing long-term funding to local development agencies including CDECs, CDCs and SADCs.

The emphasis therefore is on a territorially based public programme, backed up by a multi-partner approach relying on multi-activity methods of intervention that are likely to fit in far better with insertion initiatives. These programmes are, however, still at an experimental stage, and their budgets are very small compared with other programmes.[24] However, these

---

[24] Until 1996, insertion measures linked to local development, provided by the two levels of government for Québec (Provincial and Federal) did not exceed 10% of the total budget for Québec, and 15% for Ottawa.

emerging policies may have a more lasting impact. Their initial effect is to impose an imperceptible shift in the way problems are predominantly presented. A second effect is they allow a medium-term intervention process to be introduced (funding over five years, for example). Third, these policies are representative of a broader trend towards regionalisation involving all the social actors (businesses, trade unions, community organisations, citizens). Here we are faced by a different policy that calls for a more interventionist state likely to have more structuring effects for local authorities. This latter type of policy is based on a double dynamic that is already operating: a grass-roots economic and cultural movement built around concepts of partnership, community, local development, social contract, etc. In fact this dynamic permeates all the major players in Québécois society – not merely bodies with social aims (trade unions, co-operatives, voluntary organisations) but also many businesses and public institutions, alongside an increasingly significant proportion of those in the social professions, in both the public and voluntary sector sectors who are questioning the traditional forms of social intervention that have come out of the local authority mechanisms set up for social transfer.

5. Conditions for the Success of Insertion Initiatives

Research on the conditions for success in Québec, Canada and the USA has managed to identify a number of preconditions for successful project start-ups.[25] They can be summarised as follows:

(a) A local population that has a certain level of social cohesion. Insertion initiatives get results where a feeling of belonging to a local community is already widespread.

(b) A significant level of active voluntary organisation membership. A pre-existing active voluntary organisation membership favours the emergence of insertion and local development initiatives. The ability of voluntary organisations to home in on new needs and appropriate strategies is just one of the vital ingredients.

(c) Scope for collective entrepreneurship. Above and beyond the presence of voluntary organisations, an enterprise culture facilitates the emergence and development of initiatives for insertion by economic

---

[25] Favreau and Lévesque (1996); Fairbairn (1991); Christenson and Robinson (1989); Perry (1987).

means; the ability to make proposals, an organisational culture (bringing together the objectives of economic viability and social requirements, rigorous management and strategic planning).

(d)   Local institutions (local government, etc.) that are in favour of the new area-by-area partnership approach are another factor in encouraging the launch of projects.

(e)   National-level public authorities who are open to experiment: insertion initiatives need state financial support without constraints.[26] The limited nature of certain aid, the inflexibility of many programmes and the increasing uncertainty of agreements demotivate project leaders. The fragmentation of responsibilities between different ministries and services is also a very major obstacle.

6.   Voluntary Organisations, Insertion and the Social Economy: Prospects

6.1. Social Mobilisation, Insertion and Local Development: from the 1960s to the 1990s

During the 1960s and the 1970s social mobilisation in Québec was basically oriented around the state, within the two-pronged structure of the nation state, under the impulse of a movement – which crossed class boundaries – to win Québec national status within the Canadian confederation, and the welfare state propelled by strong demand from social movements. During the 1970s and 1980s this broad movement, in the worst cases, fragmented into a multitude of groups with category-based interests.

However, with the arrival of the 1990s state-based concepts and national spaces seemed to be losing headway to regional space as a framework for reference or belonging. A society fragmented by the slump started to rebuild itself from the bottom, through local communities and the regions. This new dynamic certainly raised a new type of challenge to those running projects within the voluntary sector, such as the partnership method, rigorous business management, efforts towards self-funding, the creation of economic information networks, and the promotion of services, etc.

---

[26] Valadou (1995).

In a more general fashion, the sector of the voluntary sector movement, which is active in the fight against unemployment, has a place at the heart of the new solutions to the crisis in unemployment, the welfare state, and local communities in difficulty. It lies at the intersection of: the relationship between the state and civil society, the relationship between local communities and development, and the new relationship between the 'economic' and the 'social'. This new dynamic also falls within the more general framework of a social contract that is coming into effect – at enterprise level between management and the trade unions, at regional level between local authorities and central government, and at local (village or urban community) level between citizens, their local community and the state, and in environmental issues between local communities, the State and businesses. The voluntary sector and the social economy enterprises that it promotes, are finding themselves at an ever-increasingly sensitive point in a society which is in the process of constructing itself. It is at the intersection of the 'local' and the 'global'; and it operates in spaces where the new techniques of social transformation are emerging, a space that no other sector of society really occupies.

6.2. The Current Period – Transition

The last decade (from 1990 to today) can primarily be seen as a period of social experimentation. First because the state is looking for new avenues to counter social exclusion, and second because the social movements are also looking for new avenues. This period has given rise to a vast proliferation of experiments, a multiplicity of areas for intervention, methods and forms of bringing people together. This period is also characterised by a certain effervescence: strong motivation of those involved, a call for more 'economic' expertise, proliferation of activity-based projects, local development, enterprises for social integration by economic means, and community development funds, etc. All developing in a somewhat chaotic fashion, in such a way that 'networking' has become a vital necessity.[27] In brief, we are witnessing a move, little by little, into a new phase dominated by the synchronisation of initiatives around a core of

---

[27] The Québec government is indirectly encouraging this. It has opened a social economy workshop, calling on various associative networks involved in the fight against unemployment within the framework of a socio-economic summit held in 1996 with its group of partners (employers, trade unions, voluntary organisation movements and women's organisations).

local development. In all likelihood this will ease the passage of experiments and developments.[28]

6.3. Conditions for the Widespread Implementation of Insertion Initiatives and Local Development

On the macro-social level two conditions seem to us to be essential for further progress by the social economy in the field of insertion. The first is tied in with the relationships that these initiatives will have with the public authorities; the second is their relationships with the trade union movement and the big co-operatives.

The voluntary sector movement, insertion and the public authorities After ten years of experiments, are matters progressing or has a plateau been reached? In the first instance, as a general rule, it has been a struggle to obtain public funding. Central government support for these initiatives has tended to confer a largely experimental and localised nature on them. However, the arrival of new public measures for insertion and local development has raised some hopes that this will change.[29] At the least, to project organisers and to many of those doing research into the relations between the voluntary and public sectors, this seems to be the most appropriate strategy.[30]

Second, the recognition of insertion and local development initiatives by public authorities is currently a central issue of social thinking: if they get significant levels of support from the public authorities these experiments could come to fruition in new bodies for assistance to development across all the neighbourhoods and regions in difficulty. Here we are thinking of the model for local development set by the CDECs.[31] The public authorities cannot provide ad hoc assistance (the 'shadow state'), but must commit themselves to long-term support not confined to aid for start-ups, since in the case of development the duration of support is more important than the level of finance committed to launching initiatives.[32] Public authorities also need to get rid of their centralising attitude and recognise these experiments by opening the way to their

---

[28] In 1996 and in 1998, two consecutive colloquia of the Institute for Training in Community Development (IFDEC) brought together all the networks engaged in insertion and local development work, thus revealing the state of current transitions.

[29] Ion (1990).

[30] Vaillancourt (1999).

[31] Favreau (1994c).

[32] Diaz (1994).

institutionalisation. Our hypothesis is that when these experiments become institutions, they will be able to generate innovative solutions to the crisis of employment and the welfare state 'by occupying an intermediate space at the intersection of the links between the state and civil society with those between local communities and development and the relationship between the economic and the social'.[33]

The voluntary sector movement, insertion, and trade unions and co-operative bodies New ties between the voluntary sector movement and the trade union movement have sprung up at local and regional level with the new CDEC and SADC groupings serving as intermediaries to lead the fight against unemployment and exclusion. On the one hand trade union activists serve on the managing bodies of these local development agencies, while on the other the unions have set up venture capital funds to maintain and create employment.

The *Fédération des travailleurs de Québec* (FTQ), the most important trade union confederation, has set up a fund that now has shareholders measuring in the tens of thousands, investments in more than 100 businesses (SMEs in Québec), thus maintaining or creating more than 40,000 jobs since it was set up in 1983. The *Confédération des syndicats nationaux* (CSN)[34] followed the FTQ's lead in 1996 by creating its own fund specialising in support for social economy enterprises.

Among the co-operative financial institutions the stress is not on local development and the fight against unemployment, but a certain number of local savings banks have taken this line with support from the general management of the *Mouvement desjardins*. The latter, moreover, has released substantial sums to support local and regional development funds together with funds from trade union organisations. Beyond insertion, the bridge the great institutions of the social economy and the new initiatives allows a restoring of the 'social' in the former, and in the latter an economic base that it often lacks. For lack of a consolidation of this bridge and lack of a recognition of such partnerships by public bodies, the insertion initiatives and local development initiatives set up by the voluntary sector movement, which have so far tended to develop in terms of the solidarity economy, risk being ghettoised as just an element of 'neo-philanthropy', or as mere subcontractors for certain public employment aid policies.

---

[33] Favreau (1994b).

[34] The CSN is the cousin of the French CFDT, in terms of its origin, its Christian culture, its social composition and its left-wing orientation.

References

Aubry, F. and Charest, J. (1995), *Développer l'économie solidaire. Éléments d'orientation*, Confédération des syndicats nationaux (CSN), Montréal.

Bélanger, J.-P. (1995), *Les Organismes communautaires du réseau: un secteur de l'économie sociale à consolider et à développer*, working document, Ministère de la Santé et des Services sociaux, Québec.

Bélanger, P.-R., Boucher, J. and Lévesque, B. (1994), 'L'Économie solidaire au Québec; la question du modèle de développement', in J.-L. Laville, (ed.), *L'Économie solidaire, une perspective internationale*, Desclée de Brouwer, Paris, pp.139–175.

Boucher, J. and Favreau, L. (1994), 'L'Évolution du discours de la CSN sur les stratégies syndicales', in Bélanger, Grant and B. Lévesque, *La Modernisation sociale des entreprises*, Coll. Politique et Économie, Presses de l'Université de Montréal (PUM), Montréal.

Castel, R. (1995), *Les Métamorphoses de la question sociale*, Fayard, Paris.

Christenson, J.A. and Robinson J.W. (1989), *Community Development in Perspective*, Iowa State University Press, IA.

Conseil des affaires sociales (1989), *Deux Québec dans un. Rapport sur le développement social et démographique*, Conseil des affaires sociales, Gaétan Morin, Boucherville/Québec.

Conseil de la santé et du bien-être (1996), *L'Harmonisation des politiques de lutte contre l'exclusion*, Conseil de la santé et du bien-être, Gouvernement du Québec, Montréal.

Defourny, J. (1994), *Développer l'entreprise sociale*, Fondation Roi Baudoin, Brussels.

Defourny, J. and J.-L. Monzon Campos (eds) (1992), *L'Économie sociale entre l'économie capitaliste et l'économie publique*, CIRIEC/De Boeck Université, Brussels.

Diaz, H. (1994), 'L'Innovation sociale, une intruse structurelle', *Économie et humanisme*, no. 328, pp. 20–26.

Gouvernement du Québec (1995), 'L'Emploi, travaillons-y ensemble', Gouvernement du Québec (proposition du gouvernement du Québec à ces partenaires socio-économiques), Quebec.

Fairbairn, B. (1991), *Co-operatives and Community Devlopment (Economics in Social Perspective)*, Center for the study of Co-operatives, Saskatoon.

Favreau, L. (1994a), 'L'Économie solidaire à l'américaine: le développement économique communautaire', in J.-L. Laville (ed.), *L'Économie solidaire, une perspective internationale*, Desclée de Brouwer, Paris, pp. 93–135.

Favreau, L. (1994b), 'Mouvement associatif et ONG à l'heure des partenariats', *Co-opératives et développement*, vol. 25, no. 2, pp. 7–26.

Favreau, L. (1994c), 'L'Approche de développement économique communautaire au Québec et aux États-Unis', *RECMA*, no. 253-254, pp. 166–175.

Favreau, L. (ed.) (1999), 'Économie sociale, développement local et économie plurielle', *Revue économie et solidarités*, vol. 30, no. 1, Presses de l'Université du Québec, Sillery, Québec, pp. 1–35.

Favreau, L. and Lévesque, B. (1996), *Développement économique communautaire, économie sociale et intervention*, Presses de l'Université du Québec, Sillery, Québec.

Fournier, L. (1993), 'Le Fonds de solidarité des travailleurs du Québec, une institution financière syndicale vouée au développement de l'emploi', *RECMA*, no. 48, pp. 53–58.

Ion, J. (1990), *Le Travail social à l'épreuve du territoire*, Privat, Paris.

Laville, J.-L. (1992), *Les Services de proximité en Europe*, Syros/Alternatives, Paris.

Laville, J.-L.(ed.) (1994), *L'Économie solidaire, une perspective internationale*, Desclée de Brouwer, Paris.

Leduc Browne, P. (1996), *Love in a Cold War? (The Voluntary Sector in an Age of Cuts)*, Canadian Centre for Policy Alternatives, Ottawa.

Lévesque, B. and Malo, M.-C. (1992), 'L'Économie sociale au Québec', in J. Defourny and J.-L. Monzon Campos (eds), *L'Économie sociale entre l'économie capitaliste et l'économie publique*, CIRIEC/De Boeck Université, Brussels, pp. 385–446.

Lévesque, B. *et al.* (1995), 'Les Fonds de développement: un instrument indispensable pour le développement régional, local et communautaire', in Côté, Klein, M.-U. Proulx, (eds), *Et les régions qui perdent...?*, Université du Québec à Rimouski, Rimouski, pp. 245–270.

Lévesque, B. *et al.* (1999), 'Les Fonds régionaux et locaux de développement au Québec: des institutions financières relevant principalement de l'économie sociale', in M.-U. Proulx (ed.), *Territoires et développement*, L'Harmattan, Paris/Montréal, pp. 233–270.

Matte, Baldino, and Courchesne, M. (1998), 'Évolution de l'emploi atypique au Québec', Ministère du Travail, Gouvernement du Québec, Montréal.

Ministère de la sécurité du revenu (MSR) (1996), 'Un parcours vers l'insertion, la formation et l'emploi. Document de consultation', Ministère de la sécurité du revenu (MSR), Gouvernement du Québec, Montréal.

Perry, S.E. (1987), *Communities on the Way (Rebuilding Local Economies in the United States and Canada)*, University of New York Press, NY.

Quarter, J. (1992), *Canada's Social Economy*, James Lorimer & Company, Toronto.

Vaillancourt, Y. (1994), 'Eléments de problématique concernant l'arrimage entre le communautaire et le public', *Nouvelles pratiques sociales*, vol.7, no 2, Montréal, pp. 227–248.

Vaillancourt, Y. (1999), 'Le Tiers Secteur', *Nouvelles pratiques sociales*, vol. 11, no. 2, pp. 21–175.

Valadou, C. *et al.* (1995), *Les Entreprises d'insertion au Québec: état des lieux*, Collectif des entreprises d'insertion, Montréal.

5 Finland: Voluntary Organisations and Co-operatives for Socio-economic Reintegration in Finland

PEKKA PÄTTINIEMI, HARRI KOSTILAINEN AND
MARIANNE NYLUND

1. Introduction

In this article, we first discuss the Nordic welfare system in Finland and the pressures it has encountered – through mass unemployment and economic recession in the early 1990s. Since the Second World War, mutual and voluntary organisations[1] have mainly had a representative and innovative role providing welfare services. Their role as employers has been marginal. The recession and high unemployment during the 1990s have caused a change in their role. They are now developing active measures to combat mass unemployment. Good examples of these innovative solutions are local associations for the unemployed and labour co-operatives. Local associations of the unemployed are developing all around the country. There are about 300 of them offering support in job search and further education, for example computer skills and language courses. In addition, low-price meals are served to their members and other unemployed people. The labour co-operatives, often established through the initiative and assistance of a local association for the unemployed, are mostly multisectoral. The business idea is to hire out members' labour to other companies thereby keeping up members' work skills and contact with the labour market. Labour co-operatives offered full permanent jobs to about

---

[1] In this paper, concepts of voluntary associations/organisations, non-profit organisations and non-governmental organisations are used as parallel concepts.

3,300 persons, part-time work to about 4,400 persons in the year of 1996. It is estimated that mutual and voluntary associations will play a more active part in work reintegration during the next few years; today they employ about 70,000 persons.

1.1. Labour Market Policy, Unemployment and Associations in Finland

National regulation of the labour market and an extensive social policy in Finland and in other Nordic countries, have made steady growth of the economy possible, and increased the level of welfare for citizens. In Nordic countries, the labour market policy is seen as an integral part of the economic and education policy but also as an important part of the whole welfare state. Deregulation of the national labour market has changed this situation. The shift to more global and deregulated markets together with mass unemployment has meant that the former national strategy for the labour market has became ineffective and even rejected its earlier objectives of encouraging economic growth and social welfare (Koistinen, 1996, pp. 17–20).

1.2. The Evolution of Finnish Welfare State and Labour Markets

After the Second World War, Finnish society, regardless of the political party, concentrated on two main goals. The first goal was to industrialise the country. The second goal aimed to minimise social barriers and class differences by developing social welfare, health care and educational institutions. These goals were reached by favouring major industrial companies in wood, paper and metal industries as well as the public sector social institutions. During the 1960s and 1970s, the level of development was almost the same as other Nordic welfare states.

Esping-Andersen (1990, pp. 26–28) developed a typology of three different welfare state regimes called 'liberal', 'corporatist' and 'social democratic'. The latter regime is also characterised as a Nordic or Scandinavian model, and represents the Finnish situation. One main principle for this model is said to be the 'fusion of welfare and work', with an emphasis on reaching full employment through welfare policies.

In a social democratic and universal welfare state system, the labour market has a central role to organise welfare services for citizens. There is also considered to be a relatively equal distribution of income. This is made possible mainly through the expansive welfare state and public employment system where social policy and the labour market are interwoven in mutually interdependent institutions (Esping-Andersen, 1990, pp. 26–28, 52–53, 149).

The fusion of welfare and work is closely related to women's participation in the labour market. This is made possible by making public social services available to all citizens (Sipilä, 1997, p. 5). The high rate of employed women is a special characteristic of the Finnish welfare system, but men and women still work in different segments of the labour market. An important characteristic of the Finnish welfare service sector is, for example, the high level of female employees. The expansion of the public sector and the feminisation of the welfare state can be seen as a transition where women moved from non-paid home care work to the same kind of mainly state-paid work in social welfare and health care sectors.

Comparisons of employment and unemployment rates of women and men in Finland show that the employment rate amongst women and men is more equal than the average in the other 15 European Union countries. Until recently the unemployment rate among women has been lower than that for men, during 1999 the unemployment rate of women has been higher than that of men (Tilastokeskus, 1999).

The aim for full employment and other traditional Finnish labour market policies continued until 1991. The Finnish welfare system experienced dramatic changes caused by the economic recession that began in the first part of the 1990s. Unemployment increased rapidly from the low level of 3% in the late 1980s, to a high of 20% at the beginning of 1990s. In autumn 1999 the Finnish unemployment rate was about 9%.

The new labour market policies of the present government emphasise the creation of jobs in the small and medium sized enterprises (SME) and service sectors. The government is also committed to job-creation by supporting self-employment and promoting service co-operatives. The new employment programme encourages entrepreneurship and local initiatives.

In Finland the state, and especially the municipalities, have played a central role in providing these services. This Scandinavian welfare model guaranteed a comprehensive safety net against unemployment until the recession of the 1990s. But voluntary organisations have another role: according to Siisiäinen (1995b, p. 7), they are becoming more important in making politicians aware of current problems in a post-industrial society. Voluntary organisations and pressure groups are especially important for citizens with limited resources. It is easier to raise issues and influence a political agenda as a group than as an individual (Siisiäinen, 1995a,b).

2.   Mutual and Voluntary Associations in Finland

Associations are seen as the traditional way of tackling social problems. At the end of 19th century, mutual aid organisations for working-class people, were established in some European countries (Kendal and Knapp, 1993, p. 2; Jaakkola, 1994, p. 149). Organisations like Friendly Societies offered contingency funds for sickness, burial and old age (Riessman and Gartner 1977; Withorn, 1980). At that time, 'helping funds' were also initiated for the same purpose in Finland – to secure basic incomes for working class people and their families (Nylund, 1996a, p. 196). In England, this type of mutual aid was called 'working spirit of self-help' (Kendal and Knapp 1993, 2: ref. to Beveridge, 1948, pp. 85–86).

Finnish voluntary associations have expanded powerfully in five waves; during the years of 1880–1905, after the civil war 1918, after the Second World War, during 1960s–1980s, and finally, from 1990 onwards.[2]

The years 1880–1905 were the time of nation building. Some associations, like the Finnish Red Cross (established in 1877), the Finnish Children's Welfare Association (1893), and the Finnish Anti-Tuberculosis Association (1907) were concerned with issues of social and health care (ICSW, 1994; Jaakkola, *et al.* 1994). By the turn of the century, many associations were linked to the temperance movement (Siisiäinen, 1995b). During the aftermath of two wars (the civil war in 1918 and the Second World War), organisations for helping orphans, handicapped and war veterans were founded. Many of the associations had close connections with party politics from the time of national independence (1917) until the Second World War.

After the Second World War, Finnish voluntary associations started to act as representatives of their members' interests to government and politicians. They also organised hobbies, voluntary education, recreation, sporting activities, etc., for their members. Associations for social welfare and health have also played an important innovative role, introducing new services that were later integrated into the public sector services. During the 1960s and 1970s many associations were registered for different user groups, such as people with coronary disease, learning disabilities and hearing or visual disabilities (Siisiäinen, 1992, 1995b).

Although associations have had an important role in Finnish society, it has not been in the role of employer. In 1919 an Association Act was passed and from then a total of 140,000 associations are registered. Of

---

[2] This categorisation differs from the five cycles of protest described by Siisiäinen (1992).

these, 29% are economic or professional, and 25% are political associations. Six per cent (8000) of all registered associations were established in the field of social welfare and health during the years 1919–1994.

2.1. Associations in Health, Social, Sport and Youth Sectors

General director Markku Lehto from the Ministry of Social and Health Care has stated that 'for the long-term unemployed we need new alternatives where the third sector, and especially the associations of social and health care potentially have a role in solving the unemployment problem' (Lehto, 1997, p. 9). In addition, sport organisations are also seen as potential employers (Kauppi, 1997).

There are about 11,500 local associations that organise voluntary social work. These organisations have 1.5 million members, however, only approximately 6% of their members are actively engaging in the activities offered or are involved in voluntary work, others merely support the associations by being their members (Poteri, 1997). One of the largest national sport organisations, Finnish Sports Union (SLU) has about 6,000 member associations and sports clubs, which in turn have about 1.2 million registered members. Allianssi (the nationwide youth organisation uniting practically all major youth organisations) has 93 member organisations, most with several local organisations, and a total of about 700,000 members (Rönnberg, 1997).

Results from a study of 94 voluntary social welfare and health care organisations indicate that these organisations employ 21,000 people (Poteri, 1997). According to JH Third Sector study of Finland, it is estimated that non-governmental organisations (NGO) employ about 70,000 people (Helander and Laaksonen, 1999). NGOs contribute about 3% (15 billion FIM) of the total National Gross Domestic Income (Hietala, 1997).

The role of voluntary organisations and social enterprises can also be seen as a supplement, not a replacement for public services. In a recent survey conducted by the University of Åbo Akademi, the attitudes of 2,000 voluntary associations were studied in 47 Finnish municipalities. The results confirm that many associations are eager to supplement the basic municipal services, but not to substitute them (Pikkala, 1997).

As stated earlier, the voluntary non-profit associations have had a marginal role as employers in Finland, and they are not commonly viewed as having an important role in employing (long-term) unemployed people.

However, the risk of being excluded from work has increased dramatically, and recently, the need for self-help solutions and the role of associations and voluntary work in helping to solve the current mass unemployment have been raised in public discussions.

In February 1997, a task force consisting of representatives from various voluntary associations in Finland produced a memorandum in Parliament entitled, 'By changing the attitudes and regulations we can achieve a substantial amount of new jobs in voluntary associations'. The task force pointed out several areas of legislation that hinder associations employing new staff. In the memorandum a model of state- or municipality-supported jobs were recommended as one solution. Associations could start employing people, initially with public support, that would be reduced gradually (Allianssi, 1997). In 1997 a new substitute for the employers to employ long-term unemployed was introduced. This so-called combined support is granted for six months to associations to employ long-term unemployed. By the end of 1998, 7,000 unemployed were employed for this period solely in the sport associations.

There is, however, resistance, especially in trade unions, to this type of employment policy. There is a fear that this kind of employment policy will mean the development of a new low-paid labour market in Finnish society.

2.2. *Financing Voluntary Associations and Local Initiatives*

The Slot Machine Association (RAY) is a state-controlled association that has a legal monopoly for gambling and maintaining slot machines in Finland. The Government and voluntary organisations together manage it and decide on the distribution of RAY's profits for social and health purposes (ICSW, 1994, 5). Thus RAY has a key role in financing voluntary associations working in the field of health care and social welfare, as well as youth work. In the year of 1996, RAY distributed 1.454 million FIM to 955 social welfare and health care associations (RAY, Annual Report, 1997). These associations have over 16,000 employees and their annual budgets total over 5,000 million FIM (Salavuo, 1996).

A new target group for the Slot Machine Association is to fund associations for unemployed. This new policy can be seen in the increasing amount of funding for new types of associations from 1994 to 1997. A clear increase in the number of associations for the unemployed, applying for funding from RAY can be seen in Table 5.1. The number of accepted applications varies, the average being around 48%. The board of RAY have also suggested that one of its funding targets should be excluded groups or associations trying to reintegrate such people.

Youth organisations also receive additional funding from the state owned company *Oy Veikkaus Ab* (a company that has the monopoly for organising lottery and betting games). *Oy Veikkaus Ab* was originally founded by three sports organisations, and since 1976 is wholly owned by the state. Regulations specify that *Oy Veikkaus Ab* must allocate its profits for arts, sports, science and youth work. During 1996, it gave out 1.685 million FIM to the associations mentioned above, and 6% (103 million FIM) of that was distributed to youth work (Isaksson, 1997, p. 71).

Table 5.1 The number of associations for the unemployed applying and receiving funding from the Slot Machine Association in 1994–1997

	Number of associations applying for funding	Number of associations receiving funding	Percentage (%) accepted applications
1994	25	14	56
1995	63	25	40
1996	78	42	54
1997	150	70	47
Total 1994–97	316	151	48 (average)

3. The Performance of Associations and Co-operatives for Integration

3.1. Mutual Aid Associations – Associations for the Unemployed in Finland

Types of mutual organisations established annually have changed from traditional forms like trade unions (or mutual aid funds) at the turn of the century, to contemporary forms like self-help groups and co-operatives of the unemployed. Currently there are two major types of association developing initiatives to integrate the unemployed and other groups at risk of exclusion from the labour market and the society. These are local associations of the unemployed, and various entrepreneurial or enterprise initiatives founded or supported by the associations.

The associations for the unemployed can be seen as one example of a new type of citizen action and self-help reintegration in Finland. The

Citizen Forum[3] conducted a nation wide study of Finnish self-help groups and voluntary action centres during the summer of 1994.[4] Over 2,000 questionnaires were sent to all municipal social service centres, health care centres and mental health centres, to local Lutheran parishes (total number 598), and to national non-profit social welfare and health care organisations (Lindqvist and Nylund, 1996; Nylund, 1995, p. 25). In this chapter, only the responses of 40 self-help groups and associations for the unemployed are reported.

The goals for action, of the associations for unemployed people varied somewhat. However, four crucial themes were found. The main objectives were to decrease the rate of unemployment of members, to improve their income level (unemployment benefit), to sustain working skills, and to maintain their social, physical and mental condition. This latter goal was one of the most frequently reported.

According to the results of these questionnaires, it appears very important for the associations to promote members' working skills, by training them for the contemporary labour market. Improving language skills and computer skills is just one of the courses offered by these associations. Most courses are taught by volunteers, but some teachers are hired with a state subsidy. In addition, paid employees (often a manager and a secretary) are hired also with a state subsidy. This subsidy is paid by the local employment office for people who have been unemployed more than one year. Usually the contracts are for a minimum of six months.

To maintain the social, physical and mental condition of unemployed individuals some of the associations offer the possibility of discussion groups for self-help and mutual aid. For the unemployed it seems to be very important to meet and interact with other people in a similar life situation to share ideas, experiences and information. Giving and receiving support also strengthens members' self-confidence and identity. However, for some people it appears to be enough to have a cup of coffee or a meal during an informal and spontaneous discussion with someone. New social contacts can bring new friends or even job opportunities (Nylund, 1996b). In addition, many associations offer leisure possibilities – for sports and handicrafts. The facilities are often given free of charge by local parishes or

---

[3] The Citizen Forum (*Kansalaisareena ry - Medborgararenan rf*) is a non-governmental organisation promoting and developong the idea of voluntary work, self-help groups and self-employment.

[4] This study was funded by the Finnish Slot Machine Association. The study was not a survey because there is no register of self-help groups in Finland. Therefore, the aim of the study was to map the number and type of self-help groups in Finland.

municipalities. Low-price meals are also served by unemployed people themselves, volunteering for cooking with the help of senior volunteers (Lehtinen, 1996).

Some of the associations for unemployed people arrange courses on issues such as 'how to apply for work' or 'how to start a co-operative or a private enterprise'. These courses and seminars are usually arranged free of charge or for a minimal fee (40–100 FIM) for members. Most of the activities of these associations are performed by volunteers, apart from a few subsidised employees (they are not self-sufficient enough to employ without subsidies). Recently about half of the 300 hundred associations[5] have received funding from the Slot Machine Association (see Table 5.1), for example, to employ paid staff. Nevertheless, some active and ambitions members have started a co-operative or a private firm. The skills and knowledge acquired from these associations have encouraged them to employ themselves and develop new contacts outside the association.

Another type of associative reintegration experiment is, exemplified by the *Sirkkulanpuisto yhteisö* (Sirkkula Park Community). This local community initiative tries to integrate people with severe alcohol problems into work and society. People in the community have built proper homes for themselves and in various kinds of workshops, members produce hand made goods (amongst other things) for sale in markets.

3.2. Labour Co-operatives

The difference between associations and co-operatives is in the extent of voluntary work. Co-operatives are more market oriented and do not have the same possibilities to use voluntary work as associations, which are obliged by law to work mainly on a voluntary basis. Co-operatives are legally one form of company and they are considered equivalent to joint-stock companies. And legally a person cannot work voluntarily without pay in companies such as co-operatives. But it should be emphasised that in Finland both the Co-operative Law and the Association Law underline the one member-one vote principle.

The emergence of labour co-operatives in the 1990s is a new phenomenon. These worker co-operative types of enterprise are owned mainly by unemployed people wanting to re-enter the labour market after varying periods of unemployment. They are not traditional worker co-

---

[5] There are, in all, about three hundred associations of the unemployed in Finland. They were all established during the 1990s, and at least 220 are officially registered and member organisations of the national organisation of Co-operation of Unemployed People.

operatives but more like the Italian social co-operatives in the field of integration into work. The idea is to subcontract members' labour to other companies. Most of them work in a range of sectors; and their members are unemployed people from many professions. However, most members are from the construction sector and from secretarial services (Karjalainen, 1996). Many of the 230 labour co-operatives are formed by the initiative and assistance of local associations for the unemployed.

The first labour co-operative was established in the autumn of 1993 in Kirkkonummi, a municipality 35 kilometres west of Helsinki. The local association of the unemployed experimented as to how they could find temporary or permanent jobs for their members. They advertised that their members were willing to do temporary work and placed a notice board in their office. The experiment was successful. However, there were some problems too; notices from private individuals or enterprises offering jobs often disappeared from the notice board and some jobs offered were in the black or informal economy. To avoid these problems, the association of the unemployed called a meeting, to establish a co-operative for association members. The co-operative would then hire its members needing temporary or permanent work to households or to companies requiring labour (Suominen, 1995).

Labour co-operatives try to sustain their members' contact with the labour markets and their ability to work. They try to employ or subcontract their members for full-time work, but part-time work, and temporary working opportunities are also welcomed. 'All labour co-operatives do not see it as necessary to employ their members themselves. It is more important to offer opportunities to members, to develop their business ideas, products and marketing' (Karjalainen, 1996, p. 27). It is also regarded as a positive result if a member is employed full-time outside the co-operative and so leaves the membership. In practice, few labour co-operatives have to close their operation because most of their members become employed directly in other companies. Some labour co-operatives have additional social goals. For example, they may give preference to hiring someone with greater social needs, for a particular job (Pättiniemi, 1995, p. 75).

The labour co-operatives can be seen as a transitional phase in three alternative directions: first for the development of an ordinary worker co-operative or employee owned business; second to gradually cease to act as a business, because all active members have been employed directly by other companies, and the original purpose of reintegration of the members in the labour market has been met or third to develop their local connections to municipalities, other businesses and associations and gradually develop into local partnerships (Pättiniemi, 1999a, p. 141).

The employment effect of the labour co-operatives can be gauged from the fact that they offered at least one employment opportunity for 1,200 unemployed in the autumn of 1995 (Karjalainen, 1996, p. 33), and the following year 1996, according to Labour Ministry, labour co-operatives were giving employment opportunist to about 4,500. Today it is estimated that they give 3,300 permanent full-time jobs and employ 4,400 persons part-time (Pättiniemi, 1996b). Moreover, studies of labour co-operatives have discovered other outcomes: self-esteem of the members increased, as well as the ability to take part in the social life of a local community.

During 1997, a number of new labour co-operatives were established, especially in the small rural towns and regions. In Kainuu region, north-east of Finland, there were ten new co-operatives with 180 members. From the beginning of January to the end of August 1997, these co-operatives temporarily employed about 125 people; and 50 members were employed by other companies. Total wages paid were about 1.1 million FIM. Savings in public spending and public incomes from VAT[6] and income taxes have been about 1.5 million FIM (Nivala, 1997).

Four labour co-operatives from the south of Finland have been participating in the Haviva-Adapt project from autumn 1996 to the end of October 1997. During this time, 18 new permanent jobs have been created by these co-operatives and 52 members have got a permanent job outside the co-operatives. Thus about 48% of the 147 members have obtained a permanent new job within a year (Kostilainen and Pättiniemi, 1997).

3.3. *Other Co-operatives and Social Firms Founded by Associations*

Various groups of people with physical disabilities or mental health problems, long-term unemployed or immigrants and refugees, consider co-operatives and social firms as one solution for gaining employment and integration into the Finnish labour market. For example, some ten people with hearing disabilities have formed a labour co-operative with the assistance of their national association. Other groups of people with disabilities are also in the process of forming co-operatives to integrate their members into the labour market.

---

[6] VAT = social insurance contribution and income tax retention (Mannila, 1996, p. 46).

Currently, various associations of people with mental health and psychiatric disabilities are establishing co-operatives or other social enterprises for work integration. These social enterprises employ 153 people at risk of being excluded from normal labour markets, and 946 people in workshops (workshops in Finland are mainly owned and run by the municipalities). The projects managed by these associations and foundations have employed an additional 343 people at risk from being excluded from labour markets (VATES, 1997).

Immigrants, especially from the former Soviet Union, have established eight co-operatives with the help of their cultural associations. The aim of these co-operatives is to integrate its members into Finnish business and working life. These co-operatives are active: in import and export, the catering and restaurant business, and in child care for ethnic groups. These new co-operatives employed some 40 people in the Spring, 1999.

Another example of how an association develops different activities is illustrated here by the *Hyvä Arki* ('Good Everyday Life') association. It is an association with social purposes, for example, to employ the long-term unemployed. The *Hyvä Arki* association and its organic food wholesale co-operative, together with some local citizens established a co-operative in Espoo, a city close to Helsinki. The aim of this *Hyvä Arki* Services Co-operative is to sell community services, such as home cleaning, repairing apartments and houses of local citizens. The *Hyvä Arki* Services Co-operative also arranges temporary labour force for cleaning and kitchen services to several schools in the city of Espoo. This co-operative employs about 20 people on a full-time basis and providing job opportunities for an additional 100 for varying periods of time annually.

3.4. Community Co-operatives

In some suburbs, there is a movement to form co-operatives linked to housing estates. Three co-operatives have already been formed and about ten projects are under development. They are formed by unemployed residents, landlords, volunteers, and voluntary associations working within the housing estate. Sometimes people from municipalities and Lutheran parishes are also active as members. Usually these community co-operatives try to improve housing, develop public spaces, and provide community services, especially child care. The main clients are real estates and the municipality.

In the countryside, some village societies or voluntary committees (which total about 3,300 in number) have taken the initiative to form village co-operatives. Frequently, village co-operatives are formed by the majority of villagers and the associations work to improve and generally develop the village. Some of the main goals are to provide services for the villagers, such as local shops, post offices, banking services, primary schools and social services (Hyyryläinen, 1994, p. 53). Village societies are moving increasingly towards providing social welfare and health care services, and creating employment for unemployed villagers. Information about the employment effects of these associative initiatives is not yet available.

There are local partnership projects in 28 regions. Some of them use the co-operative formula for their organisation and work.

4.   Conclusion and Prospects

In Finland, associations are traditionally seen as representatives of various citizen groups and not as active agents in economic or social sectors. Therefore, the idea of third sector playing an employment role is new, and was first raised in the mid-1990s.

The measures for reintegrating people at risk of exclusion began simultaneously in rural villages and in major cities with high unemployment rates. The first local associations of the unemployed were established in the late 1980s; they provide reintegrative services for the unemployed. The services, such as training, to maintain and increase the working skills and other capabilities of the unemployed, aim to help their members re-enter the labour market. Both the services and the social life within the associations for the unemployed are considered important.

Labour co-operatives and other new co-operatives actively employ their members in new jobs. This takes place either within the co-operatives or in other enterprises after a 'training period' offered by a co-operative. Labour co-operatives and other new co-operatives can be viewed as new initiatives, linked both to employment policy and to the economy. In economic life, they represent a new way of viewing business, where people take control of their own lives without depending on the public sector or large private enterprises. Labour co-operatives can be seen as transitional enterprises with two purposes: first, as a first step in developing an employee-owned business; second, as a tool for their members to get out of unemployment and in to employment with wage-earner status.

However, the Finnish welfare state is still considered to have the main responsibility for social welfare and health care services. The Public sector continues with its established tradition of absorbing new ideas from the associations and including these services in the services produced by the public sector. It is estimated that the reintegrative actions of associations will grow gradually in importance and in number over the next few years.

4.1 Case 1 Labour Co-operative Itämeren Ansio *(Co-operative 'Baltic Earnings')*

In spring 1994 The Local Association for Unemployed in Helsinki arranged a meeting for its members to voluntarily plan training on 'How to establish a workers co-operative'. About 70 members attended the meeting. During the spring, a training days were arranged in the local areas near the association. The co-operative was established in June 1994 and registered on June 30, 1994.

About 20 unemployed joined the co-operative *Itämeren Ansio*. Now the co-operative has 57 members, about 30 of them being active. Members are from different sectors of the labour markets, but mainly from the construction industry (architects, technicians, and workers), translators, and people from the graphic industry.

The aim of the co-operative is to maintain and achieve a better quality of life for its members in modern society'. That means in practice the co-operative is not necessarily trying to achieve full time employment for its members, but rather to maintain the working skills and mental health of the members during their period of unemployment. The co-operative has two businesses: subcontracting its members' labour to other companies, and doing small-scale construction work for private or company clients. The development of the business has been steady and well balanced, with turnover increasing steadily each year.

Annually *Itämeren Ansio* has offered temporary work to about 25 members and 3 non-members. This totalled 4–5 person-years. During year 1997, *Ansio* employed 22 people on a full-time basis.

4.2 Case 2 Idea-Points

In 1992 some unemployed engineers, architects and economists, gathered together at the local trade union branch 'Engineers in Helsinki', considering the idea that they should pool their resources to find themselves jobs. The *Idea* project was born.

Plans were made, more trade unions joined in such as the unions of architects (SEFE), salesman (SMKJ) and technicians (TEK), and finance was obtained (50% Ministry of Employment, 50% other sources) to launch *Idea* as a two-year pilot project. The aim of the project was to:

(a) activate the participants to create jobs and find employment for themselves either as employees or independent entrepreneurs;

(b) provide custom made vocational training according to the needs of the participants in close co-operation with potential employers, training institutes and local authorities;

(c) provide a forum for social contacts, team work and the building of a network of mutual support and exchange of ideas.

The working method from the very beginning was teamwork by the participants for the participants. All staff were recruited from project activists on short term (3–6 months) contracts. Participation was totally voluntary. Groups quickly formed in various areas such as export trade, opportunities in Germany, entrepreneurial opportunities, creation of new business ideas, active job seeking and capacity building. Regional offices were established in various parts of the Helsinki metropolitan area. Space, office equipment, furniture, stationery, coffee machine – all obtained as gifts from various sponsors. At the same time valuable contacts were formed and even the first jobs created.

Very soon it became apparent that the existing support and training schemes of 1992 were totally inadequate. They were basically aimed at training unskilled people in a situation where work was abundant but skills short. But the situation had totally changed. Skills were abundant but no jobs available. New ideas were needed and many teams set up in *Idea* to design their own training courses – often a mixture of updating specific professional skills and improving general skills, (such as command of foreign languages or computer skills) this was combined with on the job training or independent project work. The pilot projects proved successful and the concept was soon adopted by the Finnish employment services.

The very success of the *Idea*-project by the end of 1994 encouraged the trade unions to continue. The project was restructured, the regional offices wound down and the activity concentrated in one location.

In spring 1995 *Idea* was renamed *Idea-Points*. It still provides support and help for independent, self-designed job seeking and employment, and encourages capacity building and career planning. It is also a meeting place and social forum for exchange of ideas and mutual support. Co-operation with the newly established Sörnäinen House of Skills broadened the scope and contact net and provides lots of new opportunities for participating in various projects and activities. The Sörnäinen House of Skills is a project trying to integrate work, small-scale production, cultural and leisure activities, housing, open centre learning, citizens' activity, all in a socially and ecologically sustainable way in the old Helsinki workers region of Sörnäinen.

Idea-Points also provides a free telephone, fax machine and computers for job seeking as well as very cheap photocopying facilities. They have a couple of small rooms that can be used for group sessions and meetings. There are newspapers, and bulletin boards for training courses, jobs, and events.

> Everybody is welcome to visit *Idea-Points* regardless of profession, language, residency or job status. We have short courses, lectures, discussions and information on various subjects related to changes in the labour market, unemployment benefits, regulations, career planning, job seeking, entrepreneurship, co-ops, creative thinking, facing changes and personal crises. We arranged a cross-cultural shrove party with African, Irish, and Greek music, Kurdish and Iraqi food, Finnish shrove buns and a discussion on the meaning and purpose of fasting in Islam and orthodox Christianity. We also give advice on various questions related to self-employment, the developing of business ideas and worker's co-ops.

Is the Idea-Points *concept working?*

Idea-Points does not require people to fill in any forms, nor does it have a follow-up feedback system. Consequently, there are no statistics on how many people have found employment, etc.

> But more and more people are finding their way here and last spring we estimated, that on average we had about 1000 visitors per month. Our seven computers are almost in constant use. Almost daily someone says 'This is great, really what I needed' or 'my phone was cut off, because I couldn't pay the bills. Now I can hunt for jobs again'. Not to mention the young man, who danced out of the phone-room 'hey, your advice was great. I called my former employer and he has work again. He hired me on the spot. Start tomorrow'. Our job hunting groups stopped meeting because everybody had either found employment or was about to start a training course as part of a focused future career plan. Various groups are gathering, contemplating new co-ops, the phones are ringing, people are coming and going, asking advice ...

References

Allianssi (1997), 'Possibilities of third sector associations to employ the unemployed', Information Leaflet, Allianssi, Helsinki.
Esping-Andersen, G. (1990), *The Three Worlds of Welfare Capitalism*, Polity, Cambridge.

Helander, V. and Laaksonen, H. (1999), *Suomalainen kolmas sektori* [*The Finnish Third Sector*], Sosiaali - ja terveysturvan keskusliitto, Helsinki.

Hietala, K. (1997), *Kolmas sektori potentiaalisena työllistäjänä* [*Third Sector as a Potential Employer*], Studies in Labour Policy, no. 176, Ministry of Labour, Helsinki.

Hyyryläinen, T. (1994), 'Toiminan aika' ['Time for action'], Line Sixtyfour Oy, Vammala.

ICSW (1994), *Social Welfare and Health Organizations in Finland*, The Association of Voluntary Health, Social and Welfare Organizations (YTY), Helsinki.

Isaksson, P.-E. (1997), 'Den tredje sektorn. En samhällsmodell för framtiden' ['The third sector. A model for society in the future'], Schildts, Vasa.

Jaakkola, J. (1994), 'Sosiaalisten kysymysten yhteiskunta' [Society of Social Questions], in Teoksessa J. Jaakkola, P. Pulma, M. Satka and K. Urponen (eds), *Armeliaisuus, yhteisöapu, sosiaaliturva – Suomalaisen sosiaaliturvan historia*, Sosiaaliturvan Keskusliitto, Jyväskylä, pp. 71–161.

Karjalainen, J. (1996), *Työosuustoiminta työllistämisen välineenä* [*Work Cooperatives as an Instrument of Employment*], Työpoliittinen tutkimus 154, Helsinki.

Kauppi, H. (1997), 'Kansalaisjärjestöjen työllistämispotentiaali' ['The potentials by non-profit organizations to employ'], unpublished report May 19, Ministry of Labour, Helsinki.

Kendal, J. and Knapp, M. (1993), *Defining the Nonprofit Sector: The United Kingdom. The John Hopkins Comparative Nonprofit Sector Project*, working paper no. 5, The John Hopkins University Institute for Policy Studies, Baltimore.

Koistinen, P. (1996), 'The lessons to be learned. The labour market policies of Finland and Sweden in 1990–96', paper presented at the International working party on labour market segmentation, *18th Conference on European Employment Systems and the Welfare State, July 9–14, 1996, at the University of Tampere*, University of Tampere, Tampere.

Kostilainen, H. and Pättiniemi, P. (1997), 'Haviva-Adapt projektin väliraportti' ['Interim report of Haviva – Adapt project'], Institute for Co-operative Studies, Helsinki.

Lehtinen, R. (1996), 'Työttömät ja vapaaehtoistoiminta' ['Unemployed people and voluntary action']. In A.-L. Matthies, U. Kotakari and M. Nylund (eds), *Välittävät verkostot* [*Intermediating Networks*], Vastapaino, Jyväskylä, pp. 107–120.

Lehto, M. (1997), 'Uusosuustoiminnalla moniammatillisiin palveluihin' ['New co-operatives a possibility for multiprofessional services'], *Sosiaaliturva*, no. 10, p. 9.

Lindqvist, T. and Nylund, M. (1996), 'En tredje sektorn behövs – Medborgararenan grundas' ['The third sector is needed – the establishment of Citizen Forum'], in S. Suominen (ed.), *Alternativa Rörelser – Välfärdens förnyare? SSKH Meddelanden 38*, Forskningsinstitutet, Svenska Social – och kommunalhögskolan vid Helsinfgors universitet, pp. 34–46.

Mannila, S. (1996), *Social Firms in Europe. Some Practical Aspects*, National Research and Development Centre for Welfare and Health, Helsinki.

Nivala, T. (1997), 'Raportti Kainuun uusosuustoiminnasta 05.09.1997' ['Report on new co-operatives on incomes and employment in Kainuu region'], Kainuu Co-operative Development Centre, Kajaani.

Nylund, M. (1995), 'Collaboration between professionals and citizen movements – self-help groups as an example', in *Social Action and Human Rights. Finnish Contributions to the European Seminar of ICSW, Lisbon, Portugal April 1995*, Finnish ICSW Committee Publications, Helsinki, no. 1, pp. 24–29.

Nylund, M. (1996a), 'Suomalaisia oma-apuryhmiä' ['Finnish self-help groups'], in A.-L. Matthies, U. Kotakari and M. Nylund (eds), *Välittävät verkostot [Intermediating Networks]*, Vastapaino, Jyväskylä, pp. 193–205.

Nylund, M. (1996b), 'Who takes of care of unemployed people? Associations and self-help groups for unemployent in Finland in 1990s', paper presented at FORSA-symposiet *Sociala förändringar och välfärd – perspektiv och alternativ i socialt arbete, 19–21 September, Göteborg*, FORSA, Gothenburg.

Pättiniemi, P. (ed.) (1995), *Sosiaalitalous ja paikallinen kehitys [Social Economy and Local Development]*, Osuustoimintainstituutti julkaisuja 11, Helsinki.

Pättiniemi, P. (1999a), 'Labour co-operatives: a self-help solution to unemployment in Finland', in *World of Co-operative Enterprise 1999*, Plunkett Foundation, Oxford.

Pättiniemi, P. (1999b), 'The future of new co-operative movement in Finland', paper presented in Seminar, *Co-operative Research Today, Helsinki, 7th September 1999*, Institute for Co-operative Studies, Helsinki.

Pikkala, S. (1997), 'Kolmannen sektorin vaikutusvalta kunnissa' ['The influence of third sector in municipalities'], paper presented at the seminar, *Third Sector 2001, Helsinki, March 20, 1997*, Åbo Akademi, Helsinki.

Poteri, R. (1997), 'Social welfare and health care organisations in Finland: challenging future', paper presented at the *Fourth Network Conference of Nordic Third Sector Research, Vasa, Nov. 7–8, 1997*, Nordic Third Sector Research Network, Vasa.

Riessman, F. and Gartner, A. (1977), *Self-help in the Human Services*, Jossey-Bass, San Franciso.

Rönnberg, L. (1997), 'NGO's in Finland and welfare', paper presented at *REEN Summer School, June 26–29, 1997, Helsinki*, REEN Network, Helsinki.

Salavuo, K. (1996), Interview in the newspaper, *Helsingin Sanomat*, Nov. 31, Helsinki.

Siisiäinen, M. (1992), 'Social movements, voluntary associations and cycles of protest in Finland 1905–91', *Scandinavian Political Studies*, vol. 15, no. 1, pp. 21–40.

Siisiäinen, M. (1995a), 'Gamla social kitt i upplösning – föreningsverksamhetens uppgång och fall?', in K.K. Klausen and P. Selle (eds), *Frivillig organisering i Norden [Organizing Voluntarily in the Nordic Countries]*, TANO og Jurist-og Økonomiforbundets Forlag, Bergen.

Siisiäinen, M. (1995b), 'Järjestöt ovat demokraattisen yhteiskunnan uusiutumisen ehto' ['Organizations are a condition for a democratic change in the society'], *Sosiaaliturva*, vol. 83, no. 21, pp. 4–8.

Sipilä, J. (1997), *Social Care Services: The Key to the Scandinavian Welfare Model*, Avebury, Aldershot.

Slot Machine Association (1997), *Annual Report*, Slot Machine Association, Helsinki.

Suominen, A. (1995), 'Uudenmaan työosuuskunta Aktio' ['Labour cooperative Aktio in the county of Uusimaa'], in P. Pättiniemi (ed.), *Sosiaalitalous ja paikallinen kehitys [Social Economy and Local Development]*, Osuustoimintainstituutti julkaisuja, vol. 11, Helsinki, pp. 80–88.

Tilastokeskus (1999), *Statistics Finland*, Official Information Leaflet 9/1999, Helsinki.

VATES Foundation (1997), 'Preliminary study on employment in the sector of mental rehabilitation', paper released on August 18 1997, VATES Fdn, Helsinki.

Withorn, A. (1980), 'Helping ourselves: the limits and potential of self-help', *Social Policy*, vol. 11, no. 3, pp. 20–27.

6 France: Voluntary Sector Initiatives for Work Integration

DANIÈLE DEMOUSTIER

1. Introduction

In France, the voluntary sector movement and the Social Economy more generally have a long tradition of defending the right to work and of searching for routes into work. Since the 19th century, workers' organisations have been promoting the universal right to work, and fighting the insecurity in working and living conditions partly brought about by market conditions, which accentuate competition between workers. These claims have led the French workers' movement, and its constituent organisations, to develop in two opposing directions.

One direction, promoting the emancipation of wage earners, emerged out of the movement of production co-operatives and co-operatives for individual entrepreneurs, the first seeking to move beyond paid employment through production partnerships, the second to avoid employee status by pooling the necessary resources for stock, organisation and distribution without this affecting the immediate sphere of production.

The other direction, the mainstream approach, integrated with the widespread movement to raise the condition of the waged class, comes about through the involvement of co-operatives, mutual organisations and voluntary organisations (which were legally recognised in 1901, but did not take on a role as employers until after the Second World War) in offering paid employment. The voluntary organisations have promoted an original route into paid employment, passing from voluntary work through hourly work, and thence possibly into permanent employment, making use of external sources of work, paying by the session, and making a variety of other contributions (employing conscientious objectors, trainees, officials on secondment, etc.).

These two approaches coincide, however, because whether they are associations of producers or users, both kinds of group have tried to improve workers' conditions, mainly through the interpenetration of training and production. In this respect they have played a part in the moves towards full employment and social improvement, which have been an overall feature of French society for 20 years.

From this point of view, given the accepted value of work as a source of personal freedom and social recognition (and not merely of exploitation and alienation) and working in a context of high labour demand, the voluntary organisations began during the 1950s to consider integrating groups of disadvantaged people into the labour market including groups with certain physical or mental conditions, or those in socio-economic situations causing them to be temporarily classified as 'socially disabled'. Two kinds of sheltered structures were thus developed to promote access to work, and were recognised in the 1970s: the *Centres d'aide par travail* (CAT), which helped their users through work experience and sheltered workshops, developed under the auspices of voluntary organisations working with the disabled; and workshops offering work to people living in temporary accommodation and social rehabilitation centres. These were organisations especially established to help into work people who were regarded either temporarily or permanently as 'unfit for work'.

Since the 1970s, the crisis in employment, with the rapid and continuing rise in unemployment that now tends to last for longer, has led the voluntary organisations to multiply their initiatives to integrate other social groups into the labour market – for example groups of people who are 'fit for work' but who have been rejected on account of their age, gender or lack of qualifications. These very varied initiatives are all characterised by setting up and recognising a special 'integration' service leading towards employment, carrying out a role formerly established by the links between families, schools and both industrial and small-scale businesses (which were used for covering the costs of different levels of productivity).

This new service was characterised by a growth in know-how, knowledge, and 'life skills', acquired against a background of productive work. It began to emerge at the point where the labour market became more selective, increasingly demanding high and wide-ranging levels of productivity and behavioural skills vital to a service economy for which the traditional institutions struggled to provide. Entering a trade, or simply 'getting a job', was no longer something that passed from father to son; schools were unable to teach the necessary behavioural, general or vocational skills; and at the same time employers continually increased their demands in step with a labour market ever more biased in their favour.

These initiatives mainly emerged from voluntary organisations for social work initiatives or training, which were particularly sensitive to the position of directly marginalised social groups. At first they made no claim to have a direct effect on the volume or the nature of employment, or to challenge the serious imbalances in the labour market; nor did they attempt to replace public policies, though they did intend to influence them and request their support.

However, as exclusion from the labour market became a long-term problem, as employment was transformed and a succession of employment policies was introduced, these initiatives became more permanently established, widening or redirecting their scope, and giving rise to a series of different types of enterprise.

This work-integration service, originally conceived as a short-term measure, as a way of accessing jobs in traditional businesses, is itself now hotly debated – torn between its aim of providing a way into normal paid employment and its transformation into a 'trap' from which people cannot escape, stuck in a vicious circle of insecurity and recurrent unemployment.

The voluntary organisations which promoted the work-integration service have been strongly challenged by this new awareness, and are trying to overcome the limits and contradictions of their primary purpose whilst continuing to defend their aim, opening up new perspectives to enable their users to remain fully involved in economic life, and so getting involved in the debate on rights *at* work, rather than simply the right *to* work.

2. Economic and Political Conditions for Integration Structures

The creation of the 'work-integration service' took place in the late 1970s during a period of worsening labour markets. Initial analysis suggested that this deterioration had come about as the result of a cyclical and qualitative imbalance in economic and demographic trends, which the public authorities tried to remedy by measures to adjust supply and demand. Slowly, especially after the 1987–1990 boom, which saw a notable rise in growth rates without any very significant decrease in long-term unemployment, public policies came to be directed more energetically at encouraging job creation, both in the commercial sector and through identifying new sources of employment in the non-commercial sector. None the less, it remained an inequitable and highly selective labour market despite varied public policy initiatives.

2.1. Labour Market Trends: Inequitable, Selective and Flexible

For the last 20 years, imbalances in the labour market have continued to worsen in France, leading to a growth in unemployment, particularly long-term unemployment; though the absolute number of jobs has not decreased, their nature has been transformed. Selectivity and insecurity at work particularly affect certain social groups that are hit by the process of exclusion and impoverishment.

The continuing growth in unemployment levels in France is fed by the contrast between a sustained increase in the working population and a weak growth in the number of jobs. The working population in France has grown from 22.3 million to 25.2 million at the same time as the number of jobs has only increased from 21.4–22 million. This results from the combined effects of a number of factors: on the one hand, the number of workers born in the post-war baby boom will not begin to drop until 2005, when they start to reach the age of retirement; on the other hand, levels of economic activity among women of child-bearing and working age is tending to increase. Thus 750,000 new workers enter the labour market each year to replace the 480,000 who are newly retired. With the return to the labour market of older women, the working population is growing by 340,000 each year. These demographic trends will slowly go into reverse.

Parallel to this socio-demographic pressure, the growth in the number of jobs is slowed both by declines in the rate of economic growth and increases in productivity, not only in industry where most jobs are lost, but also in the service sector, which is accused of failing to create sufficient jobs. It is often said that in France, growth brings few jobs. Whilst the GDP increased by 50% between 1974 and 1993, at an average annual rate of 2.1%, employment only increased by 0.3%. Despite the drop in growth rates, which have halved since 1974, the French economy remains competitive thanks to rising hourly productivity (up by 2.6% p.a. on average) and a drop in the proportion of added value going towards wages (whose share has dropped by ten points since 1983).

These increases in productivity have thus not been distributed to employees, either by way of increased wages or through a reduction in working hours, which occurs only through part-time working, entailing a loss of monthly income. Though the amount of time spent at work dropped steadily until 1983 (the date of the law on the 39-hour week), passing from 1750 to 1550 hours over a 20-year period[1] this development has since come

---

[1] Special employment issue, *Alternatives économiques*, no. 21, 1994.

to a halt due to the scant number of jobs created. Only the increase in part time work (from 8.4% of workers in 1982 to 15.8% in 1995), including a 40% increase in involuntary part-time work, has reduced average working hours, and this development has become a major engine for job creation (60% of jobs created in 1995).

The nature of jobs is therefore changing, as they are increasingly in the service sector, and becoming more technical and more insecure. Jobs in agriculture are being lost at a regular rate (1.1 million over 20 years) as older workers reach retirement age, without enough rural development – not just in agriculture – to encourage young farm workers to gain employment. Industry has lost almost 1.5 million workers, due to high increases in productivity, flat demand and the choice of financial investment, which rather than being in manufacturing, is limiting technological innovation to what are thought of as booming sectors. Only the service sectors, commercial and non-commercial alike, which already employ 70% of the working population, remain a source of employment (+3.8 million); but this is regarded as insufficient because of rising productivity in some sectors (transport, banking and insurance for example) and the difficulty of making new personal services financially viable (through public ownership, mutual aid or privatisation). This is why in 1995, out of a working population of 25 million, only 27% were labourers (down from 33% in 1982), 3% farmers (6%), 7% freelance workers (8%), but with 29.4% white-collar workers (up from 26.5%), 20% intermediate professions (17%), and 12% management and higher professions (8%).

Although the level of qualification among the working population continues to go up, there are still more than 4 million unskilled workers (one in five), with the drop in the number of unionised workers partly made up by an increased number of salaried workers without qualifications. Every year one school leaver in ten leaves the education system with no qualifications (80,000) in spite of a considerable improvement (down from 126,000 in 1981), though unskilled workers benefit less from continuous training at work. As the level of qualifications among workers rises, so too do the demands of employers, leading to a degree of over-qualification when recruitment equates efficiency closely with paper qualifications.

French employers put more emphasis on external than internal flexibility: favouring subcontracting of business activities to new and existing enterprises, use of temporary workers (whose hours have doubled in ten years), trainee posts (which have increased five-fold) and fixed-term contracts (three quarters of all new jobs: 78% of women and 68% of men are taken on under fixed-term contracts, and workers on permanent contracts now occupy only 65% of paid employment). In this way, 6% of the working population (mainly without qualifications) is currently working without job security, whilst types of employment that were once considered stable are increasingly threatened by insecurity.

These facts explain the nature of unemployment, which continues to rise even during periods of high growth, and which now totals more than 3.5 million people or 12.5% of the working population (as opposed to 3% in 1973 and 10.6% in 1985), in spite of policies encouraging early retirement and the payment of social benefits in place of earnings (pre-pensions, social integration minimum income (RMI), single-parent allowances, etc.), which affects about 1.5 million people. The frontiers of unemployment are becoming more and more hazy, given the ease with which people move through paid inactivity, paid training, insecure employment and part-time work, which all fuel recurrent unemployment.

French unemployment is not only widespread but long-lasting. As the labour market becomes more and more selective it generates a 'queue' in which the most recent arrivals (from training or employment) are taken on first. This means that the average duration of unemployment is over a year, and 25% of unemployed people have been out of work for more than a year and a half.

Unemployment is increasingly selective. Women are twice as likely to be affected as men, young people two to three times more likely than adults, those without paper qualifications three times more likely than those with; and older workers and immigrants whose qualifications are judged to be obsolete are also hit. So although since 1993 managers and graduates have been more affected than previously (with their unemployment level now at 5%) the level of unemployment among young people (23% in the 16–24 age group), women, and unqualified workers (14.2% of labourers and 14.7% of white-collar workers, amounting to nine out of ten of the unemployed) is above the national average.

Levels of employment and unemployment now fluctuate a great deal with cycles of economic activity; labour controls no longer serve to blunt the impact of a crisis. A single, three-month period is all that separates a down-turn in activity and a fall in employment. By contrast, an up-turn in economic activity does not automatically translate into an increase in employment, due to the priority given to increases in productivity; and when job creation picks up, it does not necessarily lead to a fall in long-term unemployment but to the dismissal of the casualties of growth, some of whom had been hit by earlier recessions.

This unemployment is characterised by the impoverishment of the unemployed: 40% of them are not covered by benefits, and 50% of those who do qualify for benefits receive no more than 3000 Francs per month (only 1% receive more than 15,000 Francs). These unemployed people are among the 4 million in France who have to live on an income less than half the minimum wage.

2.2. Public Policies: Diverse and Expensive

Public policies for employment try to counter some of these changes. They are mainly focused on the reduction in the number of jobs offered, and are oriented to the stimulation of demand, developing flexibility in the markets and discriminating in favour of target populations. Since 1974, when the labour market deteriorated rapidly, many measures were imposed, often involving minor adjustments, without much consistency. 'The most obvious impression is one of abrupt change reflecting the successive changes of course and shifts in policy of public authorities faced with a problem, which became more and more pressing.'[2] Shifts predominated rather than new directions, since the view of the crisis and of unemployment remained that the causes were cyclical; this meant that solving the unemployment problem was either linked to renewed growth (including through developing new markets) with 'transitional', targeted solutions; or it was to be achieved at the expense of the workers, by seeking to lower wage rates and lower social security payments by all possible means, although many economists were able to demonstrate that France had passed from a crisis of supply to a crisis of demand.

Public policy therefore tended to work at several levels: reducing the working population, making the labour market more flexible through training, mobility and careers guidance, lowering the costs of employment, and creating new businesses and jobs, etc. These will each be examined in more detail:

Reducing the working population This was achieved by raising the school leaving age (+ two months each year, affecting 120,000 more young people); early retirement (50,000 people); helping immigrant workers to return home and also repatriating them, and finally encouraging women to leave the labour market (through parental leave and the single parent allowance). These measures made it possible to reduce the real increase in

---

[2] *Institut national de la statistique et des études économiques* (INSEE) (1987), p. 76.

the working population to the level prevailing in other European countries (about 150,000 people a year).

Introducing flexibility into the labour market through training and vocational guidance   Since the job pacts for young people introduced in 1977, training has been widely used as a lever for social groups most affected by unemployment involving: long periods of training, individual training credits, and the promotion of apprenticeship contracts (whilst the 'new qualifications' scheme, which tried to achieve the qualification of young people through links with senior workers within the workplace, to 'modernise without excluding', was ended). In 1983 this policy for training went hand-in-hand with a vocational guidance policy to make the labour market more adaptable – establishing new bodies, local offices and full-time careers and information offices. There was also reform of the national employment agency, ANPE, to improve the gathering of information on available employment from businesses, which has thereby enabled to make use of public facilities, even at the cost of dealing with the unemployed.

Measures affecting the demand for labour   These were based both on a reduction in the costs of employment and on direct job creation. Reduced employment costs are today represented by employers as indispensable to business competitiveness in their struggle against competition from newly industrialised countries. This takes many forms, such as a generally tough approach to wage levels or a specific drop in costs in the case of unskilled jobs (paid at the minimum wage, the *Salaire minimum interprofessionel de croissance* or SMIC) or moves to part-time work. The approach used ranges from granting complete or partial exemption from employers' social security contributions to direct subsidies for employment.

Finally, public policies to try to give direct support to the creation of businesses, jobs and companies (differentiating between the commercial and non-commercial sectors)   In the non-commercial sector, the creation of public employment, which was begun in 1982, was rapidly replaced by a growth in temporary subsidised contracts in the local public and voluntary sectors. The *Travaux d'utilité collective* scheme, (socially useful work open to young people, organised by a local authority or voluntary organisation and paid by the state) was set up in the form of traineeships in 1984. It was replaced in 1989 by employment solidarity contracts (employment contracts of a maximum two years' duration, of which there were 378,000 in 1995, two-thirds of them in voluntary organisations), some of which could be consolidated over five years. The same aim to identify new sources of employment in the service sector, led to legislation stimulating economic demand among private individuals through tax credits to develop the domestic market (by means of a service-employment voucher). In the private sector the same objectives were followed:

(a) through help for unemployed people setting up in business (*Aide aux chômeurs créateurs et repreneurs d'entreprises*, ACCRE set up 1977); in 1985, there were 70,000 beneficiaries in 58,000 new businesses and in 1993, 53,000 beneficiaries in 49,000 new businesses;

(b) through exemptions from social security payments and later subsidies to compensate for the low productivity of unskilled employees (at the end of 1993, there were 140,000 job-training contracts and 120,000 contracts for people returning to work) and the long-term unemployed (in 1995, 150,000 employment initiative contracts (CIE) were reserved for them).

In comparison with policies for work integration these public policies were aimed at a distinct group of users, in order to bring target populations into the workforce (the young, the poorly qualified, the long-term unemployed), prior to focusing on target areas (social housing districts). They gradually drew social and employment policies together. In this way people benefiting from the social integration minimum income, the *Revenue minimum d'insertion* (RMI), whose contracts were designed to assimilate them into the world of work, have priority access to a number of assisted contracts, such as Employment Solidarity Contracts, work-integration jobs, etc. However, these measures, largely inspired by the experiences of the work-integration services, only go some way to helping them; work-integration jobs are few in number, and the social security payment exemptions are lower than those offered under the CIE scheme.

All these public schemes, characterised by an accumulation of different measures and rapidly changing administrative arrangements, are expensive. They are also of limited and relative use. The amount of public aid for employment has increased 30-fold over the last 20 years: from 10 billion Francs in 1973, it rose to 300 billion Francs in 1983, of which the unemployment benefit budget accounted for 125 billion Francs, and vocation training a further in 89 billion Francs. Assistance for recruitment costs over 35 billion Francs, and early retirement absorbs 28.2 billion Francs.

The value of these measures is relative – the shrinkage in the working population can only be temporary. If there were an up-turn in work, the 'discouraged' non-working population could be transformed into new job seekers. The results of policies involving expenditure are limited: several studies conclude that only 20 to 40% of assisted employment is in real extra jobs (out of 213,000 jobs apparently created in the private sector, 57,000 were due to substitution and 108,000 to opportunistic behaviour[3]). For the most marginalised citizens, the combination of social policies (fighting exclusion), training policies (against illiteracy, promoting qualifications), employment policies (fighting unemployment) and economic policies (encouraging business development) does not have all the anticipated results. And under pressure from financial constraints and liberal ideology, the national state is increasingly tending to transfer the burden to local authorities, and (possibly after some preliminary efforts in the non-commercial sector) to look for no more than a consolidation of employment levels in the private commercial sector. This sector, however, is not inclined to be concerned with workers who are relatively unproductive in the short term, instead it is quite ready to externalise less profitable activities and their risks onto individuals.

3.   Non-profit Organisations for Integration

The voluntary sector has a long history of mobilisation for work integration, through mutual aid, with those social groups affected by long-term exclusion, thus reflecting the history of the labour market. Having focused initially on disabled people who were regarded as 'unfit for work' in a 'normal environment' during times of relatively full employment, they have become increasingly concerned with members of social groups which are 'fit for work', but whose 'employability' has been recognised decreasingly by employers, as the labour market has deteriorated, due to a range of factors: declining 'employability', lack of experience or qualifications (in the case of the young), and other characteristics (age, sex, etc.), even including place of residence (districts with low-cost housing).

However, whilst the idea of disability, whether physical or mental, has been given a standard legal definition (through a legal body, COTOREP, responsible for vocational guidance and rehabilitation), which is supported by a united national movement built on local experience and with achievements to match its demands, there is no such consensus over the concept of unemployability, which was first defined by employers and then

---

[3] *Alternatives économiques*, special number no. 26, 4th quarter, 1995.

taken up by workers in social employment. As the shape of unemployment becomes increasingly hazy, the unemployed themselves come under scrutiny:

(a) are they intentionally unemployed?

(b) are they motivated, fit or unfit for work?

(c) are they are registered with the national employment agency ANPE?

(d) are they covered by benefits, etc.?

The unemployed are compared with the poor, or lost in the ill-defined 'excluded' population, abandoned to social services or charities.

Thus voluntary organisations, which have seen the number of people they serve increase and become more diverse, have been led to develop their services to take account both of their users and of their analysis of changes in the labour market. On the one hand, they have looked for opportunities which are appropriate to the skills of their staff and which channel the people they serve towards work integration, enabling the voluntary organisations to pass from providing training and support for the unemployed to managing directly productive work projects. On the other hand, the nature of their economic involvement depends on their analysis of changes in the labour market: whether the imbalances are structural or cyclical, whether low-skilled jobs have disappeared, flexibility or stability considerations, and whether there will be a rich supply of new jobs and areas of employment.

Spurred on by social movements and developments within existing institutions and public provisions, measures to support work integration have taken various forms. Taking the sheltered structures as a starting point, they have tried to make it easier to gain access into the open labour market. First, by attempts to move people into paid employment within co-operatives, then by trying to access paid work through maintaining and improving skills rather than acquiring qualifications (in 'work-integration enterprises' (*Entreprises d'insertions*, EI), and intermediate voluntary organisations (*Associations intermediaires*, AI), and by separating commercial and non-commercial businesses (intermediate voluntary organisations and temporary work-integration enterprises). Finally, they have found a practical expression in companies providing personal services and taking part in local developments (through publicly funded Neighbourhood Enterprises (*Régies de quartier*, RQ), and through work-integration construction projects). However, none of these new approaches have superseded the earlier versions; their rates of development have been uneven, and all have been forced to adapt.

3.1. Sheltered Work Structures since the 1950s

When the economy was in need of labour, and the opportunity to work was seen as a means of obtaining individual independence and social recognition, the voluntary organisations, encouraged by laws passed in the 1970s, explored work opportunities for people who had been taken into sheltered organisations because of a recognised disability or marginalisation that was considered to be temporary.

Since the 1950s voluntary organisation establishments for people with mental and physical disabilities were making use of *Centres d'aide par travail* (CAT) and sheltered workshops (*Ateliers protégés* or APs)[4] to offer work to disabled adults. These organisations were first recognised in 1957 and were later acknowledged by the important law of 1975 on medical and socio-medical institutions. They operated mainly in sub-contracted markets, in competition with hospital and prison workshops.

The relative productivity of the disabled people they serve distinguishes the CATs from the APs, bringing with it these differences in financing and in the status and pay of disabled workers, with a system of allowances which takes account of the workers' actual output. The CATs are socio-medical establishments welcoming workers whose productivity is less than a third that of able-bodied workers. They are financed by an overall grant, and the workers are not considered salaried staff, although they are covered by some aspects of labour regulations. They are paid partly in proportion to their output; the balance is made up by the adult disability benefit and a guaranteed income (55% of the maximum SMIC), which can bring their remuneration up to 110% of the SMIC. On the other hand, the sheltered workshops (APs) offer work to disabled people who are able to work at least 30% of normal capacity; and they are allowed to employ up to 20% of able-bodied workers. The direct wage due from the employer must be at least 35% of the SMIC and the guaranteed income brings their remuneration up to 130% of the SMIC.

Since the law of 1987, which aimed to encourage the employment of disabled people in a normal working environment, businesses have been required to employ a quota of disabled workers (6%) or else to subcontract work to sheltered workshops or make a financial contribution to a mutual

---

[4] As of 1.1.93, there were 1196 CATs providing 74,361 places, and 315 APs offering 10,205 places (cf. *Service des statistiques, des études et des systèmes informatiques*, SESI).

body, the *Association de gestion du fonds pour l'insertion professionnelle des personnes handicapées* (AGEFIPH). The latter encourages training and the adaptation of working conditions; it can also provide support for workers moving on from CATs or APs. In this way business can be indirectly led to play a part in financing sheltered workshops, whose number continues to grow, in the absence of a satisfactory response from the external market.

At the same time, the centres for accommodation and social rehabilitation (CHRS) have included rehabilitation for and through work among their aims, supplementing transitional accommodation and social support. The notion of disability, redefined in the laws and regulations of 1974 and 1976, was finally rejected (out of a fear that it would produce an irreversible situation), although it is still written into labour law and leads in practice to a diminished status for paid workers in the sheltered structures authorised by the 1979 circular. Among the latter, centres for re-education in work and effort (for short and medium-term stays) gradually came to be called *Centres d'adaptation à la vie active* (CAVA), centres for adaptation to working life. They were financed by social aid, and entitled people using them to a gratuity combined with certain other benefits. From this starting point the CHRS have broadened their activities, developing new formulas: work-integration labour site projects, work-integration enterprises, intermediate voluntary organisations, etc. In this they have been supported by their federation, FNARS.

The 1979 circular was much used by workers employed under social programmes in order to set up training and production units within their voluntary organisations, as a way of extending their social employment when they no longer receive support from the welfare system. Others, with support from Christian or trade union activists, have opted for work co-operatives in a more collective and community-based model of economic integration.

3.2. The Co-operative Experience of 1978–1983

At the end of the 1970s, when Prime Minister Raymond Barre was encouraging the unemployed to start their own businesses, there were high hopes that workers co-operatives, SCOPs, would absorb unemployment, in part by assimilating those among the jobless most hit by de-skilling: women, young people, older workers, etc. Apart from socialisation through employment, this formula was chosen so as to experiment with types of business that could combine both work integration with self-management, and work experience. Changing the setting-up conditions made it easier to use this formula: in 1978 a law reduced the minimum number of company members from seven to four, and authorised the setting up of SCOPs as limited liability companies (*Société à responsibilité limité,* SARL) as well as public companies (SA). The unemployed could extend their benefits by transforming them into social shares; local authorities regarded these initiatives favourably, and subsidised the rescuing of failed enterprises and conversion into SCOPs. But it quickly became apparent that this kind of business was not at all suited to workers without qualifications, above all when they had not firmly established these businesses, and could not develop the independence necessary to run the co-operatives quickly enough. Such businesses were more suitable for those with professional qualifications than as a means of supporting social and economic reintegration, and it proved dangerous for these members to take up management roles in a time of strong competition. The withdrawal of specially allocated public finance marked the end of this particular experimental phase. The SCOPs, whose number had doubled during the period, regrouped around a more qualified workforce, and today they seem to be reviving the link with marginalised workers in new ways: there are now SCOPs for work integration and employment co-operatives supported by SCOP regional unions.

3.3. From Intermediate Enterprises to Integration Enterprises

The greatest number of experiments for combining training with production were carried out by the voluntary sector movement. Circular 44 of 1979, inspired by the Emmäus organisation for CHRS, was quickly put to use by youth leaders and training specialists, concerned by the difficulties facing young people trying to enter the labour market. To prevent any drift, for reasons of educational psychology, towards the CATs, they joined together with professionals to set up projects including construction projects and parks maintenance. These projects were initially recognised as 'intermediate enterprises' (EI) in 1985, thanks to a circular giving them experimental support. This gave the green light to a huge increase in their numbers (focusing on young people who were to be employed for a maximum of 18 months). With the change in government, the public authorities withdrew their support in order to promote the creation of intermediate voluntary organisations (AI), though many EIs managed to survive because of the strong commitment of their partners, recourse to assisted contracts, and help from the *Direction de l'action social,* the

Fondation de France and a fund for training benefits. From 1988 the EIs once again received public financial support in the form of finance for work-integration jobs to bridge the gap between differences in productivity and cover the costs of rotating workers, and a subsidy to finance their social support work. Between 1990 and 1995[5] the number of EIs doubled, and reached about 778 in 1997 (70% being voluntary organisations); they are generally small businesses (according to a *Comité national d'entreprises d'insertion* (CNEI) survey, 48% of them employ between ten and 49 people, and 5% more than 49) with an average of about a dozen work-integration jobs (of which only 20% are taken by women) and an average turnover, in 1993, of 2.5 million Francs. In 1994[6] they signed about 20,000 contracts (5,000 permanent 15,000 for work-integration) for the management of about 6,500 work-integration jobs. Generally engaged in a broad range of activities, these businesses are now less involved in the areas in which they began; construction work has dropped from 52% to 38%, parks maintenance from 37% to 28%. They have tended to move into the services sector and industrial production. Apart from HLM – (low-rent housing estates) contracts, local authority contracts and work for private individuals, they have tended to seek out, less competitive and more specialised, niche markets, and to set up joint ventures and sub-contracting arrangements with other commercial enterprises. The move towards a wider range of business activities is also often reflected in the more frequent use of commercial articles of association (SA and SARL), the appointment of managerial staff from manufacturing (36%) and not solely from social projects (40%) or from training sectors; this change is due to pressure from the public authorities and the support of the CNEI, which represents around 400 of current EIs.

3.4. Intermediate Voluntary Organisations: Temporary Work and Domiciliary Services

The intermediate voluntary organisations (AI) were recognised in 1987 by the Séguin law, and developed in quite a different direction from that followed by the work-integration enterprises. Their aim was not to set up their own business activities, but to make unemployed people available to other employers. They began as voluntary organisations of unemployed people looking for hourly work to tide them over, so that those who had run

---

[5] See *Comité national d'entreprises d'insertion* (the work-integration enterprise national committee).
[6] cf. DARES (Ministry of Labour) (1993, 1994).

out of benefit could preserve their benefit rights. They were principally supported by local councillors who were concerned by the pressure from SMEs and craftsmen against the EIs, and anxious to find new financially viable sources of employment (taking advantage of the exemption on employers' social security charges for up to 750 working hours per person per year).

In 1997, there were 1,102 intermediate voluntary organisations offering a significant number of jobs[7] (estimated as 20,000 full-time equivalent jobs, almost 6% of hours worked in temporary employment). This is still growing steadily in line with the number of people using the service,[8] whose average working hours do not on average exceed 48.5 hours per week, and who work for private individuals, individual employers (craftsmen, farmers), local authorities or businesses. Private individuals represent two-thirds of customers but account for only one-fifth of the hours; whereas the commercial business sector provides only one-fifth of customers but half of the total number of hours. The extent of business penetration into this market has aroused opposition from the temporary work sector (*Entreprises de travail temporaire*, ETT) and led in 1992 to a law separating commercial and non-commercial businesses by creating a new classification of businesses for integration into temporary work. *Entreprises d'intérim d'insertion* (EII) which was equally open to the ETTs, worked under the same constraints as them and benefited from public finance only for work in the area of social support (one job for ten full-time equivalents). At the end of 1996, 25 such organisations had registered with the co-ordinating body COORACE, and 16 with CNEI (in total covering 1,200 full-time equivalent jobs, representing 0.4% of temporary work). A further 70 organisations were at the planning stage.

Other ways of organising fragmented work connected with local community services have been proposed during the 1990s.

3.5. Neighbourhood Enterprises *(*Régies de quartier*): between Work Integration and Local Community Services*

Between 1981 and 1985, emerging from the urban struggles of the 1970s and the public workshops on town planning that developed at that time, the publicly funded local authority enterprise at Alma Gare in Roubaix brought

---

[7] cf. DARES (1993, 1994).

[8] Estimated at 700,000 people per year by *Coordination des associations d'aide aux chômeurs par l'emploi* (COORACE), the umbrella organisation for 960 Intermediate Associations.

together local inhabitants to renovate their neighbourhood. After 1985 a second generation of such Neighbourhood Enterprises (*Régies de quartier*, RQs) came into existence, at Meaux, Marseilles, and Besançon, etc., encouraging local management in areas of social housing. Today there are more than 100 RQs (with 30 more planned), structured as voluntary organisations bringing together more than 2,000 voluntary administrators (drawn from local people, voluntary organisations, business, sponsors, local authorities) and involving more than 500,000 local people. Charged with encouraging local participation and improving the quality of life through local community services, taking part in community life and involving local people, they employ about 5,000 people a year (1,600 full-time equivalent jobs). Some work several hours a week on housing maintenance, while others work full time on projects where homes are being renovated. This latter activity can qualify for work-integration support.

Their activities are varied – supplementing the services offered by sponsoring bodies (cleaning, outdoor maintenance, minor repairs, refurbishing of buildings, security services) but also providing services to individuals (ironing, sewing, second hand clothes, writing and secretarial services, tool hire, etc.) and to community organisations (help with setting up, administration, etc.). Their average turnover is about 1.8 million Francs, with 18% coming from public money and 82% self-financed, mostly from public contracts. They are represented by a national liaison committee, the *Comité national de liaison des régies de quartier*, which has established recognition of a quality mark based on a charter, since there are no official provisions.

There are two currents lines of thought concerning these bodies. One, more concerned with community values, emphasises their role in neighbourhood social life, observing the boundaries based on the natural relationships between local people; the other, more economic approach, supports work integration by entering the markets, even if this means going beyond the boundaries of the neighbourhood.

The Neighbourhood Enterprise Repères, *La Source, Orléans*

Established in 1992 in an area of low-rise low-cost housing for 43,000 inhabitants in Orléans, *Repères*, a publicly-funded enterprise, has been promoted since its inception by a number of partners: the city authorities, sponsors and community organisations. The latter, together making up the Convergence network, have relied on a powerful associative project to 'involve local people in improving their daily life' based on three main objectives: improving social housing and the neighbourhood within the city; involving local people in social, economic and cultural life and neighbourhood activities; and putting forward schemes for the social and professional integration or reintegration of local people with difficulties.

During the first year, the enterprise developed two kinds of service. On the one hand, maintenance of common areas and the provision of caretakers, in association with the two social sponsors: (this involved 538 dwellings under OPHLM management and 1,217 dwellings managed by an HML (social housing) public company). Eighteen people were employed on permanent contracts (CDI) and six under fixed-term arrangements (CDD). Other *ad hoc* arrangements were entered into with other partners: the University, voluntary organisations, the Postal Service, etc. Alongside this, a technical supervisor built up a rapid response service (for minor repairs requiring relatively little expertise). At the same time the Neighbourhood Enterprise also developed its community leadership function by providing centres dispensing advice and administrative help to the most needy residents.

Since then, fresh activities have emerged: an outdoor service working in partnership with the local authority parks department, and a service for organising and providing local community services. A 'street service' has been running since March 1996, employing a dozen young local adults on local authority contracts (with an average age of 23); they work in pairs (one male, one female) as mediators with young people aged 8–16, and also give assistance to people with reduced mobility in 'sensitive' places (car parks, bus stops, libraries, outside schools, etc.). Supervised by a psycho-sociologist, these young people receive training in leisure organisation. With the help of volunteers (particularly from equivalent bodies) other activities have been developed on a less regular basis, such as an information campaign concerning selective waste collection, and a competition for the best balcony floral display.

The enterprise draws on a considerable number of members: 529 individual non-voting members, an electoral college of 196 active members, an electoral college of 32 institutions, as well as automatic members. On the Administrative Council, automatic members occupy eight seats, and active members 19 (ten go to representatives of voluntary organisations, and nine to individual residents – six representing the local authority housing area and three the low-rise estate). The President must be chosen from these 19 members.

In 1996 the budget reached more than 6 million Francs, of which 68% (4.25 million Francs) was in the form of services provided – 68% of which were for the sponsoring bodies. The remaining 32% came from an operational subsidy (1.9 million Francs, including 1.1 million Francs to assist recruitment). During the course of 1996, the neighbourhood enterprise signed 130 work contracts (for 97,000 hours) involving 110 employees under various different schemes: 35 CDI, 22 CDD, nine CEC, 26 CES, two qualification contracts, one apprentice contract, 20 CIE, three RMI traineeships, and 12 local authority jobs. At the end of 1996 there were 79 employees: 40 women, 39 men; 23% were under 26, 64% aged between 26 and 50, and 13% aged over 50. Whenever someone is taken on by the enterprise, even for a few hours, the hope is that he or she will 'evolve towards a better situation than before'. This perspective of dynamic change, beyond the work immediately to hand, generates great expectations among residents. The enterprise has in this way become a real centre for leadership in the neighbourhood.

3.6. *Workshops and Work-integration Labour Schemes*

Quite independently, other initiatives have also emerged within voluntary organisations, and remain legally dependent on them: these include stop-gap work for construction sites, construction work training sites or work-integration schemes – specially arranged or through subsidised contracts. For example, there are many training voluntary organisations which support the least qualified people, filling a real public need, whilst denouncing the use of 'parking lot' (poor quality) traineeships that allow unemployed people to be taken off the register without providing a real way into work. This is why, like voluntary organisations promoting social programmes and like the *Maisons des jeunes et de la culture*, they set up the construction (renovation) site training schemes to give young people initial work experience. In this way 900 such schemes involved 16,000 young people in 1992, the equivalent of 1.5 million working days; they made use of training measures, the minimum benefit provisions (RMI) and the CES.[9] Many are in rural areas, working in environmental maintenance and agriculture. This enables the CHRS to organise work activities outside its usual structures.

---

[9] *Le Monde initiatives*, 9 February 1994.

Using productive activities not with a view to professional integration but as a stop-gap measure, is not new. However, it is being done more and more systematically, even by charitable voluntary organisations, either through small sub-contracting workshops that take on labour by the day or through maintenance work carried out by young people who can be paid in kind.

This illustrates that although work remains a linchpin on which the processes of socialisation, remuneration and qualification, etc., depend, its forms have diversified considerably, even within the organisations that seek to integrate workers and try to set them on the path towards employment in the outside world.

4.   Work-integration Voluntary Organisations Reach a Turning Point

The fabric of the voluntary sector movement in France has displayed a real capacity for innovation, which continues to be evident in new experiments, some arising from their own initiatives, others in response to pressure from their users or promoted by public measures. This has taken place through initiatives from a broad range of organisations, all aimed at integrating people into the labour market, but using different approaches. These may be by spending some time in production workshops or work schemes, making a number of hours of work available to external organisations, or by creating new jobs that may be either self-financing or have the balance of remuneration made up by social income.

The role of introducing people to work has been passed back to the community by companies that were formerly prepared to accept a temporarily low level of productivity. This has generated the new companies that are viable to the extent that the community is prepared to provide cover for part of this low productivity.

These organisations promoting integration are very localised and fragmented and have not succeeded in establishing their legitimacy so as to strengthen the basis for a real policy of work integration. Internal debates concerning their role in providing a gateway to work, or areas of operation, the public they serve, and the socio-economic rationale to be developed, all reveal doubts about the very nature of the aims they are pursuing. These work-integration voluntary organisations occupy a position at the very heart of changes in the labour market, which they can influence either towards deregulation or towards a redrawing of relationships with work.

4.1. *Organisational Difficulties Despite Undeniable Successes*

After 20 years of trial and error and diversification, the organisations promoting integration have succeeded in making their work known, both in the field of social provision and in some areas of economic activity, such as genuine SMEs. However, they have been unable to make a lasting impact on public employment policy, thus their steady development cannot be guaranteed. Their emergence at local level makes them well able to respond to the needs of the public they serve, but their affiliation to their original organisations, the inflexibility of their arrangements, and the complexity of their structures, lead to a frittering away of efforts, hindering the effectiveness of local and national coordination, which could play a part in defining a valid policy for integration.

In the absence of a strong commitment from the public authorities, there is currently a decline in the rate at which work-integration enterprises are being set up, except for businesses offering temporary work (EII) (often by transforming intermediate voluntary organisations or by supplementing EI, AI or ETTs) and Neighbourhood Enterprises (supported by local authority policies). Because of this, the aims of organisations for work integration have tended to become less-and-less ambitious, even being prepared to take on the management of a few hours of work, which might not have any place in social or vocational development. Confronted with this uncertainty and doubt, some organisations are trying to go beyond the contradictions they have to face and through this very process are developing a new experimental approach.

Complex but viable businesses In spite of the inherent difficulties in establishing them, due to their carrying burdens other businesses do not finance (low productivity, lack of financial viability), the number of these enterprises has increased and their range of activities has diversified. However their development remains unstable and chaotic, dogged by ups-and-downs in business sectors and in public provision. Their choice of economic activity has often been made with reference to ease of access and management, rather than to commercial prospects,[10] making them open to poorly qualified workers, managers with little specialised experience, and promoters whose approach is not very commercial. Public measures, also have a good deal of influence on the choice of structure. To combat economic difficulties and the unreliable nature of public support, they have

---

[10] In terms of placements; this suggests that the aim is not about qualifications but changes in behaviour.

strengthened management, with the help of their federations, and diversified their activities, structures and partners, with the aid of a strongly political approach and active voluntary support.

Emploi 38

The intermediate voluntary organisation *Emploi 38* was founded in 1990 on the initiative of the work-integration voluntary organisation *Grenoble Solidarité* to offer opportunities for a working life to 60 people employed on employment solidarity contracts in various workshops (for the reception, sorting and recycling of clothes, electrical appliances, and furniture – for redistribution to people in urgent need; and for industrial sub-contracting). In 1995 these two voluntary organisations founded a third integration structure, *E3I: Entreprise d'intérim d'insertion de l'Isère* (Temporary work-integration enterprise of Isère).

Emploi 38 offers employment with private individuals (domiciliary services), with voluntary organisations, and in collectives; *E3I* offers the same service in the commercial sector: in industry, building, collective restoration projects, etc. The three voluntary organisations form an 'integration group' sharing a joint management structure, a centralised telephone exchange, and the common provision of finance and equipment. However, although their aims are identical, the finance and organisation of each group fall under different legislation and procedures. *Grenoble Solidarité* receives local authority subsidies and State aided contracts; *Emploi 38* receives little in the way of subsidies but profits from a significant level of social security charge exemptions for people in integration jobs (up to 750 hours per person per year); and *E3I*, which does not have the benefit of these exemptions, receives co-financing from the DDTE, the DDASS and the General Council, for social support services (at the rate of one support job for every ten employees in integration jobs, full time equivalent).

In terms of vocational integration, *Emploi 38* and *E3I* employed more than 500 people during 1995 (49 full-time equivalent jobs) including five permanent employees. During the same year 215 people left the scheme, of whom 54 had a permanent or fixed-term contract, (19 in domiciliary services, with training arranged by *Emploi 38* and its partners); 30 have taken advantage of a job-seeking workshop provided by permanent staff from *Emploi 38*. These two voluntary organisations bring in twice as much income as their cost to the community: they paid more than 2 million Francs in social security contributions in 1995 as against a million Francs received in subsidies (without counting the savings in benefits). The possibilities for development are many, and tend towards diversification and greater complexity for these work-integration organisations:

(a) in the personal services sector: setting up a voluntary organisation for domiciliary work so as to offer a complete range of services and increasing professionalisation in the sector; establishing a coordination service for job providers in the sector so as to 'activate the potential demand'; encouraging the setting up of associations of private employers; and a proposal for initial training to prepare employees for these new jobs;

(b) however there are also opportunities for the community to set up publicly funded enterprises providing services for voluntary organisations and local authorities, and to sign partnership agreements with businesses.

From focusing on a variety of business activities, voluntary organisations have now moved to setting up group structures for work integration, making use of several measures, which allow for mutual aid between various structures (EI, AI, EII). This has had divergent results. Intermediate voluntary organisations have enjoyed more stability and continuity, not just because they receive permanent support and automatically benefit from public measures (exemptions from social security charges), but also because they have been submitted to less economic pressure (since the temporary work market is growing strongly). Work-integration enterprises that directly manage productive activities are more exposed both to economic trends and competition, particularly in the sensitive building sector (which is itself in crisis), and to the influence of public measures (creation and allocation of work-integration posts, release of finance). Some of the EI founded at the beginning of the 1980s have disappeared or undergone radical change; today they remain fragile, seeking out niche markets or relying on solidarity within a group of work-integration organisations.

Viability also owes something to the emergence of new styles of business management, combining the leadership of workers on social schemes and – increasingly often – management with the support of parent bodies (whether or not voluntary organisations), and bringing into play a variety of partners (public, private, and voluntary sector, etc.).

Finally, setting up partnerships with commercial businesses enables them to refute the accusation of unfair competition. Of EI questioned by the CNEI, 57% have established such partnerships, the ETT have founded temporary work-integration enterprises, EIIs, relying in some cases on existing AIs, etc. However, this is only possible because these organisations are growing at a relatively slow rate. Although the level of self-financing has increased, (fluctuating between 70% and 80%, after taking account of the AI's social security charge exemptions) these bodies remain dependent on supplementary public finance, which compensates mainly for the extra costs of work integration such as chronic low productivity, rotation of workers in insertion jobs (which they may occupy for a maximum of two years), and their subsequent follow-up. Assistance for these aspects is available through the agreements governing insertion jobs, through social charge exemptions and through financial help for social support. Overall, the financial balance sheet is rather favourable compared with that of other measures, and the cost-benefit ratio for public finance shows a credit balance, after taking into consideration savings on benefits and social charges and tax receipts.

However, these businesses remain rather uncommercial, and lack their own funds to meet the needs of cash-flow and ensure steady growth. The banks' fear of committing to an unprofitable venture, acts as a brake on the supply of funds because the businesses can offer no security. The guarantee funds offered by the *Institut de développement de l'économie sociale* are not really suited to small voluntary organisation structures, which has led some local authorities to set up their own integration guarantee funds and to consider establishing risk-capital companies. Using their own capital, development first takes place through diversifying internal activities, and then through adapting structures in order to qualify for or comply with various measures. But apart from a few extreme examples, internal economic integration or expansion remains a difficult process, not so much because of management inexperience but because of questions relating to mobilisation and development strategies.

The movements associated with these initiatives are calling for research and development to stimulate collective entrepreneurial activity, anticipate business trends, and help in setting up projects – enabling their work to be carried out within a collective approach to economic development.

Uncoordinated experiments These enterprises, which have arisen out of local movements and institutions, try to co-ordinate social schemes (which must take account of their users' needs) with artisan-type production, without, however, the support of a sectoral structure, due to the wide range of activities in which they engage. They remain fragmented, even relative to their original area of employment. Geographically, their spread is very uneven: more than 50% of EI are concentrated in five regions, not necessarily those most affected by unemployment. Co-ordination around existing arrangements (hostels, AI, EI), while helpful for negotiating financial or tax advantages with the public authorities, bears no relation to user needs or their economic activities. Because of this, whether locally or nationally, the existing forms of inter-institutional co-ordination are plagued by debates about their purpose, which prevents co-operation, building bridges and the coherence of the whole. Practical studies have shown that the structural divisions do not correspond to a strict classification of either users or activities. Certainly some slight differences separate the people served by the AI (more women, older and better qualified) and the EI (more men, younger, less experienced), but this is due more to the nature of their activities (personal services contrasted with building and parks maintenance) and the way their structures originally developed (local development or social schemes). Homogeneity is better defined in terms of the recruitment and partnership networks organised round each structure than by the measures that set it up.

If structuring through measures such as UDEI and ADAI[11] provides no basis for development, they can nevertheless set up rules for sharing markets and territory, whereas the *Commissions départmentales pour les activités d'insertion* merely grant approval and play no part in regulation. Few work-integration enterprises are integrated into local economic integration plans; on the other hand, schemes for work integration are sometimes drawn up at regional level, which is relevant to economic development. This is why some voluntary organisations combine their work on the structural effects of economic activity, particularly to gain market access and to place their clients.

These local difficulties are transposed to the national level with each new grouping: *Fédération nationale des associations d'accueil et de réadaptation sociale* (FNARS) for hostels, CNEI, COORACE, and the *Comité national de liaison des régies de quartier* (CNLRQ); and even more so in *Coordination inter-réseaux de l'insertion par l'économique* (CIRIE) that succeeds neither as a collective representative nor as a pressure group. Further, having arisen mainly out of social schemes (or more broadly out of the world of voluntary organisations for the jobless), these structures have no links with bodies working for employment (trade unions and voluntary organisations for the unemployed); despite the involvement of some Enterprise Committees that intervene in an utilitarian fashion to make

---

[11] *Union départementale des entreprises d'insertion; Association départmentale des association intermediaires* – the umbrella bodies for work-integration enterprises and intermediate associations respectively.

access to certain markets easier (such as some employee services), or to provide finance or guarantees.

Unlike the movement to help physically and mentally disabled people into work, these organisations have not managed to use their local experiences to build up a national movement, combining demands and achievements to publicise the legitimate right of the unemployed to work.

Is this the cause or the effect of weak representation? Policy measures to promote work integration through economic activity remain at the edge of social policy. Shared between the Ministry for Social Affairs and the Ministry for Labour, such measures are concerned with the minimum insertion income (RMI), local authorities, social measures, and the fight against unemployment, but never economic policy (nationally or locally) in spite of questions about the development of certain activities (such as their economic viability, organisation, qualifications relating to new types of jobs or trades). Long-term unemployment, or the unemployment that comes with exclusion, is lumped together with questions of poverty, territory, a lack of social links, unemployment, but never with the structure of economic activity itself.

4.2. Questioning Roles and Purposes

The work-integration enterprises were established to provide a transition towards the stable labour market and have been judged accordingly, though their creation coincided with the deterioration of the labour market,[12] which devalued them in the eyes of their detractors and considerably weakened the impact they might have had as examples to other 'excluding' enterprises. However, they continue to emphasise their role as a gateway to work rather than an unemployment trap, and to bear witness to the fact that exclusion is not fatal if the various political and economic parties involved show the will to fight it.

A gateway to work: essential but not enough This function is an essential one, because it expresses resistance to the idea of unemployability and de-skilling; and it reflects the need to bring the process of accessing employment into the social sphere (through collective structures, with public finance) for those without family ties or access to school and qualifications.

---

[12] Even during a period of growth when employment grew (as in the period 1987–90), long-term unemployment receded only slightly (see Section 1).

However, it remains dependant on the recruitment criteria operating in the labour market (which permanently exclude the most disadvantaged people), and on the regulations set out in public measures. For assisted contracts, the criteria may concern age, sex, place of origin, level of qualification, how long a person has been out of work, and the source of finance.

The accumulation of public measures opens up opportunities for a very flexible approach to the time and location of this transitional stage:

(a) as to type and length of the contract: trainee positions, living in, temporary salaried positions (in the CES or insertion jobs); full-time, half-time, or just for a few hours (either on a temporary basis or with an RQ) are all options;

(b) as to place: in workshops, labouring sites, with a business or a private individual, in the neighbourhood;

(c) as to the type of social support given: assistance and follow-up tailored to individual needs;

(d) as to the aims of training: social qualifications, pre-qualifications, internal or external qualifications for new trades.

The efficiency of the structures is the subject of controversy over which criteria to apply when judging them. There are traditional divisions over judging the outcome for people at the end of the schemes, and there are difficulties in measuring the nature and the durability of any solutions that have been reached. Thus in 1992 the CNEI announced a rate of job placement of 43% (CDI, CDD, and CES) to which must be added the 15% who leave the scheme to go on to further training; by contrast 37% find no permanent solution by the end of their time with an EI. The FNARS network, in a 1991 survey, involving 14,800 people, registered a rate of 35% for people leaving to go into work and 9% into training. A few years later, in 1995, E. Maurel's study of the Drome department was more pessimistic, giving the figure for people going into work at between ten and 20% (except for the AI, whose figures were automatically better,[13] since people usually leave when they find an alternative solution and not after a set period of time). However, organisations are increasingly using more personal criteria linked to social development, measured by how much

---

[13] As an illustration, *Emploi 38* announced in 1995 that out of 215 leavers (43% of registered members), 22% found a CDI or a CDD, 10% an assisted contract (generally a CES) and 9% went on to training.

progress an individual has made. Finally, other measures take account of indirect effects of human, social and economic costs that are avoided through work.

Nevertheless, it seems that there are only limited opportunities for work integration in the outside world, because of changes in the labour market itself: most jobs are on temporary contracts, and most jobs are occasional, or part time, and half of them are in the non-commercial sector. Work-integration organisations mainly manage a local pool of labour, operating in a secondary labour market, and going through successive periods of recurrent unemployment.

Real evidence, but under-publicised   However, they provide evidence that employability is a process for meeting supply and demand, and not an irreversible condition. This, therefore, gives the lie to the idea of social disability: illustrating that the process is linked at one and the same time to the need to adjust to the norms of working life, and the demands of employers who tend to favour the overqualified when taking on staff.

They also provide evidence that SMEs can combine different levels of productivity according to the motivation of employees, supervisors and the structures themselves, on a non-profit basis. They carry the risk of lower productivity of some workers, compensated through mutual assistance and less directly by public financial aid; in this way they assume once more the functions that are not considered directly profitable, such as education and training.

But this evidence remains too little publicised to have much influence on company behaviour. Though these structures are exemplary, they cannot be reproduced automatically. Their effect is marginal, compared with the extent of public need: 24,000 full-time-equivalent jobs compared with nearly a million people on the RMI or a million long-term unemployed. The cost of financing them is negligible in terms of public policies (500 million Francs out of an employment budget of 300 billion Francs), and calculations show that they bring in more revenue to the state in taxes and contributions than they cost.

Unable to cross the critical threshold, they do not succeed in exerting pressure on other firms nor in having a knock-on effect, despite the existence of the *Association nationale des entreprise pour l'insertion*, their national association, or the business association *'Agir contre l'exclusion'* ('act against exclusion'), both of which also attempt to confront the problem of work integration.

The debate on unfair competition, which was settled by the public authorities gave rise to a degree of movement in two of their areas of activity: the construction sector, and temporary work. Thanks to the concern they have shown for transparency, work-integration organisations were able to gain at the same time the support of the public authorities, the establishment of co-operation between businesses (for sub-contracting, co-working, and recruitment), and incentives to spread the practice of work integration. This was achieved either through integration clauses written into public contracts (and recognised in an agreement between the HML (social housing) union and the building federation) or through regulations, such as the authorisation granted for temporary work firms to set up temporary work-integration enterprises. By contrast the attempt to support the creation of employers' associations for work integration and qualification (*Groupements des employeurs pour l'insertion et la qualification*) was less successful and some local experiments involving work-integration contracts managed by an integration enterprise jointly with another company, seem to have been abandoned.

All this shows the need for strong and determined intervention on the part of the public authorities, going beyond mere public finance (through regulation, privileged access to public contracts, etc.); since currently they most often make use of integration structures in a trivial way, confining them to the margins.

Confronted with the risk of increasing insecurity at work, and the trivialising use of these structures, the work-integration voluntary organisations are torn between several alternatives:

(a) to retreat, discouraged by the size of the problem, and accept a certain social dualisation; this retreat is expressed by dismissing their users with a clinical approach to 'social disability', falling back on low capital production in sheltered housing (CHRS) or within the neighbourhood, and so sustaining an extended domestic economy;

(b) to adopt an emergency approach, allocating hourly work on a temporary basis even at the cost of lowering prices and charges to ensure stop-gap work in a survival economy;

(c) to manage insecurity, adapting to the demands of the market, by sustaining a secondary labour market and recurrent unemployment in a subsistence economy;

(d) to create new stable jobs in the commercial or non-commercial sectors by choosing the most productive activities and training the most productive workers in a growing economy;

(e) organising insecurity, by setting up new work collectives and restructuring working hours in a changing economy.

4.3. To Manage or Reorganise Insecurity? – Transcending the Contradictions

The process of integration into work may be considered as both reductive and transforming. Reductive because it involves restricting the need for qualifications to the simple acquisition of skills, confining business activities to sub-contracting, and transforming the definition of a job to the organisation of a few hours of work. But it can equally be seen as a means of transcending educational deprivation by changing the relationship between training and production and diversifying apprenticeships; as a way of revitalising the 'integration' enterprises (which employ workers regarded as unproductive, and engage in unprofitable activities), as an opportunity to redefine people's relationship to work, and to experiment with ways of breaking down the divisions in social time (production, training, leisure, etc.).

Revitalising an infrastructure of small local enterprises   Between craft industry and SMEs, domestic service and service to the public, new enterprises are emerging that organise local activities and transactions with a local work force. These enterprises are able to train new workers and combine technical and inter-personal skills, management and partnership qualities; they are also able to take on a labour force rejected from employment in industry, but potentially available for future work.

These enterprises are also laboratories for newly emerging activities: providing community services for a local population only partially credit-worthy, enabling experiments with new technologies which are not immediately profitable, producing new organisational innovations based around a wide range of inter-connecting activities. They therefore function as laboratories as well as providing opportunities for integration.

They are structured around new collective employers with political/ideological views, they supplement cottage industries with the support of a collective structure, and internal local partnerships (represented on an administrative council) or external ones: upstream (opening markets) or downstream (offering job placements), and promoting co-operation rather than competition.

An all-round approach to the impact of job loss However, innovation can go beyond internal organisation, to tackle the way in which social time is currently organised. The hazards of severing links with work, income, and social rights are all borne individually. Work-integration voluntary organisations that are already trying to bring together the functions of production and training (under conditions of full employment, rather than traineeships) can also try to overcome situations of individual insecurity.

First, through a collective approach to individual situations, establishing work collectives for heteronomous production: with greater collective integration in social life, in work organisation, and in relationships with the environment.

Next, through seeking to make jobs and contracts permanent, with professional status, combating the fragmentation and rotation of work. This can occur by transforming employment solidarity contracts (*Contrats-emploi-solidarité*) into consolidated employment contracts (*Contrats-emploi-consolidé*), lasting from two to five years, for 20 to 30 hours per week, on integration labour sites that thereby become real places of production; or else by increasing working hours through employer groupings, and having more than one job.

Finally this can come about through attempts to break down the divisions in social time.[14] Anxious to protect the rights of their users, many voluntary organisations calculate hours of works and income so as to preserve all their acquired rights; some voluntary organisations, however, go further. For example:

(a) a policy of voluntary part-time working: in the Rhône-Alpes region, the *Université du temps choisi* encourages employees to make available a half-time job that can be taken up by an unemployed person, leaving them free to pursue some voluntary, or creative activity. The loss in earnings is partly funded by the Regional Council to make it more financially acceptable;

(b) an Intermediate Voluntary organisation plans to establish five-year contracts with workers on work-integration schemes in small-scale companies to cover successive periods of training, family activities

---

[14] Experiments with the 'work contracts' recommended by the Boissonnat report.

and periods of productive work, and it is trying to set up the appropriate finance;

(c)   through sharing the risks of setting up in business; new employment co-operatives bring together qualified employee-entrepreneurs, unqualified employees, permanent employees and people planning to set up businesses so that they can examine the different formal structures that might reduce the mutualised costs.

5.   Conclusions: Participating in the Debate on Work

The work-integration schemes have gone through an initial phase and have adapted; they have succeeded in showing the unemployed need not have to be assisted through the traditional field of social action on account of being 'socially disabled' and excluded from society.

As the labour market has worsened, the number of initiatives has increased but sometimes with reduced aims: from 'working differently' to organising short-term jobs, or dividing up the hours of work. They have been accused of setting up the right *to* work in opposition to rights *at* work,[15] or of fostering the ideology of labour at a time when opportunities to work were disappearing, except for a growing body of poor and insecure workers. But after 20 years of feeling their way, they have also illustrated that there can be places for experimentation in social change, rather than simply for managing social problems; and they have raised the question of integration, then that of relationships with work, then the issue of the structure of work and of tomorrow's enterprises. With the risk of fragmenting into separate groups, or fossilising in a devalued sector, these organisations have had to pursue their experimental approach in order for to appeal to society and show that 'unemployability' is a relative concept, and that other ways of organising labour and business are possible.

It might well be thought that as well as benefiting the people whom they employ, these transitional enterprises can produce truly educational enterprises, which are more democratic because involving people working in partnership is innovative and valid in socio-economic terms. However, for this to be achieved, public policies are needed which link social action (on living conditions and income), labour policy (on working conditions) and economic choices (on the direction of production and the distribution of wealth). The voluntary organisations that have mobilised to sustain this process of integration provide an illustration of some of the choices open to

---

[15] *Le Monde économie*, 16 December 1994.

a changing society that may or may not have the desire to offer the same rights to all its members.

References

Abela, P. (1994), *Une politique pour l'emploi*, EPI, Desclée de Brouwer, Paris.

Alphandery, C. (1990), *Les Structures d'insertion par l'économique*, a report to the Minister for solidarity, health and social protection and to the Minister for labour, employment and vocational training, La Documentation Française, Paris.

Alphandery, C. (1995), *Insertion sociale et économie*, interim report from the CNIAE, Ministry for integration and the fight against exclusion, La Documentation Française, Paris.

Alternatives économiques, see the special issue on employment, HS no. 21, and 'Les chiffres de l'économie et de la société', HS no. 26, 1995–96.

Boissonnat, J. (1995), *Le Travail dans vingt ans*, report of the committee of the *Commissariat général du Plan*, Editions Odile Jacob, Paris.

Conseil national de l'insertion par l'activité économique (CNIAE) (1992), *Insertion par l'économique, répertoire des concours techniques et financiers*, CNIAE, Paris.

DARES (Ministry of Labour), reports 1993 and 1994 on structures for integration, DARES, Paris.

Demoustier, D. (1990), 'Structures d'économie sociale et insertion par le travail', in *Revue de l'économie sociale*, no. 22, Proceedings of the 10th conference of the Association d'économie sociale.

Dugelay, H. (ed.) (1995), *Guide pratique du rmi et de l'insertion*, ENSP, Paris, 6th edn.

Eme, B. (1995), *Politiques publiques, société civile, et pratiques d'insertion par l'économique*, CRIDA-LSCI, Paris.

FONDA (1996), 'L'Emploi au service du projet associatif', in *La Tribune de la Fonda*, no. 118, May.

Institut national de la statistique et des études économiques (INSEE) (1987 and 1993), *Données sociales*, Paris.

Institut national de la statistique et des études économiques (INSEE) (1995), *Enquête emploi*, Paris.

Le Monde économie (1994), 16 December.

Le Monde initiatives: see 'Les Banlieues de l'emploi' 2 June 1993; 'Les Entreprises d'insertion en péril', 4 May 1994; 'Les Doutes de l'insertion', 25 January 1995; 'Solidarités actives', 29 November 1995; 'Les Entreprises d'insertion sur le qui-vive', 10 April 1996.

Maurel, E. and Mansanti, D. (1993), *Activités économiques d'insertion, essai d'analyse comparée*, GREFOSS, Internal report.

Maurel, E. and Mansanti, D. (1996), *Approche territoriale de l'insertion par l'activité économique, Departement de la Drôme*, GREFOSS, Internal report.

Merckaert, A. (ed.) (1995), *Entre social et entreprise, création d'entreprise et insertion*, L'Harmattan.

On sheltered structures for the disabled:

Blanc, A. (1995), *Les Handicapés au travail*, Pratiques Sociales, Dunod, Paris.

On centres for accommodation:
Alfandari, E. and Maurel, E. (eds) (1996), *Hébergement et réadaptation sociale*, Série Actions, Sirey (see particularly Lafore, R., 'L'Insertion par l'économique dans l'aide à l'hébergement et à la réadaptation sociale', pp. 74–92).

On work-integration enterprises:
Comité national des entreprises d'insertion (CNEI) (1994–95), *Annuaire national des entreprises d'insertion*, CNEI.

On intermediate voluntary organisations:
Problèmes économiques (1988), 'L'Activité des associations intermédiaires', 8 June.

Économie et humanisme (1992), 'Chômage: société recherche créativité', no. 321, April-June (survey carried out in conjunction with COORACE).

On neighbourhood enterprises:
Économie et Humanisme: see 'Pour des quartiers citoyens', no. 322, 1992; 'Citoyens et acteurs pour un développement solidaire', no. 334, 1995.

Plan urbain les régies de quartier: expérience, développements. Regards de chercheurs (1994), La Documentation Française, Paris.

Pour (1989), special issue, 'Les Régies de quartier', GREP L'Harmattan.

Territoires, régies de quartier, une entreprise citoyenne (1995), no. 361.

Documents of the national federations and committees of *Comité national des entreprises d'insertion* (CNEI), *Coordination des associations d'aide aux chômeurs par l'emploi* (COORACE), *Comité national de liaison des régies de quartier* (CNLRQ), *Fédération nationale des associations d'accueil et de réadaptation sociale* (FNARS), *Coordination inter-réseaux de l'insertion par l'économique* (CIRIE), *Fédération nationale des centres sociaux* (FNCS).

On production co-operatives:
Demoustier, D. (1981), *Entre l'efficacité et la démocratie, les co-opératives de production*, Edition Entente, Paris.

Demoustier, D. (1994), 'Les Co-opératives de production', *La Découverte*, Repères no. 20.

7 Germany: Work Integration through Employment and Training Companies in Berlin and its Surrounding Region

KARL BIRKHÖLZER AND GÜNTHER LORENZ

1. The Emergence of Employment and Training Companies (BQGs) in Germany

1.1. The Development of the Labour Market in the Region

More than any other area, the region Berlin-Brandenburg can be regarded at present as an almost ideal illustration of the problems and challenges confronted by labour market, social welfare and economic policies throughout Germany. In this region two formerly divided economic and social systems are coming together; systems that are to all appearances united in a political-administrative sense but that are very far from being so in their economic and socio-political realities. However, it is the negative aspects of the global transformation process affecting all national economies East and West, which are surfacing more clearly here. Divisions in economic development has not only opened up the gap between rich and poor, but has also considerably sharpened the spatial disparities, between zones of prosperity on the one side and areas in crisis on the other.

Before unification, West Berlin had achieved the status of a crisis region with its annual industrial redundancies of between 3,000 and 4,000 and an unemployment rate of 10% on average since 1983 (Senat und Magistrat, 1990, p. 29; Kisker and Heine, 1987); while a proportion of the remaining jobs could only be retained in the city through a high rate of subsidy from Bonn. After unification East Berlin, one of the former GDR's industrial centres, experienced dramatic de-industrialisation within a very few years, affecting up to 80% of the jobs in the metalworking and electro-technical industries. With the loss of academic and administrative functions in the former capital city of the GDR, almost every other member of the workforce had been affected by the 'Abwicklung' ('winding up' – Newspeak for being made redundant). These figures reflect the average rate of job losses for all regions of eastern Germany, although some regional differences have emerged, worst hit are certain rural areas, especially Brandenburg and Mecklenburg-Vorpommern (Birkhölzer *et al.*, 1994).

Thus the situation in the Berlin-Brandenburg region can be said to have arisen from the merging of three crises, with the only hopeful note the eventual transfer of the 'capital city' status and functions from Bonn to Berlin. However, those working on the construction sites of the future capital come from almost every country in Europe while the unemployment rate among Berlin construction workers has hit a level of 29.2%. This means that the 'Berlin Boom' is passing most of the region's inhabitants by, in a similar fashion to the way the registered growth rate in Germany has no positive effect on the labour market situation. On the contrary, economic and socio-political data (January 1997) confirm on an impressive scale the thesis of 'jobless growth' (Aaronowitz and DiFazio, 1994):

(a)   The total number of registered unemployed, 4.66 million, reached its highest point in 1996 since the end of the Second World War despite an economic growth rate of 1.5% (*DIW-Wochenbericht*, 1/2, 1997, p. 10). Since then, the official unemployment rate decreased until 1998 to 4.19 million, in a time when the economic growth rate again achieved a level of 2.8% in the last quarter of 1998.

(b)   On a geographical basis: unemployment rate in the FRG was running at 11.9% in western Germany (1998: 10.9%), and at 19.9% in eastern Germany (1998: 17.4%); the rate in Berlin was at 15.2% (East Berlin 14.8%/West Berlin 15.5%), in 1998 it was at 16.1% (East Berlin 17.4%/West Berlin 9.3%); in Brandenburg it was 18.5% (1998: 15.2%); the West Berlin borough of Kreuzberg had the highest unemployment rate in the town with 28% and during 1998 was as high as 30.8%.[1]

Since the region has been facing the problem of mass unemployment for more than ten years now, it has a wide spectrum of experiences to draw

---

[1]   Sources: Federal Employment Office and Regional Employment Office Berlin-Brandenburg, for January 1997 and average rates for 1998.

upon, both from state employment-promotion policies, and strategies and concepts from self-help and grassroots-level initiatives.

Crisis regions often register early on what will subsequently affect wider society; and at the same time, they are like laboratories in which possible measures and strategies can be tested and their successes and failures observed. This applies in particular to the development of *Beschäftigungs-und Qualifizierungsgesellschaften*, known in Germany as BQGs for short, which have taken on increasing significance in the struggle against unemployment since the beginning of the 1980s.

1.2. The Development of Labour Market Policies in Germany: From Passive to Active Strategies

During the post-war period in the Federal Republic of Germany (indeed as in most of Western Europe) economic and social policy was under the influence of Keynesian ideas and concepts. One of its central tenets was 'full employment' (*Vollbeschäftigung*), which Keynes defined as being an unemployment rate of under 5%. A specific German variant of this model developed under the influence of Catholic social teaching, was the idea of the 'social partnership' (*Sozialpartnerschaft*) between employers and employees, with the 'neutral state' as the third partner. A whole range of social institutions based on this tripartite model were set up, mainly in the area of labour market and social policy, such as the Federal Labour Office (*Bundesanstalt für Arbeit*), the 'employment placement services' (*Arbeitsvermittlung*), the 'unemployment insurance system' (*Arbeitslosenversicherung*), the pension and health insurance bodies, and the vocational training structure. Only 'social assistance' (*Sozialhilfe*), a kind of legally guaranteed minimum income for those in need, i.e. for all individuals who – in accordance with the 'subsidiarity principle' (*Subsidiaritätsprinzip*) – had no claim on any other party for support, remained the exclusive responsibility of the local authorities.

The system's ability to function, however, was dependent upon full employment remaining a political objective or, to put it another way, the principle of the social welfare state and the principle of full employment were inextricably linked. Unemployment was seen as a temporary phenomenon, normally resolved within the one-year period envisaged by the unemployment insurance structure. Within this period, the unemployed person could draw benefit amounting to around two-thirds of his or her previous wages or salary. Only in exceptional cases involving very difficult situations would the unemployed individual end up dependent upon social assistance and thus directly upon the public purse. As the goal of full employment, ultimately part of economic policy, unemployment was a subject of little or no interest for labour market policymakers. They were completely occupied with providing the economy with the required personnel through recruitment, vocational advice and training. 'Further education and retraining measures' (*Fortbildungs-und Umschulungsmaß-nahmen*) became the most important instrument in adjusting the profile of the workforce in line with technological shifts and changes.

Long-term, structural unemployment was not envisaged by this system and the labour market policies were completely unprepared when it hit them: in 1951 the unemployment rate was 12% as a result of the effects of the war; in the 1960s and at the beginning of the 1970s, however, the rate had dropped to 1% and West Germany had to all intents and purposes become a country looking for immigrant workers. But in the middle of the 1970s the figure was once again around 5% and since then, despite statistical manipulation, it has been rising continuously (BMWi, 1994, pp. 6–7). One thing which should have worried people, but apparently didn't, was that amongst the unemployed the number of long-term unemployed was steadily growing. In the German context this means being without work for more than a year, which is the maximum period the individual can draw 'unemployment insurance benefit' (*Arbeitslosengeld*). Beyond this (and in the case of no insurance benefit having previously been earned) the person affected slides down into the ranks of 'welfare recipients', having entitlement only to the financially reduced 'unemployment assistance' (*Arbeislosenhilfe*); the final station on the journey is 'social assistance' (*Sozialhilfe*), which the local authorities are obligated to provide.

Labour market policy in Germany is still Federal Government policy, determined by Federal legislation such as, the Employment Promotion Act (*Arbeitsförderungsgesetz*/AFG) and, to an extent, the Federal Social Welfare Act (*Bundessozialhilfegesetz*/BSHG). The principles which applied during the first years of the Federal Republic have been subject to little change: the creation of jobs is still the task of economic policy-making, while labour market policy is meant to restrict itself to its placement service activities. Amazingly, the situation did not change even as the rise in unemployment at the end of the 1970s brought about the first instruments of a 'active labour market policy' (*Aktive Arbeitsmarktpolitik*), e.g. the 'Employment Creation Measures' (*Arbeitsbeschaffungs-maßnahmen*/ABM) based on the AFG, and the 'Help towards Work' (*Hilfe zur Arbeit*/HzA) programme geared to the BSHG, although here there have been new grant guidelines over the years targeted towards certain classes of unemployed (see Appendix).

The basic idea was, to replace the usual passive benefit payments, and make the funds available to enterprises or institutions as wage/salary cost subsidies, on the condition that they create extra jobs for the unemployed. One aspect was that normal profit-making enterprises would contribute 20–25% of their own resources; while organisations officially recognised as operating for the public benefit (i.e. not-for-profit, in German *gemeinnützig*) could apply for up to 100% of wage/salary costs as grants. This programme was and is subject to wild fluctuations depending on shifts in labour market and budgetary perspectives. Recently financial restrictions and the disbursement regulations have tightened to such an extent that the whole programme is becoming increasingly unattractive for potential employers. In particular, the new reformed version of the AFG, introduced in 1997, is designed to put a large question mark over the complete range of active labour market measures. The background to this is the fact that, despite all the financial investment, nothing has altered the continuous rise in the unemployment rate. For a long time nobody has denied the necessity for a thoroughgoing reform of the instruments available to active labour market strategies. While conservative parties and the majority of the employers' associations tend to want to get rid of this whole approach, or at least drastically reducing its application, the opposition parties, together with the majority of the trade unions, the charitable organisations and the unemployed organisations, are preoccupied with structural errors in the legal framework that, in their view, render the objectives of this basically legitimate approach either difficult or impossible to achieve.

The key point of the criticism is that:

(a) the measures are temporary (as a rule between six months and a year, under certain circumstances two or maximum three years);

(b) they involve exclusively individual-targeted funding with the goal of improving the job chances of the individual on the normal labour market.

In this context we had the emergence of the 'second labour market' (*Zweiter Arbeitsmarkt*), a term that in the German-speaking countries, means an intermediate labour market acting as a bridge, back to the so-called 'first labour market' (*Erster Arbeitsmarkt*) – and not in any way establishing itself as an independent new sector. In reality, however, given the unemployment figures, the second labour market has long since become a permanent fixture, while the funding guidelines still cling to the fiction of an 'interim solution' and grant neither institutional nor project-oriented support to the organisations of the second labour market that could lead to sustainable jobs in this sector (with the exception of certain new funding programmes in individual *Bundesländer*, which are dealt with later in this study, see Section 2).

1.3. The Development of Local Employment Initiatives

The idea of a third sector of the economy was and is foreign to the social institutions of the German Federal Republic. Associations and citizen associations are seen more as a supplementary factor in the cultural or leisure fields than as fundamental institutions in the core areas of work and the economy. The German concept of the 'social partnership' has no place for voluntary organisations and citizens' associations, and the same applies to the system of the 'charitable welfare institutions' (*Wohlfahrtsverbände*), where, the privately directed but overwhelmingly state-financed charities enjoy a monopoly. Within this established framework, citizens' initiatives appeared to be superfluous and only entered the public consciousness in the 1970s with the appearance of the so-called 'alternative' and 'green' movements (Birkhölzer *et al.*, 1990).

Thus, the new employment initiatives did not in any sense emerge as an instrument of state labour market policy; neither had they been explicitly conceived of within that framework, and this still applies today to the Federal Government level – the latest developments on the level of the *Bundesländer* will be examined below.

On the contrary, the emergence of local employment initiatives in general and BQGs in particular represents a reaction on the part of citizens to the absence of a specific set of employment creation instruments for reintegrating the unemployed into the world of work. Such instruments appeared unnecessary during the period of prosperity, and state-interventionist job programmes became completely out of fashion in the wake of neo-liberal economic thinking at the beginning of the 1980s (and not only in West Germany). Job creation would, so the line went, be left to economic policy and growth-promotion measures, while social policy would manage the job of dealing with consequences of unemployment. And while the social security systems proved they were able to function quite well (i.e. as long as the unemployment rate could be kept under 10%), it is the instruments of economic policy that have essentially failed completely (Hanesch *et al.*, 1994).

However, at the Federal government level the average figures and the associated problem did not appear very dramatic, especially when compared with the situation in other EU countries. But what was overlooked was the way in which the rise in unemployment was not spread equally across the country, but was showing concentrations in certain sectors (coal, steel, shipbuilding, armaments) and their corresponding locations. What appeared in a context of averages as minimal became catastrophic when the local and regional dimensions were examined: Saarland, the East Ruhr, Ostfriesland, Bremen, the North German coastal region, Mittelfranken, Oberpfalz, and last but not least West Berlin – although here it was hidden under a blanket of subsidies (Birkhölzer *et al.*, 1990; Kisker and Heine, 1987). In these crisis regions local protest movements began to form themselves, and went in search of new political alliances of local actors as well as constructive solutions for the plant/workplace and the local area. It is certainly no accident that this was the background against which the first BQGs were founded (Bullmann *et al.*,1986; Bosch and Neumann, 1991; Kaluza *et al.*, 1991).

2. Types of BQGs

2.1. Definitions and Distinctions

Although the term 'employment and training company' (*Beschäftigungs- und Qualifizierungsgesellschaft* – BQG) is used quite often now, no clear definition or uniform understanding of it can be found either in the praxis on the ground or in the academic literature. It is therefore necessary for the purposes of this study clearly to delimit the meaning of the term.

The term 'BQG' is applied in this study as a collective name for a multiplicity of institutions with different names depending on their regional origins and the period in which they were set up, but whose common objective was or is the reintegration of unemployed people into gainful work. Some have described themselves explicitly as BQGs, while others have chosen other names often with only the words 'work' or 'employment' that indicate the desired objective. After the unification of Germany, in the new Bundesländer, we frequently find the 'Employment Promotion and Structural Development Company' (*Arbeitsförderungs-, Beschäftigungs- und Strukturentwicklungsgesellschaft* – ABS). As a rule of thumb, institutions identifying themselves as 'BQG's are somewhat older and were most likely to have been founded in West Germany before unification, whereas 'ABS' organisations emerged after unification with the assistance of the Treuhand Authority, primarily from large East German industrial plants that had been 'wound up'. Nevertheless, the term BQG is being used in the East, in particular by sister organisations of former West German bodies, while the term ABS (or variations of it) has in the meantime taken root in the West as well. The terms 'initiative' or 'project' usually describe self-help groups organised by those directly affected by unemployment. To extend the confusion, new terms have appeared that relate to the terminology utilised in the funding guidelines of various *Bundesländer* such as 'Employment Promotion Enterprises' (*Arbeitsförderbetriebe*, Berlin), 'Employment Promotion Companies' (*Arbeitsfördergesellschaften, Brandenburg*), 'Social Enterprises' (*Soziale Betriebe, Niedersachsen*), 'Gainful Employment Promotion Enterprises' (*Beschäftigungsfördende Erwerbsbetriebe*, Hamburg), and many more. Unfortunately, this has not let to any uniform description being accepted, or even to a term enjoying majority usage.

Therefore in this study all these types are termed 'BQG',[2] where they fit the following working definition that distinguishes them from other types of institution:

(a) BQGs are economically active enterprises with legal status, i.e. are corporate entities under civil law;

(b) whose objective is the reintegration of unemployed individuals into gainful employment;

(c) they seek to achieve this on the basis of regular training and/or employment contracts that as a rule run for a limited time, and are rarely of a permanent nature;

(d) and on the basis of mixed financing from their own turnover as businesses, as well as from grants from public and private sources, including donations and/or work done in an honorary capacity.

In this context, the BQGs are intentionally distinguished from, for example:

(a) social or charitable institutions in which the individuals concerned are not members of the workforce, but rather are users or clients;

---

[2] Throughout this study therefore we use the German names in italics together with a literal English translation. We would like to point out, however, that these translations need not have any specific relation to existing English terms.

(b) purely educational or training measures where the work dimension is absent;

(c) activities devoted to job-finding or employment placement without the institution itself engaging in economic activity;

(d) compulsory state or 'community work programmes' without proper employment contracts.

Clearly, in view of this multiplicity – not to say confusion – of terms it is exceptionally difficult to form a comprehensive (especially in the quantitative sense) picture of the current state and development of BQGs. The following individual 'lines of development' can however be discerned.

2.2. BQGs in West Germany before Unification

The BQGs arose in West Germany at the end of the 1970s and beginning of the 1980s as a 'crisis response' at the local and regional levels. Their number remained low and, until the end of the 1980s, they had achieved no real resonance on the national political scene. As academic researchers also had only limited interest in what was happening in the regions and localities, this period has produced a series of individual case studies, but no empirical research encompassing the totality of the phenomenon.

If we first examine the subject on the basis of the initiators or 'actors', we can distinguish three types:

(a) initiatives from members of a workforce at the plant level,

(b) social-pedagogic or social welfare initiatives at the local and/or municipal level, and

(c) self-help initiatives emerging from the new social movements.

BQGs absorbing redundant staff from plant closure (Auffanggesellschaften)
In the metalworking and electro-technical plants (including steel and shipbuilding) threatened with mass redundancies, it was primarily the 'Working Groups for Alternative Production' (*Arbeitskreise Alternative Produktion*) that had been established by the IG Metall shop stewards and union representatives who, stimulated by the example of the 'Alternative Workers' Plan' in the British armaments company Lucas Aerospace (Lorenz, 1995; Wainwright and Elliott, 1982), developed the approach represented by the slogan 'Employment plan, not social welfare plan!' (Bosch and Neumann, 1991; Schomacker *et al.*, 1987). Whereas the traditional trade union strategy for redundancies had always involved

securing the social protection of those members under threat by negotiating compensation payments, often in conjunction with early retirement measures or other social benefits, here for the first time a strategy of economic intervention was formulated: creating or saving jobs via innovation in the area of socially or ecologically useful production and/or the orientation towards local or regional requirements. Examples of the latter include maintaining and extending the commuter rail transport network, such as was envisaged by the 'employment plan' developed by the workers during the closing of the AEG rail engineering works in the borough of Wedding in Berlin (Breede *et al.*, 1983).

It was in such circumstances that the terms 'employment companies' (*Beschäftigungs-gesellschaften*) and 'employment and training companies' (*Beschftigungs- und Qualifizierungsgesellschaften*/BQGs) were formulated, in the sense of:[3]

(a) enterprises designed to absorb those who would otherwise be made redundant;

(b) financed from assets, which otherwise would have to be spent on a 'social plan';

(c) supplemented by funding from the labour market and social security budgets, which would otherwise be burdened with the costs of unemployment and the social problems it causes;

(d) commissioned with the task of developing new areas of work, as well as marketable products or services, and/or;

(e) of developing alternative professional (or other) prospects for the people affected.

The final objective in this list brought 'training' into the title, and in the course of time the emphasis has shifted more and more over to (re-)training measures. As these were congruent with current instruments of labour market strategy, it was considerably easier to obtain funding for such operations than for the incomparably more difficult task of developing new products and services, an objective for which labour market policy at that time showed little interest. The plant-oriented initiatives began radically to decline in importance towards the end of the 1980s, due mainly to their dependence upon short-term funding and to the lack of support from the unions' own head offices – a by no means insignificant reason.

---

[3] Source: Beywl *et al.* (1993); Birkhölzer (1993).

Although their limited numbers condemned them to irrelevance at the beginning of the 1990s, the BQGs that grew from plant-level workforce struggles have nonetheless done pioneering work, and this model became the example to follow for the 'employment promotion and structural development companies' (*Arbeitsförderungs-, Beschäftigungs- und Strukturentwicklungsgesellschaften*/ABSs) in the industrial complexes of East Germany that were threatened with being 'wound up' (Beywl *et al.*, 1992).

BQGs as reintegration enterprises for the socially disadvantaged (Wiedereingliederungsbetriebe) A second line of development owes its origins to initiatives emerging from groups connected with the churches (*Neue Arbeit*/'New Work Initiative'), traditional charity organisations and political campaigns, in cities and communities hit by mass redundancies and industrial decline. In these regions growing 'new poverty' and declining income levels forced people earlier than elsewhere to think about new ways of financing social support (BAG, 1994; Freidinger and Schulze-Böing, 1993).

In such situations, encouraged by models from the ecumenical movement, the idea of employment companies was taken up as a tool for:

(a) combining social support and economic activity so that

(b) the economic activity helped finance the social support on the one hand, and

(c) on the other, socially disadvantaged people were offered the possibility (at least temporarily) of working, earning a wage and improving their lives.

Therefore, even temporary involvement in regular work and wage-earning with a BQG could have a therapeutic function.

BQGs of this kind have established themselves primarily in the areas of personal, public and infrastructural services, with an emphasis on the recycling sector. This has led to accusations of illegitimate competition, primarily from crafts organisations and small and medium businesses, and has led to the BQGs being pushed into areas of activity that (due to low rates of profitability and status) nobody else wants to handle. This means that the BQGs thus affected suffer not only discrimination against their workforces, but also risks to their economic survival.

*BQGs as self-help enterprises run by unemployed people and other social groups (*Selbsthilfeunternehmen*)* A third line of development has come out of the 'new social movements' – the women's movement, the ecological movement, citizens' initiatives concerned with development and social problems, neighbourhood and local community projects, tenants' organisations, homeless and squatting campaigns, self-managed enterprises, new co-operatives and last but not least unemployed self-help groups. This area is without doubt the most confusing of all and the one with the least statistical data. Nevertheless, it is the one with not only the longest but also the widest range of experiences dealing with employment initiatives of every kind. One could claim that the idea of the BQG was born here, long before initiatives at plant level in industry brought the term itself into use. While the 'new social movements' in the 1970s, were largely dominated by protest activities which were primarily meant either to provoke or to frustrate state reaction, by the end of the decade parts of this movement had developed a new orientation towards the search for low-level but constructive solutions, particularly with regard to economic self-help. West Berlin was a centre of such developments, which is why this region has some of the longest-lasting and most successful BQGs (Birkhölzer *et al.*, 1990) – the examples in the Appendix each represent one of the basic types dealt with here.

What differentiates the BQGs of this type from the previous types is their organisational structure. They are supported by a membership base that is either identical with the staff working there or the people using the product or service, or is at least open to them as well. This leads to a considerably higher level of identification with 'their firm' among the employees, which they see less as a temporary stop-over and more as their own workplace with (at least hopes for) long-term prospects for them. BQGs of this kind have, as a rule, a greater proportion of staff working in a voluntary capacity or as part-time workers, as this holds out the possibility of getting a permanent position, should the circumstances permit.

According to different assessments (e.g. Kaiser, n.d.), towards the end of the 1980s there were around 4,000 BQGs in West Germany employing a total of between 80,000 and 90,000 people. We regard these figures as being far too conservative as the parameters within which the data was collected were too narrow to really take in the whole spectrum. In 1992, for example, in western Germany alone there were 80,000 individuals in ABM programmes and 250,000 in training schemes (Brinkmann, 1995); In addition there were those individuals funded by the BSHG and other schemes (Lindner *et al.*, 1992) about whose distribution among the BQGs and other sponsor organisations little is known. The relationship between the number of BQGs and the estimated number they employed suggest, however, that they are more likely to be small-scale enterprises.

2.3. *The Situation in Eastern Germany after Unification*

In order to understand the following account fully, it is necessary to recall to mind that the unification of the two German states came about through the 'accession' (*Beitritt*) of the East German *Länder* to the legal and economic system of the Federal Republic. This involved, in reality, the transferring of all West German structures and institutions onto the 'New Bundesländer' as they had become known – in the areas of labour market and social policy as in all others. Also in this transfer were BQGs and their sponsor organisations, which began opening branches in eastern Germany. To that extent the landscape of East German support/sponsor organisations did not offer anything novel, but rather presented a faithful image of West German structures, including the typology of redundant workforce absorption companies, reintegration enterprises and self-help enterprises.

Unification inevitably brought along in its train dynamic and dramatic processes of economic change often against the will of the actors concerned, and eventually affecting the whole of Germany. In particular the Treuhandanstalt was presented with an almost insurmountable task, i.e. to privatise and to put back into economic shape the entire former state productive assets. Patently obviously, both objectives could not be achieved simultaneously. Thus the Treuhand Authority decided to give priority to privatisation, a goal that was by and large achieved by the time it was closed down in 1995 – with disastrous consequences for the second objective, however (Priewe and Hickel, 1991): between 1990 and 1993 alone 4.5 million jobs were lost, or 47% of the 1989 total. Included in that figure is the 80% of industrial jobs that vanished (taking both the Berlin and country average). This 'success' was bought with a deficit of about 150 billion Marks that the Treuhand left to its successor institutions.

Despite emigration and the development of several hundred thousand commuters, particularly among the younger part of the workforce, despite the retreat (mostly on the part of women) into the 'reserve army of labour' and despite almost a further million sent into early retirement, by 1992 there were still 2 million without regular work (Brinkmann, 1995).

In this situation BQGs were, for the first time, put into action as an officially accepted instrument of labour market and social policy. We may distinguish between two phases:

(a) the setting up of companies to absorb redundancies from 'wound-up' industrial complexes (the so-called ABS organisations), and

(b) the emergence of 'employment promotion enterprises' and 'social enterprises' among others, as instruments of a new kind of regional labour market and structural development strategy (from 1993/4).

ABSs as a special development track pursued in eastern Germany One of the preconditions for their emergence was the issuing on the part of the Federal Labour Office of extensive special regulations for the five new *Länder* (Brandenburg, Mecklenburg-Vorpommern, Sachsen, Sachsen-Anhalt and Thüringen) and East Berlin. These made the rules for claiming employment promotion funding considerably easier by, for example, waiving the limitations on areas of activity, generously extending the measures up to three years, and lifting the restrictions on generating more income. Also, BQGs were, for the first time, invited to establish small and medium-size business enterprises. All forms of BQGs were able to make use of these privileges. However, establishing new BQGs as specifically East German initiatives was hindered by the absence of institution-targeted (as opposed to individual-targeted) funding mechanisms.

Things were different at plant level: in 1991 there was a framework agreement in place between the new *Länder*, the unions and employer organisations, and the Treuhand Authority, for establishing companies to absorb those made redundant by the privatisation process (i.e. for ABS). On the model of the earlier West German BQGs resources should be invested in the setting up of new enterprises instead of in social plans; these enterprises would be taken over and run by groups from the workforce itself (Knuth, 1995). The parent company (or the Treuhand Authority) would participate in the operation by making available capital grants or loans, workspaces, buildings and land, and machinery. However, the exact conditions would have to be negotiated anew from case to case.

Within just a few years there was a boom in ABSs – up to 400 – with approximately 160,000 employees with wage/salary subsidies (Brinkmann, 1995; Knuth, 1995). Unfortunately there are very few really reliable statistics on this area of activity as the Labour Offices' statistics, although they list the number of funded individuals/jobs against the funding type, do not show the distribution of those individuals across the range of sponsor organisations such as BQGs or ABSs. Also the total number of people supported by wage/salary costs funding of all kinds is subject to considerable fluctuation, from 300,00 in 1991, rising to a high of 400,000 in 1992, and falling to 250,000 by 1994 (Brinkmann, 1995; Knuth, 1995). In 1996 it oscillated between 280,000 and 300,000, and due to the reform of the AFG legislation the 1997 figure is expected to reach an all-time low (*Wirtschaftsbulletin Ostdeutschland*, 1/97; *Was Nun?*, No. 43, 1997). On top of those figures there are 220,000 to 240,000 in training schemes and 45,000 to 50,000 in various other funded schemes (in 1996, *Wirtschaftsbulletin Ostdeutschland*, 1/97). The distribution of these figures across ABSs, other BQGs and the various other sponsor organisations cannot be determined at the present moment. It appears to be the case, however, that the proportion of employees with salary/wage costs subsidies in ABSs has continuously increased to the extent that 50% of all such grants accrue to ABS bodies, whereas pure training schemes in ABSs only play a minimal role and are usually carried out by other institutions (including other BQGs) (Grass, 1993), with the result that the share held by ABSs of the total funding available is only one-third (Brinkmann, 1995).

In the light of the meagre data available, it is not surprising that exact empirical analyses of ABSs almost non-existent. One of the rare exceptions (Grass, 1993) deals with the founding phase of the ABSs in eastern Germany only. There it is clear that, along with the enterprises from which the original ABSs emerged, it was local government that was primarily involved in the setting up of ABSs.

Whereas the ABSs, in their initial phase at least, were positioned close to their parent plants in the economic and technical/professional senses, the majority of them moved over the course of time further away from their origins, and today they orientate themselves overwhelmingly towards local and/or municipal objectives (see the case study '*ABS-Brücke*' in the Appendix). This suggests that the inclusion of 'structural development' can without doubt be justified, even if the practical activity behind the term has not involved much more than the clearing and decontaminating industrial property for future investors or the environmental improvement of brown coal mining areas and other derelict industrial land. Large-scale ABS organisations with several thousand employees are active in this sector; their similarity with certain work programmes of the 1920s and 1930s cannot be disguised, i.e. after finishing the 'emergency works' concerned, they become superfluous or be radically reduced in size. It would appear that a medium-size enterprise is more effective if municipal responsibilities are to be taken over on a long-term basis.

BQGs as instruments of regional labour market and structural development policies   The structure of labour market policies in those *Bundesländer* hit by crisis after the Wende period (upheaval in the GDR and unification) reveal two basic inadequacies:

(a)   on the one hand, the 'short-termism' of the grant measures in particular the lack of funding possibilities for the period 'after ABM';

(b)   on the other hand, the individual-based funding logic and the lack of institution-based funding possibilities.

Thus, at the *Länder* level, there were supplementary regional labour market programmes, such as the 'Labour Market Framework Programme' (*Arbeitsmarktpolitisches Rahmenprogramm*/ARP) for Berlin, or the 'Training and Employment for Brandenburg' (*Qualifizierung und Arbeit für Brandenburg*) programme. In these programmes, BQGs were designated for the first time as bodies to be funded systematically as institutions of 'the state-supported labour market' (official terminology), and for the first time possibilities of institution-based funding were envisaged that would also make grants available for administration and material costs as well as for management and supervisory staff. For the purpose of distributing these resources in a targeted fashion state agencies (*Landesagenturen*) for employment and training were established such as seven the 'employment and training support units' (*Servicegesellschaften*) in Berlin (with somewhat decentralised areas of responsibility) and the *Landesagentur für Struktur und Arbeit*/LASA in Brandenburg. These agencies were also assigned such basic tasks as the development of a regional labour market and structural development strategy, as well as various research and educational responsibilities, arising out of the fact that this was completely new territory for the public administrations of the *Länder* concerned.

Subsequent to the first period of intensive promotion of BQGs and of ABSs, the hopes of creating new jobs via 'business start-ups' turned out to be hollow: the quota of actual businesses started remained under 2%. On the other hand, many projects which had prospects of success simply could not be brought into the realm of economic self-sufficiency within the time available. What was required was a facility for further funding at a low rate, which could act as a stimulus for the development of long-term, sustainable economic activity. A reform of the Employment Promotion Act (AFG) did reflect this to a certain extent, in that new paragraphs on funding were introduced that permitted a combination of income from economic activity and part-subsidy of jobs (at a fixed level), as long as long-term unemployed – including individuals whose ABM contracts had ended – were taken on. At the same time, however, the areas of activity open to grant support were limited to youth work, social services and environmental needs and the chances of generating income by engaging efficiently in more lucrative areas of business were thus neutralised. This means that new funding possibilities can only be exploited with co-financing from the *Länder* level (from the youth work and social and environmental services budgets). (The AFG 249h and 242s schemes are now integrated into the new SAM scheme.)

Nevertheless the basic idea of stimulating economic activity through wage costs subsidies for the employment of long-term unemployed people and other 'target groups' turned out to be innovative. Not least due to the influence of the debate on the 'social economy' in the European context, a lively exchange of opinion ensued on the subject of the introduction of 'social enterprises'. The representatives of the BQGs in particular came to see their long-term prospects within this conceptual framework.

Institutions describing themselves explicitly as 'social enterprises' were first established in Niedersachsen (*Soziale Betriebe*) at the end of 1991 due to passing of relevant state legislation. These enterprises engage in economic activity that, like the Italian social co-operatives of type B, primarily employ socially disadvantaged people, long-term unemployed and other 'target groups'. They are integrated into a structure of reducing financial support, for a period of up to five or six years, with the goal of economic self-sufficiency; the steering and supervision responsibilities rest with the a state agency (*Landesgesellschaft zur Beratung und Information von Beschäftigungsinitiativen*, LaBIB, 1994).

In Berlin the term 'social enterprise' provoked strong political resistance. Despite this, it was possible to extend the ARP programme by including a modest, but essentially similar, measure called 'Employment Promotion Enterprise' (*Arbeitsförderbetrieb*). There are in principle no restrictions on its areas of activity, however a 'certificate of approval' is required from the local crafts and commercial institutions in order to avoid undesirable competition. One other version, conceptualised but hardly ever tested in practice, is the 'urban enterprise' (*Stadtbetriebe*), which in a similar way would take on municipal and/or infrastructural responsibilities. (*Senatsverwaltung für Arbeit und Frauen*, 1994).

Currently, the following models are also in operation under various different names:

(a) *Beschäftigungsfördende Erwerbsbetriebe* (Hamburg)

(b) *Marktorientierte Arbeitsförderbetriebe* (Mecklenburg-Vorpommern)

(c) *Soziale Wirtschaftsbetriebe* (Nordrhein-Westfalen)

(d) *Sozialorientierte Erwerbsbetriebe* (Sachsen-Anhalt)

(e) *Arbeitsmarktorientierte Betriebe* (Schleswig-Holstein)

(f) *Soziale Betriebe* (Thüringen).

In contrast, Brandenburg does not regard it as especially helpful to introduce, alongside the already existing categories of BQG and ABS, further categories with special funding guidelines. Rather, it wants to integrate all existing forms under the collective term 'Employment Promotion Companies' (*Arbeitsfördergesellschaften*) with equal status for its future policies. The argument is that the introduction of new categories will only make the funding landscape more complicated and more opaque.

BQGs and the concept of social enterprise Since the introduction of the 'social enterprises' (*Soziale Betriebe*) in Niedersachsen, there has been a debate in Germany on the question of what is understood by the term. The Niedersachsen model defines a special case, while all the BQGs portrayed in this study could also be described by the term 'social enterprises'. The discussion at the European level encompasses a similar multiplicity of extremely varied institutions, all with their historical and national idiosyncrasies. In this context, for reasons of comparability, we have to make use of a working definition for which there is some consensus. At least three criteria are regarded as being constitutive of BQGs:

(a) the existence of an enterprise engaging in economic activity and with a legal status,

(b) whose objectives are clearly of a social nature,

(c) and are not designed to maximise private profit.

According to these criteria, every non-commercial BQG would be classed as a 'social enterprise', i.e. almost all of them apart from a few exceptions.

Their legal status is generally either the 'registered association' (*eingetragener Verein*/e.V.) or the 'company with limited liability' (*Gesellschaft mit beschränkter Haftung*/GmbH). Both legal titles also exist in a form recognised as being 'for the public benefit' (*gemeinnützig,* abbreviations: gn.e.V. and gGmbh), which confers tax advantages. Unfortunately it is precisely this legal recognition of operating 'for the public benefit' and its current interpretation by the responsible tax and revenue authorities which prevents the development of economic activities. For this reason the recognised special status (for associations and for companies) of 'for the public benefit' is only used by a minority of organisations; the majority manage with clauses in their constitution or in the articles of association to direct the institution towards socially beneficial goals and exclude the possibility of surpluses accruing to private individuals. Outside of these stipulations complete participation in the economic life of the society is possible. German law definitely reveals a gap here, as 'social enterprises' are forced either to waive possible tax breaks or to restrict their freedom of economic activity.

The legal status of 'co-operative' (*Genossenschaft*) is hardly ever used. To explain this would be moving too far from the parameters of this study. However, due to their specific history co-operatives in Germany, East and West, are regarded as being anything but 'social enterprises'.

3. Evaluation: Results Achieved by BQGs

When assessing the achievements of the BQGs, it makes sense to distinguish between

(a) internal results which affect the relations of the BQG to its members and/or its participants, and

(b) external results, which affect the role of the BQGs in labour market and structural development strategies.

3.1. The Relationship between BQGs and their Target Groups

The BQGs offer the unemployed the only alternative for them to get to grips with their status, which they normally experience initially as individual bad luck, and to contribute to changing their situation. This motive plays a bigger role than any other in the establishment of local employment initiatives in general and of BQGs in particular. Interviews indicate that unemployed people have a very realistic view of their own chances of finding work and do not regard a job in a BQG as a guarantee of employment later; rather, they see temporary employment as a step back into the world of gainful work. Unemployment is far more than the loss of a job and income, it is a form of social exclusion, and BQGs are experienced as a chance to once more take part in the process of social production.

Therefore, BQGs are always viewed by their founders as having their own value that cannot be judged merely by external criteria of success. They are among other things a way of taking practical steps with one's life during a period of unemployment. That applies across the board to the 'self-help enterprises' (*Selbsthilfeunternehmen*) and the first workplace 'absorption companies' (*Auffanggesellschaften*) in West Germany, which had to fight for their very existence against external opposition. The situation after the Wende was similar: the setting-up of BQGs and ABSs was not granted 'from above' but had to be pushed through 'from below'. There are differences between the founder generations and those who came afterwards, and so the relationship of the members or participants to 'their' BQG is particularly important. Without any doubt, those BQGs that are member-based have an advantage over those that are structured as social-pedagogic or social welfare institutions: even if the latter can obtain support from their umbrella organisations (churches, charitable bodies, municipal authorities) in case of difficulty or conflict; in our experience the member-based BQGs are more stable and less likely to lurch into crisis; and, they are in a position to deal more effectively with changing external circumstances.

A further distinction involves the type of members or participants. Plant-level redundancy absorption companies and self-help enterprises are more likely to represent a 'normal' cross-section of unemployed individuals (from a workforce, a town or city neighbourhood, a region, etc.), whereas the 'reintegration enterprises' (*Wiedereingliederungs-betriebe*) concentrate right from the start on certain social groups. This 'target group orientation' is indeed desirable from the point of view of labour market and social policy, but can produce problems. The majority of such cases reveal organisational structures reflecting the traditional welfare institutions, in which a body of socially responsible people decide *for* but not *with* the unemployed persons concerned what they should do and what is good for them. This engenders an internal division of the staff into a small group with permanent positions – the management and supervisory personnel as a rule – and the majority of those working under temporary employment and training 'measures'; the management personnel tend to represent the BQG as a matter of priority *vis-à-vis* external bodies and, if appropriate, *vis-à-vis* the paymasters, and only as an afterthought *vis-à-vis* its own participants. As trade union representation is likely to be undeveloped in such BQGs, they are characterised by a kind of patronage and/or a social worker – client relationship, which give rise to disciplinary problems and lack of motivation for the temporary employees.

The target group orientation can also produce internal economic problems. It leads to the dilemma in which, on the one hand, income has to be generated by economic activity, but on the other it cannot be generated in sufficient quantity to secure lasting economic survival. On the one hand, employing target groups allows you to obtain higher wage costs subsidies, yet on the other, precisely this group needs supervision that causes higher costs and in turn renders the required economic performance difficult to achieve. BQGs of this type are always operating on the edge of economic survival, and the danger is definitely present that goal conflicts will be worked out to the disadvantage of the employees, their wages or their working conditions. A particular problem is posed by the tendency to employ the greatest possible number of 'disadvantaged' people for economic reasons, without having the necessary staff and resources to look after them all properly. Negative examples of 'rotation enterprises' are not unknown, in which a high level of fluctuation and minimal supervision of the employees offer no real chance to anyone.

In contrast, the workplace 'absorption companies' (*Auffanggesell-schaften*) were able to devote themselves to quality economic and technological activities on the basis (at least in part) of their highly qualified staff and access to resources. Part of the East German ABSs' work, for example, in the area of environmental technology is at a very high level of development, offering long-term possibilities of economic survival. Unfortunately, there are tendencies where key personnel leave to seek better positions elsewhere or to set up their own businesses, after the ABS has served them as a development centre for free. As this tendency is officially supported by standard labour market policy, the ABSs are continually losing exactly those staff which they require to compensate for deficit areas and thus for their long-term stability. Furthermore, ABSs have also had to let some of their high-skill personnel go due to the short-term nature of the subsidy policy. As long as ABSs are only seen as provisional labour markets that is no problem – it becomes one, however, with a change of perspective to long-term existence.

'Self-help enterprises' (*Selbsthilfeunternehmen*) are, as a rule, more likely to be geared to long-term perspectives and less subject to fluctuations of staff. But this objective runs counter to the structure of the funding available. They end up in the dilemma of not being able to fulfil their member's expectations of permanent employment because, for example, the period of financial support was not long enough to create a sustainable job or to secure a suitable post-project funding input. Here too, the way out tends to be, securing the finance for 'core staff' by continually taking on 'rotating participants'. Although in this case it is not a freely chosen tactic but one forced upon groups by the logic of the grant structures, it naturally causes the same problems: divisions among the workforce, a welfare syndrome, motivation and performance problems, and last but not least an economic risk connected with the inevitable growth in the size of the enterprise.

Work in a voluntary capacity is found throughout the management levels of all BQGs, and rather less on the ground in the enterprises. It has, particularly in the self-help enterprises, more the character of non-voluntary, unpaid work performed when earnings are insufficient or financial gaps need to be bridged. Very often members of staff remain – due to lack of alternatives – with 'their' enterprise even when no possibility of funding remains.[4]

3.2. The Labour Market and Structural Policy Effects of BQGs

BQGs make a not inconsiderable contribution to relieving the strain on the labour market. Currently, at a rough estimate, they employ around half a million people who would otherwise be unemployed, which would mean that the unemployment figures would climb to over 5 million. BQGs also contribute in corresponding degrees to tax revenues, social security contributions, the spending power of the citizens at large, as well as to local net production figures.

BQGs have, particularly in crisis regions, a significance for the regional economic structure which cannot be rated too highly. In many of the regions of eastern Germany badly hit by de-industrialisation BQGs are not only the biggest employers, but also the largest source of orders for the local economy. In addition, BQGs carry out on the local and regional levels socially necessary tasks ranging from caring for the elderly to looking after national monuments, from ecological rehabilitation measures to improving living conditions, from parks, cycle and rambler paths, 'soft' tourism, youth or health centres and regenerative energy plants to municipal development

---

[4] Several project managers work in a voluntary capacity. A case came to public notice recently of the voluntary manager of a large project who was officially registered as unemployed, and told she had to pay back her unemployment benefit as she was not 'available for work'. She took the Labour Office to court, and won her case (*Was Nun?*, 31 and 36, 1996).

workshops or regional training centres – all in all, goods and services which would otherwise not be available.

To that extent, BQGs are especially suitable for taking over activities for which the public sector has no capacity and for which the private sector has no interest. In reality they are not engaging in competition but rather represent a necessary complement to the local economic structure, above all in the following areas:

(a) nutrition and housing

(b) decentralised systems for utilities, energy, transport and waste disposal

(c) community-orientated services

(d) local culture

(e) local leisure activity and tourism

(f) improving and maintaining the infrastructure.

Against that, the central question of the reintegration of unemployed people cannot be answered so clearly. That depends upon whether we regard the BQGs merely as a transitional labour market or as an instrument for long-term reintegration. BQGs are divided on this question – as is more recent labour market policy (which is dealt with below).

Let us begin with the ability to return unemployed persons to a traditional job in what German terminology calls the 'first labour market'. According to the Federal Labour Office (Brinkmann, 1995) 59% of all people financed via ABM programmes have found employment after the termination of their ABM measure (17% with the sponsor organisation for the measure, 40% in another enterprise and 2% as self-employed). The figures say nothing about the special contribution of the BQGs but only about the 'success' of one of the funding programmes used frequently by the BQGs. Against that, 25% are said to have become unemployed again immediately after the measure finished; where the remaining 16% (not a negligible proportion) went is not disclosed. Despite that, a success rate of 59% is exceptionally high and the corollary, a failure rate of 25% exceptionally low. With the failure rate of pure training schemes at around 45%, the results of employment-oriented measures in comparison are almost twice as good.

However there is something wrong with the entire equation, as these apparently successful job-finding activities, have no visible consequences for the total unemployed statistics. Clearly the support organisations have to show job-finding successes if they want to keep on being contracted to carry out the measures. Even if the success rate were really that high in reality, this would only prove that participating in ABM offers a short-term improvement in the individual's chances in the labour market, and nothing about a sustainable reintegration into gainful employment. It suggests that a job-rotation carousel is being set in motion, in which periods of temporary employment are relieved by periods of unemployment and periods of participation in employment promotion measures – a phenomenon which has reported by people caught in this so-called 'ABM career structure' (König *et al.*, 1987).

Long-term reintegration of the unemployed would only be possible under one key condition – that the number of vacancies is actually increased by new and supplementary areas of employment. This leads to the question whether BQGs could be the tool to achieve the necessary broadening of the labour market. Potentially, the answer could be yes, as many BQGs can have innovative projects for developing new fields for employment (see the case studies in Appendix). The bottleneck occurs before the realisation of that potential, as the current conditions only allow the BQGs in exceptional cases to carry out such projects. This raises the question whether the various political decision-making organs have really grasped the potential significance of the BQGs.

4. Public Policy towards BQGs

The development of the relationship between BQGs and public policy has already been sketched (Section 2); the fact is that they are inextricably linked and both sides have had, over the years, to undergo an intensive process of learning and change.

Until the dramatic increase in the unemployment figures in East Germany in 1990/91 BQGs were hardly noticeable in government policy, and, then only on the local and regional levels. Subsequently, the attitude to BQGs was sometimes ambivalent, sometimes contradictory: at the beginning the thinking in the Federal Government, as well as among the *Länder* governments, was that BQGs (ABSs and the others) would only be a temporary phenomenon that would become superfluous when the expected economic upswing in eastern Germany got under way. Correspondingly, all funding instruments were geared to short-term objectives (see Appendix).

In the meantime, however, the view in those *Bundesländer* undergoing particular hardship matured to the extent that BQGs are now seen as being required for a considerably longer time than originally envisaged. And some *Länder* have introduced extra programmes that permit institution-related funding of BQGs with a more long-term structure (the maximum is five to six years, in Niedersachsen).

At the same time, however, the economic situation of the same *Länder* has worsened so noticeably that the programmes cannot, be funded to the extent required. Parallel to this we see a growing conflict of interest inside the *Länder* administrations between the departments responsible for economic development and those in charge of labour market and social policy. The consequence of this is the attempt to cut costs but also to bring more and more people into the programme, i.e. to try and spread a smaller sum across a greater number of people. This would only be possible if either the financial contribution from the Federal Government could be increased or if the BQGs own economic resources could be improved – or both!

A proposal from the eastern *Bundesländer* to reform the Federal legislation accordingly was not only rejected, but the Federal government began to cut the total funding available, cap the maximum grant levels and the length of time for which they were available, and to make the allocation rules more difficult. As the *Länder* were not able to compensate for the loss of income, the BQGs affected had either to let people go or cut back on pay or supervisory support for their members. Economically, such actions are not common sense, as cuts in the funding for active labour market strategies automatically mean increases in the spending on passive measures.

One other possibility remains – to improve the economic basis of the BQGs by, for example, easing access to the general market and to public tenders. Such attempts meet considerable resistance from chambers of commerce and similar organisations, but nonetheless do take place at the local level via official or unofficial agreement between the actors. Thus the economic activity of the BQGs, always operates in a grey, or half-illegal, zone.

In general terms, the acceptance of and political support for BQGs diminishes continuously as one moves from the lower (local government) to the upper (Federal Government) levels. Though possible at the lower level, for example via the formation of local partnerships, it is often blocked due to the legal and financial dependence at the higher levels (Bullmann, 1991).

Similar contradictions are to be found in the relationship between economic and social policy. It is always proclaimed that the division between the two is being removed, for example in the programmes in the new *Länder* promoting social and employment enterprises, but there is very little evidence of this in the praxis.

5.   Conditions for the Success of BQGs

Despite an apparent continuous development over more than 15 years, the future of BQGs is, at the present moment, more than uncertain. Everything revolves around the question as to whether and how the BQGs can contribute not just to a provisional, but rather to a long-term broadening of the labour market. Thus the quality of the employment in BQGs will become a key condition for their success, both internally and externally.

BQGs are more dependent than traditional enterprises upon the commitment of their staff. To that extent the current tendencies visible in sinking wages and worsening working conditions as a result of cost saving measures are distinctly counter-productive. The increasing pressure from outside can only be compensated for by greater effort on the part of the workforce. We would expect, therefore, that the BQGs that have a long-term chance of survival are those that offer a high level of participation and internal democracy.

The quality of their work is, for the workforce, probably of equally great significance. This does not have to do with formal seniority, but concerns the feeling that they are engaged in meaningful activity, as well as offering a chance of personal development.

These two elements can hardly be found any more within the classical structures of training and re-training programmes, which tend to be 'qualifications in the fog' (Brinkmann, 1995), or in the traditional fields of employment. The key issue can no longer be 're'-integration into traditional employment structures. Sustainable reintegration into gainful work in the past was essentially only possible where the BQGs were concerned with developing new fields of employment. This realisation is now seemingly shared at the Federal level, at least within the parameters of a new research programme called 'Employment through Innovation' (*Beschäftigung durch Innovation*), which is being put together at the present moment.

There is certainly much disagreement over where such employment-promoting innovation is to be found. The majority of the academic labour market and employment specialists are still looking for solutions in the industrial sector and/or the high-technology areas. The majority of the BQGs, however, have in practice orientated their efforts towards the needs at the local and regional levels. The potential for employment found at these levels has been verified in an impressive manner by the European Commission in their publication on 'Local Employment'.

A number of experiences informed that study, not least of which were those of the German BQGs. The most successful BQGs were those that had succeeded in anchoring themselves in local or regional networks. The forms these take are many and varied, ranging from 'round tables' (*Runde Tische*) on local 'alliances for work' (*Bündnisse für Arbeit*, with the collaboration of the trade unions and employer organisations) to fully fledged local partnerships (with the local authorities) (Birkhölzer and Lorenz, 1997). This strategy provides one of the few possibilities of actively countering the negative consequences of restrictive budgetary policy on both the Federal and *Länder* levels.

BQGs, due to their grass roots origins, suffer from a chronic lack of capital and an inadequate supply of resources of all kinds. Obtaining these on the capital market is often either impossible, or economically prohibitive. Consequently, BQGs are dependent upon strategies of co-operation with others, for example, by forming 'co-operative alliances' for joint administration and utilisation (or mutual exchange) of resources, such as local exchange and trading systems. Other possibilities include co-operation agreements with local authorities or institutions to use or take over unused lands, buildings or workspaces, or for free use of facilities such as colleges and other public educational institutions (*Was Nun?*, No. 34, 1997). As mentioned already, private donations and work in a voluntary capacity is indispensable in this situation. The necessary precondition is the clear, legally binding commitment of the BQGs to serving the community and doing so on a not-for-profit basis.

The finance structure of a BQG, like the combination of social and economic objectives requires, a special kind of social management, for which traditional management techniques are not appropriate. What is missing here is both the systematisation of knowledge gathered in praxis and an appropriate means of further education and support.

Similarly for developing social marketing – unmet needs at the local and regional levels often have the disadvantage that there is in sufficient spending power available to make meeting them commercially viable. At the same time, meeting these needs could be a foundation for regular employment and training structures, but these could not be financed through their income alone. Such deficits would have to be compensated for, through specific agreements, using public funds via savings in the cost of administering unemployment and other social welfare responsibilities.

There are already enough examples of BQG practice which prove that such models are not only economically viable but also offer great advantages to both sides. What is still lacking, at least in Germany, are appropriate tools of social accounting and auditing, which can make the economic significance of such enterprises transparent and comprehensible.

6. Conclusions

'Employment and Training Companies' (BQGs) represent the most important contribution to developing a culture of social enterprise in Germany (Bonas, 1996). They owe their origins and growth to an economic and social order that is helpless in the face of rising mass unemployment, and yet cannot or will not admit this. Thus, large sums are allocated to labour market and social policy measures, which are structured in such a way as to prevent them achieving sustainable results. So, on the one hand BQGs are becoming an indispensable element of public labour market and social policy, and on the other they are looked down on, blocked or discriminated against when they try operate. They are needed, it would appear, but not wanted, and even now large numbers of politicians and large sections of the public seem to assume that they will disappear as soon as the 'old order' has been re-established.

Our investigation of the conditions for success indicates that social enterprises in general and BQGs in particular require a specific socio-economic environment for their further development. This is noticeably lacking in Germany; at the most there are a few structures being set up in a few places. Even the academic debate emerging around the terms 'social economy' and 'third sector' is still in its infancy. In this situation the prospects for the BQGs are still completely open, although the political framework appears extremely unpromising. The social consensus upon which the Federal Republic was built is in danger of breaking up. The split runs right through the whole society, including the churches, trades unions and charitable organisations, and no-one can predict what will remain of the German 'social welfare state' after its restructuring. Budgetary cuts hit the classic forms of socio-economic integration first and, amongst the BQGs, threatened the survival of the 'reintegration enterprises' with their heavily subsidised 'bridging projects'. On the other hand, the principle of economic self-help inevitably gains in significance.

Thus, the BQGs in their current form face the alternative of either gaining official recognition as social enterprises with long-term responsibilities, or sinking back into political insignificance. As no positive developments can realistically be expected at the national level, the better chances are clearly at the local level for the time being. Future developments will depend upon the decisions made by the Bundesländer.

Appendix

ABS Brücke

ABS Brücke (ABS-B) a redundancy absorption company at plant level, was formed was formed as a BQG at the time of the '*Wende*' (1989). Employment in the metalworking and electro-technical industries in the region, was reduced from 85,000 to 15,000 people by 1992. In the firm *Narva*, a large manufacturer of light bulbs, 2,000 people were made redundant. From a workforce of 5,000, 1,000 are working with *ABS Brücke*.

Narva like all other companies in the ex-GDR had provided social services for its workforce and even for their families and residents in the area (medical treatment, food/catering, child care, etc.), *ABS-B* has also attempted to provide such services; they have since extended their activities across the entire borough of Friedrichshain and two other boroughs in West and East Berlin.

ABS-B has established businesses employing 620 people are employed in 45 projects in the following fields:

(a)   construction/conversion of apartments and premises,

(b)   social services for elderly people,

(c)   children's and youth projects.

ABS-B sees itself as a bridge ('*Brücke*') between unemployment and work, between old and young workers, between East and West. *ABS-B* has four subsidiaries, the fourth of which, '*Bildungsbrücke*', still survives as a normal commercial company (GmbH = plc) because of high subsidies for training measures in East Germany.

The association acting as a holding company and umbrella for the enterprises and projects is *Avran (Narva* spelt backwards). Other private companies which bought premises in the ex-*Narva* complex, like *Syrius* and *Priamos*, could not keep their promises and now only employ 50-60 employees. A comparison between these and the *ABS-B* enterprises shows a high performance on the part of the latter concerning job creation and other social objectives.

Problems faced by *ABS-B* are: the revolving-door effect of ABM subsidies (so that only 20% of workers from *Narva* are still employed in *ABS-B*); the lack of support from politicians for social enterprises; and the hostile attitude from the chamber of commerce towards ABSs/BQGs in general.

Atlantis

Atlantis, (a reintegration enterprise) is a non-profit limited company producing eco-technical products and offering ecologically oriented services. Parallel activities include providing training and employment for otherwise unemployed people.

Fields of activities are the development, planning, installation and maintenance of:

(a) solar-thermal water heating systems, etc.,

(b) photovoltaic equipment for the electricity generation,

(c) wind energy systems for generating electricity and operating water pumps,

(d) equipment for combined heat and power systems, etc.

The social objectives of *Atlantis* are training and social work, creating jobs in environmental fields and involving people in product development.

Atlantis trains women and men from different backgrounds for the ecological labour market. The training is tailored to practical work and is complemented by seminars in the subjects of environment/energy and work. In addition, social workers offer counselling and help with personal problems and work conflicts for employees.

Since being founded in 1989, *Atlantis* has created 450 new jobs in the Berlin borough of Kreuzberg and an additional 100 in Brandenburg. The subsidiary *Atlantis in Brandenburg* is based at the Centre Kesselberg (in Neu-Zittau) and operates on the model of *Atlantis* in Berlin; they produce botanical purification systems as well as a 37 kW wind turbine. Another branch is based in Potsdam and runs a car-sharing service.

Through training people who are involved in product development such as rotor blades for windmills, *Atlantis* not only provides development skills but also tries to open up new markets (which are however predominantly market niches). It also promotes SME development to a limited extent and is thus involved in restructuring the local economy.

In 1994 it started an *Arbeitsförderbetrieb* (employment promotion enterprise) in Berlin-Kreuzberg in order retain its income and reinvest surpluses in the company. Fifty employees manufacture solar power equipment and wind energy systems, conduct projects to save energy in public buildings, and operate a catering service.

Atlantis is financed by regional and European employment and environmental promotion schemes and (via its *Arbeitsförderbetrieb*) by its own sales income. As *Atlantis* sees it, its state support reduces the social costs of unemployment and of the destruction of the environment and is thus an investment for the future. *Atlantis* has shown that from a fiscal perspective, cost-effective jobs for the unemployed can be created and result in considerable social and ecological benefits. Unfortunately by the beginning of 1999, this social enterprise went bankrupt because of liquidity problems which were caused – besides other reasons – by delayed payments of ABM money from the Employment Exchange Office.

Zukunft Bauen e.V.

Since 1983, *Zukunft Bauen e.V.*, a self-help enterprise, has been developing projects in the West Berlin. It started as a registered association (e.V.) in the borough of Wedding and has established two subsidiaries (*Zukunftsbau gGmbH* and *L.I.S.T. gGmbH*), operating in four further boroughs in East Berlin. With 12 projects, *Zukunft Bauen* provides the following services:

(a) vocational training/qualification;

(b) housing rehabilitation, management and supply;

(c) social care and counselling.

Formerly, these services were for a group of socially excluded young people (from the squatters' movement) but they now take in young families with low incomes, single parents and other disadvantaged young people, most of them without any school certificates.

The social objectives of the projects are:

(a)   improving the situation of disadvantaged groups and their livelihoods,

(b)   improving the quality of life in urban neighbourhoods,

(c)   the long-term stabilisation of the so target groups.

The goal of *Zukunft Bauen* is to give disadvantaged young people work, training and income for a three-year period to enable them to work on the 'first labour market' afterwards and to live independent of social security benefits. From 370 persons employed currently, there are skilled project staff (social workers, trainers, supervisors etc.) and six managing directors, all of them in permanent positions.

Since it began, *Zukunft Bauen* has managed to organise an internal democratic structure for decision-making based on a core workforce and the management staff. In recent times, particularly since the workforce has more than doubled in size, a new model is under discussion.

The *Zukunft Bauen* project combine operates with 30 different sources of finance, mainly subsidies and *Pflegesätze* (fees for social care and supervision determined by social welfare and juvenile legislation) from the social services and youth affairs departments of the boroughs and the Berlin senate. The employees do not work on the basis of employment support schemes like ABM. However, 25% of the annual turnover comes from the project combine's own economic activities, especially in the areas of building and renovating houses.

References

Aaronowitz, S. and DiFazio, W. (1994), *The Jobless Future. Sci-tec and the Dogma of Work*, University of Minnesota Press, Minneapolis and London, pp. 37–40.

BAG (*Bundesarbeitsgemeinschaft Arbeit e.V.*) (1994), *Aufgaben und Ziele von Beschäftigungsgesellschaften. Grundsatzpositionen der BAG Arbeit*, BAG-Arbeit, Berlin.

BAG (*Bundesarbeitsgemeinschaft Arbeit e.V.*) (Hrsg.) (1996), *Qualitätssicherung und Innovation – Zukunftschancen von Beschäftigungs-, Qualifizierungs- und Vermittlungsgesellschaften. Jahrestagung der BAG am 2. und 3. Mai 1996 in der Evangelischen Akademie Hofgeismar*, BAG-Arbeit, Berlin.

Baur, M. and Kühnert, U. (1996), 'Arbeitsfördergesellschaften im Land Brandenburg und ihr Beitrag im Strukturwandel', in: *WSI-Mitteilungen*, Jg. 49, H. 3.

Beywl, W., Helmstädter, W. and Wiedemeyer, M. (1992), 'Arbeitsförderungsgesellschaften in den neuen Bundesländern. Perspektiven einer strukturellen Reform', *HBS-Manuskripte*, no. 89, Düsseldorf.

Beywl, W., Helmstädter, W. and Wiedemeyer, M. (1993), 'In die beschäftigungspolitische Abseitsfalle? Die Gesellschaften zur Arbeitsförderung, Beschäftigung und Strukturentwicklung in den neuen Bundesländern', in *Politik und Zeitgeschichte*, vol. 35, pp. 31–39.

Birkhölzer, K. (1993), 'Lokale Strategien zur Beschäftigungs- und Strukturpolitik in Krisenregionen', in *Regionale Arbeitsmärkte und Arbeitsmarktpolitik in den neuen Bundesländern, IAB-Mitteilungen*, Nürnberg.

Birkhölzer, K. (1999), 'Local economic development: a European-wide movement towards more economic democracy and social justice', *Local Economy 1*, 1999, edited by Local Economic Policy Unit, London, pp. 43–54.

Birkhölzer, K. (1999), 'A philosophical rationale for the promotion of local economic initiatives', in A. Twelvetrees (ed), *Community Economic Development: Rethoric or Reality?*, Community Development Foundation, London, pp. 15–22.

Birkhölzer, K. (1999), 'Development dilemmas in Berlin and the eastern part of Germany', in A. Twelvetrees (ed), *Community Economic Development: Rethoric or Reality?*, Community Development Foundation, London, pp. 278–286.

Birkhölzer, K. and Lorenz, G. (1997), *The Role of Partnerships in Promoting Social Cohesion. National Report on Germany*, Working Paper Series, The European Foundation, Dublin.

Birkhölzer, K. and Lorenz, G. (1998), 'Germany', in C. Borzaga and A. Santuari (eds), *Social Enterprises and New Employment in Europe*, Regione Autonoma Trentino-Adige, Trentino, pp. 255–279.

Birkhölzer, K. *et al.* (1990), *IFP Lokale Ökonomie. Zusammenfassung der Forschungsergebnisse*, Berlin.

Birkhölzer, K. *et al.* (1994), *Beschäftigungs- und Strukturpolitik in Krisenregionen. Ein internationales Symposion*, Berlin.

Birkhölzer, K. *et al.* (1997), *The Contribution of Social Enterprises to Community Economic Development. Country reports from Britain, Germany, France, Italy, Sweden and Spain*, European Network for Economic Self-help and Local Development/TechNet, Berlin.

Bonas, I. (1996), 'Neue Unternehmenskultur: Soziale Unternehmen in Deutschland', Beitrag auf der Fachkonferenz 11-12.5.1995 beim Europäischen Parlament in Brüssel, in *Handlungsstrategien gegen Arbeitslosigkeit, Armut und soziale Ausgrenzung aufg regionaler und lokaler Ebene*, Dokumentation, TRION, Hamburg, pp. 72–81.

Bosch, G. and Neumann, H. (Hrsg.) (1991), *Beschäftigungsplan und Beschäftigungsgesellschaft*, Köln.

Breede, W., Cremer, D. and Winters, E. (1983), *Hochschule und Betriebe. Darstellungen, Analysen, Erfahrungsberichte am Beispiel der Produktionsstätte AEG-Brunnenstraße*, Technische Universität Berlin, Berlin.

Brinkmann, Ch. (1995), 'Arbeitsmarktpolitik in Ostdeutschland. Eine Zwischenbilanz nach 5 Jahren Transformation', in *Beschäftigungsobservatorium Ostdeutschland*, 16/17, pp. 4–9.

Bullmann, U. (1991), *Kommunale Strategien gegen Massenarbeitslosigkeit. Ein Einstieg in die sozialökologische Erneuerung*, Opladen.

Bullmann, U., Cooley, M. and Einemann, E. (1986), *Lokale Beschäftigungsinitiativen. Konzepte, Praxis, Probleme*, Marburg.

Bundesministerium für Wirtschaft (BMWi) (Hrsg.) (1994), *Standort Deutschland. Auftrag Zukunft*.

European Network for Economic Self-Help and Local Development (ed.) (1997), *Community Economic Development and Social Enterprises. Experiences, Tools and Recommendations*, 16 pages, Technologie-Netzwerk, Berlin.

Fischer, H. and Helmstädter, W. (1995), 'Arbeitsförderungsgesellschaften im Land Brandenburg. Stellung und Strategie im arbeitsmarktlichen Konzept', in *Arbeit und Sozialpolitik*, Jg. 49, Heft 3/4.

Freidinger, G. and Schulze-Böing, M. (Hrsg.) (1993), *Handbuch der kommunalen Arbeitsmarktpolitik*, Marburg.

Gesamtberliner Landesregierung von Senat und Magistrat (Senat und Magistrat) (1990), *Bericht über die Lage der Berliner Wirtschaft*, 19, Senatsverwaltung für Wirtschaft, Berlin.

Gesellschaft zur Information und Beratung örtlicher Beschäftigungsinitiativen und Selbsthilfegruppen gGmbH (GIB) (Hrsg.) (1995), *Soziale Betriebe* (*GIB-Info*, November 1995).

Grass, B. (1993), 'Beschäftigungs- und Qualifizierungsgesellschaften. Bericht einer Wiederholungsbefragung in den neuen Bundesländern', in *HBS-Manuskripte*, 104, Düsseldorf.

Hanesch, W. *et al.* (1994), *Armut in Deutschlan*, Der Armutsbericht des DGB und des dpw, Reinbek b. Hamburg

Hildebrandt, R. (1997), 'Der Sozialstaat ist ernsthaft in Gefahr', in *Der Tagesspiegel*, no. 83 (3.2.97).

Institut für Arbeitsmarkt- und Berufsforschung (IAB) (1996), 'Informationen aus dem IAB', 17, Neue Bundesländer.

Kaiser, M. (n.d.), *Qualifizierungs- und Beschäftigungsinitiativen in der Bundesrepublik Deutschland. Herausforderungen an eine lokale Beschäftigungspolitik*, Manuscript, n.d.

Kaiser, M. (1992), *Gesellschaften zur Arbeitsförderung, Beschäftigung und Strukturförderung (ABS-Gesellschaften) als Träger arbeitsmarktpolitischer Maßnahmen*, IAB-Werkstattbericht, no. 10, Nürnberg.

Kaluza, H., Pollmeyer, B. and Tehler, G. (1991), *Kommunale/regionale Arbeitsmarkt- und Beschäftigungspolitik. Ein Leitfaden für die Praxis*, Bremen.

Kisker, K.-P. and Heine, M. (1987), *Wirtschaftswunder Berlin?*, Berlin.

Knuth, M. (1994), *Zwei Jahre ABS-Gesellschaften in den Neuen Bundesländern. Ergebnisse einer schriftlichen Befragung im November 1993*, Institut Arbeit und Technik, Wissenschaftszentrum Nordrhein-Westfalen, Gelsenkirchen.

Knuth, M. (1995), 'ABS-Gesellschaften zwischen Abbau und Aufbau', in *WSI-Mitteilungen*, H. 7/95.

Knuth, M. (1996), *Drehscheiben im Strukturwandel. Agenturen für Mobilitäts-, Arbeits- und Strukturförderung*, Berlin.

König, D., Krüger, H. and Schröder, U. (1987), *Eine Zeitlang gehöre ich dazu. ABM und zweiter Arbeitsmarkt*, Hamburg.

Landesgesellschaft zur Beratung und Information von Beschäftigungsinitiativen (LaBIB) (1994), *Soziale Betriebe. Vom Plan zur Tat. Bausteine für die Betriebsgründung*, Hannover.

Langkau, J. (1990), 'Die Zukunft selbst gestalten: Beschäftigungs- und Qualifizierungsgesellschaften in der Phase der wirtschaftlichen Neuordnung', *Wirtschaftspol. Diskurse*, 11, Bonn.

Lindner, H. *et al.* (1992), *Schaffung von Arbeitsplätzen für Sozialhilfeempfänger durch Beschäftigungsgesellschaften*, Gutachten im Auftrag des Bundesministeriums für Arbeit und Sozialordnung, Thüringen.

Lorenz, G. (1992), Europäische Strategien der alternativen und lokalen Ökonomie. Berlin 1992 (IFP Lokale Ökonomie, Heft 11).

Lorenz, G. (1995), *Zur Konzeption einer Socially Useful Economy. Die britische Debatte im Kontext der Strukturpolitik des Greater London Council 1981–1986*, vol. 2, Egelsbach/Frankfurt/St. Peter Port.

Lorenz, G. and Birkhölzer, K. (1997), 'Intermediate labour market initiatives in Germany'. in *Local Economy 2*, 1997, pp. 160–165.

Müller, Ch. (1992), *Beschäftigungsgesellschaften*, Bonn.

Priewe, J. and Hickel, R. (1991), *Der Preis der Einheit. Bilanz und Perspektiven der deutschen Vereinigung*, Frankfurt.

Schomacker, K., Wilke, P. and Wulf, H. (1987), *Alternative Produktion statt Rüstung. Gewerkschaftliche Initiativen für sinnvolle Arbeit und sozial nützliche Produkte*, Köln.

Senatsverwaltung für Arbeit und Frauen (Hrsg) (1994), *Arbeitsförderbetriebe für Berlin. Zwischen Zielgruppen- und Marktorientierung*, Regionale Arbeitsmarktpolitik, Berlin.

Stiftung Bauhaus Dessau; Europäisches Netzwerk für ökonomische Selbsthilfe und lokale Entwicklung (Hrsg.) (1996), *People's Economy – Wirtschaft von Unten. Approaches Towards a New Social Economy in Europe*, Stiftung Bauhaus Dessau, Dessau.

Wainwright, H. and Elliott, D. (1982) *The Lucas Plan. A New Trade Unionism in the Making?*, Allison and Busby Ltd., London.

Periodicals:

Beschäftigungsobservatorium Ostdeutschland, Hrsg.: Europäische Kommission, Generaldirektion Beschäftigung, Arbeitsbeziehungen und soziale Angelegenheiten (Wissenschaftszentrum Berlin).

DIW-Wochenbericht, Wochenbericht des Deutschen Instituts für Wirtschaftsforschung, Berlin.

IAB-Werkstattberichte, Hrsg.: Institut für Arbeitsmarkt- und Berufsforschung der Bundesanstalt für Arbeit, Nürnberg.

Informationen aus dem IAB (Neue Bundesländer), Hrsg.: Institut für Arbeitsmarkt- und Berufsforschung der Bundesanstalt für Arbeit, Nürnberg.

Was Nun? Erfahrungen und Informationen aus Arbeitsförderungsgesellschaften und Projekten, Hrsg.: PAULA e.V., Berlin.

Wirtschaftsbulletin Ostdeutschland, Hrsg.: Hans-Böckler-Stiftung, Düsseldorf.

8 Italy: The Impressive Development of Social Co-operatives in Italy

CARLO BORZAGA *

1. Evolution of the Labour Market and Employment Policies in Italy

Since 1973, Italy, like most developed countries, has seen its employment situation deteriorate almost uninterruptedly. The unemployment rate, which at the end of the 1960s had settled at around 3.5–4.0%, progressively rose to 12% in the mid-1980s. After falling to 7.5% in the period 1986–91, the rate rose rapidly to its present 12%. As in other countries, this increased rate of unemployment in Italy has been due both to a slowdown in the growth of employment – attenuated until the early 1980s by the *Cassa Integrazione Guadagni* (Redundancy Fund) – and to an increase in the female activity rate, that has been only in part off-set by a decline in the male rate.

However, in order to understand certain specific aspects of the Italian case one should bear in mind that, at the time when rates of output growth began to slow down after the first oil crisis, Italy was the European country with the lowest rate of economic activity and therefore, independently of the unemployment rate, it had a lower proportion of its population in employment compared to other European countries. Since this difference of activity rates was mainly due to a low female activity rate, one may note that in Italy, at the beginning of the 1970s, the majority of the labour force was made up of men in the middle age range. This helps explain certain features of the Italian labour market, and in particular the high degree of protection afforded to the employed, due both to the efforts of the trade

* The author is grateful to the *Consorzio Gino Mattarelli* and the *Istituto Nazionale della Previdenza Sociale* (INPS) for providing the data and to Flaviano Zandonai for his work in processing them. I also wish to thank J. Defourny for his helpful comments. I alone am responsible for any errors or omissions.

181

unions and to the laws regulating the labour market, above all the *Statuto dei Lavoratori* (Workers' Statute). The increase in activity rates in the labour market, where the employed have enjoyed special protection, has made entry to the labour market difficult, thus leading to unemployment rates of women and young people higher than in other European countries. As a result youth unemployment became the principal target of labour policies in the late 1970s and early 1980s.

Principal among these policies were the following: at the national level, subsidised work/training contracts, and the introduction of greater flexibility in the management of occupational mobility and employment relations; and at the regional level, measures in support of enterprise creation.

The work/training contract, first introduced experimentally in 1978, was generally adopted in 1983 and subsequently was widely used, to the extent that in the period 1984–1990 the contracts approved accounted for more than 80% of job entrants.[1] This contract, restricted to young people aged between 16 and 29, lasts for two years, and provides for a reduction in social security contributions – total exemption in the early years and a 50% reduction subsequently – which in Italy amounts to about 30% of the gross wage. The massive use of this measure by firms, however, did not produce a net increase in employment, except to a rather modest extent during the years of recovery (1986–1991).

Several flexibility measures were introduced starting from the early 1980s. Their main aim was to reduce the degree of protection guaranteed to employees and to encourage their employment in other firms, thereby also reducing the public expenditure required to finance the *Cassa Integrazione Guadagni*.[2] Very limited and largely ineffectual, however, were attempts to reform and increase the efficiency of the employment services, which are still being organised as they were in the 1950s.

The combination of these two policies has facilitated the adoption by firms, especially the most innovative ones, of more selective human resource management practices for recruitment and labour turnover. Such initiatives have in fact been assisted, on entry by the training/work contracts and, on exit by early retirement policies and by the possibility of retiring after only 35 years of work. The result was a replacement of older

---

[1] This figure has been calculated by the author.
[2] A fundamental measure in this process was the reform of *Cassa Integrazione Guadagni* in 1993.

workers by young ones.³ At the same time, the high level of youth unemployment, even among highly educated and skilled young people, enabled firms to maintain production in the more developed regions in the north of the country, even during the economic recovery of the second half of the 1980s. As a consequence, the economic and occupational recovery did not induce firms to relocate to the southern regions and did not generate new migratory flows from the South.

The third employment policy was for measures in support of the creation of new firms. With the exception of national-level measures in support of youth entrepreneurship in the Southern regions, this consisted mainly of a myriad of regional measures, all characterised by limited financial resources and therefore supporting often structurally fragile initiatives. However, this legislation is noteworthy for having benefited a number of local initiatives, including those for the work integration of disadvantaged people.

2. Labour Policies for Disadvantaged Workers

Public policies in support of the work integration of disadvantaged people implemented in Italy after the Second World War can be divided into two categories: those initiated by the government and those by the local administrations (regional, provincial and city councils). The former have worked in two areas: application of Law 482 of 1968 for persons in situations of greatest disadvantage, and recruitment incentive measures in favour of the relatively disadvantaged categories.

The first comprehensive measure in Italy to help people with occupational difficulties was Law 482 of 1968, designed to promote the employment of civilian invalids, including the disabled, widows and war orphans. This law established a quota system that required firms and public bodies with more than 35 employees to hire a quota of disabled people equal to 15% of the overall workforce. However, from the beginning, Law 482 has been applied bureaucratically and half-heartedly, and it has been largely ineffectual. In subsequent years the effectiveness of this law was more and more conditioned by numerous factors:

---

³ Some calculations of the numbers of adult workers replaced by young workers are contained in Borzaga (1993), and in Contini and Rapiti (1994).

(a)   rapid changes in the labour market after 1973–74 and in particular the reduction of manpower in medium-large firms and its increase in small firms not subject to the quota system,

(b)   the growing number of large firms in crisis or restructuring and therefore exempt from the quota system,

(c)   job placement agencies frequently mismatching worker's occupational characteristics and the type of job offered by firms (Buzzi, 1991),

(d)   the lack of training of most of the disabled registered at the job placement agencies,

(e)   the resistance of firms (especially to hiring those with mental disabilities), and the consequent widespread evasion of the law.

As a consequence, the rate of unemployment of those entitled to being hired under law 482 of 1968 was 37% in 1982 and had risen to 50% during the 1990s.

After several unsuccessful attempts, the Parliament reformed the law in 1999.[4] The new law reduces the quota of the disable workers firms with more than 50 employees must employ from 15% to 7%, but requires firms with 15–35 employees to employ one disadvantaged worker and firms with 35–50 employees to employ two disadvantaged workers. The law also provides for several incentives to the firms and creates a specific fund to finance these incentives and any other innovative practices in favour of the employment of disable workers. The new law will come into force in January 2000.

Given the limited effectiveness of national legislation, regional governments attempted to remedy the situation with their own laws, especially during the 1980s. These laws introduced incentives for firms undertaking to respect the quotas, promoted vocational training for the disabled, and financed forms of sheltered employment and work-integration initiatives. However, these regional measures also proved to be largely ineffective.

In addition, since the policies implemented by the local administrations differ in their objectives, in the amount of resources allocated and in the instruments used, their effects are unevenly distributed across the country, with marked disadvantages in the southern regions. Due to the local administrations' lack of jurisdiction over employment issues, the principal limitation of these policies is that they are conceived of as

---

[4] The new law is n. 68 of 1999.

social and welfare policies rather than labour market policies. They therefore address only those whose disadvantaged position in the labour market is due to disability or severe marginalisation, thus excluding those in long-term unemployment because of a lack of schooling, vocational skills or work socialisation.

3.   Birth and Growth of Social Co-operatives

The first social co-operatives, which were free private initiatives, appeared at the end of the 1970s; they were designed to overcome the shortcomings of public policies, by creating paid jobs for disabled people who would otherwise be difficult to employ via the quota system. The promoters of these first co-operatives were groups of Catholic volunteers motivated by a belief in the importance of social commitment, as well as groups of parents and groups of practitioners in search of social policies as alternatives to institutional ones. A decisive boost to the growth of the co-operative formula came with the law concerning people with mental illness, which reduced the number of them institutionalised in mental hospitals: since the quota system did not apply to the mentally ill, their only chances of employment lay in sheltered employment and social co-operatives.

The spread of social co-operatives, moreover, was part of the broader development of the non-profit sector (Borzaga, 1991; Barbetta, 1996) intended to provide social and welfare services as alternatives or supplementary to public services. In fact, alongside the work-integration social co-operatives, other co-operatives and voluntary organisations that offered welfare services were created and grew. Many co-operatives offered a combination of both welfare services and work integration.

However, the use of the co-operative formula for this kind of activity encountered a number of difficulties. These were due mainly to the predominant interpretation of the concept of mutual assistance, which the Italian legislation on co-operatives interpreted in the narrow sense as restricted to a single category of members only, and to the consequent difficulty of justifying the presence in the membership not only of the disadvantaged workers but also of volunteers, often in substantial numbers. These difficulties slowed down the development of the phenomenon in provinces where the Courts applied the mutual assistance principle most strictly. This resulted in pressures to adapt the legislation on co-operatives.

After wending its way through parliament, in 1991 a law was passed that gave specific recognition and a regulatory framework for social co-operatives. Confirming what had been achieved in previous years, law 381 of 1991 acknowledged social co-operation to be an instrument for the pursuit not of the members' interests but of the community's general interest in human enhancement and the social integration of citizens, and consequently accepted that both voluntary members (up to a maximum of 50%) and members using the services delivered by the co-operative could be part of its membership, in addition to worker members.

The law distinguished between two types of social co-operative – those delivering social, health and educational services, and those providing work integration for disadvantaged people – indicating that the two ends could not be pursued jointly by the same society.[5] The law therefore specified that 'disadvantaged persons' were certain well-defined categories: those with physical or mental disabilities, drug addicts, alcoholics, minors from problem families, and prisoners on probation. At least 30% of the workforce employed in the work-integration social co-operative must belong to one of these categories and the disadvantaged workers, if possible, must be members of the co-operative. Decisions relating to hiring disadvantaged workers are taken by the co-operative itself, unless it has specific commitments to public bodies.

The law prescribed forms of tax relief for social co-operatives, and gave the disadvantaged workers employed in the work-integration co-operatives exemption from social security contributions. In addition, the work-integration social co-operatives have direct access to public contracts, initially without competition from other firms. This rule was immediately contested by the European Community because it was deemed in breach of the regulations on competition. The problem has been resolved by the law enacted on 24 January 1996 to implement the Community directive, article 20 of which establishes that the public administrations may include in its tender conditions a contractual obligation to use (employ) a pre-established percentage of disadvantaged people. Since it is unlikely that a for-profit firm will accept such a clause, the new law should work to the advantage of work-integration social co-operatives in a manner not substantially different from previously.

---

[5] This sharp distinction between the two types of social co-operative was probably due to the legislator's desire to clearly distinguish between initiatives aimed at work integration and those supplying welfare services; a distinction that was not made in many social co-operatives and sheltered employment initiatives.

In contrast to what has happened in a number of European countries, the facilities granted to work-integration co-operatives have not provoked objections or accusations of unfair competition by the employers' associations. Indeed, at least so far, the growth of the non-profit and social co-operation sector has been viewed positively by private firms as a way of reducing the state's presence in the economy. Experiments have been conducted in some forms of collaboration, especially in management training for social co-operatives. As regards the work integration of disadvantaged people, an interesting experimental agreement is that between employers' associations and the provincial consortium of social co-operatives in Treviso. This agreement was approved by the Ministry of Labour and provides that firms guaranteeing a given number of orders to work-integration social co-operatives may benefit from a reduction in the number of disabled workers that they are obliged to hire by law 482 of 1968. Despite several proposals being discussed in Parliament, the law 68 of 1999 did not state the possibility of using an agreement of this type in a more general way.

Approval of Law 381 of 1991 has accelerated the development of social co-operation in general, and of work-integration co-operatives in particular. And it has also helped to clarify objectives and organisational structures by rendering an obligatory separation between work-integration activities and social service delivery. The law has also been followed by regional support laws and by the stipulation of a collective work agreement, which has introduced forms of wage and work-time flexibility for people taking part in work integration. This work contract provides that the working hours of disadvantaged workers may initially be much lower than the normal amount and may be gradually increased as the worker acquires the necessary skills. Moreover, the contract states that the starting wages of disadvantaged workers may be lower, even by up to 50%, than those of other workers, and that they must reach the level of the latter within a certain number of years (usually three years). Furthermore, some regional laws provide that some groups of disadvantaged workers, especially the disabled, may work in social co-operatives for limited periods of time (6–12 months) receiving work-grants directly from the regional government.

Approval of the law has also promoted the full recognition of social co-operation by the Italian co-operative movement, and therefore its full integration into the movement. Today, as well as being represented in the main Co-operative Associations, social co-operation is organised into local consortia in over one-third of the Italian provinces and these in turn belong to a national consortium. At their respective levels, the consortia perform all the functions for which individual co-operatives lack the resources: general contracting, training, social policy proposals, research and development, promotion, assistance and consultation. Both social services and work-integration co-operatives belong to the local consortia.

The policies adopted by the local authorities have also encouraged, though often haphazardly, the development of work-integration co-operatives, in terms of both quantity and efficiency. In particular, the following factors have been important in influences on the numbers and strength of initiatives: the grants paid to encourage the start-up of new schemes and to boost existing ones; measures designed to reduce the labour cost of work entrants; and the prioritisation of co-operatives in the allocation of public works contracts. The efficiency of such measures has been enhanced by the increasingly close – though not always straightforward – links between Employment Agencies and co-operatives.

4.   Variety of Models

As they were formed to meet the needs of people with different characteristics and problems, and promoted by members of diverse entrepreneurial culture and professional skills, and due to the lack of precise regulations until the 1991, the social co-operatives for work integration are markedly heterogeneous. Their principal differences are concerned with:

(a)   legal form: although law 381 sharply distinguishes between social co-operatives supplying social services and social co-operatives for work integration, there are still some co-operatives that engage in both;

(b)   the composition of the membership: in some cases this consists of both volunteers and workers or workers and users, in others only of worker members, in still others only of the users' relatives;

(c)   types of workers involved in work integration: in some cases they all belong to the same category of disadvantaged people, in other cases they are mixed;

(d)   objectives: some co-operatives, especially those operating with disabled people, run themselves as enterprises intending to provide stable integration of these workers into the co-operative's activities, maximising their productivity in order to stay in the market even with this particular type of disadvantaged workforce; while others seek to integrate disadvantaged workers into open employment after a period of training.

This latter aspect is of particular interest. Without denying the validity of both objectives, and while maintaining that in both cases social co-operatives should provide substantial training, the more interesting and innovative formula seems to be the one that seeks subsequently to integrate disadvantaged workers into open employment. Whereas the former type of co-operative differs from traditional forms of sheltered employment only because it is – at least in theory – able to pay disadvantaged workers better, the second fills a major gap in Italian policies for the work entry of disadvantaged people – that of 'on-the-job training'. It is well-known that one of the shortcomings of the obligatory quota system was the lack of training for disadvantaged workers – and after massive technical progress in all productive sectors, this is even more so today. These difficulties cannot be overcome in all cases by school training schemes or by short periods of training in firms, since neither of these approaches is able to provide general skills, like the ability to concentrate for long periods, the capacity to handle stress, relational skills, and the capacity for independent decision-making. These abilities are learnt more easily and better through direct work experience, especially if it is combined with specifically targeted training.

5. Social Co-operation for Work Integration: Features and Results

In recent years in Italy, a number of research studies have examined social co-operation in general and work-integration social co-operatives in particular (Borzaga, 1988, 1994). An idea of the size and features of the phenomenon can be drawn from the following data, provided by the National Institute of Social Security (INPS) and from two postal surveys carried out in 1993 (*Consorzio Gino Mattarelli*, 1994) and in 1996 (*Consorzio Gino Mattarelli*, 1997).

According to information provided by INPS – to which the work-integration co-operatives must report the hiring of disadvantaged workers receiving relief on social security contributions – at the end of 1998 the number of work-integration co-operatives amounted to 1,463 and employed 11,319 disadvantaged workers out of a total labour force of 23,104 employees. Table 8.1 summarises the evolution of the number and employment levels of work-integration co-operatives since 1993, i.e. two years after approval of law 381. However, one should not be misled by the sustained growth between 1993 and 1994, given that the figures refer both to new co-operatives and to those that regularised their position in that period by notifying INPS of disadvantaged workers hired or by separating work-integration activity from the delivery of social services. More realistic data on growth is that registered between 1994 and 1998. The employment results of the work-integration co-operatives are good, particularly considering the fact that, in the same period, the number of employees enrolled on the obligatory placement registers (under law 482 of 1968) diminished.

The figures on the number of disadvantaged employees set out in Table 8.1, however, do not account for all the integration activity performed by co-operatives. Many co-operatives employ people on work-integration projects who do not receive regular wages but do receive contributions from public bodies (work grants, apprenticeships, etc.). These people are not included in Table 8.1.

Table 8.1   Social co-operatives for work integration: 1993–1998

	1993	1994	1995	1996	1998
Number of co-operatives	287	518	705	754	1463
Annual rate of growth (%)		80.5	36.1	6.9	39.3
Total employment	4501	7115	9837	11,165	23,104
Annual rate of growth (%)		58.1	38.3	13.5	43.8
Disadvantaged workers employed	1675	3204	4686	5414	11,319
Annual rate of growth (%)		91.3	46.2	15.54	4.6
Employees by co-operative	15.7	13.7	13.9	14.8	15.8
Disadvantaged workers by co-operative	5.8	6.2	6.6	7.2	7.7
Disadvantaged workers in total workforce (%)	37.2	45.0	47.6	48.5	49.0

Source: National Institute of Social Security (INPS).

The average work-integration co-operatives is rather small with 13–15 employees, including an average of 5–6 disadvantaged workers; their percentage of the total workforce is above the minimum fixed by the law but still lower than 50%.

In 1996[6] most co-operatives (63.7%) had between 31% and 60% of disadvantaged workers in the total workforce. (If supported employment is classified as those co-operatives with percentages of disadvantaged workers higher than 70%, then in both 1993 and 1996 they formed a distinct minority – respectively 11.7% and 16.4%.)

It is also interesting to analyse the distribution of total workers and the number of disadvantaged workers in work-integration co-operatives. Although a small number of co-operatives have more than 50 employees, the majority are medium-to-small in size and employ fewer than 15 disadvantaged workers. Many of the larger co-operatives were set up following the closure of the psychiatric hospitals and employ workers with mental disabilities.

Work-integration co-operatives are not distributed uniformly across the country. They are strongly concentrated in the northern regions, and especially in areas characterised by large numbers of small firms. It is in these areas of great entrepreneurial dynamism, low unemployment rates and strong social cohesion, that the spontaneous phenomenon of social co-operation has found fertile ground for development. Moreover, trends towards production decentralisation have enabled the work-integration co-operatives to grow and consolidate by becoming subcontractors of firms in their area. Finally, the greater sensitivity of regional administrations and municipalities to the work situation of disadvantaged people has guaranteed support for co-operatives, and this has often resulted in these local bodies allocating contracts to the co-operatives (for maintenance of public buildings, green areas, the collection and recycling of waste, etc.). It should also be noted that approval of law 381 has stimulated the formation of work-integration co-operatives in the southern regions, as evidenced by the growth registered between 1993 and 1996 (from eight to 53 co-operatives).

The postal surveys conducted by *Conzorzio Gino Mattarelli* in 1993 and 1996 were based on addresses compiled by the two main national associations *(Lega and Confederazione delle Co-operative)*. The questionnaire was returned by 110 work-integration co-operatives in 1993, and by 138 in 1996. The figures set out below refer only to these co-operatives and provide comparative data from both surveys. The findings (Table 8.2) substantially confirm the results of the analysis of the INPS data until 1996. However, it should be noted that the co-operatives replying

---

[6] The fact that, in 1993, 34.4% of co-operatives had workforces comprising less than 30% of disadvantaged workers confirms that in that year the regularisation process was still under way and that it was practically completed by 1996.

to the questionnaire have a lower percentage of disadvantaged workers than the figures drawn from data on co-operatives as a whole (cf. Table 8.1).

Table 8.2 Work-integration co-operatives in 1993 and 1996 (survey by *Consorzio Gino Mattarelli*)

	1993	1996
No. co-operatives (responding)	110	138
Total employees	1387	3179
Disadvantaged workers	1095	1123
Employees per co-operative	12.6	23.0
Disadvantaged workers per co-operative	9.9	8.1
Disadvantaged workers in total workforce (%)	44.1	35.3
Total members*	5199	3808

* The co-operatives have some members who are neither workers (disadvantaged or not) nor volunteers, but who are simply interested in supporting or being involved with the co-operative. After the passing of Act no. 381 of 1991 the number of these has progressively declined.
Source: Consorzio Gino Mattarelli (1994, 1997).

The data confirm that the first social co-operatives were created towards the end of the 1970s and that they developed most strongly during the 1980s. This expansion has continued in recent years. It should also be stressed that most of the co-operatives answering the questionnaires had been in existence for more than five years (and some of them for more than ten years), and this demonstrates their ability to survive in the market.

Many co-operatives integrate people with various forms of disadvantage into work. However, the data confirm that the majority of the co-operatives replying to the questionnaires (see Table 8.3) are concerned with the work integration of the disabled or the mentally ill. These are followed, in order of importance, by marginalised adults, and prisoners, who, often only because of the opportunities offered by the co-operative, can serve sentences other than imprisonment. Between 1993 and 1996, however, there was a decline in the number of co-operatives engaged in the work integration of the physically disabled (from 33.4% to 19.8%), but an increased commitment to prisoners and drug addicts.

Table 8.3 Types of disadvantaged workers in social co-operatives

| | 1993 | | 1996 | |
	n	%	*n*	%
Disabled people	108	33.4	66	19.9
With mental disabilities	60	18.6	62	18.7
Teenagers	14	4.3	14	4.2
Prisoners	21	6.5	41	12.3
Drug addicts	48	14.9	62	18.7
Immigrants (non-EEC)	15	4.7	21	6.3
Disadvantaged adults and others	57	17.6	66	19.9
Total*	323	100.0	332	100.0

* The total is higher than the number of co-operatives in the samples because some co-operatives employ more than one type of disadvantaged worker.
Source: *Consorzio Gino Mattarelli* (1994, 1997).

Work integration is achieved mainly through environmental maintenance activities, in particular of public green spaces, often under contracts with public bodies, and subcontracted craft and assembly work, usually for industrial firms (see table 8.4). However, personal services (but not normally social services) are also widespread. The co-operatives' business therefore comprise the sales of products and services to both public bodies and private customers.

Table 8.4 Work-integration co-operatives by industry (% distribution) in 1996

Agriculture	19.3
Craft	19.3
Commercial services	13.8
Industry	9.4
Other services activities	38.2

Source: *Consorzio Gino Mattarelli* (1994, 1997).

Most of the social co-operatives, especially the older ones, had voluntary members who were regularly involved,[7] albeit contributing relatively low weekly working hours compared to that for worker members. Bearing in mind that the majority of volunteer members consisted of males in the central age range (35–55 years), engaged in indirect functions such as administration and finance, personnel management and training, it is

---

[7] Volunteers also include relatives of disadvantaged workers only if they work directly in the activities of co-operatives and without remuneration.

evident that their major contribution to the co-operative was entrepreneurship, often in support of a younger paid workforce.

6.   The Effectiveness of Work Integration

The quantitative data set out in the previous section are not enough to assess the effectiveness of social co-operatives. However, two more detailed studies, conducted on smaller samples, help to establish the match between objectives and results.

6.1.   The Individual Work-integration Experience in 33 Co-operatives

The first study is a survey conducted in 1994 on a sample of 33 social co-operatives operating in four regions of northern Italy. Most of these co-operatives are engaged in a single activity (64% of cases), largely in the following areas: maintenance of public and private green spaces, cleaning services, carpentry, farming, construction, and waste collection.

The income of the co-operatives studied are as a consequence rather differentiated. Averaged over the three years examined, the volume of sales can be broken down as follows: 53.6% from contracts with local administrations, 39.0% from contracts with private bodies, and 8.4% from public subsidies for work-integration initiatives. None of the co-operatives examined depended solely on income from public bodies.

On 31 December 1993, the number of people working in the co-operatives surveyed amounted to 751, of whom 375 were ordinary workers, 255 were disadvantaged workers, and 121 were volunteers. The number of disadvantaged workers and that of ordinary workers remained substantially the same during the three-year period considered, with a constant disadvantaged/total workers ratio of 42–44%.

Between 1991 and 1993 the percentage of disadvantaged people fully integrated into work increased;[8] and for the year 1993 the figure was above 24%. A job was found within the same co-operative in 63% of cases and in the open labour market in the remaining 37% of cases. In addition there was a fall in the incidence of work-integration failures, which in 1993 was below 15%.

---

[8] In the research, only the workers with a long term work contract or with a two-year training/work contract have been considered fully integrated into work.

Analysis of the data[9] on the characteristics of the disadvantaged workers shows that there was a markedly larger percentage of men (76%) than women (24%). Just over half (54%) were younger than 30, while more than 80% had only elementary school-leaving certificates. Almost all (88%) joined the co-operatives in the 1990s (particularly in 1992/3), with most coming from outside the normal labour market (67% of cases). The previously employed and/or unemployed accounted respectively for 12% and 20% of the entire sample. In terms of disadvantage, the largest group consisted of the disabled (119) – mainly those with mental disabilities (60% of cases) – followed by drug addicts (106).

The wages of the disadvantaged workers In the majority of cases, disadvantaged workers have been hired according to the provisions of the agreement between social co-operatives and trade unions (52.6%) or other types of employment contracts (7.6%), or on the basis of *ad hoc* contracts (19.0%). Of these 31.7% received a reduced wage (starting wage) as envisaged by the agreement. Only 3.3% of them received no form of remuneration at the beginning of the work-integration process, and only 17.4% received a lump-sum payment (work grant). Over time, the number of disadvantaged workers paid according to the social co-operative contract of employment has increased (to 67.0%), while the percentages of workers receiving lump-sum payments (7.9%) or no wage at all (0.8%) have diminished.

At the time of the interview, 41.9% of disadvantaged workers earned more than one million lire per month and therefore not much less than an ordinary worker, who earns an average of about one and a half million lire. While, 42.3% earned between 500,000 and 1 million lire, and only 15.6% earned less than 500,000 lire. However some disadvantaged workers do not receive wages at all, but receive a subsidy from the local authority (work grants); and for the first three years of work, the work contract for social co-operatives allows the payment of lower wages to low-productivity disadvantaged workers than that fixed by the contract.

Average working hours amounted to 30–32 hours per week. The working hours increased with the disadvantaged worker's length of service in the co-operative. It was higher for certain categories of worker (prisoners, the marginalised) and lower (*ca* 22–26 hours) for those with physical and mental disabilities.

---

[9] For each of the disadvantaged workers entering a co-operative in the period January 1991 to December 1993 a file-card was compiled to assess the characteristics and effectiveness of the work-integration process. A total of 466 file-cards were thus collected.

The situation of the workers at the end of the integration process The analysis of the degree of effectiveness of the integration process gives some interesting results.

Of the 466 disadvantaged employed by the co-operatives surveyed, At the end of December 1993, 32% were still undergoing work integration while the remainder, having completed the process, had either taken up stable employment with the co-operative (26%) or had left it (42%).

The main cause of them leaving – which occurred in most cases (55%) after just over 12 months with the co-operative – was dropping out of the integration scheme (50% of cases); on the other hand just over 44% left the co-operative because they had completed the scheme. Of those leaving the co-operative on completion of the integration scheme, 66% actively joined the labour market: 79% to take up employment while 21% were in search of work. There were very few cases of participants returning to inactive roles outside the labour market (15%).

This analysis provides one of the first assessments of the success of the work-integration process. Taking into account the number of participants achieving stable integrated within the co-operative (120) plus those gaining outside employment (46), but excluding those still taking part in integration, one may conclude that the work-integration process has had a positive outcome in 52% of cases. The figures relating to dropping out of the integration scheme and to the number of people unemployed or becoming inactive (122 subjects in total) show a 39% probability of failure.

A small number of 24 workers had to remain in the co-operative despite the fact that external work integration had been originally been envisaged for them. The failure to achieve the integration in the open labour market was due to either lack of opportunities arising or rejection by potential employers.

The average amount of time taken by the disadvantaged workers to complete the integration process and taking up stable employment in the co-operative, (based on figures for about 38% of those in stable employment) was 18 months.

The evolution of personal skills The survey finally attempted to assess the professional development of disadvantaged workers by analysing the development of the resources and skills required for performing a job. For this analysis, an experimental grid was constructed which enabled measurement of the development of the disadvantaged worker's occupational and social skills, covering the following areas:

(a) work skills

(b) cultural skills

(c) relational skills

(d) professional skills.

In the interviews, a five-point composite scale was used to analyse and assess each worker's skills both at the beginning and at the end of the integration process. Scoring was graduated as follows: none = 1, low = 2, medium = 3, medium-high = 4, high = 5.

The average level of the occupational skill possessed by disadvantaged workers on entry to the co-operative and calculated on all skill areas was 2.5 (Table 5). In terms of different skill area, the lowest scores were recorded for 'professional skills' area and for the ability to respect task execution and learning times.

Skill assessments were made on 31 December 1993 for those still undergoing work integration and, at the time of their departure from the co-operative, for the others who left the co-operative during the year; these reveal a general improvement in all the abilities considered.

The increase in the overall score from 2.5 to 3.1 (Table 8.5) highlights an improvement in the disadvantaged workers' ability from a low to an intermediate level. For none of the abilities, however, were medium-high levels of ability recorded. The best progress was made as regards skill in the use of tools, independence in the performance of tasks, and ability to respect task execution times.

Disadvantaged workers achieving stable employment in the co-operative, and particularly those who found employment in the open labour market, obtained higher-than-average scores. Those entering the external labour market possessed a medium-high ability to use tools and to socialise. Workers quitting the co-operative registered a lower level of professional development.

Analysis of the data in Table 8.5 using multinominal logic regression (Borzaga, 1996) shows that the probability of success in integrating disadvantaged workers into the co-operative or into the open labour market is positively influenced mainly by the abilities of disadvantaged workers entry to the co-operative, and by those abilities acquired during the integration process. However, the specific aims of the co-operative and the way in which its activities are organised also seem to influence the probability of success.

Table 8.5　Disadvantaged worker skills on entry to the co-operative and their development

	Beginning of process	Completion	Range of variation Min.	Max.
Work skills area	2.4	3.1	1	5
- respect for times	2.3	3.0	1	5
- respect for rules	2.6	3.1	1	5
Cultural skills area	2.5	3.1	1	5
- ability to learn	2.4	3.0	1	5
- ability to concentrate	2.5	3.1	1	5
- cultural ability	2.7	3.2	1	5
Relational skills area	2.8	3.3	1	5
- ability to socialise	2.8	3.3	1	5
Area of occupational skill	2.2	3.1	1	5
- ability to use tools	2.2	3.1	1	5
- ability to work independently	2.3	3.0	1	5
Overall	2.5	3.1	1	5

6.2. A Cost-Benefit Analysis

The second study, linked to a detailed cost-benefit analysis, was carried out in the county of Trento by the local *Agenzia del Lavoro*. It examined 115 disadvantaged workers involved in ten work-integration co-operatives between 1992 and 1995 (Marocchi, 1999). This survey is interesting because it assessed an experiment whereby the *Agenzia del Lavoro* met the expenses of co-operatives arising from training disadvantaged workers – specifically, part of the labour cost of both disadvantaged and ordinary workers who received on-the-job training, and the costs of hiring trainers.

Of the 115 disadvantaged workers examined, 87 had completed the work-integration programme. Of these, 43 (53%) found steady work, 32 in enterprises other than the co-operative, and the rest in the co-operative itself. Two-thirds of those who found permanent employment had been in work for at least two years. The work-integration programme lasted between 1.6 years for those who found work in ordinary firms, and 2.4 years for those who were hired on a permanent basis by the co-operative.

The cost-benefit analysis yielded distinctly positive results, even with very restrictive hypotheses. Even by taking account only of monetisable benefits and using diverse discount rates and hypotheses on the duration of the working lives of the work-integrated people, the cost-benefit analysis confirmed that the costs sustained by the *Agenzia* were entirely repaid in the form of higher taxes and social contributions, and that the disadvantaged workers and their families obtained greater benefits. However, the benefits obtained by the co-operatives were much more limited, indeed almost nil. This, though, is in line with their nature as non-profit organisations whose principal goal is not the accumulation of capital but maximisation of the number of people integrated into work.

In conclusion, the survey confirms that work-integration co-operatives have progressively consolidated and spread. They are able to achieve the goals that they set themselves adequately but not entirely. Bearing in mind the large number of disadvantaged workers involved and the satisfactory success rate, both in the improvement of work skills and in work integration, the co-operatives interviewed displayed at least three important shortcomings.

First, a rather limited ability to achieve entry of disadvantaged people into the open labour market on concluding their work-integration period. This is due to at least two factors: first, labour demand selectivity and the refusal by firms to hire disadvantaged workers even if they have previous experience of work in a co-operative; second, the absence of systematic relations between co-operatives and firms, and the inefficiency of the public job placement services. With the data available it is impossible to establish which of these factors is most influential.

Another weakness is the prevalence of production activities with extremely low technological and skill content; although this reduces the time taken by disadvantaged workers to reach adequate levels of productivity, it hampers their professional development.

Finally, the co-operatives still pay too little attention to the importance of enhancing the specific occupational skills of disadvantaged workers.

Some of the survey findings indicate that some co-operatives are organising themselves to overcome these limitations, in some cases with the help of the local consortium. However, if this is to be accomplished, the policies designed to support them need to be thought ever again.

7. Conclusions

Italian work-integration co-operatives seem sufficiently well-established in terms of both their numbers and the amount of disadvantaged workers in employment. They have obtained legal recognition, with the associated benefits of funding and reputation. And they have been able, although still only partially, to achieve the objective of the work integration of disadvantaged individuals. More specifically, work-integration co-operatives guarantee – in a relatively short time and for a significant percentage of disadvantaged people – greater employability through an effective improvement in their work skills and professional abilities so as to enable their stable reintegration into the labour market, although this still occurs too often within the co-operatives themselves.

This evolution of the work-integration co-operative is a real and evident innovation in the Italian labour and social policies; yet its potential has still not been fully grasped either by the economic policy-makers or, often, by the co-operatives themselves. The latter have in fact demonstrated that work can be a real alternative to welfare benefits and sheltered employment; and that it is possible to implement, in private and voluntary form, schemes that have to date been deemed workable only by public institutions or by the imposition of compulsory quotas.

Although the experimental phase has now been completed, the further strengthening of social co-operation is conditioned by numerous factors, both internal and external to co-operatives themselves. The key issue is the role to assign to these initiatives, which are still too closely tied to welfare policies. Their consequent marginalisation influences their qualitative and quantitative development, and reduces their interest to enterprises and economic and labour policy-makers. It is evident from the foregoing analysis that social co-operatives should also be attributed a role as an instrument of active employment policies. If this recognition is achieved, it may give rise to a number of positive outcomes.

The first of these positive outcomes would be a better specification of their objectives by the co-operatives themselves, given that they are still often unsure of their role, and a clarification of their relationships with the employment agencies. This would spur them to adopt a more entrepreneurial role, balance the mix of disadvantaged and normal workers to ensure a better economic performance, to improve relatively underdeveloped training activities and to gain access to employment incentives and facilities.

In this way the co-operatives could develop closer relationships with enterprises and workers' organisations; the success of work integration, in fact, depends on the possibility of establishing flexible contracts with the workers undergoing integration, and gaining trade union support; it also depends on relatively easy labour market re-entry by workers who have successfully completed the integration process – and to achieve this a good network of contacts with firms is necessary; in addition firms could help co-operatives by outsourcing work to them.

Another useful policy measure could be extending the typology of disadvantaged people eligible for work-integration initiatives to include certain categories of the long-term unemployed not affected by specific disabilities; this extension would increase the overall efficiency of such schemes.

Finally, the recognition of the economic value of the training activities conducted by work-integration co-operatives would make them eligible for training grants, including those provided by the European Community; and this would both strengthen social co-operatives and improve their commitment to training activities.

References

Barbetta, G.P. (ed.) (1996), *Senza scopo di lucro. Dimensioni economiche, storia, legislazione e politiche del settore nonprofit in Italia*, Il Mulino, Bologna.

Borzaga, C. (1988), 'La co-operazione di solidarietà sociale: prime riflessioni su un settore emergente', in *Sociologia del Lavoro*, no. 30–31, Angeli, Milano, pp. 266–301.

Borzaga, C. (1991), 'The Italian nonprofit sector. An overview of an undervalued reality', *Annals of Public and Co-operative Economic*, vol. 62, pp. 695–702.

Borzaga, C. (1993), 'Progresso tecnico, domanda di lavoro e disoccupazione: gli aspetti qualitativi. Un primo approfondimento', *Politiche del Lavoro*, no. 22–23, pp. 257–284.

Borzaga, C. (1994), 'La co-operazione sociale di inserimento lavorativo: un'analisi dell'efficacia e dei fattori di successo', *Rivista della Co-operazione*, no. 18, pp. 73–96.

Borzaga, C. (1996), 'Social co-operatives and work integration in Italy', *Annals of Public and Co-operative Economics*, 67-2, pp. 209–234.

Borzaga, C. (1999), 'Introduzione. La cooperazione sociale di inserimento lavorativo: quale ruolo e quali politiche di sostegno?', in G. Marocchi, *Integrazione lavorativa, impresa sociale, sviluppo locale. L'inserimento lavorativo in cooperative sociali di lavoratori svantaggiati come fattore di crescita dell'economia locale*, Franco Angeli, Milano.

Buzzi, C. (1991), 'Immagini e valutazioni del mondo imprenditoriale sull'inserimento lavorativo degli handicappati', *Impresa Sociale*, no. 1, pp. 28–34.

Consorzio Gino Mattarelli (1994), *Primo Rapporto sulla co-operazione sociale*, Edizioni Consorzio Gino Mattarelli, Milano.

Consorzio Gino Mattarelli (1997), *Secondo Rapporto sulla co-operazione sociale*, Edizioni CGM, Milano.

Contini, B. and Rapiti, F. (1994), 'Young in, Old out: nuovi pattern di mobilità nell'economia italiana', *Lavoro e Relazioni Industriali*, no. 3, pp. 20–56.

Marocchi, G. (ed.) (1999), *Integrazione lavorativa, impresa sociale, sviluppo sociale*, F. Angeli, Milano.

Organisation for Economic Co-operation and Development (1992), *Employment Policies for People with Disabilities. Report by an Evolutation Panel, Labour Market and Social Policy Occasional Papers*, no. 8, OECD, Paris.

9 Spain: A New Social Economy Still Inadequately Known and Recognised

ISABEL VIDAL[1]

1. Very High Unemployment and Limited Social Protection

The unemployment level in Spain is particularly high. In 1998 it stood at 19.36%, twice the European Union average. This high level is due first to the increase in the working population at the beginning of the 1980s, following the population explosion of the 1970s and the gradual appearance of women on the labour market. However, it is due above all to the inadequacy of the Spain economy to generate jobs.

Spain has a working population of 16.2 million people aged between 16 and 65 years and an activity rate of 63% (in 1998), the lowest of all the countries of the European Union. The lack of job prospects partly explains why young people and women are late entering the labour market.

Out of 3.1 million unemployed people, only 1.5 million received unemployment benefit in 1998 (49%). Women and young people are worst affected by unemployment. Although they delayed entering the labour market, in 1998 the level of unemployment among young people stood at 36% for the 16–24 age group, while unemployment among women reached 26%. These groups, having contributed less, draw little benefit from social policies.

1.1. The Inheritance of the Franco Era

To understand the context in which the policies aimed at fighting unemployment were born, it is necessary to take into account the main events in the development of social protection in Spain, at least as regards

[1] For writing this chapter, the author has received financial support of the R&D National Plan of the Science and Technology Inter-Ministerial Committee of the Spanish Government (SEC97-1309).

the guaranteed income. Compared with the other countries of Europe, this development occurred belatedly and at different speeds.

During the first 30 years of the 20th century, small-scale mechanisms were set up to provide protection in old age. The Second Republic (1931–1936) saw the first attempts to create a modern social security system, but the civil war put an end to this. The 1940s and 1950s saw the introduction of a few, fairly limited mutual social security systems. A genuine, modern system of social security finally emerged in the 1960s. However, there was still no efficient system of collecting the taxes and social security contributions necessary to finance the social security system.

The regulatory system under Franco was characterised by major state intervention in the economy and industrial relations. From the end of the 1950s, the state tried to combine modernisation and economic liberalisation on the one hand with the maintenance of social order on the other. One fundamental component of this strategy was the principle of job security, based mainly on substantial protection for workers faced with arbitrary redundancy.

The principle of stability became the central axis of labour law. Widespread continuous and stable employment acted as a functional substitute for a system of social benefits which remained under-developed for many years. No universal system of a guaranteed minimum income was established independently of participation in the labour market and the prior payment of contributions by workers.

In such a situation, the state contributed to the rigidity of the labour market and tolerated the establishment of a system of salary supplements within companies themselves. These mechanisms offset the inadequacies of the social benefit system and the employment policy took on the functions of the social policy. In other words, public guarantees of stable employment reflected the inadequacy of the welfare state under Franco. According to Gonzalez and Calvet,[2] the system ruled over by Franco was no more than a 'proto social state'.

1.2. Modernising Social Policies

Lessenich[3] believes that the distribution of roles between the state and the market and the configuration of social rights in Spain have undergone fundamental changes over the past 20 years. Spanish society has moved on

---

[2] Gonzalez and Calvet (1991).
[3] Lessenich (1996).

from 'despotic corporatism'[4] to a democratic and pluralist political system and therefore from a system based on an authoritarian guarantee to one of concerted deregulation.

As of 1976, Spanish social policies were characterised by an increasing desire for 'modernisation'. Liberalisation and democratisation spread to the labour market. The state reduced its level of interventionism and built up a legislative framework within which interest groupings could be organised. It also gradually passed the regulation of industrial relations over to the regional governments.

The 1970s was also a period of transition from a situation of full employment to that of a rise in the level of unemployment, accompanied by the need to create and develop the financial mechanisms needed to cover social expenditure. These mechanisms took shape at the end of the 1970s and developed rapidly during the 1980s, a period when the state of the Autonomous Communities was created. The Spanish state is now made up of 17 Autonomous Communities that are responsible for the administration of employment policy, while the central administration retains the tasks of devising and financing this policy. However, some of the autonomous governments plan and regulate employment promotion measures that are financed by their own budgets and reserved for citizens living in their territory.

However, financial restrictions led to various reforms of the normative employment framework (*Ley Basica de Empleo*, 1980). The first of these, which was a general reform, took place in 1984 and was followed by partial amendments. As from January 1994, the reduction of social cover was confirmed by new provisions aimed at reducing the expenditure incurred by unemployment. This has led to a fall in the number of people on benefit, thus breaking the rising trend recorded since 1988. In point of fact, all these reforms have tightened the conditions governing entitlement to unemployment benefit and reduced the amount of the benefit compared with the worker's previous salary.

So what happens to unemployed people who are excluded from the benefit measures provided for at national level? Social services systems run by the municipal authorities and subsequently the governments of the Autonomous Communities developed substantially in the 1980s. General guidance services were set up as a third line of protection alongside those of social security (on a contribution basis) and social assistance.

---

[4] Sarasa and Moreno (1973).

When the first European Community proposals regarding a guaranteed minimum income appeared in 1988, all the countries of the European Union already had specific legislation with the exception of Spain, Greece and Portugal. As of this date, Spain took various initiatives to make good this deficiency. A minimum family income system was set up in the Basque region in 1989. Over the next two years, similar provisions, bearing different names and governed by different criteria, were adopted in the other Autonomous Communities. However, the national government did not reinforce the initiatives of the Autonomous Communities or establish a new framework guaranteeing the equality of all Spaniards before the law. Thus it did not envisage the possibility of integrating these minimum income systems into the national social security system for those who do not pay contributions to this system.

The situation on the labour market and the reductions in protection against unemployment have provoked a flood of people or families seeking a minimum income from the social services. In other words, the marginal groups of the population threatened with exclusion are currently increasing sharply.

However, unlike other more advanced societies, extreme poverty in Spain is tempered by very widespread family solidarity and highly developed forms of black economy which soften the effects of unemployment. But the transition from a rural society to an urban society, the arrival of women on the labour market and the increase in the number of poor single-parent families are all signs that Spanish society is moving towards the general model of economic and social development in the most industrialised countries in Europe.

2. The Response of the Social Economy to the Employment Crisis

In the fight against unemployment, the rare active policies of the Spanish state are based on the social economy in the broad sense of the term, that is chiefly associated workers' co-operatives (*cooperativas de trabajo asociado*), workers' limited companies (*sociedades anonimas laborales –* SALs), associations and foundations.

2.1. Associated Workers' Co-operatives and SALs

During the second half of the 1970s, a period that coincided with a sharp rise in unemployment and a poor protection system, workers rediscovered workers' limited companies. These were recognised in 1986, ten years after they first appeared. Unemployed people and those with poor job security used SALs and associated workers' co-operatives, along with various forms of self-employed work, as formulas likely to provide them with an income to meet their needs.

However, during the 1980s, the development of the policy of unemployment benefit partly overshadowed the leading role of associated workers' companies in the creation and preservation of jobs. Workers' motivation to create or maintain a job declined when they were offered the guarantee of unemployment benefit. The main measure in the active employment policy during the 1980s was the possibility granted to those receiving unemployment benefit of capitalising this benefit in order to create their own business. This capitalisation option was subsequently withdrawn from those unemployed people wishing to work on a self-employed basis, but was maintained and even increased for associated workers' co-operatives and SALs.

2.2. Initiatives to Integrate Disabled People through Work

As from 1993, the largest share of public finance went to the Professional Integration Programme for disabled people. This was the result of a process introduced earlier on, as until the 1970s disabled people were the responsibility of the family and remained at home. As from the 1980s, the families of these disabled people began to join forces and found associations that were subsequently transformed into foundations and co-operatives. The aim of these parents' associations was to create employment structures for their children and residences for disabled people without families. People were faced with a collective need that was not covered by the public or the private sector. Civil society took the initiative and set up productive structures intended to meet this need. The state then recognised this service and created the financial basis to support these initiatives.

It is important to note that these professional centres for disabled people are not necessarily set up within the framework of the social economy. The professional centre is considered to be an instrument belonging to a parents' association or to members of the family. It may adopt the legal status of a workers' limited company or a limited liability company.

2.3. Social Integration Associations, Charitable Trusts and Co-operatives

As from the 1980s, associations, small charitable trusts and associated workers' co-operatives emerged to deal with the problems of people who are socially excluded owing to long-term unemployment or the lack of rights to benefits. However, these social-integration initiatives are still not legally recognised. In the 1970s and until the mid-1980s co-operatives and workers' limited companies created jobs for those excluded from public job protection policies, but now these integration iniatives have been extended further to replace the job protection policies.

The San Fermin Project Association *in a District of Madrid*

The *San Fermin Project Association* is a non-profit association located in the Usera municipal district to the south of Madrid. This association was set up by the people of the San Fermin district with the twofold objective of community support and development and socio-employment integration.

The project beneficiaries are mainly people from the district, and in particular young people in a situation of social risk (up to 14 years) and young people aged between 18 and 25 who receive the minimum income and are looking for their first job.

The association undertakes three types of activity: a prevention programme for young people at social risk, a vocational training programme for young people receiving the minimum income and the management of the San Fermin civic centre.

In 1993, a total of 60 young people benefited from the prevention programme, 45 young people aged between 18 and 25 benefited from the vocational training programme and around 350 were assisted by the civic centre.

The association benefits from various forms of public finance: it has a contract with the Usera municipal council to provide social services, a contract with the Madrid Institution for training, and subsidies from the Community of Madrid for the vocational training programme.

Today, between 200 and 300 social-integration enterprises share this objective. They have set up their own representative structures and are grouped together within the Spanish socio-employment promotion and integration network (REPRIS), the alternative and mutually supportive economy network (REAS) and the Spanish Association of recycling companies[5] in the social and mutually supportive economy (AERESS). These three federations represent almost 90 enterprises that focus on the socio-employment integration of the socially excluded, from the long-term unemployed to young people who have not completed their vocational training, and including former prisoners and single-parent families, and often unemployed women with dependent children. In 1998, this group of enterprises comprised almost 1,000 jobs and 2,000 people had benefited from their integration activities.

These entrepreneurial initiatives are usually created by members of a promotional group. This group often consists of professionals, housewives, religious figures, the people of a particular district who decide to join forces to combat poverty in their community, and in particular social exclusion. These are therefore voluntary initiatives led by a group of private individuals. The promoters often join the activity that has been set up and become paid employees. However, in this type of experiment, in some cases the group of promoters may be employed elsewhere. In this case they act as the impetus and guarantee the founding values of the project.

These experiments traditionally assume the legal statuses of the social economy: associations, foundations and associated workers' co-operatives. The statuses of limited liability company or limited company have not yet been used, but will no doubt be developed in the same way as entrepreneurial initiatives in the field of the integration of disabled people. In fact, the promoters of these initiatives will probably use legal forms specific to the conventional trading sector to facilitate their activities as businesses.

Generally, such initiatives appear at a local level and involve a specific district. For example, the *San Fermin Project Association* in Madrid (see inset) is a district association, while the *Engrunes Foundation – Miques Co-operative* was set up in 1981 by a parish community in a district severely affected by unemployment and poverty in a suburb of Barcelona. These are local initiatives, often backed by the Church, which play a special role in the fight against poverty in Spain. It may even be said to be the institution that has done the most in this area, even if the example of the *San Fermin Project Association* bears witness to the role played by lay initiatives. In addition, these are mainly urban organisations, even though a few such bodies are appearing in rural areas.

---

[5] These are enterprises that develop waste and recycling activities.

These initiatives develop a wide range of different activities, from remotivating the people they work with, to actual economic activity, and including the creation of aptitude for work skills. The information we received from the Spanish Association of recycling companies in the social and mutually supportive economy (AERESS) about 22 of its associated enterprises gives some details of the social-integration enterprises in Spain (CIES, 1998, 1999). Of the 738 people working in these 22 enterprises, 70% are men and 30% women; 73% of these people have an employment contract; 19% of these people are volunteers, the rest receive a grant. Forty-two per cent are aged between 26 and 35, 27% between 36 and 45, 21% between 46 and 65 and 10% are under 25-years-old. These enterprises undertake economic activities involving the collection of second-hand goods provided free of charge, the storage and repair of the goods collected, the sale of repaired goods, and various gardening or horticultural activities. In 1998 they recovered 32.1 million kilograms of waste, including 18 millon kilograms of paper.

The 22 enterprises that are AERESS members concentrate on the collection of bulky goods and clothing, ten of them focusing on collecting paper from private households, seven from shops, five in containers. Of these, three also recover waste from buildings sites and two collect tin cans. These activities are often accompanied by restoration work. For example, electrical household goods, furniture and computers are repaired with a view to selling them on the market. Only a few of these enterprises have a shop. The bulkier goods collected are broken up and the various metals they contain are extracted.

To undertake these economic activities successfully, in 1998 these 22 enterprises[6] recorded expenditure in excess of 1500 million pesetas[6] (9 million euros). The enterprises of the group AERESS operate in the market. CIES (1999) shows that in a sample of 22 sets of accounts for 1997 and 1998 financial years, the private market provided 45% of income. Retail trade accounted for 35% and wholesale 10% of income. The public market represented 32% of income. Thus 77% of income comes from market-related activities (public and private). Subsidies represented 18% of income, whilst private donations accounted for 5%. These are therefore above all trading structures that sell goods and services on the market and which have to be profitable and competitive if they wish to pursue their company aims.

---

[6] Around 160 pesetas equivalent to 1 euro (August 1997).

The Engrunes Foundation *and the* Miques Co-operative, *Parish Community Initiatives*

The *Engrunes Foundation* and the *Miques Co-operative* were set up by the Christian community of the Saint Matthew Parish in the La Plana district of Esplugues de Llobregat, in Catalonia. Their aim is to ensure the social and employment reintegration of excluded persons.

The two organisations have their own objectives The *Engrunes Foundation* focuses on social integration, while the *Miques Co-operative* concentrates on the employment integration of those who have received social and therapeutic assistance from the *Engrunes Foundation* and have benefited from the type of economic of activity this foundation undertakes and possible agreements with public administrations.

These projects are intended for a variety of population groups: men aged between 40 and 60, who have aged prematurely and have a long history of exclusion behind them, very isolated people who are no longer accustomed to working and have a very low self-esteem, who are dependent on alcohol and have very limited personal resources; the beneficiaries of the inter-departmental minimum income integration programme of the Generalitat of Catalonia or the programme to combat poverty and exclusion implemented by the Barcelona municipal authorities.

Activities are developed in social fields (group dynamics, support services, training workshop) and economic areas (collection, storage, restoration and sale of second-hand goods, maintenance and construction of housing, renovation of parts from abandoned cars). In 1998, there were 123 beneficiaries with a support staff of 31 people – 70% men and 30% women.

The project benefits from some agreements with diferent local and regional governments. In 1998 income was 253 millon pesetas (1.5 millon Euros), of which 56% was from public markets.

---

3. Results and Outlook for Social-integration Enterprises

Unlike special education and employment centres for disabled people, as mentioned above, social-integration enterprises are not recognised by law. Nevertheless, like any other enterprise, they have obligations and the bodies that finance them require guarantees in the form of assets that they usually do not possess, in order to grant them credit. Consequently they often suffer cash flow problems and have to accept a higher degree of insecurity. As regards decision-making, ideological principles predominate.

One of the main problems facing these initiatives is the ultimate integration of their own workers into the conventional labour market. In fact, they run the risk of having to keep them in work owing to the high level of unemployment and the inadequacy of the job creation capabilities of the Spanish economy.

To overcome this problem, social-integration enterprises support the creation of small co-operatives and various forms of self-employed work. Every year, the 90 or so organisations in the three federations referred to above each succeeded in developing between two and three small co-operatives of four or five workers, resulting in the creation of around 1000 jobs. It is the social-integration enterprises themselves that provide the initial equipment, the management training, the initial capital, sometimes even the first lorry – often a second-hand one – and a small warehouse at a low rent. All this makes it possible to begin collecting and restoring goods with a view to selling them, thereby securing a revenue for the new enterprise.

3.1. The Slow Development of Public Policies

The emergence and development of social-integration enterprises follows a logic similar to that of any other social initiative. First of all a group of people decide to get together and undertake an economic activity in such as way as to achieve its goal. Once the enterprise achieves a certain level of results, the public authorities begin to take an interest.

Social integration enterprises are very much a minority movement in Spain and they are active in an area in which it is relatively difficult to recognise them. They are not yet in a position to arouse genuine interest on the part of political leaders responsible for social or employment policies. Moreover, they are working in a country in which the development of the state as the main service provider dates back only 15 years, since the establishment of the Autonomous Communities.

Since the public policies designed to fight unemployment have yielded poor results in terms of social-integration, politicians responsible for employment and social services have started to take an interest in these initiatives. Although they are marginal and have only limited resources, they have clearly succeeded in achieving genuine integration. Consequently, from the 1990s, at local level and in the Autonomous Communities, the administrations have begun to support these initiatives by giving them a few specific subsidies. At the moment, and in the near future, the hopes of the social-integration movement are founded on the possibility, in the Autonomous Communities, that the governments may grant a minimum salary linked to the integration activity. This would be the clearest and the most effective way of recognising the activities of these social-integration structures.

On the other hand, the major claim made by the social-integration enterprises movement on the central administration concerns regulations governing their recognition that would determine the conditions they would have to fulfil to obtain recognition and their terms and conditions of incorporation. Such regulations would have to take into account the specific type of industrial relations that are established between the worker on the integration programme and the enterprise. They would also have to define the role of the central administration (Ministry of Employment and Social Security) and the autonomous administrations, particularly as regards social support for workers on integration programmes.

3.2. The Need for Joint Responsibility and Transversality

In the fight against social exclusion, the concepts of 'joint responsibility' and 'transversality' have an important role to play if the best possible results are to be obtained. Let us look at each of these concepts.

What does the term 'joint responsibility' mean when applied to the field of social exclusion? It means that all the social and economic players must play an active part, each in their respective areas, all guided by the wish to solve the problem. Simply allowing a social initiative to develop is not sufficient if there is no real involvement on the part of all the social players.

At the moment, in this fight against exclusion, the social-integration enterprises movement is calling in particular for greater involvement on the part of the various levels of the public administration. In addition, as we have already said, these initiatives are faced with the need to become conventional job creators in the legal frameworks of co-operatives or through self-employment.

The concept of joint responsibility is also vitally important in terms of the behaviour of financial institutions. As suggested by the various experiments studied by Vidal,[7] the easiest way to obtain finance for the development of these initiatives would be to establish a financial body

---

[7] Vidal (1996).

designed with their needs in mind that would operate as part of an overall project.

In an overall approach to the fight against exclusion, the concept of 'transversality' is also essential. This involves promoting solutions that are not sectorial or vertical, but which are horizontal, in which the principle of proximity plays an important role. Until now, the Church or those anxious to ensure social justice have been considered responsible for those who are excluded. Local or Autonomous Community administrations have responded superficially and on the basis of a principle of assistance (public charity). This shows that in Spain the issue of exclusion is not yet seen as a sign of the inefficiency of the economic system.

Since the concept of assistance has prevailed in the various approaches to the issue of exclusion, social service officials are responsible for resolving the social and personal problems resulting from long-term unemployment. This is the wrong approach to the problem. Social exclusion is not exclusively a matter for social services. It is the responsibility of all the social players including, among the institutions, those responsible for employment, housing, industry and finally social services.

Social exclusion is the outward expression of an imbalance. It bears witness to the fact that the concepts of the market and efficiency do not work well enough or require external institutional or social action to avoid or attenuate the imbalance around the people excluded.

3.3. Outlook

Looking at the movements currently found in the various countries of the European Union and those at work in some of the Autonomous Communities in Spain, there is reason to hope that the social-integration enterprises in Spain will achieve greater recognition among the various levels of regional and local administration. Moreover, this institutional recognition is already implicit when certain public works contracts are awarded, such as for the upkeep of gardens or buildings. In the medium term, the central administration too will eventually introduce regulations to facilitate the development of these initiatives aimed at social integration through work.

Similarly, among the conventional enterprises, various players will no doubt develop a certain degree of joint responsibility with regard to the problem of exclusion, even if this happens far more slowly that we could wish. In this respect, tax incentives will probably play an important role, in particular as regards the easing of social charges for those on integration programmes.

Finally, there is reason to hope that active employment policies will facilitate the future development and consolidation of the social-integration enterprises as established instruments in the field of job creation.

References

Aguilar, M., Gaviria, M. and Laparra, M. (1995), *La caña y el pez. El salario social en las comunidades autónomas 1989–1994*, FOESSA Foundation, Madrid.

Centre d'études du changement social (CECS) (1996), *España 1995, una interpretación de su realidad social* (polycopié), CECS, Madrid.

Centre d'Iniciatives de l'Economia Social (CIES) (1998), AERESS report, CIES, Barcelona.

Centre d'Iniciatives de l'Economia Social (CIES) (1999), *Informe Socio-Económico de las empresas miembros de la Asociación Española de Recuperadores de la Economia Social y Solidaria (AERESS), 1997–1998*, CIES, Barcelona.

Conseil économique et social (CES) (1996), *Economia, trabajo y sociedad. Memoria sobre la situación socioeconómica y laboral, 1995*, CES, Madrid.

Esping-Andersen, G. (1990), *The Three Worlds of Welfare Capitalism*, Polity, Cambridge, UK.

Fundescoop (1994), *Medidas de formación y fomento de pymes y autoempleo en la Unión Europea* (survey financed by EUROFORM), Madrid.

Gonzalez, J. and Calvet, J. (1991), 'Crisis, transición y estancamiento. La política económica española, 1973–1982', in M. Etxezarreta (ed.), *La reestructuración del capitalismo en España. 1970–1990*, Icaria Editorial, Barcelona, pp. 133–175.

Lessenich, S. (1996), 'España y los 'regímenes' de Estado de Bienestar', *Sociologia*, no. 13, pp. 147–161.

Rojo, E. and Vidal, I. (1994), 'Mercado de trabajo y políticas de fomento del empleo autónomo en los países miembros de la U. E.', in *Información Comercial Española. Revista de Economía*, no. 729, Ministerio de Comercio y Turismo, Madrid, pp. 61–73.

Sarasa, S. and Moreno, L. (1993), 'The Spanish "Via Media" to the development of welfare state', working paper no. 93/3, Institut d'Estudis Socials Avançats, CSIC/Université Pompeu Fabra, Barcelona.

Trigo, J. (1994), *Economía y empresa en España*, 2nd edit., Ediciones 2000, Barcelona.

Valle, V. (1995), '1996: Budgets prorogés et réformes différées', *Cuadernos de información económica*, no. 104, pp. 3–8.

Vidal, I. (1987), *Crisis económica y transformaciones en el mercado del trabajo. El asociacionismo en el trabajo en Cataluña*, Diputation de Barcelone, Barcelona.

Vidal, I. (1992), *Mapa de Catalunya de serveis socials. Les iniciatives socials a Catalunya en làmbit de les persones disminuides* (survey conducted at the request of the Generalitat of Catalonia), Generalitat of Catalonia, Catalonia.

Vidal, I. (ed.) (1996), *Inserción social por el trabajo. Una visión internacional*, CIES, Barcelona.

Vidal, I. and Perri 6 (eds) (1993), *Delivering Welfare: Repositioning Non-profit and Co-Operative Action in Western European Welfare States*, CIES, Barcelona.

Vidal, I., Rojo, E. and Trigo, J. (1992), *Estudio socio-económico del emprendedor procedente de la capitalization de las prestaciones por desmpleo*, Interministerial Commission of Science and Technology, Barcelona.

10 Sweden: Co-operative Development Agencies as a Means of Bridging Recent Failures of the System

YOHANAN STRYJAN AND FILIP WIJKSTRÖM

1. Introduction

The Swedish third sector's relative size is comparable, in economic terms, to those in other Western countries (Lundström and Wijkström, 1995; Stryjan and Wijkström, 1996). However, its composition, the organisation forms traditionally employed, and their mode of operation, deviate from the norms accepted in other industrialised countries. This situation has to do with general features of Swedish society at large, with the role assumed by social-economy/third-sector organisations within it, and with the labour market policies pursued by successive Swedish governments from the 1930s onwards. The traditional Swedish model ideally presupposed full employment and continuous industrial expansion, facilitated by a well-functioning labour market that is maintained by state 'active labour market policy'. It did not legitimate the social economy's involvement in job-creation (nor, indeed, endorse the concept of job creation by other than market means). Consequently, the sector's role thus far in insertion/reintegration tasks, and in job creation in general, was relatively limited, and oriented in a different way than in other industrialised countries.

As the Swedish model's performance sagged, emerging problems of 'excess' labour were met, to start with, partly by way of a further expansion of the public sector,[1] and partly by an array of stop-gap measures. However,

---

[1] Thus, the industrial labour force declined by 120,000 between 1973 and 1983. In the same period, public sector employment grew by 279,000 (*Arbetsmarknadsdepartementet*, 1984).

as the public sector, too, entered a phase of downsizing, amidst an economic crisis, and unemployment figures passed the 10% mark, the pretence of an active labour-market policy could no longer be sustained. Consequently the developments of the 1990s were marked by a greater openness to non-traditional solutions (by Swedish standards), and by an increased role for social economy organisations, both as employers, and as facilitators of new job-creation. This new attitude has not been significantly modified by current economic upswing, at least not where the field of insertion is concerned.

Future third-sector engagement in labour-market insertion and employment creation in Sweden will, none the less, take place in an environment that is substantially different from that in most other European countries. The attitudes and strategies adopted by the organisations concerned are somewhat different as well. Swedish voluntary organisations have traditionally focused their resourcefulness primarily on *activating* people, rather than *employing* them. As a logical extension of this attitude, the current expansion strategy of the sector sets a premium on the proliferation of new, independent organisations, rather than on the expansion of those already existing (cf. Jobring, 1988). The presentation below gives a general description of the Swedish situation, and sketches out some case studies.

1.1. Employment, Insertion, and the Swedish Model

Popular movement organisations played an important role in establishing the Swedish model. Co-operative movements in particular contributed to the economic and social integration of traditional society's marginal groups: the rural and the urban poor, and laid the institutional foundations for the Swedish welfare state. Historically, the Swedish welfare state represented the most extreme position as far as the level of aspirations regarding the universality of the welfare state's coverage, and the degree of public sector involvement in the production of welfare are concerned. Though the basic ingredients of the Swedish model are far from extraordinary in themselves, the model's specific combination of normative assumptions and institutional practices is probably unique. It is useful to open the discussion by a brief review of some of its normative underpinnings (Stryjan and Wijkström, 1996).

Collectivism and individualism Society at large (rather than households) is considered the major producer of welfare.[2] Welfare policies are primarily an issue of distribution. Somewhat at odds with its collectivist spirit, the model also contains a fiercely individualistic slant. Entitlements are strictly individual, and were often purposefully decoupled from any affiliation to any collectivity, or even family.

Equality and exclusion A strong egalitarian emphasis is applied to both ends of the scale. Welfare measures are primarily targeted on socially sanctioned *needs*, rather than on the *needy*. Ideally, the model could be perceived as a general insurance scheme (Hedborg and Meidner, 1984), safeguarding *average* welfare for the *entire* population, rather than *baseline* welfare to targeted *problem groups*. Thus, the public sector managed the upmarket segment of welfare. Non-profits catered mainly to low-visibility segments. As we shall see later, this focus on the average impaired capability to recognise new and/or marginal problem groups.

Welfare and employment The right to employment was (and, in many ways, still is) part of the normative core of the Swedish Model (Stryjan, 1994). Grossly oversimplifying, we could say that welfare policy was seen as a matter of *distribution* of a collectively produced good, in accordance with societally set entitlements. Employment is a central ingredient of these entitlements. In other words, welfare is truly general only in as much and as long as employment is general as well. This makes full employment into a prime boundary condition for the model's coherent operation. Or, put in another way, it is the normative glue holding the model's elements together. At the micro level, it is also a central element of identity.[3]

The provision of employment was expected to occur in the sphere of production; primarily through the workings of the labour market, and is not considered an element of welfare policy proper. The setting of full employment as a societal norm (a formulation subtly different from that of defining unemployment as a major societal problem) has none the less led to the state assuming an increasing responsibility for employment policies,

---

[2] As Abrahamsson and Broström (1980) point out, Swedish Social Democracy has historically striven for the control of distribution. The control of production was best left in the hands of business. The distinction between production and distribution, however, verges on industrial physiocracy: only industrial production was considered 'production proper'. The productive aspect of services was never fully acknowledged. The view that welfare is a societally distributed good contrasts with the current view of households as central producers of welfare (Netten and Davies, 1990).
[3] The frequency of sole-proprietorships and self-employment in Sweden is rather low.

that was enacted on two levels: at the macro-level, the state assumed the role of a facilitator of a smoothly functioning labour-market. At the micro-level, it assumed responsibility for the social overhead costs that worker mobility entails. These principles are stated as early as 1944, in the opening pages of *The Labour Movement's Post-war Program*. Programmatically, unemployment was considered an individual (rather than systemic) and temporary (rather than endemic) affliction, definitely not as a manifestation of exclusion. Individual re-entry into employment was considered a question of rehabilitation. In a manner of speaking, *every* person losing his job was entitled to be 'inserted' into employment. Such rehabilitation and reintegration measures were traditionally considered part of the state's employment policy sphere, to be executed by labour-market authorities, through an array of strictly *individual* measures: trade reschooling and mobility grants for the ordinary unemployed, placement subsidies for the disabled and sheltered workshops for those that could in no way be fitted in the ordinary labour-market. Co-operatives and other third-sector organisations were *not* being viewed as a major policy tool in this field (Stryjan and Wijkström, 1996, 1998).

The model built on the assumptions of a homogenous society, a growing economy, and full employment. The far-reaching integration of society that made the model a working proposition rather than a pious fiction was largely achieved, historically speaking, through the contribution of popular movements and co-operative organisations. The popular movements, that initially were explicitly non-establishment, evolved, from the late 1920s onwards, into committed builders of a new society. In a sense, they succeeded in moulding society into their, initially 'alternative' vision. For the optimistic social-engineers of the 1950s it might, indeed have seemed that problems of marginalisation were given a definitive solution. This profound optimism is probably the best explanation of the fact that the responsibility for maintaining and developing the system was handed over, nearly frictionlessly, to the state. In return, the movement organisations obtained a significant say in the further development of the system, and the setting of entitlements (Stryjan and Wijkström, 1996). The function of *voice* gradually displaced that of active *involvement*.[4] The new *modus vivendi* had two significant weaknesses, which became evident with time:

---

[4] The terms are borrowed from Hirschman (1970), and Hirschman (1982), respectively. For a model integrating involvement in the Hirschmanian framework, see Stryjan (1989), ch. 4.

(a) it largely depended on continuous expansion of the welfare system; co-responsibility for cutbacks is not an attractive proposition;

(b) by making the movement organisations into custodian of past achievements, it impaired their sensitivity to the emergence of new problem groups. New, 'alternative' movements of the late 1970s and 1980s voiced a sharp criticism of these characteristics. However, due to their essentially middle-class character, they too, initially failed to attract and mobilise the newly marginalised.

1.2. The Social Economy in Sweden

The scope and composition of the social economy in Sweden have been the subject of considerable discussion (Boli, 1991; Stryjan and Wijkström, 1996; Lundström and Wijkström, 1997). Neither the term 'Social economy', nor the Anglo-Saxon category of 'non-profits' have a clear parallel in Swedish rules of incorporation and the Swedish institutional set-up. Consequently, taxation and incentive structures do not induce existing organisations to assume benefit-maximising organisational attributes of a type that would be familiar to, for example American researchers. On the other hand, the concept of 'popular movement' (*folkrörelse*) that is essential for the understanding of this organisational sphere, lacks a clear correspondent in non-Scandinavian tradition (Stryjan and Wijkström, 1996). To an extent, the sector also lacks a clear understanding of itself. Many organisations profess an affinity to popular movement ideas, or identify themselves as such movements. In keeping with this tradition, the attitude towards philanthropic activity is overwhelmingly negative. Nonetheless, a sizeable subgroup of organisations has its roots in 19th century philanthropic organisations, and sports distinctly more conservative political and ideological affinities. A population that would approximate accepted notions of a social economy would consists, roughly, of:

(a) established co-operation;

(b) Popular (folk) movements, and non-profit organisations;

(c) new co-operatives, especially in the social welfare services;

(d) foundations, a group that certainly fits under the 'non-profit', and, possibly, 'third-sector' labels.

Organisations in the first three clusters normally incorporate under the economic- or voluntary (*ideell*) association form. In this respect, Sweden is often described as a thoroughly organised nation. There are nearly 200,000 associations in Sweden (SOU, 1987, p.21).[5] About 145,000 of these are affiliated to regional or national organisations. A further 50,000 local associations are not connected to any national or regional umbrella organisation. The degree of association membership among the population is high, both absolutely, and in comparison to other industrial nations (Pestoff, 1977; Curtis *et al.*, 1992). Organisations on the national level have between 31 and 32 million memberships, which means that the average Swede is a member of approximately four organisations (SOU, 1987; Wijkström, 1995). Only one out of ten Swedes is not a member in any association. Studies indicate that nearly 50% of the Swedish population are active to a varying degree in 'their' associations.

The total number of foundations in Sweden is estimated at about 50,000 and they represent a considerable amount of accumulated wealth. Lundström and Wijkström (1997) estimate the number of active non-profit foundations at 15,000. Some of these are actively engaged in the production of services (and, thus can unproblematically be included in the 'non-profit' category), and/or maintain a popular movement profile, loosely fitting into a 'social economy' category.

1.3. The Social Economy and Employment

Lundström and Wijkström's (1997) estimate that the Swedish non-profit sector in 1992 consisted of roughly 200,000 organisations. Of these, more than 84% were small – without any employees at all. Less than 0.5% had 20 or more employees. These larger organisations also stand for over 80% of the total operating expenditures of the sector. In 1992, Swedish non-profit organisations employed, in different forms, about 100,000 persons, placing the sector's share at somewhat below 2.3% of the labour force.[6] The FTE (full-time equivalent) is 83,000 person-years (Lundström and Wijkström, 1997); these figures do not include the commercial operations of consumer and farmer co-operatives). Despite their comparative weight, the direct contribution of most established organisations to labour-market insertion is rather low. The overwhelming majority of those employed are, on the contrary, professionally trained personnel. Less skilled tasks are

---

[5] This figure includes ca 20,000 economic associations (established co-operatives, new co-operatives, and commercial establishments), not all of which can be considered to belong to the social economy, or to be non-profits.

[6] This figure doesn't fully discount extreme part-time assignments, and probably overestimates the sector's labour-force share somewhat.

often managed by voluntary labour. Significantly, the volume of voluntary work is estimated at 300,000 person-years, over three times the volume of employed personnel.

The Swedish traditional division of responsibilities in the employment field acknowledges the role of two, and only two parts: government, as a facilitator of jobs, and 'the Business Community' (*näringslivet*), as an actual creator of jobs (Stryjan and Wijkström, 1996). This division of labour virtually cut off voluntary organisations from 'job creation' in the ordinary sense of the term. Furthermore, it motivated a self-imposed limitation on the state's part as far as support for such initiatives on the sector's part is concerned. It was perceived as legitimate for the state to interfere in big industry crises (through direct support, subsidies, and, at times, even 'owner-friendly' nationalisations[7]); a pattern replicated at local government level (Brunsson and Johannisson, 1982). Support for third-sector organisations, on the other hand, was largely conditional on it *not* generating any jobs. Support measures, or subsidised workforce were, in principle, not to be used for tasks that 'could have been carried out by commercial organisations'. Organisations that use such labour, it was argued, would have an unfair competitive advantage over those that do not. In other words, a job could be publicly financed (wholly or partly) only if it was possible to prove that it was not really necessary. Throughout the 1970s and the 1980s, social enterprises' impact in this field was concentrated on boundary cases and 'non-market' jobs, mostly under various labour market board temporary job-placement programs. Since 'problem groups' were not accepted as a legitimate statistical category, and 'illegitimate' phenomena tend not to leave a clear mark in public statistics, defining these organisations' contribution becomes a complex task. In certain niches, however, predominantly regional policy and countryside development, public activity aimed at job-creation started gaining acceptance from the early 1980s onwards. As we shall see below, the development in these fields provided a new blueprint for the sector's activity.

---

[7] It has been remarked that the largest volume of nationalisations in Swedish modern history was accomplished by the Centre and Centre-Right governments of the 1970s. Social-Democratic governments, arguing that the party's major mission is in the field of redistribution, not of production, traditionally took a dim view of nationalisations.

2. Towards a New System?

As the assumptions of a growing economy and full employment that form the foundations of the Swedish model became increasingly untenable, problems and problem groups became visible. The first issue of the sort to come to public awareness was the progressive deterioration of living conditions in the countryside. The structural rationalisation of the 1970s has all but eliminated the traditional industrial and mining estates,[8] leaving a large number of small, isolated, and now companyless company towns in its wake. An amalgamation of small municipalities into bigger territorial units, initiated in the 1950s, and intended to strengthen and upgrade local government, led, in parallel to a further drain of services from peripheral villages.

In the early 1980s, disillusionment with attempts to 'remedy' the countryside's problems by subsidising the migration of jobless from the countryside to metropolitan areas, where the jobs were,[9] and of companies to the countryside, where the jobless were, the notion of genuinely local development was gradually accepted. A number of highly publicised local projects (e.g. 'The Norberg Model', see Bäckman *et al.*, 1982; *Arbetsmarknadsdepartamentet*, 1984) helped to set the trend. The first co-operative development centres (LKUs), in Jämtland and in Värmland arose in the early 1980s from such local initiatives.

Yet another indicator of system trouble, a surge in youth unemployment in the early 1980s, provided a stimulus for a program against youth unemployment, launched jointly by the government, established co-operation, and trade unions. The program constituted, in a double sense, a major departure from Swedish labour tradition, by endorsing, in principle, two traditional anathemas:

(a) the involvement of state organs (in this case SIND, the State Industry Board) in direct job creation; and

(b) the formation of worker co-operatives, an organisation form that both Swedish labour movement and consumer co-operation traditionally treat with the utmost suspicion (see Stryjan, 1996a).

The program included youth worker co-operative training programs (see, e.g. Axelson, 1985) and, at the national level, a Co-operative Council

---

[8] Primarily within steel, mining and glass industries. The tradition of industrial estates was in part a result of the sparse population patterns, and in part a carry-over from the 17–18th centuries.
[9] A policy that came to be nicknamed '*flytlasspolitiken*' (the removal-van policy).

(*Kooperativa rådet*), was formed, consisting (at that stage) of representatives of the government, established co-operation, and trade unions.[10] The initiative roughly coincided in time with the emergence of the first LKUs. The two developments came to converge in 1986 in a program, much inspired by UK experience, that institutionalised Council support for LKUs.

Ironically enough, by the time the program became operative, the youth unemployment of the early 1980s virtually vanished (temporarily, as it turned out) in the overheated labour market of the late 1980s. Consumer co-operation's involvement also waned somewhat (Jonnergård and Svensson, 1990). The new situation resulted in the LKUs essentially re-inventing themselves, looking for new tasks, and, not the least, for new members and sponsors. In doing that, they may have laid the cornerstone for a new model.

2.1. The Co-operative Development System

The most noteworthy feature of the Swedish situation at present is, the scale of genuine grass-roots formation, of self-help organisations that are called into being by local stimuli, and not initiated by, nor affiliated to national organisations. The creation of innovative solutions to new problems often entails higher transaction costs than the replication of established models. It is at this point that the availability of support structures plays a decisive role.

An interesting group of new support organisations in the voluntary sphere are the volunteer centres. Created in the early 1990s, after a Norwegian model, the centres are designed to facilitate voluntary activity and to link prospective volunteers with existing tasks. To our knowledge, however, the centres do not engage in the formation of new organisations, or in employment initiatives. The most salient and successful support structure presently in operation is the nationwide network of co-operative development agencies (CDAs, or, LKUs in Swedish).

Currently (1999) there are 26 LKUs in operation,[11] employing a nucleus of 70 co-operative consultants, as compared to 1989 when there were 11 employing the full time equivalent of 4.5 people (Jonnergård and Svensson, 1990). Every LKU is an independent association constituted by

---

[10] Appointed personally, not *ex officio*; significantly, other associations and popular movements were not invited to join.

[11] The breakdown of organisational memberships, below, pertains to 21 LKUs only (Stryjan and Wijkström, 1998).

local organisations (legal persons) within a county. The circle of members, that originally was restricted by statute to established co-operative enterprises, was widened in 1990, under pressure from then existing LKUs, to include other associations, and (optionally) organs of local government. The aggregate composition of the body of LKU members is presented in the table below.

Table 10.1 Members of local LKU associations, 1996

Type of organisation	N
Consumer co-operatives	45
Farmers co-operatives	35
Housing co-operative associations	46
Bank and insurance co-operatives	31
Co-operative kindergarten and schools	239
Other new co-operatives	145
Political organisations	31
Trade unions (local chapters or districts)	26
Municipalities	69
County councils	12
Voluntary study associations	35
Other associations	32

The LKUs mandatory task is to promote co-operative development through information dissemination, advisory work, and education about the co-operative business form. Job creation is one natural consequence of this orientation, though the LKUs field of operation also includes conversions of existing organisations, and the design and development of voluntary solutions for service provision that do not contain formal job creation. Though the explicit mandate of LKUs is not to combat exclusion, nor confine their operations to excluded groups, groups on the brink of exclusion were always seen as important potential users of LKUs' services. Since their inception, LKUs were active in local development in the countryside, in immigrant suburbs in the larger cities, and in youth groups. An evaluation of the LKU system from a job-creation perspective was carried out by the Swedish Accounting Bureau (*Riksrevisionsverket*, RRV) for 1992 (RRV,1993). The LKUs had, at the time, a joint turnover of 20 MSEK; 300 new co-operatives were started, with a combined turnover of about 500 MSEK, and 1300 jobs were created with the LKUs' assistance or through their initiatives, at an average cost of 11,000 SEK per job. By comparison, The National Labour Market Board's (AMS) cost per job created 1992 was 72,450 SEK.

The economic crisis of the 1990s brought a rising public awareness of problems of social exclusion, especially in the metropolitan areas. In a near reversal of the integrative drive of the 1940s–1950s, the shrinking welfare state of the 1990s is now seen as continuously spawning new 'problem groups'. Naturally, this view is, to some degree a matter of altered perceptions: most of the problem groups now acknowledged as legitimate targets for insertion projects did, definitely, exist also in the seemingly 'integrated' 1970s and 1980s. Increasing awareness of urban problems has induced the government, in 1995, to appoint a committee for metropolitan areas, and allocate funds for urban community development programmes in the metropolitan areas. Given their previous initiatives, the LKUs were well positioned to take advantage of this new openness, and increase their engagement in the field. Due to the newness of these initiatives it has not been possible to provide any statistical data as yet.[12]

The major directions/target-groups for LKU engagement at present are:

(a) local/countryside development,

(a) problematic residential suburbs,

(c) youth groups/young unemployed,

(d) immigrant and second-generation immigrants.

LKUs act either in response to local initiatives, or by initiating projects themselves. The aim of the action is to promote independent development, and not to start, own or manage enterprises, nor to directly employ the target population. Due to the way LKU activity is financed, their engagement is on a strict project-basis. Its results, though, are expected to be sustainable. (For further details on LKUs see Appendix.)

Countryside community development Countryside community development is a distinct category of LKU activity, not the least spatially. In this case, the aim is invariably to mobilise the community's own resources in upgrading its own, social and economic environment. The creation of new sources of income, the upgrading (or stopping the deterioration of) local

---

[12] To the extent statistics of new co-operative formation are at all available, they do not distinguish between different categories of co-operative initiatives, and the types of groups forming them.

services, and the facilitation of voluntary organisation can be seen, in this case, as elements of one and the same task.

Huså Community Co-operative

Huså is a peripherally located village in Jämtland, some 20 km from the nearest metalled road. In the 1970s the community was facing slow attrition. There was virtually no local employment, returns from agriculture are meagre, and inhabitants sought employment in the neighbouring towns (some of which are major ski resorts). Due to depopulation, the community lost its school and the only grocery was about to close down. A community theatre project provided the nucleus for mobilising the remaining inhabitants, and generated a flow of tourists, that helped to retain the grocery. The idea of establishing a ski lift, in order to attract tourists in wintertime as well emerged in 1982. The lift co-operative was constituted in May 1983, with the aid and active co-operation of the newly established Jämtland LKU, that helped both with internal organisation and with mobilising credit. The lift was clear for operation in December 1984, thanks to a massive contribution of voluntary labour. At present, the village can boast of a winter restaurant and a summer café, a spate of tourist activities, a goat dairy farm and shop,[13] some 50–60 chalets and a youth hostel. Some of these activities are shouldered by the co-operative, others by private persons or companies (e.g. a tourist hotel in a nearby locality), in co-ordination with, or on lease from, the co-operative. The school was reopened. The number of inhabitants increased, from 100 to 150.

Making economically active members stay in the community, or attracting new ones, often leads to the spontaneous creation of jobs. A new school or a kindergarten (or, as the example below illustrates, a community theatre play) are at least as important elements in this process as the establishment of a business venture. The Huså community co-operative, is somewhat of a textbook case – see box (Mårtensson, 1985, Stryjan, 1994b; Lorendahl, 1995).

The local impact of village co-operatives in the county of Jämtland has been evaluated by Lorendahl (1995). The six co-operatives explored in the study[14] generated between two and ten jobs each. The actual impact of such co-operatives on small communities and the spinoff effects they generate

---

[13] The dairy is affiliated to *Jämtspira* – a regional co-operative in which, too, the Jämtland LKU played an important role. See Stryjan (1993); Stryjan and Fröman (1991).

[14] All in all, there are over 100 new co-operatives in Jämtland county.

go well beyond this small direct effect, as the example of Huså, above, illustrates.

Urban Development Countryside development efforts address a section of the core population, that is now in the process of being marginalised. Problems of marginalisation are, however, most manifest in the urban areas, and in demographically peripheral groups of newcomers and outsiders; be they biological newcomers – new age cohorts about to enter the labour market, or ethnic outsiders: first and second-generation immigrants. Owing to a high degree of residential segregation, these categories tend to flow into each other. Problematic residential suburbs tend to have a high percentage of immigrants and higher youth unemployment rates. Immigrant youth are more likely to be unemployed, etc. This also applies in a positive sense: projects that target a neighbourhood have implications on the situation of problem groups residing in it. Obversely, projects that target a problem group would tend to locate, and have positive spinoffs in the immediate neighbourhood.

The type of initiatives undertaken in urban community development can be illustrated by the case of the *Galaxen* community centre, situated in one of the most socially problematic Gothenburg suburbs. The association runs a community centre, a playground, and a farm enclosure. The association has five employees,[15] and 220 members, in keeping with the association's statutes, pledge 25 hours voluntary work per year. A further 200 pay dues and are supporting members. In 1994, members put in 7,000 hours' voluntary work in improvements and maintenance of the premises. It is quite likely, given the social structure of the neighbourhood, that many of those involved are unemployed, or refugees that lack work-permits. About ten temporary workplaces in maintenance and improvement of the neighbourhood were created in 1996 through an imaginative (and as it would appear, somewhat irregular) conversion of social benefits. While the association's activity provides a regular workplace for five employees, this is quite secondary to its main purpose: mobilising, and knitting together the social fabric of the neighbourhood (see box for details).

---

[15] More precisely: revenues from a municipal contract to operate the playground finance the wages of three employees. Two employees at the community centre are partly supported by labour-board funds, and partly by the revenues the centre generates.

The Galaxen Ideel Association[16]

The case described below contains fairly little actual 'job creation'. In the course of the association's development four municipal jobs were, in fact, phased out, to be replaced with three jobs, with the association as the employer. A fourth job was created, with municipal funds. From a trade union view the example could rather be seen as an illustration of job downgrading. However, the association's central goal never was to generate employment. Its engaging in a job saving operation was motivated by a concern for the service itself, not for its producers. The municipality's decision to close the playground set the conditions for the rescue operation.

The *Galaxen* playground is located in West Bergsjön, a Gothenburg suburb. It has been in operation since 1970, the year the suburb was completed. The entire Bergsjön area is notorious for social problems and high rates of youth criminality. Official unemployment is 12.9%, and youth (age-group 18–24) unemployment is 18.5%.[17] W. Bergsjön, is situated slightly separated from other areas, and consists of 2000 flats. The service infrastructure is highly limited.[18]

The *Galaxen tenant association* (*ideell association*) was established by the neighbourhood's tenants in response to rising social problems. The association's initial aim was to develop free time activities for the neighbourhood's youth. As there are neither public nor commercial premises in the neighbourhood, finding suitable premises for youth activity was a major problem. Eventually, the park and leisure departments consented to lend its 30 sq.m. shack at the playground for weekly youth dances, run by the association. Indirectly, this led to an increasing involvement of the association in the operation of the playground.

The playground, too, gradually changed character. From its initial concentration on carpentry and construction activities, it changed focus to farm animals, becoming somewhat of a farmyard in miniature, with cows, chicken, pigs, goats and geese. Members of the association volunteered to care for the animals over weekends and holidays.

With time, the association redefined its aim, to include meaningful occupation and creative leisure time for the neighbourhoods' adults as well. The association's activities outgrew the limited premises, and after some years'

---

[16] The information in this section is based on information from Sven Bartilsson, Kooperativ Konsult, Gothenburg, an article in *Vår Bostad*, 9, Sept. 1996; and a case description in SOU (1996b).

[17] *Vår Bostad*, 9, Sept. 1996, p. 36.

[18] By way of services (private and municipal), the entire suburb can boast three shops, two kindergartens, one kiosk, and the playground.

improvisations, it decided to build its own community centre. About 40% of the total outlay of 2.2m. SEK were obtained through grants from the state, the municipality and the housing corporation. The remainder was raised by the association: 600,000 SEK from its revenues of lotteries and ticket sales from its own activities, and a 700,000 commercial bank loan (guaranteed by the housing corporation). The house was inaugurated in 1990.

In late 1989, while the community centre was nearing completion, the municipality announced its intention to close down the playground. The decision was due to budget cuts, and a continuing downsizing of the park and leisure departments. The playground and was staffed, at the time, by four of the department's employees. The association negotiated a takeover as a subcontractor to the municipality.

In 1996, the association employed three people in the operation of the playground and in taking care of the animals. Wages are covered by the contract fee. All additional work is carried out on a voluntary basis. An expansion for horse riding is planned. Two additional employees (one partly financed by a labour-market grant) run the community centre's activities, including a cafeteria. Recently, some catering and conference activities were started as well. An environmental project covering the whole of Bergsjö was started 1996,[19] and includes ecological construction, and recycling. This year, the association has also been organising employment, on temporary contracts, for unemployed refugees housed in the neighbourhood.

Organisation – The association does not consider itself a co-operative 'in the traditional (i.e. economic) sense', and chose not to incorporate itself as an economic association. It has 220 ordinary members. Members pay a yearly due, and pledge a minimum of 25 hours' voluntary work per year. Voluntary tasks may include cleaning, maintenance of the the neighbourhoods' expanding communal facilities, the tending of farm animals, and organisation of youth activities. In 1994, the association's members contributed 7000 hours voluntary work, well over the stipulated minimum. 'Volunteer overtime' is rewarded in a symbolic manner (T-shirts or sweatshirts with the association's logo on). The association has no ambition to recruit all tenants as members. In a sense the formalised work pledge instituted in 1991, is a threshold that helps keeping membership figures down to those committed. The association's activities are, however, open to all inhabitants.[20] A status of 'supporting member' that entails no work pledge and no voting rights is also available. In addition, the association has encouraged and indirectly stimulated the activity of other local associations in the neighbourhood.

---

[19] *Vår Bostad*, 9, Sept. 1996, pp. 36–39.

[20] The association chairman, quoted in a *Vår Bostad* reportage states: 'we had 350 members before we decided on a work pledge'.

Support   The association has received, over the years, a great deal of support from various sources: the state (through the General Donations Fund), the municipality, and the housing corporation. Current environmental projects are supported by the Department of Environment. Though the attitude was in general positive, all projects were initiated locally. External support emerged as matched finance to internally generated resources, as project finance awarded to locally formulated projects, or as credit guarantees on loans taken by the association. Substantial, non-pecuniary help was also extended by officials that volunteered know-how on project formulation, and on access to funds. Though it is obvious that the project would never have achieved as much as it did without the support and goodwill it met, there is no doubt that local initiative played a crucial role.

The case also illustrates Swedish social economy organisations' tendency to involve individuals in different fashions: as employees or volunteers, and in different organisational and economic contexts. In a fashion that is almost the obverse of the philanthropic tradition, volunteers are recruited, in this case, by and from the target group, while outside 'helpers' and 'experts' are engaged by the community as consultants, on a paid contract basis.

There are clear parallels between the methods developed for countryside development, and those now applied in urban community development. In both cases, the prime focus is on *community*, and its social capital. It is realised that, in the longer run, the major portion of resources required to sustain development will have to come from the members of the community themselves. The development of local services, and general improvement of the residential area provide a suitable nucleus for mobilisation, from which further development may arise.

Projects that target specific groups   In parallel with community development in problematic neighbourhoods, which have employment creation as a spinoff, there is an increasing tendency to develop projects that facilitate self-employment (preferably in co-operative forms) in such neighbourhoods, with community enhancement as a spin-off. Some such projects explicitly target specific ethnic groups; e.g. Romany, Greek, or Turkish kindergartens; Swahili trading companies, etc. Others address immigrants in general, such as the ongoing '*Vägen till vattnet*' project, that aims to develop tourist services in the Stockholm Archipelago by and for immigrants.

Integration programs for unemployed youth form a specific category, in which trade skills training and work practice are integrated with education in running a co-operative and basic business skills. The largest such project in enterprise form, *Tippen*, a recycling co-operative in Stockholm, offers 39 youth places. The *3&fler* program operated as a combined course and 'co-operative nursery' for business projects that are initiated by the participants themselves.

2.2. The Authorities: Support and Obstruction, Tolerance and Control

It is difficult to give an unequivocal assessment of the authorities' attitude to the projects described above. Appearances notwithstanding, the administration of the Swedish welfare state has never been a monolithic, centralised structure, that may be reoriented by decree. We can better regard it as a 'soft state' (Stryjan and Wijkström, 1998), in which various elements of both central and local structures are endowed with considerable formal autonomy. This autonomy, and the absence of compelling sanctions at the centre's disposal were previously balanced by a strong common ethos (Anton, 1974) that enabled the central state to steer by recommendation, rather than by decree. This common ethos is presently withering away, and giving way to a considerable diversity. Initiatives at the local level thus encounter a complex web of instances and attitudes, rather than one distinct authority: the municipal and county administrations, on the local government level; and at the national level county branches of national (autonomous) boards and authorities, such as the county labour market authority, health and unemployment insurance, and taxation authorities. The policies these different bodies pursue, and the rules they implement (with a considerable degree of local latitude) are often incompatible, and at times outright conflicting (Stryjan, 1996). A recent state enquiry finds that administrative practice in the fields of employment, job-creation and integration often reflects deeply seated reservation towards co-operative ventures (SOU, 1996a). Successful initiatives normally require joint financing from a number of bodies, and an endorsement from a few others (so that a grant from one authority won't be taxed away by another, or cause the recipient to lose his or her social benefits from a third one). Their success depends on lucky configurations, and on local actors' proficiency in weaving local alliances, and in inspiring local officials to bend traditional practices so as to accommodate unconventional initiatives.

3.   Concluding Remarks

The Swedish economy is characterised by a combination of a relatively undeveloped private service sector, with a highly sophisticated mature industry, dominated by a small number of large enterprises, whose recruiting practices have become increasingly selective. Employment openings, especially in the service branches, or for skilled and semi-skilled industrial workers and artisans have to be created by those concerned. Discussing the social economy's role merely in terms of job creation would, however be an oversimplification. The strength of the organisations we are dealing with lies, actually in their skilful blending of different (employment and non-employment) work inputs, in order to accomplish a broad range of tasks. Rather than integration in the narrow sense, the experiments we are dealing with, are geared to create a blend of 'non-jobs', carried out on a voluntary basis, and regular jobs, mainly within emergent small businesses. We should consider their impact in a broader perspective, which includes, besides employment/insertion, impacts on:

(a)   the quality of services,

(b)   quality of life for service users, and/or of the unemployed,

(c)   impacts on the community.

The Swedish social economy has strong roots in the popular movement tradition (Stryjan and Wijkström, 1996). Organisations, especially those that have regarded themselves as being, or belonging to, a popular movement, have traditionally focused their resources primarily on *activating* people, rather than on *employing* them (or were exposed to censure whenever failing to do so). This stance was due partly to ideological considerations, and partly to limitations imposed by the state (including the extremely high cost of regularly employed labour, under the existing taxation system). This strategy was highly appropriate, as long as the organisations were acting in a strongly job-centred society, with a high level of labour market participation and low unemployment. The increasing salience of job integration/insertion, both as a response to societal issues, and problems experienced by an organisation's members, motivates an increased involvement in the field of employment. In the particular Swedish situation, it is important to distinguish between this involvement's two components: as employer, and as an agent of integration. The sector's increasing prominence as an employer only rarely creates new jobs, though it may indeed contribute to saving, or enhancing existing, threatened jobs, and opening them for individuals that might otherwise have been excluded. Genuine job creation for marginalised groups predominantly takes the form of facilitating independent job creation by those affected. In other words, effecting empowerment, rather than substituting present dependence on the welfare system with new forms of dependence.

The complex, and basically unfriendly environment in which the experiments described in this paper have developed, may be changing now, as both problems of exclusion, and the social enterprises' contribution in combating them are winning an increasing recognition. It is, however, too early to talk about a breakthrough. Given the specific nature of Swedish public administration, this process of reorientation may, be complex and take some time. Presently, the total central and local government expenditure (including project funding) on the entire co-operative development system is merely a fraction of the funds spent on employment stimulation measures for business (tax breaks for new employment are estimated at 2.6 milliard SEK[21]) and well below the amounts spent on a medium-size industrial closure. While there is a well established institutional praxis of supporting employment in conventional enterprises, and some (if insufficient) routine procedures to encourage self-employment and sole ownership business, the activity of social enterprises in the field is still subject to administrative whim (SOU, 1996a). The institutionalisation of social enterprises' contribution would require steps both at the symbolical/political and the administrative level:

(a) At the political level the problem is largely a matter of legitimacy: the fact that social enterprise alternatives provide viable ways out of exclusion still remains to be recognised.

(b) At the administrative level social enterprises' legitimation problems are largely caused by their tendency to defy established administrative categories that order Swedish existence, e.g. the separation, between enterprise and association, volunteering and wage employment, unemployment and illness, etc. Put differently: whatever social enterprises do, cannot be accounted for in proper administrative terms. A further development of the sector would require dealing with the water-tight partitions that separate different income-support and employment-support categories, and between different forms of

---

[21] The study in question suggests that these benefits merely contribute to a 'churning effect' in which subsidised workers displace regular employees, with hardly any new jobs generated in the process (*Metro*, 17 January 1997).

economic activity. This may be accomplished either by increased flexibility at the county and local branch level of the authorities involved, or by clear, unambiguous rules for the conversion of, for example unemployment benefits into business-start grants, wage subsidies, personal income and capitalisation for one's own co-operative, etc.

Some visible shifts have recently taken place at the symbolic level; the trends they outline are inconclusive and at times contradictory. Thus a post of secretary of state for integration issues was created in 1996, and replaced in 1998 by a new state authority for integration issues (*integrationsverket*). A government circular (of September 12 1996) instructed county governors to explore possibilities for facilitating small business creation, this time explicitly including LKUs and social movement organisations in the circle of organisations to be involved in the process. Though county governors' powers are highly limited, this initiative did help bring clarity to the local scene, and resulted in the formulation of county development programs, by joint parties that included third-sector actors alongside business community.[22] These developments increase the legitimacy of social enterprises, and, through the creation of new fora for policy co-ordination, may pave the way for an adjustment at the administrative level as well.

Appendix   FKU: The Association for Co-operative Development, and its Members[23]

The FKU (*Förening för kooperativ utveckling*) is a network, presently (1999) associating 26 local co-operative development agencies (CDAs, in Swedish LKUs). The LKUs, the organisation's members, are all fully independent secondary co-operatives. Their main aim is to promote co-operative development, Job creation is a natural consequence of this orientation, but not a mandatory goal.[24] While the first LKUs emerged

---

[22] None the less, co-operative initiatives and proposals contributed by third-sector organisations were pointedly excluded from the final draft of the Stockholm county program.

[23] The study is gratefully derived from the text of an address by Elisabet Mattson, Kooperativ Konsult, Gothenburg, and information from Jan Forslund, KIC, Stockholm; the (1996) chairman, and vice-chairman, respectively, of FKU.

[24] The National Accounting Bureau's 1993 evaluation states explicitly: 'The primary objective of an LKU should be the development of co-operative activity in various sectors. ... to create co-operatives, not, e.g. create employment' (RRV, 1993, p. 5).

spontaneously, through local initiatives, the rules of formation have been institutionalised by now, and provide an interesting combination of local embeddedness with central support measures.

Local commitment This is the first and necessary condition for the emergence of a LKU. An association is established, by locally based organisations belonging to established consumer and farmer co-operation, local government agencies and, increasingly, by new co-operatives. The specific local constellations vary from case to case. The potential availability of matching support from national organs, has clearly motivated and reinforced local initiatives in this field. The initiatives themselves were invariably local. No LKU was ever established through government initiative, or missionary intervention from another county.

Central support Once local financial support pledges by member organisations and local government organs are secured by the founders, these provide the LKU with an entitlement for matching finance (roughly the equivalent of one full-time employee) from the co-operative council. Together, local and central funding form the LKU's baseline operating budget. It provides for employment of a skeleton staff, and finances the LKU's mandatory activities, namely the dissemination of information to the public, and providing initial counselling services free of charge to the general public and would-be co-operators.

Local expansion the baseline operating budget provides the LKU with a financial backbone. It does not limit its scope of operations. On the contrary, LKUs are both allowed and encouraged to expand their networks, introduce new operations and services, on fee, project or contract basis, and mobilise new sources of financing. In 1992, state grants accounted for 24% of the LKUs joint turnover. In some of the most established LKUs the percentage of state funding was as low as 11%. Revenues from own activities account for an increasing portion of the turnover. New operations may be organised either as autonomous projects, or through the expansion of the LKUs permanent staff. Such projects may be directed to a variety of target groups, and may include: counselling services for prospective co-operative founders, and help in takeover negotiations; training in basic business skills for the general public and new business starters; training in business development and professional help in contract negotiations for operating co-operatives; training in collective business skills for young unemployed; training programs for local development counsellors, and community activists; design of new organisation forms in neighbourhood services or in the care of, for example, mentally handicapped, or mental patients, etc. The new services created either cater to the needs of the association's present (primarily new co-operative) members, or aim to further broaden the LKUs membership base and contact network. The sources of financing vary greatly; training programs may be commissioned by various bodies within (local or national) authorities, co-operative enterprises, or financed by fees from the participants themselves. Currently, a number of programs are also supported by matched EU financing. In 1993, 76% of the LKUs turnover was generated from fees and project financing. This portion has probably increased since.

Organisation and governance Every LKU is an independent organisation, constituted by juridical persons. With one exception (the Värmland LKU, established in 1983, before the form was institutionalised), all are incorporated as associations, three of which are *ideell*, the remainder economic. In 1996, the LKU associations had, between them, over 700 members. Typically, new co-operatives constitute over half of the body of members. It is also worth mentioning that LKUs are one of the few organisational arenas in which consumer co-operation and farmer co-operation co-exist in a fairly conflict-free and fruitful manner. The association is headed by a board whose members are mostly recruited from the member organisations and the LKUs active counsellors. There are no uniform rules regulating the composition of the board, and the proportion of representatives of old and new co-operatives and politicians may vary considerably. The board has, formally speaking, the ultimate responsibility for the LKUs operation. It is the formal counterpart in wage negotiations, and sets broad policy lines for the LKU. It also provides a venue for contact with related organisations. Operational management is normally entrusted to the LKUs employees, who also have a considerable say in formulating the LKUs strategy.

Operation There were 21 LKUs in operation (1996). The number is likely to increase by further two in the near future. By the end of 1987, there were eight LKUs, their number rose to 18 in 1992. In principle, the target coverage is one LKU per county. This principle is not strictly adhered to (the Stockholm county has had two fully fledged LKUs since 1994).

Table 10.2   **The LKUs in 1992**

LKU	Start year*	Turnover KSEK	State grants KSEK	%
Blekinge	1987	1434	300	21
Dalarna	1987	1631	300	18
Gävleborg	1992	500	0	0
Gothenburg	1987	1691	300	18
Jämtland	1982(87)	1539	300	19
Kronoberg	1991	400	200	50
Norrbotten	1988(91)	570	300	53
Roslagen, KUR	1992	550	200	36
Skaraborg	1991	553	250	45
Skåne	1987	1600	300	19
Stockholm, KIC	1987	2000	300	15
Koopus	1986	680	200	29
Värmland	1983(86)	2753	300	11
Västerbotten	1986	700	300	43
Västernorrland	1991	690	300	43
Älvsborg	1986	1330	300	23
Örebro	1984	745	300	40
Östergotland	1992	600	300	50

Source: RRV (1993).
* Actual starting year. Formal start in parentheses.

Between them, the LKUs employed a nucleus of *ca* 70 people in 1996 (as compared to 35 in 1993). Additional employees may be engaged on temporary basis in various projects, run by respective LKU. As employers, LKUs coordinate their wage negotiations through KFO, the co-operative employers' federation. Wage scales and wage setting standards developed by KFO in consultation with the LKUs help to reduce tensions around wage setting and employment benefits. Though there is no explicit common policy towards growth adopted by all LKUs, the general attitude is rather restrictive, the tendency being rather towards the creation of satellites and project groups, further increasing organisation density.

The FKU network The LKUs have maintained a loose contact network from their very inception, mostly by periodical meetings and, eventually, a newsletter. Though informal co-operation forms developed quite early in the process, the network members jealously stressed their independence and local embeddedness, according first priority to local, rather than national networking. The motivation to create, or to join a national organisation was, to begin with, quite low. The pressure to create a firmer organisation increased gradually, with increasing population density, and with the network approaching a full national coverage. A national organisation, the FKU, first emerged in 1994. An important stimulus for this step was provided by Sweden's accession to the EU, that heightened the LKUs need for representation outwards, at both national and international levels.

The FKU association has no permanent staff, and does not run its own projects. The posts of chairman and vice-chairman (currently held by Gothenburg and Stockholm, respectively, are expected to rotate. Other organisational matters (such as organising and hosting LKU meetings, formulation of internal policy guidelines, etc.) are often handled by *ad hoc* delegation. On the whole, the FKU has no ultimate say in the internal affairs of a member LKU. Through its position as a member of the Co-operative Council, however, and its accumulated prestige, it has become somewhat of an informal accrediting institution for would-be LKUs.

References

Abrahamsson, B. and Broström, A. (1980), *The Rights of Labor*, SAGE, Beverly Hills, London.

Anton, T.J. (1974), *Governing Greater Stockholm*, University of California Press, Berkeley, Los Angeles, London.

Arbetsmarknadsdepartamentet/Bergslagsgruppen (1984), *Local Initiatives for Employment Creation in Fagersta, Skinnskatteberg and Norberg*, Stencil, government printers, Stockholm.

Axelson, U. (1985), *Arbetskooperativet Klingan*, Brevskolan, Stockholm.

Bäckman, G., Londström, F., Londström. S. and Olsson, S. (1982), *Norbergsmodellen*, Mimeo, Örebro University College.

Boli, J. (1991), 'Sweden: Is there a viable third sector?', in R. Wuthnow (ed.), *Between States and Markets. The Voluntary Sector in Comparative Perspective*, Princeton University Press, Princeton.

Brunsson, N. and Johannisson, B. (eds) (1982), *Lokal Mobilisering. Om industriers kommunalpolitik och kommuners industripolitik*, Doxa, Lund.

Curtis, J.E., Grabb, E.G. and Baer, D.E. (1992), 'Voluntary associations membership in fifteen countries: a comparative analysis', *American Sociological Review*, vol. 57, pp. 139–152.

Haviva (1997), *Growth Opportunities for Co-operatives in the Stockholm Regio*, KiC, Stockholm.

Hedborg, A. and Meidner, R. (1984), *Folkhemsmodellen*, Tema nova Rabén & Sjögren, Stockholm.

Hirschman, A.O. (1970), *Exit, Voice and Loyalty*, Harvard University Press, Cambridge, MA.

Hirschman, A.O. (1982), *Shifting involvements. Private Interests and Public Action*, Martin Robertson, Oxford.

James, E. (1989), 'The private provision of public services: a comparison of Sweden and Holland', in E. James (ed.), *The Nonprofit Sector in International Perspective. Studies in Comparative Culture and Policy*, Oxford University Press, New York.

Jobring, O. (1988), *Kooperativ rörelse*, Koperativa Institutet, Stockholm.

Jonnergård, K. and Svensson, C. (1990), *Kooperationens utvecklingssystem. En utvärdering av verksamheten efter tre år*, Publication Ds 1990:1, Allmäna Förlaget, Stockholm.

Loord-Gynne, U. and Mann, C.-O. (1995), *Vad blev det av de enskilda initiativen? Rapport till ESO*, Publication Ds 1995:25, Finansdepartamentet, Stockholm.

Lorendahl, B. (1995), 'Nya Kooperativ och lokal utveckling', in P. Aléx, I. Normark, Y. Schörling, Y. Stryjan and B. Wikström (eds), *Kooperation och välfärd*, Kooperativa Studier, Stockholm, pp. 69–94.

Lundström, T. and Wijkström, F (1995), 'Från röst till service? Den svenska ideella sektorn i förändring', *Sköndalsinstitutets skriftserie*, no. 4, Sköndalsinstitutet, Stockholm.

Lundström, T. and Wijkström, F. (1997), *The Nonprofit Sector in Sweden*, Manchester University Press, Manchester and New York.

Mårtensson, B. (1985), *Bykooperativ i Bredsjö och Huså*, Glesbyggdsdelegationen and Kooperativa institutet, Stockholm.

Metro (1997), 17 January.

Netten, A. and Davies, B. (1990), 'The Social Production of Welfare and Consumption of Sosial Services', *Journal of Public Policy*, vol. 10, pp. 331–347.

Pestoff, V. A. (1977), *Voluntary Associations and Nordic Party Systems*, Department of Political Science, University of Stockholm, Stockholm.

Putnam, R. D. (1993), *Making Democracy Work: Civic Traditions in Modern Italy*, Princeton University Press, Princeton.

RRV (1993), *Utvärdering av stödet till lokala kooperativa utvecklings centra*, Report F 1993:23, Stockholm.

SOU (Statens offentliga utredningar) (1987), *Ju mer vi är tillsammans*, Publication SOU1987:33, Allmänna Förlaget, Stockholm.

SOU (Statens offentliga utredningar) (1988), *Mål och resultat – nya principer för det statliga stödet till föreningslivet*, vol. 39, Stockholm.

SOU (Statens offentliga utredningar) (1996a), *Attityder och lagstiftning i samverkan*, vol. 31, Fritzes/offentliga publikationer, Stockholm.

SOU (Statens offentliga utredningar) (1996b), *Kooperativa möjligheter i storstadsområden. Underlagsrapport från storstadskommittén*, vol. 54.

Stenius, K. (1995), *From Common to Anonymous. State, Local Government, Third Sector And Market in Swedish Alcohol And Drug Treatment*, Stencil, Stockholm School of Business, Stockholm.

Stryjan, Y. (1989), *Impossible Organisations: Self-management and Organizational Reproduction*, Greenwood Press, New York, Westport, London.

Stryjan, Y. (1993), *Cooperatives in a Changing World: Membership and Adaptation in Swedish Farmer Cooperation*, Report 65, Swedish University of Agricultural studies, Uppsala.

Stryjan, Y. (1994a), 'Co-operatives in the welfare market', in Perri 6 and I. Vidal (eds), *Delivering Welfare*, CIES, Barcelona.

Stryjan, Y. (1994b), 'The formation of new cooperatives: theory and the Swedish case' *Economic and Industrial Democracy*, vol. 15, no. 4.

Stryjan, Y. (1996a), 'Systemskiftets irrgångar', *Research Report*, no.1, Stockholm School of Business.

Stryjan, Y. (1996b), 'Personalkooperativ: bättre än sitt rykte', *Kooperativ Årsbok 1997*, Kooperativa Studier, Stockholm.

Stryjan, Y. and Wijkström, F. (1996), 'Co-operatives and nonprofit organisations in swedish social welfare', *Annals of Public and Co-operative Economics*, vol. 67, no. 1, pp. 5–27.

Stryjan, Y. and Wijkström, F. (1998), 'Chapter XIII: Sweden,' in C. Borzaga and A. Santuari (eds), *Social Enterprises and New Employment in Europe*, Regione Autonoma Trentino, Trento, Italy.

Vår Bostad (1996), 9, September.

Wijkström, F. (1995), 'Den ideella sektorns roll', in P. Aléx, P. Normark, I. Schörling, Y. Stryjan and B. Wikström (eds), *Kooperation och välfärd*, Föreningen Kooperativa Studier, Stockholm.

11 United Kingdom: Labour Market Integration and Employment Creation

ROGER SPEAR

1. Historical Development of Active Labour Market Measures

In terms of overall policy the UK situation has been marked by emphases on improving the functioning of the labour market (LM), deregulation and increasing LM flexibility; this has involved eliminating minimum wage levels, reducing employment protection (and the power of trade unions), thereby making it easier to 'fire' people, and a shift towards a more enterprise-focused system of employee relations and training; government policy has also shown a concern to reduce welfare dependency – by increasing work incentives, encouraging job-seeking activity, reducing the number of people permitted to receive benefits and reducing the relative level of benefits in relation to wages. This more recent attack on welfare dependency may also have had some effect on size of the 'black' or informal economy. One of the key problems addressed is how to increase demand for low-skill labour, and an important motivation behind deregulation has been to increase demand for low-skill labour by reducing its price. As the aggregate level of unemployment has fallen there has been a greater emphasis on targeting types of disadvantaged people (especially long-term unemployed) and disadvantaged areas/communities. There has been some discussion of large-scale benefit transfers to employment subsidies particularly for long-term unemployment, but nothing more substantial than a few small programmes of this type. An emerging theme in current debates (possibly informed by discussions in continental Europe, motivated by the Delors report – see EC, 1995) is the role of the social economy in providing socially and environmentally useful work, and work in new service sectors. None the less, central government policy has focused more on making the labour market

243

work better than stimulating demand for labour and raising skill levels. This theme has continued with the government under Tony Blair, though the commitment to the EU Social Chapter has moderated the approach to a degree.

In addition it should be noted that although the major player in labour market intervention is central government; the delivery of its programmes has been decentralised and contracted out to Training and Enterprise Councils (TECs or Local Enterprise Companies, LECs in Scotland); these bodies are not publicly accountable and are dominated by private-sector interests. Local government, the co-operative and voluntary sectors, and of course the private sector also play important roles, and they may place greater emphasis on increasing skills/training, demand and promoting equality. At the local level, use is made of other sources of funds (such as government programmes for urban/environmental regeneration, social services budgets, etc.) for the development of community-based projects often with work integration as a major objective. Such projects often take the form of partnerships between local government and the independent sectors. Another major source of funding for training and an important influence on policy are the various programmes of the European Commission, which many labour market integration projects utilise.

With regard to active labour market policies that include wage subsidies, job creation, schemes integrating workers into trading enterprises, a major active LM measure during the 1980s was the Community Programme. This was a temporary work programme providing mainly low-paid and part-time jobs; mainly organised through voluntary organisations and local government, it had more than 300,000 people on the programme at its height in 1986/7. They worked on community projects such as services for disadvantaged groups, environmental improvement, refurbishing community buildings, home insulation, etc. (and a variety of other projects including crime prevention and tourism). Criticisms of the scheme were that it provided low-paid, part-time jobs so it was unattractive to older people and those with dependants (two-thirds were under 25); lack of capital finance and a relatively low training budget meant that jobs provided fairly low-grade work experience, and allowed only limited skills development. However, it had reasonable job entry rates (28% immediately after leaving the programme – though CP participants had above average qualifications).

There were other active labour market measures in place alongside the Community Programme, for example there was a scheme for 20,000 people to be employed in the voluntary sector; 50,000 young people secured jobs supported by employment subsidies; 100,000 people were supported in their attempts to start their own businesses through the Enterprise Allowance Scheme (for one year, benefits could be transferred to help create a self-employment subsidy, but participants had to raise £1000, as start-up capital, in many cases through a bank).

There was a gradual run-down in expenditure on training and job creation programmes, until the early 1990s and an increasing interest in more coercive 'Workfare' programmes (as in USA). There was also an increasing emphasis on job outcomes i.e. training programmes were funded on the basis of job entries at their conclusion – which focused training organisations on selecting the most job-worthy applicants. But as unemployment rose with the recession in the 1990s, a renewed investment in job creation, temporary work programmes and employment subsidy schemes took place. These included Community Action – a programme to provide work experience on projects benefiting the community – participants received benefits plus a supplement.

More recently with declining unemployment (currently around 5%), there has been a renewed focus on the long-term unemployed; for example, through employment subsidy measures and additional (temporary) benefit/wage allowances to individuals, i.e. supplements to wages, or temporary supplements to benefits for those doing part-time work. There are workfare-type pilot schemes underway involving supplements to benefits for those undertaking work, and cuts to benefits to those who refuse without good cause.

In the New Deal (currently underway), the Government is committing up to £3.5 billion over four years (drawn from a 'windfall tax' on privatisation). It offers options to go for full-time education and training (including self-employment options), for environmental improvement, or for voluntary sector work; but, like 'workfare', it takes sanctions against those who refuse to participate (usually terminating benefits). It targets young unemployed people (18–24 year-olds who have been claiming unemployment benefits for six months), lone parents, the long-term unemployed (for two years or more), and people with disabilities. Other measures such as family tax credits aims to help people avoid 'poverty traps', where it is more economic to live on benefits than to take a low paying job. And the Single Gateway scheme (currently being piloted) aims to facilitate transitions between statuses by providing a 'one-stop shop' for unemployed people to access information on work, benefits, tax credits, training, housing and other government services.

2.   Typology of Different Forms of Employment Creation Initiatives

Although the most common use of active labour market measures may be through conventional organisations employing an unemployed person temporarily or permanently, it is arguable that this would tend to select the most employable category of the unemployed. For such organisations work integration is peripheral to their aims; whereas for the initiatives considered in this section, integrating (often more disadvantaged) unemployed people into work is usually a major aim. It is in this area that the social economy usually plays a major role. Very often local community based organisations (co-operatives and community business) are highly effective in assisting less employable (more disadvantaged) groups due to local knowledge and networks; voluntary organisations are effective through their specialist knowledge in supporting specific groups of people or types of need. In some cases, these initiatives may have used some of the national government programmes discussed in Section 1, but local authorities and (frequently larger) voluntary organisations have their own programmes and resources.

However, it is not easy to identify and comprehensively classify the different types of voluntary sector and co-operative initiatives, projects or enterprises of interest. Some make use of government programmes, others do not. Their legal form does not help identification and classification since they may use company law or friendly society law or industrial and provident society law (and many voluntary organisations will also be registered as charities). And finally a common approach is to classify the initiatives according to how they are generally labelled and recognised, bearing in mind that given the flexible legal framework there may be considerable diversity within each category and overlap between categories for example community business may use volunteers and be registered under the same law as voluntary organisations. Because of these identification and classification difficulties data is rather limited and unreliable. The latter approach to categorising the voluntary and co-operative sectors is used here, but use is also made of data from development agencies and federal organisations. The following are common types of initiatives that are widely known and well established –

namely co-operatives, community business, and voluntary organisations; in addition consideration will be given to a more recent innovative initiative – intermediate labour market organisations.

The section below gives some measure of the range and scope of labour market integration initiatives in the voluntary and co-operative sectors in the UK. However so diverse are the legal forms that it is only possible to get statistics on the major forms – co-operatives and community business, and an approximation for certain types of work integration enterprise in the voluntary sector. Most of these initiatives in the UK are small (the average size of worker co-operatives is about ten workers), community businesses tend to be larger, and voluntary sector organisations are varied with some larger organisations.

2.1. Co-operatives

Co-operatives in the UK are formed either under company law or friendly society law. There is no specific co-operative law though there is considerable interest and activity associated with drafting co-operative law for future government legislation (largely through the work of a co-operative lawyers association). Co-operative federations and sympathetic professionals have drafted model rules for a variety of types of co-operative under the two types of law mentioned above. The predominant type of worker co-operative is a highly collectivist one with nominal shareholding (£1). Some people have argued this overburdens the financial structure with debt, and there has been an increase in employee share ownership plans (ESOP)-type structures that allow substantial levels of employee ownership (this has been seen particularly in municipal privatisations of bus services). Future co-operative legislation (nationally, and possibly through a European Co-operative Statute) would moderate this tendency if reserves could be capitalised and used as security for bank loans; there would also be the advantage of reduced risk of degeneration of the co-operative to a private company (sometimes for personal gain).

During the 1980s the UK saw in its worker co-operatives one of the most rapid growth rates of any co-operative movement in Europe (though from a small number – see Table 11.1). This was partly due to the high levels of unemployment and a concern by local authorities to create jobs, but also due to developments in the more radical co-operative movement of the 1960s and early 1970s. This rapid expansion of worker co-operatives was from a small base and the sector is still small. These worker co-operatives are generally small with an average size of five workers in 1989 rising to an average of ten workers in 1993; they are in sectors of the economy with low capital entry costs (54% in services, 20% in retail/wholesale, and only 18% in manufacturing (Hobbs and Bartlett, 1989)).

Table 11.1   UK worker co-operatives and jobs in co-operatives 1976–1992

Year End	No. of co-operatives	Annual growth (%)	No. of jobs	Annual growth (%)
1976	105		3350	
1980	355	36	4500	8
1984	915	27	7850	15
1988	1403	11	8500	2
1992	1115	–6	10,800	6

Source: Cornforth and Thomas (1994), and Co-operatives Research Unit (1989, 1993).

Most co-operatives are new starts (approx. 90% in 1986) with co-operative workers recruited from the ranks of the unemployed – a relatively high proportion of them are women and from ethnic minorities, partly due to targeting such groups in inner city areas where many co-operative support organisations (CSOs) are located. It was estimated in 1988 that there were 217 women-only co-operatives, 126 ethnic minority co-operatives, and 112 co-operatives with a special policy of employing people with disabilities (Hobbs and Bartlett, 1989). However a proportion are job-saving rescues (with greater size and capitalisation). With regard to jobs being saved, it is worth noting the significant growth of employee ownership during the last five years. Some of these have saved jobs through buy-outs, rescues of failing businesses, and conversion of businesses with retiring owner managers (for further an examination of these issues, see Spear and Voets, 1995).

During the 1990s, growth tailed off substantially, and the numbers appear to have stabilised after a decline during the recession. The Industrial Common Ownership Movement (ICOM – the worker co-operative federation), which provides registration documents for many co-operatives estimates that it was registering about 17 new co-operatives per month in 1988, 14 new co-operatives per month in 1989, and ten per month in 1990, with an increase again during the recession in 1990; but failures during the recession, while possibly less than anticipated in comparison with small firms, have reduced overall numbers, and the subsequent rate of formations has declined with the level of unemployment. In 1995, ICOM registered 90 new co-operatives, and about 85 new co-operatives in 1996, while they registered 42 worker co-operatives in 1999, interestingly an increase on the 28 registered in 1998, and with a number being in new technology sectors (Internet/IT). But part of this decline is apparent, due to the fact that ICOM is registering a declining proportion of co-operatives (for example in 1996 it is estimated another 85 co-operatives were formed independently of ICOM, by CDAs, which are experienced enough to carry out the legal requirements themselves and are under pressure to save costs).

However, estimates based on a survey by the Co-operatives Research Unit (CRU; see Table 11.1) indicate that co-operatives weathered the recession well with numbers in 93/94 roughly comparable to 1986 levels, and indeed employment continued to increase from 8500 jobs in 1988 to 10,800 jobs in 1992 when the last comprehensive survey was conducted. With reducing unemployment, it would seem likely that overall numbers have declined somewhat due to declines in the formation rate (due to fewer co-operative support organisations), while the failure rate has probably also declined (but at a slower rate) due to increasing maturity of the sector (but these are only estimations of trends).

The most important influences on the number of new co-operatives being formed have almost certainly been declining unemployment and a reduction in development support. Since 1988 the numbers of CDAs has declined and the funding for most continuing CDAs has also been cut – due partly to reductions in local government budgets. Although there are (in 1999) about 38 co-operative support organisations that are members of ICOM, only about half of these are well-established, but amongst these there are some which have very strong development capabilities.

Social Co-operatives In the UK the social co-operative picture is less developed than many other European countries – most of the social co-operatives are worker co-ops. There appear to have been very few if any attempts to set up user co-operatives in the welfare sector, though there has been significant interest. Co-operatives have also for many years been active as employers of people with disabilities. It is important to differentiate between two types of social co-operatives – social care co-operatives providing care like home care, and social employment co-operatives that provide employment for disadvantaged groups (often with support – hence the term supported employment); the two categories may overlap to the extent that social care co-operatives may employ people with disabilities or disadvantages. Social care co-operatives arise largely from the restructuring of the welfare state, but they also play a role in providing (often part-time) employment for women many of whom are returning to the labour market.

Social co-operatives are generally similar to traditional worker co-operatives, but there are some differences. First, because of the nature of the service (personal) and the democratic nature of co-operatives there is a tendency for users to have some level of participation in the affairs of the co-operative, though often this may be consultative rather than formal. Second, in the social-employment co-operatives the status, terms and conditions of employment of people with disabilities is problematic and tends to be different to other members due to the risk of losing their state benefits. In some cases they are volunteers and in others employees, but in neither case are they paid normal wages; they are usually only paid expenses to avoid the risk losing benefits if they were ever made unemployed.

Wrekin Home Care Co-operative

The co-operative was set up in 91/92 as a result of a Wrekin Council initiative, similar to the *Walsall Home Care Co-operative* model. A steering group was set up to help the co-operative get established. They received a start up grant of £10,000 and started with ten members/carers, and they were self-financing within 18 months. There are currently about 80 carers most work 20–25 hours per week; they come from various backgrounds – full-time jobs, retirement, some with home care background, some with informal care experience; most are aged 30 to 50 years old.

They provide home care services every day of the week, including 24 hours a day cover and operate in urban and rural areas in and around Telford. Their work is mainly domestic including: preparing breakfast, washing, personal care, and miscellaneous such as dog walking; but not nursing care.

The co-operative doesn't advertise its services but gets most of its business through word of mouth and referrals from social services, and hospitals, etc. Its clientele are mostly older and disabled people paid via social services contracts or privately via clients' benefits, though some private clients are not on benefits. The co-operative does about 6000 hours care per month, of which 2700 hours are from direct payments by clients and 3300 hours are from social service contracts; this represents 280 private clients and 122 social service clients; and entails 1800 visits per month.

They rent space in a community centre from the council – for their office and a big room they have converted for a day-care service. All carers are members of the co-operative; they are self-employed for private clients and employed for social service contracts, which makes life a little complicated for accounts and administration. Carers pay the co-operative an hourly levy on their work, and this covers administration (by full-time staff), training, assessments, etc. At the annual general meeting the carer members elect a management committee that meets once a month. An informal meeting also takes place once a month where any member can come and air views, complaints, etc. Decisions are mostly taken by consensus. The full-time staff cover most administrative tasks, assess clients needs, advise clients on benefits, and organise carers matching them to clients, providing training, doing accounts, etc.

New carers attend a training course over a number of weeks that covers most aspects of what is required of them, including being a co-operative member. By the end of course they become members.

In 1995 they decided to open a day-care centre; this took a long time to get established, but it is now very successful – they provide lots of activities for their clients in a very pleasant environment.

There has been considerable activity in the area of social co-operatives (providing employment and/or care for people with disadvantages or disabilities), and an informal network of social co-operative support organizations has operated for much of the 1990s. The following table provides data on community service co-operatives, most of which may be considered social co-ops. Although the crèche co-operatives appear to form the majority, the numbers of home-care co-operatives has increased substantially since 1992, and an ICOM survey revealed 49 care co-operatives in 1998; and there were a similar number of nurseries in 1992, and by the mid-1990s it was estimated that about 25% of all new co-operatives registered were social co-operatives (But these were also registered by CDAs).

The figures (Table 11.2, overleaf) do not show the 20 or so social-employment co-operatives in the manufacturing and retail sectors, or the co-operatives with special policies favouring the employment of people with disabilities. Co-operatives have for many years had a good record as employers of people with disabilities. Some of the most well-known successful examples are Daily Bread, a well-established Christian wholefood retailer and wholesaler employing some people recovering from mental illness (operating in Cambridge and Northampton); Pedlars Sandwiches, a catering co-operative employing people with mental illnesses; Adept Press, a printing business employing people with hearing impairment; and others that focus on employing people with learning disabilities.

Table 11.2 Community Service Co-operatives (1992)

Training (including social)	3
Crèche/playgroup	40
Miscellaneous (cleaning)	27
Welfare (residential)	5
Home care	49 (1998)
Environmental/recycling	14
Total	97

2.2. Community Business

Community businesses first started in rural areas – most notably in the Highlands and Islands of Scotland in the mid-1970s. They were highly successful here as a way of mobilising local communities to provide services such as transport and shops. Community businesses typically take the form of a holding company structure with projects run as trading subsidiary companies. The holding company is registered as a company limited by guarantee with charitable status, thereby allowing members of the community to take a share (at a nominal price of £1) in the community business and thereby own and control it. A development function is typically provided at the holding company level, and this spawns various projects that are usually registered as conventional companies (limited by shares) but wholly owned by the holding company to ensure accountability. Development support may alternatively be provided through an external agency. This model was successfully transferred to inner city areas, most extensively in Glasgow and the rest of Scotland from the late 1970s, and then into Wales. It has been taken up in the rest of the UK, as an approach for addressing problems of exclusion and disadvantage in depressed inner city areas, in order to establish and strengthen community structures and services. It has been used elsewhere in initiatives that might benefit from (a sense of) community ownership such as City

Farms and Community Transport. Community businesses share many of the principles of co-operatives and have gradually increased in number.

Table 11.3 Community businesses (estimated figures)

	1995 UK
Trading companies	400
No. staff/trainees	3500
Turnover (£m)	30

2.3. Voluntary Organisations

Although the voluntary sector plays a major role in supporting disadvantaged groups in society, its role in in labour market integration and employment creation is much smaller, though statistics are not readily available. There appears to be an increasing interest in employment, though the majority of initiatives are training and advice projects. The following types of initiative may be discerned:

(a) training or advice projects;

(b) work initiatives with training for people with disabilities (often by charities serving that group);

(c) work initiatives with training for people recovering from mental illness (often by charities serving that group);

(d) community regeneration projects creating jobs (full and part-time), often run by development trusts;

(e) multi-project community based organisations (such as settlements) that often have training projects and sometimes employment projects;

(f) housing associations with employment, training and advice projects.

To complicate matters, the above categories are not mutually exclusive. The first category may be carried out by a wide range of voluntary organisations including small and large charities, and for wide range of target groups including young people and ethnic minorities. The second and third categories are self-explanatory; a traditional strength of the voluntary sector (which includes charities) is that they often specialise in supporting a particular target group.

There are over 160 development trusts – 'enterprises with social objectives that are actively engaged in the regeneration of an area – a valley, a housing estate, a town centre or a wasteland – whilst ensuring that the benefits are returned to the community'. They are partnership organisations often involving public, private and community partners in funding and governance; they promote and manage a variety of types of projects, including managed workspaces of small enterprises, environmental improvement, community transport, training and advice to small businesses, housing improvement, city farms, etc.

Settlements are multi-purpose organisations committed to tackling poverty and injustice in urban and inner city areas. They are trusts governed by trustees, and many have been established over 100 years, having been endowed with a large property to house their projects and provide some income. They carry out a wide range of projects, some of which are related to training and work integration. Many operate in poor inner-city areas and support ethnic minorities amongst others.

Housing associations have become the major vehicle for social housing (gradually replacing public housing in many areas), they are becoming more and more involved in social and economic projects associated with their tenant communities.

It is extremely difficult estimating the considerable and diverse contribution of voluntary organisations to work integration. In general terms, the voluntary sector is much larger than the co-operative sector in the UK, but the co-operative sector has a solid history of work-integration initiatives, while the voluntary sector is better known for its social and community work. However, it is clearly making a major contribution in the area of training, and there is an increasing development of work-integration initiatives (including social firms that aim to provide real jobs with reasonable pay whilst trading in the market (ECHO, 1997)). The community care legislation with its greater emphasis on local government contracting with the independent sector has given a major boost to such activities, particularly for people with disabilities and those recovering from mental illness. Voluntary organisations (including large charities) specialising in supporting such groups are probably the largest players in the field. Similarly for voluntary organisations associated with young people, though the emphasis here has been more on training and job placement/seeking advice. On the other hand, as unemployment declines, disadvantaged communities often with very high unemployment have been an increasing focus of attention, and more general or multi-purpose community-based voluntary organisations have often made major contributions. In addition the voluntary sector continues to play a substantial role in welfare provision, and thereby offers another route for employment; this can be seen particularly in home-care initiatives that voluntary organisations promote, although some of these projects are largely staffed by volunteers.

2.4. Intermediate Labour Market Organisations

In the UK recently there has been considerable interest in intermediate labour markets. These are: 'waged or salaried, full or part-time jobs with training, which are only available to unemployed people for a limited time period, and where the product of their work has either a direct social purpose or is trading for a social purpose where that work or trading would not normally be undertaken' (Simmonds and Emmerich, 1996). The key features of these initiatives are that they: are intermediate (leading to the normal labour market), and waged (paying the rate for the job), provide temporary employment, trade for a social purpose, and provide added value (i.e. avoiding substitution/displacement effects). It could be argued that such initiatives are a development of the Community Programme, but the differences are that training is more integral, they are more closely and overtly linked to the local social economy, and they have more community control. For example, Glasgow Works in July 1995 was co-ordinating 19 projects employing 232 people; it helped set up these projects with small local partnerships, which then managed the very varied projects – these included security services, childcare, a community/schools theatre company, electrical goods refurbishment, environmental improvement, tourist services, and health projects.

Some commentators argued that ILMs should be a key part of a national strategy to address the problems of the unemployed (Hutton, 1995; Commission for Social Justice, 1994), and indeed this has become part of the Governments national policy. But for ILMs to become well-established requires the development of the following: a system of benefit transfers to help pay the costs of the employing organisation together with greater flexibility in the benefits system and associated programmes; the development of the capacity of social economy to serve as a local instrument of such initiatives; good links with local regeneration agencies to help ensure initiatives operate within local regeneration strategies and improve links with local labour markets; and for similar reasons training and guidance needs to be available through competent local training providers.

The Wise Group

The Wise Group is a Scottish charity, set up in 1983, (and for a period it was extended into the UK through franchising arrangements). Initially it provided an ILM programme delivering training and work experience for the unemployed through insulating the homes of older and disadvantaged people. It has since expanded to provide a wide range of innovative employment and training services: including ILMs, conventional skills training (for call centres, retail, etc.), employer intermediary (employment recruitment), and assistance with job search including an 'After Care' service to support ex-clients in new jobs. Its ILM work delivers community benefits including environmental improvement, waste collection, building, security, office administration, etc. In 1995 it had 560 trainees, 230 staff, and a turnover of £14m, while in 1998 over half of its ILM programme participants (i.e. 574 people) went onto jobs; in terms of services delivered 3237 homes were made more secure, and 5022 homes benefited from its energy services. It is funded from a variety of local, national and European public funds, but earns a proportion of its income from trading/contracts. It was estimated (Simmonds and Emmerich, 1996) that the gross cost of a participant's place with the Wise Group ILM programme was £14,000, but taking account of benefit savings and tax receipts this reduces to £6000 p.a.; this compares favourably with a total cost (1996) of about £8500 to keep someone unemployed.[1]

---

3. Factors Influencing the Effectiveness of Initiatives

This section considers factors influencing the effectiveness of the initiatives discussed in Section 2. It emphasises the importance of a development function and examines the varied ways in which this is carried out.

3.1. Assessing Effectiveness

A commonly expressed issue when judging the effectiveness of these labour market integration initiatives is that of mismatched expectations.

---

[1] *Source:* Finn (1996); Simmonds and Emmerich (1996).

Public authorities often have high expectations for projects working for disadvantaged groups; this may be partly due to overblown promises by those seeking funds. It applies not only to the success rates (of people moving on to regular jobs), but also to the need for continued finance and support for the initiatives. It applies not only to individual projects, but also to types of initiative, so one can see fashions and lifecycles of types of initiative as their true cost and effectiveness gradually becomes apparent, and 'new' types of 'more promising' initiatives emerge. In some cases the new initiatives are better, but the risk is that expertise will be lost, effective projects will close and the wheel will be re-invented.

In assessing effectiveness it is important to reflect that most of the initiatives referred to in this chapter are concerned with some of the most disadvantaged individuals and communities; they are also effective at targeting and attracting such individuals onto their projects and securing community support. In addition they do not just provide training and jobs, but often also deliver community benefits in the form of local services and less-tangible benefits like more positive attitudes/beliefs amongst disempowered individuals and communities.

3.2. Projects, Communities and Networks

Most of the LM integration projects in this chapter share an orientation towards the local community and the social economy. This is partly in the belief that social and economic relations can be restructured positively for individuals and communities; but it is also based on the belief that rethinking how policies and programmes are accessed, makes sense economically and socially. And a particularly important feature of many initiatives is re-integrating bureaucratically differentiated policies and programmes at the local level.

This process of decentralisation and reintegration at the community level, allows good use of local networks and knowledge through community or user group involvement/participation and partnership. It also allows for projects to be directed towards specific local needs and local regeneration strategies. However in practice this is not always easy! It takes considerable leadership skill to maintain active community involvement beyond the excitement of the initial period. And there are often issues around professional management to be resolved – first, to make sure it develops rapidly, but second, that it does not dominate other community and ethical concerns, or squeeze out volunteer enthusiasm and involvement.

3.3. Contextual Framework

The organisational and policy context of these labour market initiatives is dynamic and complex. There are many organisations, networks, and funding programmes to negotiate. Many projects seek multi-partnerships and multi-sourcing of funds. Some rationalisation might reduce the costs of setting up, and make it easier for smaller groups to enter the system. Given this level of complexity and the changing nature of policies and funding programmes, it is not surprising that the entrepreneurial/development function is becoming professionalised, with specialist consultants, development organisations and support capacity in local authorities. Most initiatives described here have had or continue to have close links with a development function whether it be the holding structure of settlements and community business or the development agencies of co-operatives (see below).

Another relevant factor in the contextual framework is the way in which support may be made more amenable to these initiatives. For example one particularly useful forms of support (public or private) is in the provision of an asset base (such as property) which may be used to assist core funding, and develop a longer term perspective; the settlements and some community business provide examples of this. Ways of making the use of benefits more flexible is important for many disadvantaged groups, and can greatly assist the viability of schemes. And access to local government contracts plays an important role for many of these initiatives, particularly in the early stages. Finally although the need to fund development infrastructure seems to be accepted, the level of funding necessary is still contested in many cases.

3.4. Development Function

One important consequence of the hotch potch of policy measures associated with labour market integration initiatives is that new professional competences have been developed both to prepare and manage funding applications for potential projects, and to establish multi-partner relationships particularly to address the multi-faceted nature of problems faced by disadvantaged communities. Thus the development function associated with these initiatives can be very demanding and complex. In many ways local agents carrying out development can be at the leading edge of moves to rethink the employment/welfare relation, and rethink the way in which communities can be regenerated.

One of the most interesting development models has been the UK's distinctive and highly effective system of co-operative support – it has also been a model for a number of other countries such as Sweden. The term co-operative support organisation is used to describe a range of usually quasi-autonomous organisations working mainly to support worker co-operatives, but also sometimes for community businesses, credit unions, housing and other co-operatives. They serve a number of functions – first, institutionalising the entrepreneurial process; second, overcoming other barriers to forming co-operatives, e.g. access to finance; third, as agents of state social/labour market/small firms policy – to work with targeted groups of unemployed, and existing co-operatives creating jobs and providing training and advice; and fourth, representing them and negotiating for resources.

The first CSO was set up in the late 1970s, by 1988 there were 90 CSOs, a majority quasi-autonomous local co-operative development agencies (CDAs), but their number and their resources have declined drastically to around 25 now. Most CSOs have to make annual funding applications and have between one and five staff, mainly with generalist skills though with some specialists. The CDAs have management committees with most comprising a majority of co-operative representatives, plus community, council, and trade union representatives. This highly decentralised form of local co-operative support has been very successful in setting up co-operatives amongst its target groups – those unemployed who are disadvantaged in the labour market – low and old skill people, ethnic minorities, and women. Most CSOs are strongly committed to a bottom-up strategy – this involves intensive non-directive work facilitating a group of people to develop their own business plan and start up their own co-operative business.

Similar development functions and strategies can be seen in the other types of initiatives. Community business often have a separate development function (or development trust) associated with them. They and development trusts have a major strength in securing multi-partnership support for community based initiatives; this can be seen in their varied sources of funding, their many partnered governance structures, and in the variety of project they usually promote. The holding company type structure is common to several types of initiatives, community businesses, settlements, and development trusts, and offers central management services as well as a development function. Settlements (and often development trusts too) in most cases have endowed funds usually in the form of a large multi-purpose building that they can use both as a source of income and to support (and house) their projects. The proximity of similar projects has considerable advantages for management, development and training – for example, some development trusts run managed workspaces as a basis for supporting the development of new enterprises for the unemployed – providing training, advice, management services, and a sense of community of interests. Other voluntary sector initiatives serving specialist groups often have advantages of size and resources and are able to draw on the resources of their own organisation for development activities.

4.   Conclusions and Prospects

The UK labour market policy is marked by an emphasis on placement and job search to make the market work better. None the less, it is recognised that the LM integration initiatives described here achieve some degree of support because they are effective with the more disadvantaged in society. And they may be supported for economic as well as social reasons (the anti-inflationary effects of bringing inactive or excluded people into the labour market, particularly for youth and long-term unemployed). The relatively low cost of measures to improve the operation of the labour market (such as job-search training, and better matching vacancies to unemployed) has been more prominent than the much more costly labour market integration measures for more disadvantaged groups; though problems of deadweight (vacancies already existing and likely to be filled) and displacement are relevant here but rarely seriously addressed.

The policies relevant to labour market integration initiatives are quite diverse. First, there is the question of level – local, regional, national, European; second, there is the fact that some agencies are sectoral in targeting specific groups; and third, there is the intersecting policies of the labour market, benefits policy, enterprise (or small firm) policy, urban policy, and welfare policy. There is enormous variation in policy and practice in each of the above areas and levels. As argued above, an emphasis on more flexible labour markets has not been matched by a more flexible benefits policy. Small firms have received an ideological boost during the Thatcher years, which makes setting them up more acceptable, but resources have not matched rhetoric; although they might offer higher growth rates (Birch, 1979), many are in more marginal sectors of the economy, with higher failure rates than large firms. In the welfare sector changes in government policy for the provision of public services (at local and national level) have opened up opportunities for co-operatives and non-profit organisations. Such initiatives may well be limited to sectors that have low market entry costs, like home care, but the co-operative and not-for-profit form should have advantages of trust and quality in a sector where the involvement of staff and clients is valued.

The strengths of co-operatives are their clear market orientation combined with a strong ethical base – a commitment to democratic practices, equal opportunity policies, and strong links with the local community; they also benefit from a locally based support structure of co-operative development agencies. Community based initiatives (community business, settlements, and development trusts) are good at targeting disadvantaged communities; they tend to have better structures for involving a range of influential local partners and giving a clear sense of community ownership and control; usually they have closer links with projects (than CDAs) – which may be reassuring to funders; and they often also have the benefit of being able to draw on volunteer skills and energy. Large voluntary organisations have a tradition and strength of supporting specific groups; they have the advantages of size (access to resources) and specialisation. Intermediate labour market organisations have a well-defined philosophy for giving transitional support for both communities and disadvantaged groups. They have a clear specification that has been gradually refined, over the years. The important characteristics are: developing recognisable skills, real wages and jobs (some element of trading), delivering social/community benefit with close community links (operating in the social economy). They generally make use of community based structures; and as with co-operatives the 'strawberry field' model is the one most commonly used for growth (new independent growth becomes established in adjoining areas).

Given the complexity of the policy framework and the support required for these initiatives, the development function fulfils an important role – through specialist development agencies and/or holding structures. It is also important that initiatives find ways of meeting the twin challenges of social and economic effectiveness – through operating within local economic strategies, and focusing on growing social economy sectors.

Policy improvements include: making the benefit system more flexible and adaptable to LM integration initiatives; exploring ways of creating new endowed resources such as multi-purpose buildings that will provide a secure basis for longer term projects; examining ways of developing longer term funding arrangements (the short-term nature of many current projects is problematic); reducing transaction costs of organising projects by for example simplifying funding contexts and bidding procedures to fund projects (especially to facilitate multi-funded projects); opening other government programmes (and simplifying them) to LM integration initiatives, e.g. small firm support; and opening public bodies more to contracting relations with such projects (e.g. in the welfare sector, and for other 'public' services).

References

Batsleer, J., Cornforth, C. and Paton, R. (1991), *Issues in Voluntary and Non-profit Management*, Addison Wesley, Wokingham.

Birch, D. (1979), *The Job Generation Process, MIT Program on Neighbourhood and Regional Change*, MIT, MA.

Butler, R.J. and Wilson, D.C. (1990), *Managing Voluntary and Non-profit Organisations: Strategy and Structure*, Routledge, London.

Commission on Social Justice (1994), *Social Justice: Strategies for National Renewal*, IPPR, London.

Cornforth, C. and Thomas, A. (994), 'The changing structure of the worker co-operative sector in the UK: interpretation of recent trends', *Annals of Public and Co-operative Economy*, vol. 65, no. 4.

Cornforth, C., Thomas, A., Lewis, J. and Spear, R. (1988), *Developing Successful Worker Co-operatives*, Sage Publications, London.

CRU (1989), *Directory of Co-operatives*, Co-operatives Research Unit, Open University, Milton Keynes.

CRU (1993), *Directory of Co-operatives*, Co-operatives Research Unit, Open University, Milton Keynes.

CRU (1996), *Strategic Management in the Social Economy – Learning and Training Pack*, Co-operatives Research Unit, Open University, Milton Keynes.

EC (1995), *Local Development and Employment Initiatives, An Investigation in the European Union*, SEC 564/95, European Commission, HMSO, London.

ECHO project (1997), *Social Firms*, Garant Publishers, Leuven/Apeldoorn.

Employment Policy Institute (EPI) (1995), *The Limits of Active Labour Market Policies*, vol. 9, no. 6, EPI, London.

Employment Policy Institute (1996), *Employment Audit*, Issue 2, Autumn, EPI, London.

Finn, D. (1996), *Making Benefits Work*, Centre for Local Economic Strategies, Manchester.

Griffiths, R. (1988), *Community Care: Agenda for Action. A report to the secretary of State for Social Services*, HMSO, London.

Hobbs, P. and Bartlett, W. (1989), 'Sharing in recovery, small firms, producer co-operatives, and job creation in Europe', *10th National Small Firms Policy and Research Conference, UK.*

Hutton, W. (1995), *The State We're In*, Jonathan Cape, London.

ICOM (1998), *Co-operating in Care*, ICOM, Leeds.

LAURA (Land and Urban Analysis Ltd) (1990), *Community Business*, Dept. of Environment, HMSO, London.

Laville, J.-L. (1994), *Services de Proximité*, CRIDA, Paris.

Macfarlane, R. and Laville, J.-L. *et al.* (1992), *Developing Community Partnership in Europe*, Directory of Social Change, London.

Paton, R. (with Duhm, R. *et al.*) (1989), *Reluctant Entrepreneurs – The Extent, Achievements and Significance of Workers Takeovers in Europe*, Open University Press, Milton Keynes.

Philpott, J. (ed.) (1996), *Working for Full Employment*, Routledge, London.

Sikking, M. (1989), *Co-operatives with a Difference*, ICOM, Leeds.

Simmonds, D. and Emmerich, M. (1996), *Regeneration through Work*, CLES, Manchester.

Spear, R., Leonetti, A. and Thomas, A. (1994), *Third Sector Care*, CRU, Milton Keynes.

Spear, R. and Voets, H. (1995), *Success and Enterprise*, Avebury, Aldershot.

PART II: THEORETICAL ISSUES

12 The Specific Role of Non-profit Organisations in the Integration of Disadvantaged People: Insights from an Economic Analysis

CARLO BORZAGA, BENEDETTO GUI AND
FABRIZIO POVINELLI*

Introduction

The growth in unemployment that has affected almost all developed countries in the last 20 years has had a more particular impact on 'less favoured' or 'disadvantaged' workers, i.e. workers with physical or mental disabilities, with socialisation problems or simply unfit to work. At the same time, traditional employment policies designed to assist these types of workers became less effective, due to the decrease in employment opportunities and to the increasingly selective demand for labour. Over the same period a number of new private initiatives aiming at tackling the problem of disadvantaged workers' employability have taken place in various countries. Some of these initiatives are presented in this book.

In this chapter we shall examine the nature and the role of the productive organisations whose explicit aim is to integrate less favoured people into society through the workplace. These organisations include those generally characterised by a lower proportion of disadvantaged workers within their workforce – often under 50% – if compared with more traditional approaches to the phenomenon, such as protected employment. The enterprises we will focus on are mainly engaged in genuine productive activity or on-the-job training of less favoured workers.

* The authors wish to thank Dr Giuseppina Valenti for her assistance during the compilation of the bibliography.

On the theoretical side, the debate that has accompanied the development of these enterprises has not yet revealed to what extent there is any real innovation in social integration through work for less favoured people. Here, we wish to make a contribution to this debate by proposing an interpretation of the role of these organisations not merely from the redistributive point of view (work and income redistribution) but also from the perspective of a more effective allocation of society's human resources.

We start our contribution from the observation that the failure to achieve the integration of disadvantaged people – besides being open to criticism from an ethical or civic point of view insofar as it prevents them from participating in a broad range of normal social activities – is a source of inefficiency because of the waste of potentially productive resources that it implies.[1] Furthermore, society faces steadily rising costs of ensuring an income to those who are unable to provide it for themselves.[2] Currently, the obstacles to the employment of disadvantaged workers can be summarised as the interaction of two phenomena. On one hand, there is a lack of information on the real abilities of disadvantaged workers, their effective productivity, and the conditions required for the full realisation of their productive potential. On the other hand, there is the negative effect of institutional and social constraints to employment. Among these, the fact that the costs and risks of integration through work are essentially borne by the employer, while the benefits are largely reaped by both disadvantaged people and society as a whole.

Given these limitations and institutional constraints, there is clearly a logic behind discriminatory behaviour by employers against disadvantaged workers. However, if these people are offered suitable employment and have received appropriate training to carry it out, there is no reason why they should not achieve levels of productivity comparable with (or even superior to) those of other workers.

Policies for the integration of the various categories of disadvantaged workers – particularly disabled people – have tried to remove the barriers that have caused exclusion from the employment in different ways.

In many countries, including Italy, these measures have primarily consisted of the legal requirement that conventional businesses take on a certain proportion of disadvantaged employees, and of the provision of subsidies. These policies have, however, proved largely ineffective, and

---

[1] Provided, of course, that the employment of disadvantaged people is not substituting for other types of workers (Smith, 1986).
[2] Thornton and Maynard (1986).

their failure can mainly be explained by information asymmetries. The authorities in charge of labour policies have only a limited knowledge of the real ability of enterprises to take on such workers. As a consequence, enterprises alone may be in a position to assess the productivity of these workers. This information asymmetry constitutes an obstacle to the utilisation of significant levels of publicly funded incentives, and to trade unions' willingness to accept substantial pay reductions for workers in order to compensate for the increased costs of training and the increased risk taken by the employer.

This is the background to the present study of the new organisational forms that aim to integrate disadvantaged workers through work. We are aware that these organisations operate within a tight legal framework regarding the allocation of any profits made and the adoption of legal forms to protect this goal. Our key hypothesis is that these requirements can both enable the organisations to bypass the obstacles to invest in disadvantaged workers' training mentioned above and sustain the confidence of the public administrations and trade unions. Furthermore, if these bodies manage to achieve a certain degree of reputation, they may be in a position to ensure conventional businesses real improvements in the abilities of those workers who are being integrated during their training, thus reducing both the costs and the risks of further integration into conventional businesses. In this way, this particular type of enterprise helps improve the smooth functioning of a segment of the labour market.

To develop the arguments supporting this hypothesis, we shall do the following: an analysis of the costs and risks that businesses face when taking on new staff (Section 1), the definition of the concepts of 'disadvantage' and 'disadvantaged person' in the labour market (Section 2), a more thorough investigation of the reasons why businesses tend not to employ disadvantaged workers (Section 3), a look beyond the constraints faced by these workers to examine traditional policies for integration through work (Section 4), and finally the analysis of the specific role played by organisations specialising in the integration of disadvantaged people and subject to laws prohibiting the distribution of profits (Section 5).

1. Business Choices and the Costs and Risks of Work Integration

The following analysis starts from the notion that the labour market is characterised by information imperfections and asymmetries due to varying constraints and human capital. These elements make it impossible to compare the functioning of this labour market with one operating under conditions of perfect competition. Because of these features of the labour market, a business wishing to recruit staff under advantageous conditions has to make two kinds of investment.

The first type of investment is an 'investment in selection'. This is a matter of recruitment or selection processes. It consists of identifying the worker who comes as close as possible to the requirements of the enterprise. The more inadequate or imperfect the information available, the more expensive the selection process.[3]

The second type of investment is an 'investment in training'. Once the worker considered most appropriate has been selected, a business must provide her with some training (specific, and general) so as to equip her with the skill necessary to do the job efficiently and correctly.[4] The less has been spent on the selection stage – or, in other words, the less precise has been the selection process – the higher are, on average, the costs of training.[5]

There is considerable uncertainty over the prospects for recovering these investments, which are expensive and not always predictable.[6] Such investments are fruitless if, for instance, the worker proves incapable of developing the necessary knowledge or of using it properly, or leaves the firm.[7] It is thus understandable that a firm restricts this investment with respect to the socially better workers.

In the first phase of the selection process, a business generally makes use of a 'candidate profile', setting out parameters or requirements that are relatively cheap and easy to monitor (for example, possession of a specific qualification).[8] In the second phase, the firm passes on to the real process of choosing between pre-selected candidates. The use of crude indicators such as 'expected productivity', based on past experience or experience of the market, enables the business to limit costs, perhaps considerably. However, this approach also runs the risk of excluding workers capable of high

---

[3] Spence (1974).

[4] Mincer (1962, 1991).

[5] Oi (1962) defines the costs of *hiring* (including the cost of the selection process) and *training* as fixed labour costs, which converts them into 'quasi-fixed production factors', i.e. 'factors the overall cost of which is partly variable and partly fixed'.

[6] Ritzen (1991).

[7] A business generally recovers initial training costs by paying the worker a wage lower than the real value of his or her production; to succeed in covering the costs of the initial training phase the trained (and sufficiently productive) worker must remain in the firm for a certain length of time (Becker, 1980).

[8] Spence (1974).

productivity (statistical discrimination).[9] In this case, not only does business profitability suffer, but also the effective use of the resources of society as a whole.[10]

At the training level, according to traditional assumptions, a business is only willing to finance the costs of specific training that cannot be acquired in another firm. General training costs continue to be at the worker's expense whether in full-time education or on-the-job (paid for through wage levels lower than productivity).[11] In both cases a firm will try to reduce costs by choosing workers among the best trained, who are likely to be those able to learn fastest. A close correlation has in fact been observed between the level of a worker's education and the amount of training she must be given at work. Therefore, businesses tend to increase the human capital of workers who already have a good level of education, since their training period is generally shorter and therefore cheaper.[12] This results in a more segmented labour market. On the one side, there are educated workers able to profit from further training. On the other side, there is an underclass of ill-educated workers who may or may not succeed in getting a job but who receive very little further training and thus remain at the bottom of the ladder in terms of both jobs and wages.

In sum, the selection and training processes increase the gap between 'less productive' or 'risky' workers and those who are more suitable to start with, affecting their prospects for jobs, wages and career development.[13]

---

[9] Phelps (1972).

[10] Ritzen (1991); Booth and Snower (1996).

[11] Becker (1980). This statement is only valid if we accept the hypothesis of complete information. If we abandon this hypothesis, the picture is different. If some people possess more information than others (asymmetry of information), a business may benefit from partly financing the general training of a worker with the aim of investing in information. Recent empirical analyses confirm this assumption (Bishop, 1991). It could be said that the main 'value' of a trained worker as opposed to a new one in need of training depends not just on the result of the training investment but also on the information acquired on the characteristics and productivity of the worker. In the beginning this value is unknown; staff in charge of training progressively (and to a considerable extent) get an idea of these aspects later (Acemoglu and Pishke, 1996). Stevens (1996) has developed a more detailed model, without clear distinction between general and specific training; he comes to different conclusions as to the choice of businesses to allow training investment.

[12] Arulampalam *et al.* (1996).

[13] OECD (1994).

2. The Concepts of 'Disadvantage' and 'Disadvantaged People' in the Labour Market

A worker may be defined as 'less favoured' or 'disadvantaged' in the labour market if she shows any characteristic that puts her in a position of disadvantage in comparison with other workers.[14] The most common cause of disadvantage is linked to some handicap, that is, 'any limitation or deficiency in the ability to develop an activity, according to the manner or parameters which are thought of as normal, which is due to physical or psychological infirmity or impairment'.[15] If functional limitations lead an individual to become 'disabled', the amount of work she can do and the range of work she can undertake are effectively reduced, as compared with a worker regarded as 'not disabled'.[16] However, incapacity (or reduced capacity) in a given activity also depends on a number of environmental and socio-cultural factors (lack of socialisation, poor education) that interact with the functional limitations of the individual.[17] These factors alone may be enough to restrict a worker's employment opportunities. We can thus use the wider concept of 'disadvantage' to cover 'disabled' people in the traditional sense of the term as well as people who are faced with systematic limitations in performing the job according to accepted standards. This includes not only former drug addicts and ex-convicts, who are regarded as typical disadvantaged people, but also those with little work experience, poor education or obsolete qualifications.

The presence of limitations, whatever they may be, does not usually lessen the worker's productivity in the exercise of range of functions that he or she may fulfil, and does not definitively impair her social and occupational development. Some limitations may be overcome in a number of ways: adapting the job itself (possibly without incurring excessive costs);[18] through suitable training, whether in full-time education or at work; or simply through the concept of 'adapted' employment.[19] Nevertheless, 'disadvantage' generally leads to lower pay, or a narrower range of job that the individual is able to undertake.[20] This means lower

---

[14] Other writers refer to workers who are 'hard to place' (Erhel *et al.*, 1996).

[15] World Health Organisation (1980); Scarpat (1993); Johnson and Lambrinos (1985).

[16] Baldwin and Johnson (1995).

[17] Berkowitz and Berkowitz (1990); OECD (1994).

[18] Baldwin and Johnson (1995).

[19] Erhel *et al.* (1996).

[20] Stern (1996).

productivity compared with what may be regarded as normal,[21] and/or less flexibility at work. On the other hand, there are relatively few people for whom integration to work is completely impossible. For example, it has been observed that many people who are incontestably regarded as 'disabled' (people who are deaf or hard of hearing, or who are partially sighted; paraplegics and mentally retarded people) cannot only undertake numerous kinds of tasks but can even reach a level of productivity equal or actually higher than that of many 'not disabled' people in a given line of work. It must also be remembered that all 'non-disabled' people have limitations or even serious difficulties in carrying out some manual or non-manual tasks, too.[22]

On this basis two 'categories' of disadvantaged people in the labour market may be distinguished.

First, we find a number of people whose productivity falls consistently below normal levels, i.e. lower than that of other workers in any job and impossible to change, regardless of any 'adapted' post or training process.

Second, there is a majority of people whose average productivity is lower than that of other workers but who may be effectively employed as a result of a selection and training process.[23]

For most disadvantaged people, therefore, the main obstacle to overcome for satisfactory integration in the work force is the singling out of a suitable job that enables them to use their existing abilities and to develop the abilities in which they are deficient in the most efficient way. It is then possible to overcome the lack of productivity (qualitative and quantitative), as compared with the demands of labour.[24]

3. The Problems Posed by Occupational Integration of Disadvantaged People

Having made a general analysis of the costs and risks of hiring a new worker, and having defined the concept of 'disadvantage', we now discuss the specific difficulties connected with the integration process.

First, for some categories of disabled workers, integration through work implies accepting the costs of adaptation of the working environment.

---

[21] Haveman *et al.* (1984) regard an individual as 'normally productive' when he is able to 'engage in work that is sufficient to earn a living'.

[22] Stern (1989).

[23] Lepri and Montobbio (1994).

[24] Erhel *et al.* (1996).

The most widely known example is the elimination of barriers caused by the layout of the workplace. However, taking on disabled workers can imply a whole series of more complex logistical and organisational changes. The costs associated with these changes do not apply to the majority of disadvantaged workers, and may subsequently be compensated for by public subsidies when workers are taken on.[25] We will therefore disregard them.

Second, the labour market excludes workers who are systematically and permanently less productive than conventional workers, even where perfect information exists.[26] The inevitable fall in productivity caused by employing these people implies that they can only be taken on if permanent subsidies are offered to the firm. The decision of the public authorities on whether to grant this type of subsidy – and to ensure that the levels set are appropriate – is not an easy one, since there is a danger that firms will behave opportunistically.

Finally, for all other disadvantaged workers, the deficit in production can be curbed if a personalised selection and training process is provided. Their exclusion from production is essentially motivated by increased costs and risks that the firm would have to accept during the selection and training process.[27] These costs are relevantly increased by imperfect information and institutional rigidity.

First of all, during the selection process, the costs incurred in drawing up an appropriate job description for a disadvantaged worker and in ensuring that it corresponds to a job vacancy within the company are higher than the costs of identifying a position for a non-disadvantaged employee. The business must thus allow for longer and more difficult trial periods, under special supervision by 'personnel specialists'.

Furthermore, the training process is more expensive in the case of a disadvantaged worker because of the additional general training it requires, particularly in developing interpersonal skills. As noted above, an enterprise is not generally willing to finance the costs of general education unaided. In most cases, the worker will also need longer, or more intensive,

---

[25] Collignon (1986) highlights the possibility that the expense of these improvements may in some cases lead to improvements in the overall productivity of the enterprise. For example, the elimination of architectural obstacles which is needed for the employment of paraplegic workers can also improve access to buildings for other workers and clients.

[26] Except where the pay offered and requested is close to zero. As Erhel *et al.* (1996) have observed, 'hard to place' workers can be considered as non-competing groups.

[27] For example, see Wadensjo (1994) about the broader issue of the ever-increasing effect of 'fixed labour costs' for enterprises that expect to cover them unaided.

specific training in order to reach satisfactory productivity levels.[28] In addition, a worker having a relatively low level of 'human capital' (in the sense used by economists) usually turns out to be slower in acquiring new skills.[29]

It is important to stress that a high proportion of disadvantaged people, when selected for appropriate functions and adequately trained, can be as useful to the company as worker. However, it is extremely important that those who have gone through the special selection and training process should receive some kind of certification, issued by a credible institution, to accredit the working skills gained. If this is lacking, there is the risk of prolonging the discrimination against these people by referring to their inherent characteristics (physical or mental handicaps, history of prison or drug addiction, complete absence of traditional vocational training, etc.) rather than to their newly acquired skills. This implies that a disadvantaged worker who has acquired higher than average productivity (actual or potential) can still suffer systematic discrimination during recruitment procedures based on signals alone.[30] Indeed, it has been observed that discrimination (statistical or based on prejudice[31]) can trigger off a vicious circle, preventing disadvantaged workers from having access to the labour market – except for a marginal fashion – and so losing the chance of using their skills and changing the external signals which disadvantage them.[32] This is demonstrated more forcibly in periods of high unemployment, when

---

[28] In numerous instances the precise skills required to carry out a given task are less important than a high level of socialisation (OECD, 1994).

[29] A further factor is the recovery time – that is, the period of work in the enterprise needed to recover the investment in training the worker. Recovery time tends to be longer for a disadvantaged worker than for a conventional employee; the risk of her quitting work is higher because of the difficulties encountered in adapting to an ever-increasingly competitive working environment, often on top of a generally less stable state of health. On the other hand, a disadvantaged worker will be less likely to leave the job deliberately for another with a different employer.

[30] In this instance discrimination does not take the form of a refusal to employ the disadvantaged worker, but of reduced pay. On 'financial discrimination' against handicapped people, see Johnson and Lambrinos (1985); Baldwin and Johnson (1994, 1995).

[31] 'Discrimination based on prejudice' is used where a category of persons is excluded on the basis of prejudice against them, ignoring assessments of their productivity. The phenomenon is worsened because it is not necessarily the employer who holds the prejudice; it is enough for other staff or clients to be prejudiced for it to be judged inopportune to take on a disadvantaged person.

[32] Tarling and Wilkinson (1996).

firms are more likely to choose other workers with more favourable characteristics, real or assumed.[33]

4.   The Limitations of Policies for Work Integration of Disadvantaged People

In the past, work integration policies for the disadvantaged mainly concerned the disabled, even though structurally and conceptually they were often so elastic as to be often extended to much broader categories. These programmes have been changed as other labour policies have been developed. Different solutions have also been adopted in different countries. In the light of the preceding analysis, here follows a summary of the most common types of solution,[34] and their respective limitations.

4.1. Regulatory Policies

The purpose of regulatory policies is to influence the behaviour of employers towards disadvantaged people by imposing constraints, duties and obligations on businesses. The most common type of regulation in western European countries is the imposition of quotas, thus obliging businesses (except, in general, the smallest firms) to employ a certain number of disadvantaged people.[35] Instead of subsidising employment costs, these regulations simply forcibly transfer them to companies. Businesses, especially if they are unable to recoup these costs from customers (for example, because they are in competition with firms in other countries where such an obligation does not exist), try to avoid this obligation to recruit. For this reason such policies have proved ineffective, especially since the 1970s.[36]

4.2. Compensation Policies

These policies propose to compensate for the (real or presumed) productivity gap of disadvantaged workers, reducing the recruitment costs,

---

[33] Although this is the situation in the majority of European economies, it should still be noted that the steady decrease in the numbers of young people joining the active population as a result of falling birth rates over recent decades could lead to a deficit in human resources for the economic system, and hence increase the need to make use of the potential offered by 'disadvantaged' or 'secondary' workers (OECD, 1992).

[34] Schmid and Semlinger (1984).

[35] Emerson (1988).

[36] Schmid and Semlinger (1984).

so as to encourage employers to engage such workers voluntarily. There are several variations on these policies.

The first consists of training and vocational guidance before recruitment, with the aim of meeting the deficiencies in general education of the individuals concerned and identifying the most suitable kinds of work. A limitation of this kind of intervention is that vocational training, particularly when it is provided through 'special centres' or 'special classes', is often structured solely as a function of the characteristics of the people receiving the training without taking sufficient account of the demands of labour.[37] In this case, there remains the problem of bridging the gap between the training given to workers and that required by businesses.[38] Additionally, the more disadvantaged unemployed people are, generally the less inclined they are to take part in training programmes[39] and even if they do take part in them their employment prospects remain poor.[40] In some cases, training programmes can be counter-productive or lead to stigmatisation. This is because taking part in a training programme can be interpreted by employers as a signal of low productive potential.[41] Finally, in some countries businesses often regard the public vocational training system as unreliable, and the qualifications it confers as lacking credibility.

Another variation is that of economic incentives for recruitment (wages policies or subsidies). Policies of this kind encourage employers to take on workers with difficulties in integration, compensating the firm for low initial productivity and the most significant training costs. As it always happens with subsidies there are several effects (substitution, relocation, 'creaming off', etc.) that raise the cost to the public purse of every new job created for a disadvantaged person. The problem then is to identify the unjustified payment of subsidies to crafty or lucky employers.[42] This is even more important, since the objective is to achieve integration simply by lowering labour costs, and in this case the subsidy must be very high. It goes without saying that the payment of a significant financial incentive to recruitment is justified insofar as the individual's working capacity is tangible, verifiable and measurable.

---

[37] Breda and Rago (1991).
[38] Erhel *et al.* (1996).
[39] Raam *et al.* (1993).
[40] Pedersen and Westgerard-Nielsen (1993).
[41] Dolton (1993).
[42] Gui (1990).

4.3. Substitution Policies

With substitution policies, the government does not intervene in the traditional labour market. It rather promotes directly work integration of targeted people (usually disabled) in the public sector, in sheltered employment or in *ad hoc* businesses. In other words, it creates a demand for labour 'outside the market', i.e. a 'substitute labour market'.[43] There are nevertheless omissions in policies of this kind, particularly where working conditions are aimed more at providing an occupation than at genuine production. In this case, instead of encouraging real social and occupational integration for disadvantaged people, measures of this type result in creating ghettos, tying many people, capable of playing an active part in the normal labour market, to separate production structures.

4.4. Innovative Measures

Recent years have seen the birth and the spread of new kinds of measures that differ from the traditional approaches.[44] Among these are more personalised employment services, measures to target employment, and various forms of 'supported employment'. These new measures present some interesting features. Above all, they guarantee a business that the work will be carried out by the person concerned, with support from an assistant, according to methods that ensure a normal standard of productivity. Additionally, the degree of support and help at work received by a disadvantaged person is tailored to her personal requirements, case by case. Special importance is given to on-the-job training, which is reflected in intensive one-to-one training with a qualified instructor. These policies have been implemented primarily in public or semi-public bodies, or in non-profit organisations.[45] Although it is true that these measures have features that help overcome the labour market failures discussed above, they are also exceptionally expensive.[46] People involved in these occupational integration programmes may also become the victims of stigmatisation's negative effects.

---

[43] Schmid and Semlinger (1984); Seyfried and Lambert (1989).
[44] Scalvini (1995).
[45] Kierman and Stark (1985); Burkhauser and Hirnoven (1989).
[46] Particularly when these measures are carried out by public bodies.

5. Non-profit Organisations Specialised in the Rehabilitation of Disadvantaged Workers

Since the 1980s, non-profit organisations have been set up and have gradually spread, with the aim of promoting the occupational integration of disadvantaged people. They may be distinguished from regulatory or compensatory policies insofar as they do not aim at creating jobs for these people in conventional businesses, but instead at setting up new companies to train and employ them on a temporary or permanent basis. They may also be distinguished from substitution policies, including sheltered employment, both because of their specifically business-like nature and their more ambitious aim of achieving full productivity from rehabilitated workers. However, they have often made use of the kinds of assistance for training and occupational integration that are characteristic of supported employment. Their structure varies from country to country, usually taking the form of co-operatives or voluntary organisations.

In Italy, these initiatives at first favoured the stable integration within the organisation of people with physical or mental disabilities. Subsequently they focused more on training on-the-job for people disadvantaged in a broader sense, often with the aim of making such people go back to the normal labour market. At present, most of these bodies offer either stable integration within the organisation, or a more limited work experience skewed towards either one or the other objective, essentially depending on the practical employment possibilities for these workers within the labour market.

These schemes are more frequently compared with ways of achieving social integration of disadvantaged people than with measures for improving their opportunities in the labour market. From a regulatory and financial point of view, too, they are more likely to be found within the framework of social policies than labour policy, since the difference between them and traditional forms of sheltered employment has not been fully grasped. In reality, these organisations are responding to the question of training disadvantaged people at and through work in a new way. They present two advantages with respect to traditional measures.

The first advantage is that these organisations can select and train disadvantaged workers at a lower cost than other businesses, thanks to certain freely available human and financial resources (voluntary work and donations) and to skills that have been developed through extensive experience in the field. This advantage enables these bodies to limit the profitability deficit often involved in employing these workers (caused by higher selection and training costs and possibly reduced productivity). When they aim to integrate workers into the normal labour market, the comparative advantage they enjoy enables them to train people so as to give them a kind of 'passport' to meet the requirements for employment in a conventional firm. If conventional companies use the services of integration organisations, no longer have to cover the costs of selection and training associated with the employment of disadvantaged people. Work-integration bodies can thus provide a sort of certificate vouching for the worker's skills, establishing and/or developing their reputation as reliable intermediate institutions. Their credibility can act as a counterweight to the prejudices to which disadvantaged people often fall victim.

Another advantage is due to the existence of strict laws concerning the allocation of any profits and the adoption of democratic and transparent structures (co-operatives and voluntary bodies). These organisations have the reputation of reliable and credible bodies both to the public authorities – who are always worried by the risks associated with financial incentives – and to the trade unions – who for similar reasons express concern when companies depart from wage norms during training periods and apprenticeships. In this respect, as established by research into non-profit organisations,[47] constraints on the distribution of profits provide a guarantee given that any credit balance will go towards consolidating the financial structure of the integration body, with the effect of strengthening its work with other disadvantaged people. The pursuit of the stated objectives is also guaranteed by a membership made up of beneficiaries and volunteers together with managers and other conventional workers.[48] As Askildsen and Ireland have shown,[49] the whole range of aims and constraints which characterise these particular institutional forms and distinguish them from profit-oriented businesses provide incentives to invest in human capital. By taking into consideration their superior propensity for actively involving workers in their training, these organisations are able to make use of the benefits of this investment in-house.

Thanks to this double advantage, integration bodies can devote themselves more effectively to training disadvantaged people and identifying the more suitable tasks for them. This unleashes an increase in productivity that may be exploited within or outside the organisation.

---

[47] Hansmann (1980, 1987); Gui (1991).
[48] In Italy, at least, the establishment of social co-operatives allows for the participation of these different groups in their controlling and decision-making bodies.
[49] Askildsen and Ireland (1993); Ireland (1994).

Integration bodies also suffer from some limitations.[50] Among them the most important probably is the 'creaming off' of the most promising disadvantaged workers to the detriment of those in greatest need.[51] 'Creaming off' can take place when workers are admitted to a training programme within the organisation, and may be motivated by the need to maintain a certain level of productivity in order to ensure its survival. It can also take place when workers leave to join the normal labour market, which is considerably more demanding.[52] That said, it is to the credit of these integration bodies that they reveal the true abilities of workers who would otherwise be condemned by the labour market. Indeed, no measures, except for direct public sector employment in sheltered workshops, can avoid 'creaming off'. Consequently, integration into the normal labour market through specialised organisations cannot be the only approach of employment policy for disadvantaged people. It must be accompanied by a range of aims and policies targeted more precisely on those people whose disadvantage is most pronounced.[53]

A similar argument can be made in the case of 'relocation effects', which can lead to a lower unitary production cost in integration bodies (taking into account the benefits paid to them) and which translates into a loss of markets and jobs in other businesses. However, risks of this kind are reduced by the fact that integration organisations are often found in sectors of the market that are not normally exploited by conventional businesses.

A third limitation, in our view, affects the efforts of disadvantaged workers to enter the labour market: an integration body, or even all these organisations taken together, cannot succeed in building up a reputation sufficient to guarantee effective opportunities for employment in the normal labour markets through their selection and training programmes. Among the valid reasons (not solely based on prejudice) for this insufficient reputation, might be the fact that the integration bodies lag behind conventional firms in technical or organisational terms. This gap

---

[50] Apart from these specific limitations, these bodies can also suffer from constraints which affect more generally all non-profit organisations such as the difficulty of checking the real allocation of profits (Ben-Ner and Van Hoomisen, 1991; Ben-Ner, 1994) and the lack of incentives for improved efficiency (Hansmann, 1996; Ortmann, 1996).

[51] Ballet (1996).

[52] Integration organisations can become prisoners of workers whose rehabilitation into the normal labour market is impossible (in some countries the law requires them to keep the worker on within the organisation). The only point at which 'creaming off' is then possible is the point of entry into training.

[53] For example the stable integration, in these organisations or others, of people who are rejected by the labour market.

goes to highlight the problems of developing vocational training that is properly recognised in the outside world.[54]

Conclusions

This chapter has considered what can be learned about the labour market and the emergence of non-profit organisations specialising in the occupational integration of disadvantaged people. This development has emerged in different European countries during the past 15 years. The question examined has been whether these bodies merely present a more socially acceptable approach (deeper commitment and better integration) through which society can care for the deprived and draw them into the system, or whether, on the contrary, their working methods also make it possible to alleviate some of the deficiencies of the labour market, particularly as regards disadvantaged workers.

Theoretical analysis and empirical observation presented in the book show the particular contribution that these organisations can make to promote the better use of human resources. Their strength lay in the reduced cost of selection and training of potentially productive but disadvantaged people, and their integration into the labour market. These people would otherwise be condemned to exclusion, given the imbalance of information concerning their true abilities and the institutional constraints affecting the allocation of profits to investment in training and selection.

If this is the case, non-profit organisations specialising in work integration of disadvantaged people are not a last resort to make up for the failure of other policies. On the contrary, they provide a measure deserving a particular place in employment policy. These organisations have a number of special features that other measures cannot reproduce, and which in our view increase their likelihood of success in the selection, training and work integration of disadvantaged workers. This measure naturally has both strengths and weaknesses. It is certainly not capable of providing the sole solution to the vast problem of integrating disadvantaged workers, but it provides a tool that lends itself particularly well to complement other measures.

For example, matching this measure with special employment subsidies, or even the introduction of compulsory quotas, could be a

---

[54] This lagging-behind may be due to inadequate capitalisation, to the lack of an enterprise culture, or to a kind of production which is too marginal to enable workers to acquire skills that can be exploited in the normal labour market.

promising route. As has already been made clear, there is less risk of abusing of subsidies within non-profit organisations. The mediation of these integration organisations can also reduce the costs and risks to business as a consequence of the imposition of quotas. Thus, certain experimental schemes in the North of Italy constitute less expensive ways of forcing conventional businesses to contribute to the work integration of disadvantaged people. Among other ideas is that of 'converting' compulsory employment quotas into undertakings made to integration organisations to buy semi-finished products or services. Beside these forms of sub-contracting, other kinds of collaboration between conventional firms and integration bodies can also be envisaged. For example, agreements concerning specific job opportunities to be made available by conventional businesses to workers undergoing training with integration organisations, even for a limited period or intermittently. This collaboration would take place without changing their normal employment status, but in the expectation of achieving the levels of productivity required by conventional companies.

Implementing such schemes requires at least a partial revision of the norms that govern the working of the labour market, and especially recruitment. These norms are currently too restrictive, insofar as their main objective is to avoid abuse on the part of conventional businesses. It is also of fundamental importance that integration bodies build up and cultivate a sound reputation in the market for their actual skill in improving the employability of disadvantaged people and in certifying their level of productivity. Finally, policy makers must be made fully aware that they have a truly innovative measure in the field of active employment policies at their disposal. This measure may prove indispensable in countering the heavy consequences for the ill-qualified resulting from the increasingly selective nature of labour demand.

References

Acemoglu, D. and Pischke, J. (1996), 'Why do firms train? Theory and evidence', *NBER Working Papers Series*, no. 5605, Cambridge, MA, pp. 1–51.

Arulampalam, W., Booth, A.L. and Elias, P. (1996), *Modelling Work-related Training and Training Effects using Count Data Techniques*, ESCR Research Center on Micro-social Change, University of Essex, Essex.

Askildsen, J.E. and Ireland, N.J. (1993), 'Human capital, property rights, and labour managed firms', *Oxford Economic Papers*, vol. 45, pp. 229–242.

Baldwin, M.L. and Johnson, W.G. (1994), 'Labor market discrimination against men with disabilities', *Journal of Human Resources*, vol. 29, pp. 1–19.

Baldwin, M.L. and Johnson, W.G. (1995), 'Labor market discrimination against women with disabilities', *Industrial Relations*, vol. 34 (4), pp. 555–577.

Ballet, J. (1996), *Les Enterprises de solidarité*, mimeo, Université de Versailles, St. Quentin en Yvelines.

Becker, G.S. (1980), 'Investment in human capital: effects on earnings', in O.C. Ashenfelter, and R.J. Lalonde (eds) (1996), *The Economics of Training*, Elgar, Cheltenham, pp. 3–32.

Ben-Ner, A. (1994), 'Who benefits from the nonprofit sector? Reforming law and public policy towards nonprofit organizations', *The Yale Law Journal*, vol. 104 (3), pp. 731–762.

Ben-Ner, A. and Van Hoomissen, T. (1991), 'Nonprofit organizations in the mixed economy. a demand and supply analysis', *Annales de l'économie publique sociale et cooperative*, vol. 62 (4), pp. 391–415.

Berkowitz, M. and Hill, M.A. (eds) (1986), *Disability and the Labor Market*, ILR Press. Cornell University, Ithaca.

Berkowitz, M. and Berkowitz, E. (1990), 'Labor force participation among disabled persons', *Research in Labor Economics*, vol. 11, pp. 181–200.

Bishop, J.H. (1991), 'On-the-job training of new hires', in D. Stern, and J.M.M. Ritzen (eds), *Market Failure in Training? New Economic Analysis and Evidence on Training of Adult Employees*, Springer-Verlag, Berlin, pp. 62–98.

Booth, A.L. and Snower, D.J. (eds) (1996), *Acquiring Skills. Market Failures, their Symptoms, and Policy Responses*, Centre of Economic and Policy Research (CEPR), Cambridge, UK.

Breda, M.G. and Rago, M. (1991), 'Formare per l'autonomia. Strumenti per la preparazione professionale degli handicappati intellettivi', *Quaderni di Promozione Sociale*, 24.

Burkhauser, R.V. and Hirnoven, P. (1989), 'United States disability policy in a time of economic crisis: a comparison with Sweden and the Federal Republic of Germany', *Milbank Quarterly*, vol. 67, suppl. 2, pp. 166–194.

Collignon, F.C. (1986), 'The role of reasonable accommodation in employing disabled persons in private industries', in M. Berkowitz and M.A. Hill (eds), *Disability and the Labor Market*, ILR Press, Cornell University, Ithaca, pp. 45–68.

Dolton, P.J. (1993), 'The econometric assessment of training schemes: a critical review', paper presented at the *International Conference of the Economics of Labour, Maastricht*, mimeo.

Emerson, M. (1988), 'Regulation or deregulation of the labour market: policy regimes for the recruitment and dismissal of employees in the industrial countries', *European Economic Review*, vol. 32 (4), pp. 777–817.

Erhel, C., Gautié, J., Gazier, B. and Morel, S. (1996), 'Job opportunities for the hard-to-place', in G. Schmid *et al.* (eds), *International Handbook on Labour Market Policy and Policy Evaluation*, Elgar, Cheltenham, pp. 1–32.

Gui, B. (1990), *I sussidi marginali all'occupazione*, Giuffrè, Milan.

Gui, B. (1991), 'The economic rationale for the 'third sector', nonprofit and other noncapitalistic organisations', *Annales de l'économie publique, sociale et cooperative*, vol. 62, no.4, pp. 551–572.

Hansmann, H.B. (1980), 'The role of nonprofit enterprise', *The Yale Law Journal*, vol. 89, no. 5, pp. 835–901.

Hansmann, H.B. (1987), 'Economic theories of nonprofit organisation', in W.W. Powell (ed.), *The Nonprofit Sector. A Research Handbook*, Yale University Press, New Haven.

Hansmann, H.B. (1996), 'Too many nonprofit organizations? Problems of entry and exit', in *Osservatorio Giordano dell'Amore, Le organizzazioni senza fini di lucro*, Giuffrè, Milan.

Haveman, R.H., Halberstadt, V. and Burkhauser, R.V. (1984), *Public Policy toward Disabled Workers*, Cornell University Press, London.

Ireland, N. (1994), 'Human capital, asymmetric information and labour-management', *Annales d'économie et de statistique*, 33, pp. 13–28.

Johnson, W.G. and Lambrinos, J. (1985), 'Wage discrimination against handicapped men and women', *Journal of Human Resources*, vol. 20 (2), Spring, pp. 264–277.

Kierman, B. and Stark, J. (1985), *Employment Options for Adults with Developmental Disabilities*, Utah State University, Development Center, Logan, Utah.

Lepri, C. and Montobbio, E. (1994), *Lavoro e fasce deboli. Strategie e metodi per l'inserimento lavorativo di persone con difficoltà cliniche o sociali*, FrancoAngeli, Milan.

Mincer, J. (1962), 'On the job training: costs, returns and some implications', *Journal of Political Economy*, vol. 70 (5), 50–79.

Mincer, J. (1991), 'Job training: costs, returns and wage profiles', in D. Stern and J.M.M. Ritzen (eds), *Market Failure in Training? New Economic Analysis and Evidence on Training of Adult Employees*, Springer-Verlag, Berlin, pp. 15–38.

OECD (1992), *Employment Policies for People with Disabilities: Report by an Evaluation Panel*, Labour Market and Social Policy Occasional papers, OECD, no. 8, Paris.

OECD (1994), *Disabled Youth and Employment*, OECD, Paris.

Oi, W.Y. (1962), 'Labor as a quasi-fixed factor', in O.C. Ashenfelter and R.J. Lalonde (1996) (eds), *The Economics of Training*, Elgar, Cheltenham.

Ortmann, A. (1996), 'Modern economic theory and the study of nonprofit organizations: why the twain shall meet', *Nonprofit and Voluntary Sector Quarterly*, vol. 25, no. 4, pp. 470–484.

Pedersen, J. and Westergard-Nielsen, N. (1993), 'Unemployment: a review of the evidence from panel data', *OECD Economic Studies*, no. 20, pp. 65–114.

Phelps, E.S. (1972), 'The statistical theory of racism and sexism', *American Economic Review*, vol. 4, pp. 533–549.

Raam, O., Torp, H., Hernaes, E. and Goldestein, H. (1993), 'Evaluation of labour market training programmes: some experiences with an experimental design', paper presented at the *International Conference of the Economics of Labour, Maastricht*, mimeo.

Ritzen, J.M.M. (1991), 'Market failure for general training, and remedies', in D. Stern and J.M.M. Ritzen (eds), *Market Failure in Training? New Economic Analysis and Evidence on Training of Adult Employees*, Springer-Verlag, Berlin, pp. 185–213.

Scalvini, F. (1995), 'L'inserimento lavorativo delle persone svantaggiate', *Impresa Sociale*, no. 21, pp. 7–13.

Scarpat, O. (1983), 'Un tentativo di analisi costi-benefici dell. inserimento dei disabili nel mercato del lavoro', *Rivista Internazionale di Scienze Ecomomiche e Commerciali*, vol. 30 (9), September.

Schmid, G. and Semlinger, K. (1984), *Labour Market Policies for the Disabled. Experiences from the Federal Republic of Germany, Great Britain, Sweden and the USA*, Wissenschaftszentrum, Berlin, pp. 1–74.

Seyfried, E. and Lambert, T. (1989), *New Semi-sheltered Forms of Employment for Disabled Persons. An Analysis of Landmark Measures in the Member States of the European Communities*, CEDEFOP Document, Luxembourg.

Smith, R.S. (1986), 'The economics of job displacement', in M. Berkowitz and M.A. Hill (eds), *Disability and the Labor Market*, ILR Press, Cornell University, Ithaca, pp. 112–126.

Spence, A.M. (1974), *Market Signaling. Informational Transfer in Hiring and Related Screening Process*, Harvard University Press, Cambridge, MA.

Stern, S. (1989), 'Measuring the effect of disability on labor force participation', *Journal of Human Resources*, vol. 24 (3), pp. 361–395.

Stern, S. (1996), 'Semiparametric estimates of the supply and demand effects of disability on labor force participation', *Journal of Econometrics* 71, pp. 49–70.

Stevens, M. (1996), 'Transferable training and poaching externalities', in A.L.Booth and D.J. Snower (eds), *Acquiring Skills. Market Failures, their Symptoms, and Policy Responses*, Centre for Economic and Policy Research (CEPR), Cambridge, UK.

Stigler, G.J. (1961), 'The economics of information', *Journal of Political Economy*, vol. 69, June, pp. 213–225.

Tarling, R. and Wilkinson, F. (1996), 'Economic functioning, self sufficiency and full employment', paper presented at the *International Working Party on Labour Market Segmentation, University of Tampere*, mimeo.

Thornton, C. and Maynard, R. (1986), 'The economics of transitional employment and supported employment', in M. Berkowitz and M.A. Hill (eds), *Disability and the Labor Market*, ILR Press, Cornell University, Ithaca.

Thurow, L. (1975), *Generating Inequality*, Basic Book, New York.

Wadensjo, E. (1994), 'Trends in labour market policies for youths with disabilities', in *Disabled Youth and Employment*, OECD, Paris, pp. 35–48.

World Health Organization (1980), *International Classification of Impairments, Disabilities and Handicaps. A Manual Classification Relating to the Consequences of Disease*, WHO, Geneva.

13 Third Sector and Social Economy Re-examined in the Light of Initiatives Promoting Insertion

JEAN-LOUIS LAVILLE

International comparisons confirm that the approach to insertion of disadvantaged workers into the labour market through economic activity has taken root. The adoption of this approach in several countries changes our view of this practice. It seems to be a real innovation, leading to the emergence of new kinds of measures, which have anticipated the limitations of active employment policies – making use of some but changing their emphasis.

So, from an empirical point of view, they provide some impulse to conceive new public policies to combat social exclusion and unemployment. Moreover, from a theoretical point of view, this new trend presents some characteristics relating it to the two traditions of the third sector and of the social economy.

Some of the national case studies included in this book focus on initiatives promoting insertion through non-profit organisations (NPOs) and voluntary sector. In these cases, a non-distribution constraint is respected. But, in other cases, the distribution of profits is only limited and privileges the participants in the activity. Rather than non-profit organisations, we can speak of 'not-for-profit' enterprises, mainly co-operatives. The beneficiaries of the enterprise's activities are members forming a group with equal rights ('one person, one vote'). This represents the latin and francophone tradition in which 'a passion for equality'[1] has been the driving force behind the social economy. The historical strength of co-operatives, together with the extensive studies of co-operation, explains

---

[1] Chanial (1997).

why this movement provided the true centre of gravity for early approaches to the concept of the social economy.[2]

This chapter reviews the hypothesis of an evolution of the third sector and a new social economy because the insertion initiatives provide an opportunity to re-examine these two traditions of third sector and social economy. It is specially interesting because it also gives some impulse to analyse the possible interactions between these two approaches in the light of new phenomena. Recently, voluntary organisations played a growing role in the social economy; it must be remembered that they often represent the largest part of the social economy, particularly in terms of jobs. However, this third part of the social economy (alongside mutual societies and co-operatives) has always posed the main theoretical problems.[3] For this reason, literature on NPOs raises major questions and is at the same time a source of inspiration for concepts of the social economy.

From the descriptions of situations in individual countries and the transversal analyses in this book, it is possible to determine just how organisations promoting insertion by economic means play a part in renewing the social economy or third sector, as distinct from the private profit sector. The establishment and the survival of these independently managed organisations cannot be explained by the presence of investors taking entrepreneurial risks in the expectation of a return on their investment. They sit squarely in the historic tradition of enterprises whose beneficiaries are never primarily involved to realise a capital gain (to use Gui's definition of the defining characteristic of the third sector[4]). In other words, the purpose of the enterprise is to 'provide a service to their members or to the community rather than to make a profit'.[5]

1. Mutual Aid and the General Interest

These not-for-profit enterprises are inspired by two distinct dynamics.

The first of these is the principle of *mutual aid* or *mutual* benefit.[6] The mutual aid dynamic presents new problems with regard to labour market

---

[2] See for example the work of Desroche (1976).

[3] Defourny (1992).

[4] Gui (1991).

[5] This was the definition applied by the *Conseil wallon de l'économie sociale* (1990) in Belgium.

[6] The question of whether it is possible to compare mutual aid and mutual benefit is not considered here. A discussion of this question is to be found in Laville and Sainsaulieu (1997).

insertion through economic activity. In the past, social enterprises were founded by individuals 'comparatively dominated in their relationships with entrepreneurial capitalists', but who nevertheless had 'the means to finance useful activities themselves'.[7] They also possessed cultural resources associated with their collective identity, for instance due to the know-how shared in worker co-operatives. The beneficiaries of insertion programmes have less autonomy and fewer resources. The initiatives they organise require support from professionals and institutional partners. In both France and Québec the failure of co-operatives set up by marginalised workers[8] and the recurrent difficulties encountered by women's catering co-operatives may in part be attributed to the fact that no appropriate support systems were developed.[9] There was also discrimination against mutual aid organisations; in Great Britain this took the form of legal discrimination, since charitable status was not extended to self-help groups, in France public policy excluded self-help insertion groups from the institutionalisation of insertion initiatives.[10]

The second dynamic operating in this field is that of *help for others* or the *general interest*. In the economy as a whole, the organisations, dedicated to the general interest, are on the increase. Insertion through economic activity is but one example. Some of these general-interest organisations reject the voluntary organisation framework to adopt the co-operative form as has happened in several experiences in Italy. In that country as elsewhere, innovations begun in the voluntary sector have led to the development of a new kind of co-operative: the social co-operative. In our view, this amply illustrates the fluid boundaries between two organisational structures whose similarities are greater than their differences, despite the view held by those who exclude co-operatives from the third sector, restricting it to voluntary organisations. If self-help is difficult when the objective is to combat exclusion, the dynamic of helping others raises the questions of paternalism, which affects all private organisations working in the general interest. It is a particular problem in insertion enterprises, given the characteristics of the target group. The huge inequalities between promoters and beneficiaries increase the danger that such enterprises will drift off course, and function on the basis of continued dependency of their participants. A charismatic leadership is a risk that

---

[7] Vienney (1994), p. 94.
[8] Barbeyer (1984).
[9] Despite the detailed proposals formulated to define appropriate support: cf. Hersent (1990).
[10] Chopart *et al.* (1998).

insertion initiatives face even more than other enterprises according to their workers' profiles. That is why certain initiatives insist on the importance of democratic internal rules because they not only defend the access to work but also the democratic relations, in a learning process allowing the participants to reach social integration and personal autonomy.

2.   Entrepreneurs and Promoters of Social Networks

The nature of the target groups for insertion initiatives raises questions about the two dynamics operating in the third sector (mutual aid and general interest). But the differences between current and earlier models of the social economy are not limited to these questions. These differences also arise from the variety of stakeholders involved in these not-for-profit enterprises. In place of homogeneous groups united by a threatened identity (nationality, way of life, craft, etc.), there are now more varied actors, whose identity is more diverse but who are united by a common awareness of the unemployment problem and the felt need for an urgent response.

The origins of insertion initiatives lie not so much in groups strongly linked by a single socio-economic identity as in a wish to provide employment opportunities for unemployed people hit by exclusion.[11] Individuals who engage in economic activities for this reason and who are convinced of the value of training for salaried work and socialising the unemployed may be described as *social and civic entrepreneurs* insofar as they regard the common good as more important than material gains.[12] However, this does not exclude a variety of motivations and competences, depending on whether those involved are activists, social work professionals, or beneficiaries. Among the founders there is almost always an individual, or a very small core of people, who share the characteristics of every entrepreneur worthy of the name: strong personal involvement, a sharp awareness of financial and commercial realities, strong leadership, motivation to promote efficiency and high returns (in the broadest sense). These innovators have good prospects to succeed in their projects, which can often upset relationships within a locality, requiring the use of

---

[11] From this point of view, experiences of insertion extend the trend seen in the workers takeovers, where participants are united by the threat of unemployment. Paton (1989); Laville (1994b).

[12] In this respect insertion through economic activity is not an isolated phenomenon, but is established in accordance with logics of action found in a wide range of European initiatives, cf. Laville and Gardin (1997), and the Commission of the European Communities (1995).

sophisticated strategies for managing relations with public and private institutions. The skills required thus go beyond those necessary for business creation. This is the source of the obstacles faced by self-help initiatives that lack the time and means to develop such skills internally and often find themselves subject to strategies imposed from outside.

From a sociological point of view, the people undertaking such activities cannot be confused with either the strategists of large organisations or the participants of traditional social movements (which may be identified in terms of the sociology of organisations or of the sociology of industrial relations respectively). Unlike strategists, they do not act in order to take control, defend, or enlarge existing territory, but to change the system through the process of creating institutions. Unlike mass movement participants, they do not initiate change solely through collective action and national mobilisation, but through small-scale community action – building durable interaction from a sense of community identity. They work on removing barriers, establishing their own area of action, and relying on a project-based approach that transcends the logic of public programmes. These actors for social change emerge during periods of crisis when the potential for development and social progress seems for them to be exhausted, and when institutional boundaries, stable during periods of growth, are shifting.[13]

Entrepreneurs in insertion initiatives try to marry an ability to mediate politically with management skills: they play the role of 'networking actors', using genuinely versatile strategies to link institutional cultures that previously had little contact. Given the size of the task facing them, social and civic entrepreneurs cannot succeed if they are isolated. They have to become co-ordinating managers of social networks, bringing together allies to join and support their project on a voluntary basis.

(a) In some cases these will be networks of experts and professionals recruited for their technical knowledge and management know-how.

(b) In other cases networks are made up of relevant officials in economic and political institutions. These people help legitimise a project, access resources from the public sector or from the private business.

(c) There are also concerned activists who want to become involved in project support networks, or beneficiaries who can make a valuable contribution to projects through informal social groups like unemployed voluntary organisations, for instance.

---

[13] Laville (1994a).

Such supporters are less closely involved than entrepreneurs and are more sheltered from risk, but they nevertheless play an essential role. If any creation of enterprise may be regarded as partly based on building *social capital*,[14] this is even more true of insertion enterprises. The representation of interests by such stakeholders is quite distinct from the way in which interests are represented in bodies engaged in collective bargaining. It relies on shared values, and its effectiveness depends on personal commitment. The socio-economic innovation begins with a common good definition expressed in the project itself and validated by the voluntary commitment of the members. Thus it becomes possible to develop a horizontal approach, where everyone can contribute to discussions not simply in terms of their status but as individuals aware of the nature of the problems, expressing a subjective point of view, integrating and transcending their social roles. Building links between systems and rationales that are usually kept apart helps to reformulate problems to make new approaches possible, and to reveal other possibilities.

This shift in the nature of social economy organisations and networks, from homogeneous groups to varied groups with a wide range of stakeholders including users, volunteers, and workers, can be seen in other areas as well as insertion. According to Borzaga and Mittone,[15] it corresponds to a new form of organisation, half-way between voluntary organisation and co-operative. The Italian social co-operatives are emblematic of such an evolution bringing together users, volunteers, and workers. This might also be seen as the expression of a new relationship between the individual and the community, where involvement is anchored in a limited field of action, where the individual not only belongs to a community but invests in it according to personal circumstances and is able to alternate between strong involvement and a relative withdrawal as dictated by his or her priorities.

More deeply, the community they refer to is the political community. Even if it is rooted in a local community, they act for a recognition of the social rights of beneficiaries by providing them work linked to social protection and status. By creating insertion initiatives, the stakeholders not only behave as entrepreneurs but also contribute to the public sphere in the sense of Habermas: 'Citizens behave as a public body when they confer in an unrestricted fashion – that is, with the guarantee of freedom of assembly and association and the freedom to express and publish their opinions –

---

[14] Putnam (1993); Coleman (1990).
[15] Borzaga and Mittone (1997).

about matters of general interest'.[16] It is the case when a public space is opened up for local dialogue based on exchanges between the various stakeholders involved. By doing so, insertion initiatives contribute to the emergence of 'dialogic democracies'[17] being included in 'the proliferation of social movements and self-help groups' opening spaces for public dialogue and developing reflexivity in civil society. They problematise 'aspects of social conduct that previously went undiscussed' or were reserved for experts. The quality of the debate they stimulate is crucial to invent innovative methods and to meet the demands for ways of integrating disadvantaged people that go beyond the inappropriate usual policies against unemployment.

3. The Relationship between Actors and Activities

The socio-economic framework in which organisations in the social economy operate is characterised by voluntary involvement and control by the stakeholders. Insertion organisations also exemplify another trend typical of the social economy today: an extension and increasing heterogeneisation of the relationship between actors and activities. However, the greater heterogeneity seen in this new social economy is very different from that in the more traditional social economy.

When the traditional model of the social economy has become more heterogeneous, it has been due to its integration inside public policies or to the adaptation of its rules to suit the markets or quasi-markets in which it operates. The result of this institutional isomorphism[18] is to strengthen the influence of elected administrators and managers to the detriment of volunteers and employees.[19] 'The enterprise then chooses those members who are most compatible with its development', which reverses the original rules, and 'the dynamic of an enterprise does not exclude a break with the social solidarities of its origins'.[20]

Structures for insertion, on the other hand, revitalise the original rules determining the relationships between their members and economic activities, because the very purpose of these activities is to provide working

---

[16] Habermas (1974), p. 49; see also Habermas (1989); and Calhoun (1992).

[17] According to Giddens' terms; see Giddens (1994), pp. 117–124; the two following quotations come from this text, p. 120.

[18] Di Maggio and Powell (1993).

[19] The major categories of participants in the 'co-operative quadrilateral' are: the members, the administrators, management and the paid employees, according to Desroche (1969).

[20] Vienney (1986), p. 117.

opportunities for people unable to find work in the labour market. Furthermore, when people other than the unemployed are asked to become involved, this is not for financial reasons but to adopt a political dimension. In this regard the Italians refer to 'extended mutuality', and in Québec the phrase 'local governance'[21] is used to designate a civic dimension that draws together people concerned with the solidarity that insertion bodies develop in a given locality.

The increasing heterogeneity of the social economy today therefore stems from two different movements. The original model of the social economy is gradually becoming less rigid, and involving a wider range of people in order to adapt to the constraints of the dominant economy. At the same time a new social economy is emphasising its fresh approach to new social questions. In other terms, at a time when the ability of the third sector to maintain its own identity is questioned, a new generation is emerging, stressing the limitations of previous forms of synergy between the state and the market.[22] In short, during the 19th century, organisations operating in the social economy challenged the fact that the rules governing economic activities were conceived separately from moral, political and religious rules. The spread of market economy and the widespread social protection associated with the development of the welfare state have gradually eroded this aspect, which was once an essential component of the third system. However, economic activities that stimulate social links have regained a relative importance at the beginning of the 21st century, as ways out of the 'crisis' are being sought, and the issue of work is being raised with a new urgency after a period of full employment in developed countries.

4. The Original Dynamic Combining Market and Non-market Resources

The reduced homogeneity of work-integration initiatives founding groups has led to an approach to project development based less on a shared identity, but rather on the precariousness of certain groups and a collective attempt to overcome it. The movement of insertion through economic activities may be defined as a collection of organisations that mobilise

---

[21] For questions of local governance, there exists international and interdisciplinary forums like *International Journal of Urban and Regional Research*.

[22] On the synergy between the state and market in times of expansion, cf. Laville (1994), pp. 41–54.

resources, set up activities and fulfil objectives that are not met by for-profit private enterprises. Thus when there is a lack of traditional entrepreneurs to provide employment for certain people, groups of individuals develop entrepreneurial capabilities and create private not-for-profit enterprises. In short, they react to market failures.

Insertion through economic activity is at the same time a reaction to state failures, principally its inability to satisfy the needs of minorities.[23] As indicated in the introduction, some insertion initiatives arise where local people can no longer tolerate social exclusion.

Organisations for insertion are in a better position than private for-profit enterprises to invest in the selection and training of workers, since the lack of a profit motive enables them to give priority to the usefulness of an activity rather than its profitability. They can also offer guarantees regarding the use of public funds, because the fact that surpluses are not privately appropriated limits the 'windfall effect'.[24] Consequently they have emerged predominantly in a local mixed economy, linked both to the market economy (because their products are sold) and to the non-market economy (because they use public funds).

Insertion through economic activity rests on the idea of two kinds of production:

(a) The initiatives produce goods or services in the market; in certain respects this resembles a constant feature in the history of the co-operative movement, i.e. the development of labour intensive business activities, giving priority to jobs for people.

(b) As a result they provide a service of insertion through training that draws on public finance to compensate for the extra costs of supervision, the lower productivity of workers on insertion programmes, and the effort involved in achieving their qualifications. This principle of public expenditure for training-insertion services has gradually been accepted, either through exemptions from taxes and social contributions as in Italy, through the assumption of part of the wage costs as in France, or through a combination of the two, as in Belgium.

The innovation, lies in this combination of market and non-market resources within the same organisation. But it also explains the barriers encountered by organisations for insertion through economic activities. Of

---

[23] For an analysis of state failures, see for example Weisbrod (1977).
[24] See the conclusions of Borzaga *et al.* in their contribution to the present work.

course, for-profit enterprises can benefit financially from various public schemes, and public bodies can sell some of their services in the market. Nevertheless a dichotomy between the market and non-market economies dominates the traditional structure of institutional systems, and runs counter to using a combination of resources as a permanent mode of operation.

Despite a growing recognition of this issue by institutions in several countries, this tension with previously established institutional frameworks persists. This is even more true since the 30-year period of expansion and prosperity following the Second World War, established a complementarity but also a clear separation between the market and non-market economies. The division between the market and non-market social economies in Belgium is one result of this. Insertion through economic activities consists of enterprises mobilising market and through state-controlled redistribution resources, in an environment that is largely hostile to such attempts.[25]

5. Regulations under Question

'The availability of free human resources', 'a membership base of voluntary workers and beneficiaries working alongside promoters and other workers', and 'skills developed through constant work with disadvantaged workers': such are the advantages enjoyed by insertion projects.[26] Although the way structures for insertion emerge and become institutionalised is known, their future development raises issues of their long-term regulation, and is inseparable from larger institutional changes.

The experiences of the social economy over the past century have shown that equality in law between members, and communal ownership of an enterprise, does not necessarily translate into democratic functioning for those involved. Sociological research on organisations in the social economy emphasises the differences in power that arises from the pursuit of an economic activity, in voluntary organisations and co-operatives alike.[27] It could even be said that the confusion between the formal equality and a real stakeholders control is a major cause of the limitations encountered in the social economy. The conviction that decision-making processes were democratic because the principle 'one head, one vote' was

---

[25] On the concept of plural economy, see Laville in OECD (1996), pp. 43–53; Laville (1999).

[26] To mention some of the important characteristics of insertion initiatives noted by Borzaga *et al.* in their chapter in this book.

[27] Among many works on this subject, see Gherardi and Massiero (1986); Laville (1989).

adopted has, for a long time, obscured an examination of the inequalities produced through the organisation of work and production. Due to complex pressures from the wide variety of stakeholders involved, the new social economy including initiatives for insertion through economic activities has now reopened the debate over how to combine economic efficiency and democratic co-operation.

Economic and sociological researches have also revealed the important influence of macro-economic regulations on the context for organisations in the social economy. External contingencies weigh upon the internal dynamics of co-operatives, and other enterprises.

The political framework for interactions between public authorities and not-for-profit enterprises is not simply a matter of legal recognition. It also draws up rules that influence their structures to such an extent that is possible to speak of a political embeddedness.[28] Historically, the specific legal structures have been unable to prevent institutional isomorphism, which has broadly speaking turned co-operatives into subsets of the market economy, and voluntary organisations into subsets of the non-market economy. Emerging insertion initiatives depend on both market and non-market resources, which are mobilised through voluntary involvement. So, when they start up, the insertion initiatives mix non-monetary resources coming from volunteers with market and non-market resources. But this initial equilibrium is fragile, because it runs counter to the separation that exists between social and economic worlds. To conclude, though the ways in which insertion initiatives emerge can be analysed from current evidence, questions concerning tendencies in both their internal functioning and their external relations remain open.

References

Barbeyer, D. (1984), *Contribution de la SCOP à l'insertion des travailleurs marginalisés*, Ronéo, Paris. (And an account of surveys of 23 bodies.)

Borzaga, C. and Mittone, L. (1997), *The Multi-Stakeholders versus the Nonprofit Organization*, Discussion paper no. 7, Università degli Studi di Trento, Dipartemento di Economia, Trento.

Calhoun (ed.) (1992), *Habermas and the Public Sphere*, MIT Press.

Chanial, P. (1997), *Pour une généalogie de l'esprit associatif en France*, Ronéo, Paris.

Chopart, J.N., Eme, B., Laville, J.-L. and Mouriaux, R. (1998), 'The welfare recipients collective action' in R. van Berkel (ed.), *Welfare Claimants in Europe*, Université d'Utrecht, Utrecht.

---

[28] Laville (1998).

Coleman, J.S. (1990), *Foundations of Social Theory*, Harvard University Press, Cambridge, MA.

Commission of the European Communities (1995), *Les Initiatives locales de développement et d'emploi*, Entuête dans l'Union Européenne, Brussels.

Defourny, J. (1990), *Efficacité économique et démocratie coopérative*, éditions De Boeck, Brussels.

Defourny, J. (1992), 'Vers une économie politique des associations', in J. Defourny, and M.C. Malo (eds), *Vie associative et fonctions collectives, Report to the Xth Congress of French-speaking Belgian Economists*, CIFOP, Charleroi.

Desroche, H. (1969), *Le Développement inter-coopératif*, Université de Sherbrooke, Sherbrooke.

Desroche, H. (1976), *Le Projet coopératif*, Éditions ouvrières, Paris.

Di Maggio, P.J. and Powell, W.W. (1993), 'The iron cage revisited: institutional isomorphism and collective rationality in organizational fields', *American Sociological Review*, vol. 48, April.

Gherardi, S. and Massiero, A. (1986), 'The impact of organizational culture on life-cycle and decision making', in *Newborn Cooperatives*, Università degli Studi di Trento, Trento.

Giddens, A. (1994), *Beyond Left and Right. The Future of Radical Politics*, Polity Press, Cambridge.

Gui, B. (1991), 'The economic rationale for the third sector', *Annals of Public and Cooperative Economics*, vol. 4.

Habermas, J. (1974), 'The public sphere', *New German Critique*, 3.

Habermas, J. (1989), *The Structural Transformation of the Public Sphere*, MIT Press, Cambridge, MA.

Hersent, M. (1990), *Femmes et insertion dans les quartiers de développement social. Bilan et orientation. Étude pour le secrétariat d'état chargé des droits des femmes*, La Documentation Française, Paris.

International Journal of Urban and Regional Research, Blackwell Publishers, Oxford, UK and Boston, USA.

Laville, J.-L. (1989), *L'Évaluation des pratiques de gestion participative dans les PME et les coopératives*, Commission of the European Communities, Luxembourg.

Laville, J.-L. (1994a), 'Économie et solidarité: esquisse d'une problématique', spécialement, in Laville, J.-L. (ed.), *L'Économie solidaire, une perspective internationale*, Desclée de Brouwer, Paris.

Laville, J.-L. (1994b), *Collectifs et coopératives de travail en Europe – éléments pour un bilan 1970–1990*, CRIDA-LSCI, CNRS, Paris.

Laville, J.-L. (1994c), 'Économie et société: pour un retour à une problématique fondatrice de la sociologie', *Sociologie du travail*, no. 2/94.

Laville, J.-L. and Gardin, L. (eds) (1997), *Local Initiatives in Europe. An Economic and Social Review*, CRIDA-LSCI, CNRS and Commission of the European Communities, Paris.

Laville, J.-L. and Sainsaulieu, R. (1997), *Sociologie de l'association*, Desclée de Brouwer, Paris.

Laville, J.-L. (1998), 'An approach of third sector and welfare mix in French-speaking countries: "the proximity services"', in *Third International Conference of the International Society for Third-sector Research*, University of Geneva, July 8–11, 1998.

Laville, J.-L. (1999), 'The future of work', *The Welfare Society in the 21st Century*, 39, Institute for Applied Social Science (Fafo), Oslo.

Macfarlane, R. and Laville, J.-L. (1992), *Developing Community Partnerships in Europe*, Directory of Social Change and Calouste Gulbenkian Foundation, London.

OECD (1996), *Reconciling Economy and Society. Towards a Plural Economy*, OECD, Paris.

Paton, R. (with Duhm, R. *et al.*) (1989), *Reluctant Entrepreneurs – The Extent, Achievements and Significance of Workers Takeovers in Europe*, Open University Press, Milton Keynes.

Putnam, R.D. (1993), *Making Democracy Work. Civic Traditions in Modern Italy*, Princeton University Press, Princeton, p. 171.

Salamon, L.M. and Anheier, H.K. (1996), *Defining the Nonprofit Sector*, Manchester University Press, Manchester and New York.

Vienney, C. (1994), *L'Économie sociale*, La Découverte, Paris.

Weisbrod, B.A. (1977), *The Voluntary Nonprofit Sector*, Lexington Books, Lexington M.A.

14 Legitimate Orders of Social Participation and the Logic of Social Change

BERNARD EME

Nothing had changed because I was there, frozen and hidden in the narrow street: no word, no light, no behaviour, no noise. This indifference, as unshakeable as the walls and the sky above me, seeped into my bones. I was struck numb with the bitterness of rejection, which I was so often to feel afterwards.

(Georges C. Glaser, *Secret et violence*, 1951)

The social economy (the 'third sector', comprising co-operatives, mutuals and non-profit organisations) and the inclusion process, especially within organisations promoting inclusion through economic activity or through work,[1] seem to go naturally together. Most of these organisations are in fact part of the social economy; they are naturally linked problematically

---

[1] The distinction that may be made between these two types of integration is irrelevant to the argument to be developed here. Fluctuations in vocabulary nevertheless oblige us to give a provisional but heuristic definition of this type of inclusion. Inclusion through sheltered economic activity and work is addressed at members of society categorised as 'in difficulties' according to the dominant social norms. The latter, through the constraints of paid employment in a commercial organisation – specific by its social aim – receive a training on-the-job in the standards of civil conduct and socialisation more generally as well as practical or vocational knowledge under the professional and educational supervision of 'tutors'. Such apprenticeships may involve: (1) individuals, with the accent on their individuality, where the emphasis is on individual adaptation to the demands of the processes of production; (2) groups of people, where the primary concern is a degree of functional socialisation, which is an effect of apprenticeship; (3) the socio-economic context of integration (businesses, local area, etc.) where the functional transformation of that environment is at simultaneously the condition for individual apprenticeships and for forms of productive socialisation. Individual adaptation, socialisation and changes in the integration environment are the three functional forms of integration through work – forms that are evidently not mutually exclusive.

where the social economy is seeking to develop alternative social models for the most deprived as a way of helping their social integration. Although these models may be extended indiscriminately to many types of people, it is widely acknowledged that most of them support categories of people 'in difficulty'[2] and were developed by organisations within the social economy. The values held by these bodies influence the whole field of work inclusion in the context of profound changes within the economy but also affecting relationships between the economy and state-controlled regulations, and in a broader sense on the relationship between the economy and society.

This chapter will not question the overwhelming evidence of a link between inclusion through work and the social economy. The analysis reveals a multiplicity of institutional forms, and a wide range of status and social identity among the individuals involved, making it difficult to discern a readily identifiable form of change. This is why the claim that inclusion through work leads to a standard set of changes through the creation of an 'intermediate economic area'[3] conceals a wide variety of developments. These diverse developments arise from complementary or competitive organisations working in quite distinct activities (social work, training, local or community development, urban social development, etc.) involving different groups of people; and these people go beyond the pre-set administrative categories based on a negative model of disability (long or very long-term unemployed, people 'in difficulties', etc.) – and thus make up a real 'black box'.[4] Similarly, the increase in the range of individual status and work identities,[5] due to these new kinds of 'inclusion jobs', leads to unintended consequences of discrimination and social inequality. As we know, 'legal status and the social identities associated with it, form part of a hierarchy closely related to status at work'.[6]

---

[2] In the case of France, see Supiot's analysis of the way in which the right to work has ceased to be universal through the construction of particular categories and the individualisation of those who have these rights leading to 'the increasing fragmentation of the legal framework affecting labour', which has contributed to 'giving precedence to individual employees over workers collectively' (Supiot, 1994, p. 97).

[3] Rosanvallon (1995), pp. 190–191.

[4] From the analysis of 19 research and study reports on integration through economic measures, and 12 other works, it can be shown that the people helped by these schemes are not well understood, and are in fact the subject of much ignorance (see Eme, 1996a, p. 63 *et seq.*).

[5] Sainsaulieu (1988).

[6] Elbaum (1994), p. 34; Schnapper (1989), pp. 3–29.

State bureaucracy has its own rules to differentiate between the roles of bodies in the social economy based on their economic form and their types of users: so in France some organisations fall into the category of non-monetary trade, or in public interest or social utility activities, which are expected to provide their product or services either free or at a very low price. Others operate in the non-competitive commercial economy, i.e. in gaps in the commercial economy overlooked by competition (niche market); while others are involved in the competitive commercial economy.[7]

Table 14.1

Reciprocal economy	Non-market economy	Market	Economy
Mutual or self-help activities	Non-commercial economy involved in activities of public interest	Non-competitive commercial economy	Competitive commercial economy
Non-monetary mutual aid bodies for integration through work	Non-profit bodies for integration through economic activity	Profit or non-profit bodies for integration through economic activity	Profit or non-profit bodies for integration through economic activity
Self-help groups	Centres for active living; insertion work sites	Intermediate voluntary organisations	Insertion enterprises; neighbourhood associations

In day-to-day practice, these distinctions and divisions are blurred. The same activities can simultaneously support non-profit public interest bodies, non-profit organisations working in the non-competitive market, and profit or non-profit bodies in the commercial market. Some non-profit organisations, working within local voluntary organisations for work integration, set up profit-making subsidiaries under commercial articles of association.

The result is explosive change, both historically and socially. This change cannot be regarded as forming the basis of a social movement

---

[7] In France a Ministry of Labour circular of April 1985 defined intermediate enterprises (which later became work-integration enterprises) as 'real businesses creating lasting jobs and producing goods and services under market conditions ...'.

leading to an 'alternative' approach to social change. Touraine's concept of a social movement derived from historically defined forces cannot account for these dynamic patterns of change. Touraine's social movement concept operates through identity, opposition and totality, i.e. through a conscious assertion of identity (identity), in a central conflict (opposition) around the challenge of a cultural model and for the appropriation of values set in a historical perspective (totality).[8]

In contrast the movements for inclusion are made up of a complex variety of impulses arising in different professional fields and pressure groups. Those involved, working either professionally or as volunteers, come from many different cultural, political and socio-professional backgrounds. The rather weak affirmation of identity through such organisations does not produce a truly central conflict in society. On the other hand, the impetus towards change is built up in a heterogeneous pattern, through the aggregation of local social movements each establishing their own particular kinds of organisation in their localities.

In the first section we move beyond the diversity emerging from change at the local level, to reconstruct some common principles, which bring into question the universality of standards for integration; it thereby begins to establish a new approach to the issue of inclusion through economic activity. The social economy brings to bear fundamental mechanisms, different from conventional standards, and makes it possible to find a place in the commercial economy for deprived people.

In the second section we establish the conceptual basis for 'legitimate orders of social participation'; and in the third section we attempt to determine the various 'legitimate orders' that have been brought into play since the middle of the 1960s, through an analysis of the different processes of change resulting from measures for inclusion through work. The various legitimate orders of social participation that have been analysed show that inclusion takes many forms, and broadly reflects the different aspects of functional integration in society. But a profound change has taken place: what originally led to a sort of 'natural' integration into society or in the system or in the nation state (all equivalent terms in a classic integration theory) is now fragmented, and now leads to many different kinds of inclusion. Like light, the social and political integration is diffracted into many forms of personal inclusion where people must enter into structures or groups temporarily and have differentiated

---

[8] Touraine (1993; first published 1973).

activities. Some of these still have little legitimacy, e.g. socially useful activities.

Integration in classic sociology is defined as the integration of society itself. By integrating itself, society links its different parts and the individuals, and makes them interdependant. This is how individuals integrate into social groups because of institutional processes (the interiorising of norms and values, symbolic violence, and so on). Integration is based on a global and holistic vision of society: it is a system, a state, an industrial world building a whole, giving a social and symbolic place to the individual. Whereas, inclusion means that the individual must give her or himself a place in society. It could therefore appear that the idea of inclusion reveals the difficulties and the limits involved in applying and reproducing a classic universal model of integration that does not function anymore. This idea brings into play, in a problematic manner, the differentiated forms of functional integration of individuals (and these have doubtful legitimacy). In future, conflicts of legitimacy arise in relation to the extent of integration of individuals in society.[9]

1. Principles of Integration through Economic Activity

The notion of inclusion, which has emerged in public policy and in civil society over the last 20 years,[10] is, from a general point of view, and in its more specialised form as inclusion 'through economic activity' or 'through

---

[9] It will be understood that in order not to over-burden this account only implicit reference has been made to the 'double level' theory of society of Jürgen Habermas, who considers society at once as a system for the systematic integration of the individual regulated by action through a raft of measures, and as a life-world recreated through communication. Systematic integration refers to the practical non-normative co-ordination of actions, where each is a function determined by processes primarily directed at the success of the consequences of an action; a social instinct without norms comes into play, which by-passes the awareness of those involved and regulates their decisions avoiding subjectivity. In life-worlds the social integration of each person is utilised (standards for 'belonging', solidarity), constantly constructing personal identity (the socialisation of social beings and their subjectivisation, their capacity for engaging in interactive processes) at the same time as cultural reproduction takes place (the transmission of knowledge, outlines of interpretation, resources for comprehension and the attribution of meaning) (see Habermas, 1987).

[10] For the social construction of integration based on the tension between these participants, see Eme (1994, pp. 157 *et seq.*; 1996b, pp. 182 *et seq.*). This tension has developed at different times and in different places in many ways, which explains the social, economic and cultural variations in schemes for integration through work.

work', a 'pre-notion' in Durkheim's sense, the use of which 'as a sociological concept risks ... leading to the introduction into the field of analysis those presuppositions of social action and the ideological principles which are at the heart of the current debate'.[11] Full of semantic pitfalls,[12] the concept of work inclusion designates as much the processes of change undergone by individuals in their transition to the labour market as the more stable changes through roles held on insecure terms in economic organisations in transitional[13] or secondary labour markets. However, if inclusion leads to these processes or roles that describe individuals and/or groups of people, it also reveals a transformation in the methods of social and public intervention in such areas as social action, training, assistance to employment, business creation, community and local development, etc. And it leads to changes to principles underlying all the practices developed in this field to allow the utilisation of new methods for individual integration.

1.1. Selectivity, Involvement and Individualisation

The first principle is that of selectivity. According to Robert Castel, the policies and practices of inclusion are to be distinguished from assimilation policies that 'proceed through general directives in a national context' by the fact that they follow 'a logic of positive discrimination'.[14] This has two different meanings according to whether it applies to specific groups of people (young people 'in difficulties', certain categories of women and older workers, the long-term unemployed, etc.), or to local areas. In the first sense, through positive discrimination, the least qualified groups who are most affected by 'selective unemployment'[15] are the focus of special policies, supplementing training, which aim at an overall qualitative and quantitative regulation of supply and demand in the labour market. Inclusion practices are more likely to target their user groups, and to put in place the means to help them overcome their social and professional difficulties. In the second sense, defined local areas – most often urban areas of social housing ('estates') that have multiple problems in terms of development, unemployment, ghettoisation, and living conditions – have

---

[11] Paugam (1993), p. 15.
[12] See Bailleau *et al.* (1990), p. 7.
[13] Schmid (1995).
[14] Castel (1995), p. 418.
[15] Gautié (1993), p. 101.

become subject to new all-encompassing regional policies, local and horizontal, based on the principle of involving everyone concerned.[16] Thus a selectivity principle that departs from the principle of universality, and relativises it, has been introduced.[17] This selectivity is not applied at the individual level; it operates at the level of groups or areas defined by failings and shortcomings in quality, resources and qualifications. These are the most deprived people, often defined in official publications as 'in greatest difficulty', or the neighbourhoods described as 'in difficulty'[18] or 'disadvantaged' or 'vulnerable', etc.

This selectivity is not enough to define fully the changes brought about through inclusion. The second characteristic is that action is based on a 'moral philosophy of involvement' of people in inclusion projects, 'so that the state takes on powers of intervention over individuals who are regarded as members of society and not merely its beneficiaries, in order to make productive participation in society a legitimate focus for their energies'.[19] Taking the French example of the RMI (*Revenue minimum d'insertion*, income support for people on integration schemes), this has a dual function providing income both from welfare and from work integration. Those who benefit from this system receive income support but are obliged to engage in an 'inclusion process contract'. Depending on their situation and their abilities, this contract contains various aims and activities for better health, or housing, or professional training and education through supported work, etc. The type of contract arrangement is developed in local 'inclusion process committees' (*Commissions locales d'insertion*), which comprise relevant local people such as social workers, politicians, council staff, voluntary organisation staff, SME managers. Here, inclusion requires 'an active approach to civic responsibility on the part of the beneficiary',[20] since in return for the benefit he or she gives an undertaking relating to their behaviour within society; for example through accepting work in an organisation for inclusion, the beneficiary moves on from welfare recipient status and voluntarily engages in an effort at inclusion. He is supposed to respect minimum constraints of production and discipline (working hours, health and safety, etc.) to internalise the

---

[16] Ion (1990).
[17] Commaille (1997), p. 79.
[18] See Supiot (1994).
[19] Donzelot (1986).
[20] Commaille (1997), p. 79.

norms, to learn the rules of the job, and sometimes (but not unfortunately always) to participate in the decision making of the organisation.

'This close association, within social rights, of the right to welfare with the right, which is also a duty, of citizenship, calls for greater responsibility from beneficiaries'.[21] This change converts those receiving benefit from passive members of society, receiving welfare payments or other benefits according to their rights, into active citizens who, in return for accepting 'positive duties' (with regard to inclusion), have a right to be socially useful and to exercise the right to a place in society.[22] In financial terms, we thus pass from passive expenditure on unemployment insurance to active support for working activities.[23]

The third characteristic of inclusion takes account of the uniqueness of individuals. Establishing work-inclusion schemes assumes an individualising approach that acknowledges individuality so as to handle it more effectively. People are no longer treated as categories, individual needs are no longer spurned; on the contrary, this approach always regards people as individuals and treats them as such. If selectivity or positive discrimination affects categories of people, the principle of individualisation emphasises individuals and the particular kind of intervention that is appropriate. From socialisation in productive structures for inclusion through economic activity, there has emerged the aim of producing 'individualised paths to inclusion' through community-based management that is attentive to the need for personal autonomy. This path is conceived ideally as a progressive evolution towards the employment market passing through rationally defined steps. It is guided (*'référent'*, *garant*) by someone from a local institution, and each step is tutored. Sometimes a local committee discusses issues relating to the evolution of the path. In most cases, these paths are quite varied; they depend on local opportunities – job vacancies, as well as the ever-changing integration process politics. In this way, pursuing the general concept of 'social individualisation', linked to the inclusion process, a principle of respecting the uniqueness of the individual replaces the 'principle of universality'.[24]

---

[21] Commaille (1997), p. 79.

[22] Rosanvallon (1995).

[23] However, the demarcation line between this and compulsory work in return for an income ('workfare') has become hard to discern.

[24] Commaille (1997), p. 78.

1.2. By-passing the Labour Regulations: the Functional Approach with Local Scrutiny

The fourth characteristic of inclusion involves using standards particular to insecure employment built into specialised inclusion structures (which may be distinguished from social work and training models). This takes place through a series of exemptions to normal labour laws so that, special regulations and new organisational methods allow the socio-technical transition between the social and the economic spheres. These organisational methods reflect certain interactive processes:

(a) a statute for temporary work exempt from ordinary legal provisions (whether paid or not) for production in a specified organisation supported by public grants;

(b) socialisation and the development of identity through introduction into a more or less sheltered working world;

(c) the acquisition of 'practical' or 'vocational' knowledge[25] via work with a training component where prominence is given to social development and supplementary training.

These characteristics are, however, also elements of an instrumental approach in which various roles must be learned so that functional inclusion in society takes place. Work integration may be defined as an apprenticeship in the different kinds of knowledge and specific skills that lead to the universal norm of integration through employment (which also confers rights). Through the use of specialised regulations (allowing positive discrimination, selectivity, individualisation, job contracts that are exempt from ordinary laws), it is possible to reach conformity with those universal standards that find their most concrete expression in paid employment in the commercial or public economy. Inclusion through economic activity may thus be seen as a technical, functional and adaptive path towards 'traditional' employment through particular intermediate structures allowing a normalising transition to integration. The structures of the social economy consequently occupy the position of socio-economic instruments forging the socio-professional transition towards other areas of economy: the market and public sector.

---

[25] For the kinds of knowledge which help to form to social and professional identities, see the analyses of Dubar (1991).

The sixth characteristic is that these models of development are increasingly constructed according to a functional logic of transition with three main elements: the first adopts a strict logic of transition through individual adaptation of people to the demands of production; the second adds to this a transition based on a productive socialisation allowing the assimilation of the functional constraints of production; finally, the third widens these two perspectives to include transition as an element in an overall approach to the context of people and groups, i.e. the adaptive transition assumes a change in the rules and standards of the host organisation (businesses, local areas, etc.).

Finally, the last characteristic of inclusion is that this functional approach is increasingly being debated by those involved locally, and (re-)constructed through local inter-organisational activity, which suggests that both local[26] and co-operative actions[27] are being revalued positively.[28] Distinctive standards for action, which are not predefined or universal, would appear to be the result of new regulations that accept the specificity of each area and the increasing contractual autonomy of members of society, i.e. 'the notion of rules, standards, models imposed 'top down' on the institutions and professionals charged with its application is now being replaced by that of a plurality of rules and models produced 'bottom up'.[29] Inclusion through economic activity is being defined in terms of a new set of standards: a more pragmatic vision emerges in opposition to the application of universal law in a bureaucratic fashion.

2. Legitimate Orders of Social Participation

In practical terms, these principles appear to restrict the range of options by giving this 'adaptive transitional model' a single universal standard at which to aim (paid employment) within a perspective of functional integration. Furthermore, they assume that inclusion through economic

---

[26] Commaille (1997), p. 135.

[27] Some people infer from this that the state plays an organisational role in this labour of society on itself, or of individuals on themselves (see, for example, Donzelot and Estebe, 1994). We believe that this takes as achieved something which remains only a hoped-for change.

[28] Because of French traditional centralisation tendencies, this change is even more important in France than in other European countries used to citizenship and decentralisation of political power.

[29] Commaille (1996), p. 187.

activity that provides training, can succeed in producing this developmental transition to employment (which becomes more and more difficult). Finally, they question the function of structures within the social economy, which ultimately is simply to produce a transitional sector for people most deprived of cultural, social and symbolic resources. The logic of this is to adapt people to work without reorganising the functioning of the enterprise. During the last 25 years, alongside this view of inclusion through work, different forms of inclusion have been developed in an attempt to reconsider the problematics of integration. Paid employment has not always been the aim of integration through work, and this opens up wider perspectives for the integration of individuals.

2.1. A Plurality of Orders in Conflicts of Legitimacy

To approach the idea of inclusion crudely, regarding it in terms of the words and images which it conveys at first sight, may lead us to wonder into what, exactly, individuals are to be integrated. As a process, this assumes the existence of at least two 'orders', two 'registers' of social membership or social participation, or, to take a still broader view, two integration 'worlds'. Let us remember that the notion of 'legitimate orders', with local but not universal validity, was developed by Max Weber in *Wirtschaft und Gesellschaft* (*Economy and Society*). Certain things are valid according to certain rules and norms within the context of one legitimate order which would have no value in another equally legitimate order. Forms of rationalisation (defined roles, functions and rules defining relations between people) would be distinguished according to the specific relationships with the rules and norms of multiple orders: 'activity, especially social activity, and even more particularly a social relationship, may take its direction, for those involved, according to the representation of a legitimate order (*legitime Ordnung*). The chance that this will actually occur we will call the 'validity' (*Geltung*) of the order in question'.[30]

From this perspective society may be imagined and described as a *Gestalt* with arbitrary limits constructed on the interdependence and interrelation of orders that are more or less legitimate. The construction of society is in that sense subject to controversies or conflicts of legitimacy around particular rationalities and values. A society is thus here regarded as a series of social orders, in other words ways of life, values and rules, brought together at various periods in conflicting or complementary ways

---

[30] Weber (1971), p. 64 *et seq.*

or in juxtaposition. Society is constructed through the always controversial interdependence of different forms of legitimacy embodied in different social orders, in the knowledge that these forms of legitimacy change with time, becoming more or less powerful.

2.2. Inclusion and the Specific Process of Transition between Orders

What are these legitimate – and non-legitimate – orders of social membership and participation constructed in inclusion schemes? First there is the order from which people come to be included, then that in which they are to be included or will include themselves. Roughly speaking, these people come from one order that must be labelled, and social actors then place them, or help them to place themselves, in another order, also requiring labelling. Still very approximately, we can say that these people come from an order regarded as not legitimate, invalid and undesirable, since either they themselves want to leave it or society wishes to remove them from it; and that they want to enter an order that is regarded as legitimate, valid and desirable. During different periods and societies, paid employment has not always been a legitimate order of social participation.

By this simple reasoning, which at this rough stage seems to validate a number of orders and rationalisations, we can refute the idea of 'exclusion', which suggests that people come from outside society (an 'elsewhere' outside society) and that they are then helped to move inside. There is no 'great outside', or 'great inside' where 'those who are not in want to be so, since they would otherwise be in a social void';[31] such a view gives a rather static representation of society. Whereas our hypothesis lends validity to the multiple societal dynamics in which there exist many 'outsides' within society itself, and, naturally, a large number of 'insides' – and these can be reconstructed from the discourse and actions of their participants. These 'insides' and 'outsides' do not always have the same meaning and change over time. What was at one given moment an 'outside' may become an 'inside', and it is the policies and positions of the people involved which determine that legitimacy or otherwise of these social spaces.

The excluded, therefore, can be found at the heart of society, in the hub of big cities, as well as in small towns and rural villages; everyone is always included in one order and excluded from other orders or worlds. To speak of exclusion in general terms of being in or out is to conceal the

---

[31] Touraine (1991), p. 8.

social, concrete, day-to-day processes through which different orders, and conflicts of legitimacy between them, develop. The (de-)validation and the (de-)legitimisation of an order and the people belonging to it from the point of view of a different order are social and cultural developments that the term 'exclusion' expresses very imperfectly.[32]

The idea of inclusion through sheltered work or work suported by public subsidies, seems therefore to mean the social process of transition between orders, one of which is rightly or wrongly considered not legitimate and the other, legitimate. But to achieve this process, integration also assumes the existence of a third state that may be called an intermediate space, or a space of mediation. This enables the subject to move between the non-legitimate order that he or she must leave and the legitimate order into which he or she is to be included. The legitimacy of this intermediate space seems to allow the technical transition of people, i.e. it gives people a function by adapting them to it. These spheres of social activity that permit inclusion are mainly functional and instrumental.

These intermediate spaces allowing the emergence of work inclusion practices form part of the institutionalised fields of action that exist more or less extensively throughout society. Through these inclusion practices, actors are continually reproducing the field itself, changing and modifying its workings and its values. These functional intermediate fields (social work, welfare services, social health services, training, local development, leisure, housing, health, etc.) are thus frequently areas subject to controversies and conflicts arising from these changing integration practices. Workers in the inclusion field criticise and deny the validity of some practices that perpetuate an order they regard as non-legitimate. In this way, in France, 'social work' came to be regarded as a way of reproducing delinquency, poverty and welfare, a means of controlling 'dangerous' sections of the population;[33] similarly, training schemes 'did not lead to employment'[34] and could only lead to further failure at school and to selection patterns that perpetuated inequalities, etc.

---

[32] See the entirely pertinent criticisms of the use of the idea of exclusion by Castel (1995).

[33] Social workers are taking up the problems thrown up by a series of sociological critical analyses that link the institutional organisation of the controlled management of impoverished or marginalised groups and their life-styles. Here we can only cite the famous issue of the journal *Esprit*, 'Pourquoi le travail social?', no. 4–5, April-May 1972, which features contributions from Michel Foucault, Jacques Donzelot, Philippe Meyer, etc.

[34] Malglaive (1985), p. 378.

The new inclusion practices thus are concerned with a legitimate, validated and desirable order and they challenge or invalidate those practices that are regarded as leading to the reproduction of what has been called the non-legitimate, invalid, unwanted order. In attempting to change practices in traditional fields by setting up instrumental spaces for mediating the adoption of new practices, integration through work institutes a functional space for economic activity that marks a break with the practices of welfare and training.

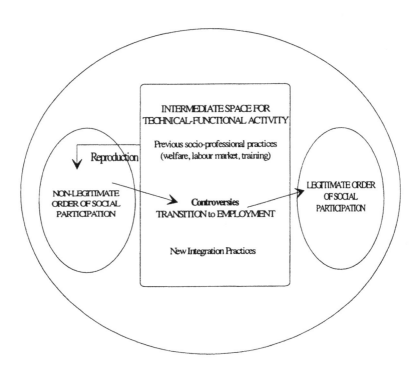

Figure 14.11. **Legitimate orders of social participation and rationales of integration**

3. Legitimate Orders of Participation by Inclusion through Economic Activity

The example of France enables us to distinguish four functional areas in which work inclusion practices have been developed. Although employment remains the dominant order, other areas have been added over time, allowing other kinds of inclusion to appear. In describing them, we will demonstrate the multiple nature of the changes that underlie these practices.

3.1. Social Work and Change through Alternative Social Models

The first functional area is that of social work, from which was first developed an order based on autonomy, responsibility and the development of individual abilities. Local workshops are created in order to include young people who are delinquent or with problems. These workshops are not well organised. And pay is not regularised – they are in informal production collectives. The objective (the legitimate order to be attained) was not work, employment or employability; what was provided was the opportunity for choice, or the conditions for individual autonomy and responsibility; with a huge range of possibilities for people to chose their own path. At the end of the 1970s and beginning of the 1980s, these workshops become enterprises, and developed the ideology of a different, alternative economy to be brought about by inclusion practitioners and others. The emphasis given to autonomy led to economic values more concerned with quality through demands for: more democratic social relationships at work, the social usefulness of the goods and services produced, and their compatibility with an ecological concern for the conservation of natural resources. 'Quality of life' had now more legitimacy than 'standard of living'. Some of the integration structures were founded by social workers and were known as 'alternative enterprises' and later as 'intermediate enterprises' aimed at an entrepreneurial model with social goals in opposition to a model of welfare or social control. Inclusion is realised though employment but it takes its meaning from a different kind of economy to that which provides its social and cultural dimensions. The legitimacy of employment does not only lie in obtaining a salary or a status but in participation in an alternative economy that challenges the values of capitalist economy. The legitimate order of social participation was based on a different society, founded on an economic democratisation that was to spread into society at large. This was the moment when inclusion through economic activity corresponded to the social economy (the 'third sector').

During these two periods the non-legitimate orders of social participation were those of delinquency and marginalism (1965–1972), then of poverty and social maladjustment (1970–1979), and finally and more extensively, that of social welfare.

The objective (the legitimate order to be attained) was not work, whether employment or any other activity. Neither employability nor employment were the aims; what was involved was providing the opportunities for choice, or the conditions for individual autonomy and responsibility. Society was not the sum of employment, but a huge range of possibilities in which people could choose their own path. If employment was implicit, it took its meaning from a different kind of economy that gave it a social and cultural dimension distinct from that of employment in the market economy. The legitimate order of social participation was a different society, founded on an economic democratisation that was to spread into society at large.

Although in France inclusion practices were born out of conflict within the world of social work (as argued above, providing an intermediate space) around 1965 – a time of economic boom. This was because the first phase of inclusion reflected an ideological crisis in the values and norms of the welfare state,[35] rather than economic changes. The crisis of welfare must be understood in the context of a challenge to the rigid and multiple forms of power and dependency developed by a state that ended up in sole control of solidarity, producing passive clients with no responsibility for the services provided. The challenge was not employment but the creation of a democratic and revitalised civil society, capable of building solidarity and responsibility in a practical way in the face of the bureaucratic Leviathan of the welfare state.

During this period, inclusion practices arose from an exploration of relevant alternative social models,[36] a mixture of functional and instrumental approaches with practices anchored in the day-to-day, in defined contexts, driven by a will to change society starting from the here and now. The apprenticeships, the success of training schemes, and practical activities, developed their foundations in informal production

---

[35] See Rosanvallon (1993).
[36] Sainsaulieu (1996).

collectives, often rooted in community solidarity or daily neighbourhood experiences working to transform social relationships.

3.2. Training and Change through Functional Local Models

The second functional area is that of training, the subject of controversies involving those working in inclusion. In short, actors in the field questioned the value of in-service training, (often referred to as 'dead-end training'), and preliminary training[37] that was supposed to mediate between the world of education and the world of production. Although actors involved with integration retained an educationalist's vision of the relationship between training and work[38] in which 'day release provides a very effective means of re-establishing harmony between training and work',[39] they were discovering or re-discovering the order of trades (or crafts) as a legitimate world in which on-the-job training took place through contact with an older trainee who 'knew the ropes' and introduced the new arrival to the accepted habits and customs of the trade. With the creation of intermediate enterprises, the old custom of apprenticeship was taken up and re-invented. The legitimate order of participation envisaged in these practices was not employment *per se* but participation, pride and solidarity in a trade. It is not employment that provides social identity but belonging to a trade. The intermediate sphere of activity provided a practical transition towards a trade, and did so through on-the-job training practices. Training schemes were challenged because they did not lead to employment, and contributed to the non-legitimate reproduction of categories of people who were regarded as 'worthless' because they had neither qualifications nor employment.

Gradually, during the 1980s, this legitimate order came to be no longer a trade *per se* but employment in the market economy. A profound shift occurred, leading to a dominant legitimate order of social participation consisting of paid employment in a social enterprise (*entreprise d'insertion*) subject to market forces whose economic objectives must be shared by those being included. The most profitable and economically competitive businesses were preferred (a high level of selectivity of employees, reduced training time, etc.).[40] The arguments

---

[37] Malglaive (1985).
[38] Tanguy (1986).
[39] Monaco (1993), p. 28.
[40] Sauvage (1988).

advanced by actors in the field changed, emphasising the need for the internalisation of economic constraints on production in a competitive environment (i.e. client relations, quality of products and services, profitability and productivity, etc.); intermediate enterprises increasingly resembled competitive commercial businesses. The non-legitimate order of social participation was now welfare through work in sheltered enterprises, which developed in niches ignored by the markets, that is a social economy previously established as a sheltered welfare economy.

Regarding the methods of change, these procedures for inclusion through economic activity are more a matter of exploring local models for practical change than of a socio-economic alternative moving towards a more democratic society. 'Alternative' takes on another meaning: the search for new organisations to bring about the social and technical transition into employment, and a practical adaptation of jobs in the commercial economy rather than challenging the social and economic system that prevents such transitions. In this approach to change underlying inclusion practices, what matters is to provide individual training in the context of a socialisation, which is designed to internalise the constraints and contingencies of a competitive economy, and so which takes account of such factors as profitability, quality and productivity as they apply to commercial enterprises. The change takes place in societal, contractual, individual and functional modes of action.

3.3. The Locality and Functional Changes in the Living Environment

The third legitimate order of social participation that emerged during 1983–1984 out of hybrid local developments in the social economy is that of the neighbourhood as a basis for roots and belonging, a space for ordinary life.[41] An entire tradition of integration practices, still developing today, has its origins in the ideology of 'living and working in the home region'. The area is developed as a social, cultural and economic whole, leading to job creation, and return of employment to the regions. From this point of view, measures and structures that develop new types of economic circulation are encouraged, keeping them as short as possible so as to cut out external, parasitic middlemen. The intermediate functional space in which integration practices are developed is that of a local economy that brings producers and consumers, employers and employees, the

---

[41] Eme (1990).

unemployed and potential employers all closer together; proximity between people has to be constantly constructed.

In this way the 'intermediate voluntary organisations' (which have no specific legal structure), make it possible to build closer links between job seeker and their various potential employers (private individuals, voluntary organisations, local authorities, and even businesses, under certain conditions). New local ties are forged between the economic players in a given area.[42] The order of social participation that is regarded as non-legitimate is that of exodus, mobility, a professional nomadism towards other regions because of 'desertification', or the 'destruction' and 'break-down' of local employment catchment areas. Individual change, through individual adaptation or functional socialisation, is linked to the wider context of functional change at local points of access to services. Both public and private institutions and organisations, and inter-institutional regulations, have been focused on achieving this. However, this form of localised change with its new rules and new standards conceals the fact that 'change is never completely "endogenous"; the cost of economic and cultural modernity is always a loss of identity and cultural community'.[43]

In all three of these functional spaces for integration, rooted in welfare, training and local development respectively, the system is developing more and more in the direction of changes within what Alain Touraine calls, in contrast with the sphere of identity, 'the instrumental universe'.[44] This progressive shift towards an instrumental rationale has as its target practical changes and adaptations on the part of individuals, their mode of socialisation and the context of their lives and work. From this perspective, inclusion increasingly denotes practical changes within functionality, a reordering at the heart of instrumentalism, and the economic world of inclusion that is part of the social economy, becomes a 'functional sub-system' of the market economy system and state power. In that way, one adapts people to the system without reanalysing the system itself, which continues to exclude people. The social economy and the inclusion economy become tools of the market economy and state power.

---

[42] Eme and Laville (1988).
[43] Quéré (1985); see also Fourquet (1989) who stresses that 'local development is always exogenous even when it is endogenous'.
[44] Touraine (1997), p. 117.

3.4. Active Citizenship and the Neighbourhood

The last legitimate order of social participation is the more political one, which might be called civic urbanism or active citizenship. Citizenship comes about in the here and now; it gives credence to 'the idea that voluntary participation in public affairs, public-spiritedness, is a component of citizenship. Whether rich or poor, man or woman, French or foreign, under age or adult, a citizen is someone who takes part in public life'.[45] Citizenship is built up in daily life through individual involvement in town affairs, at the level of the immediate neighbourhood, the district, the town, or the community.

This investment comes about through a local economy catering for inclusion, through the economic management of urban services and the management of economic fluctuations. Through economic activities (house cleaning, repairing, public garden maintenance, etc.), which allow inclusion through work in the neighbourhood we take back possession of the public space (which is no longer lived as something devaluing). To root this firmly in the economy (the functional sphere) is a means of exercising citizenship and re-inventing the often run-down city as a place of civility[46] in which individuals, through their daily experiences, acknowledge the most ordinary rights and duties.[47]

The urban public space is experienced, represented, talked about and worked in as a desirable joint asset in which, through the process of inclusion, residents re-create a civilised way of living together that appears to be the legitimate order of social participation. By contrast, the non-legitimate order was, first, the undemocratic forms of urban rehabilitation,[48] and then violence and bad behaviour that leached on the city and prevented the deployment of its creative and innovative resources. The intermediate functional sphere constructed by the neighbourhood management associations and by other bodies for inclusion through economic activity is a neighbourhood economy built with democratic aims.

However, although these inclusion structures in neighbourhoods or communities make it possible to rebuild civil linkages in which (in an autonomous fashion by contrast with institutional methods) residents can

---

[45] Madec and Murad (1995), p. 65.
[46] Eme *et al.* (1995).
[47] Pharo (1985).
[48] The first neighbourhood community association (*Régie de quartier*) was forged out of the urban struggles of the Alma-Gare district in Roubaix (see Mollet, n.d.).

express an 'ordinary citizenship' restoring meaning and legitimacy to daily relationships, this is because they operate within familiar and well-known districts. The movement from a strictly functional rationale to a logic of social inclusion rooted in the culture and processes of solidarity is taking place more and more often, in local districts,[49] and it rebuilds the 'life-worlds' of residents at the cost of changing the local identity. Social inclusion – as opposed to functional or systematic integration – always accepts the existence of life experiences whose codes, traditions, and culture are constantly redefined in relation to other life-worlds.

4. Towards a Plurality of Modes of Social Participation Based on Life-worlds?

Inclusion through economic activity, then, leads people from non-legitimate orders of participation into a diverse range of legitimate orders. But one legitimate order of social participation predominates: the paid employee in the commercial economic order, through a vision of inclusion as 'technical-functional access' to the labour market. The social economy could in this perspective be interpreted from an instrumental point of view as simply an intermediate sphere allowing movement towards paid employment. On the one hand, it adapts people to the economic market without improving their capacity to adapt. They are trained for specific work but not for changing work. On the other hand, the social economy does not challenge the extent to which the work organisation of enterprises adapts itself to the people involved in the process of inclusion. The social economy that in the past was a political project for transforming society, actually maintains the social system as it is.

The standard salarial framework as the dominant legitimate order displaces other patterns of social participation. In any case, many of the orders constructed by inclusion (the alternative economy, or place, community as sources of identity, etc.) are only regarded as legitimate by default, given their failure to link with the major order, the market economy. Here is the paradox in inclusion through work, which aims at a single legitimate order that it can rarely achieve, whilst in practice

---

[49] We repeat Michel Autès' distinction between localised approaches applied in a functional manner to districts taking account of their individual characteristics, and local approaches based on the regional experiences of residents (symbolic and cultural as much as socio-economic; see Autès (1992), pp. 287–288).

establishing a wide range of other orders of social participation, which are only legitimate for want of something better. With the new economic regulations, fewer and fewer people in the inclusion process have access to the labour market. Measured against the standard salarial framework of legitimate employment, people in inclusion positions seem to remain excluded from that order, since they can find no place in it. The idea of inclusion also means a distancing and tension in relation to the prime legitimate order of reference, which can only be paid employment within the economy.

Since they are unable to provide paid jobs in the market economy, inclusion through work schemes have instead built up their own sector of activity[50] based on structures in the social economy and dependent on the market economy, and redistribution through sub-contracting agreements or the externalisation of services. The upshot of this is the serious risk of social stratification in society overall, a situation where transition from social participation within the inclusion economy to social participation in other orders, particularly that of a paid employee in the market economy, can only take place with great difficulty. Leading as they do to a differentiation of modes of integration for individuals, these schemes can be seen as a renunciation – in the last resort – of the universal norm of integration in the market economy.

From this theoretical perspective 'inclusion' is not the opposite of 'exclusion'. Inclusion is refracted through a wide range of factors (sheltered work, training, accommodation, health, leisure, culture, etc.), which reflect the various functional aspects of the systemic integration of individuals, i.e. integration based on technical-rational and instrumental approaches aiming primarily at efficiency and success. Integration fails to change either the economic system or the state system, and the various forms of integration slice into individuals' lives as if they were so many functional aspects to be controlled by public policies. It used to be assumed that the integration of individuals into society, the system, the nation-state[51] was as a unified life-system, but this now has to be the subject of the individual's efforts to try to reintegrate his or her life experiences. Thus

---

[50] For theoretical approaches to this sector (service sector, quaternary sector, social services sector, disinterested activities), see Eme (1996c). Whatever theoretical approach is adopted, it remains the case that at present the sector is mainly developing as an integration sector.

[51] Understood as the classic, Durkheimian idea of the integration of the individual into the system 'through a process of internalisation of standards and values by individuals' (Dubet, 1994, p. 31).

inclusion is built on a multitude of processes that constantly have to be brought back together, and this gives rise to a new subjectivity in the ceaseless construction of life-projects.

However, inclusion can certainly be analysed in a more positive fashion as opening up the possibility of a number of choices of lifestyle within society. From this perspective, the other orders of social participation that have appeared as a result of inclusion practices could well support other life-styles in the future. Under circumstances of radical change, this would create the conditions for other kinds of social ties and other relationships between the economic and social spheres. Inclusion through work would take on a historic significance, having cleared the way for other forms of social participation currently non-legitimate, but which could provide the foundation for a plural social participation for citizens (in other words a legitimate plurality of, modes of living, values and standards), through which to reforge the relationship with democracy and the links between the social and political orders. Approaches that start from 'life-worlds' of individuals and that build on experiences,[52] collective values and culture, could reunite the modes of solidarity underlying social integration and the process of subjectivisation. Conditions facilitating such developments might be poor results together with instrumental logics that are no longer effective in dealing with individual adaptation, functional forms of socialisation, or the technico-rational transformation of the living and working environments.

According to this perspective, inclusion might mean the transformation of individual functional integration, which, though not an end in itself, would be a condition for the possibility of social integration. And though in the conceptual framework we have developed here 'work inclusion' is not part of the kind of social integration that 'guarantees both the coordination of actions through interpersonal relations regulated in a legitimate manner, and ... the continuity of group identity',[53] its strong point could nevertheless be renewing the functional integration of individuals. In this respect we agree with the concern of other writers 'to re-situate the individual within a social 'galaxy' and thus to go beyond the conflict between the individual and the state by reactivating intermediate structures': 'Institutions would operate not just within the narrow limits of their functional role but also play a role developing the whole social life-

---

[52] Dubet (1994).
[53] Habermas (1988), p. 406.

world'.[54] Inclusion as an intermediate sphere might then be a sphere of instrumental rationality that becomes a tool of the development of the experience of social belonging. A plurality of modes of social participation could be opened both in the legitimate area of paid work as well as in other areas of life. And the social economy might once again, go beyond its use as a support for functional inclusion, and find those values on which a project for egalitarian social integration could be based.

References

Autès, M. (1992), *Travail social et pauvreté*, Syros-Alternatives, Paris.

Bailleau, F., Léomant, C. and Sotteau-Léomant, N. (eds) (1990), 'L'Insertion en question(s)', *Annales de Vaucresson*, no. 32–33.

Castel, R. (1995), *Les Métamorphoses de la question sociale. Une chronique du salariat*, Fayard, Paris.

Cérézuelle, D. (1996), *Pour un autre développement social. Au-delà des formalismes techniques et économiques*, Desclée de Brouwer, Paris.

Chasseriaud, C. (1993), 'La Grande Exclusion sociale', rapport au Ministre des Affaires Sociales, de la Santé et de la Ville, November.

Commaille, J. (1996), *Misères de la famille, question de l'état*, Presses de la Fondation nationale des sciences politiques, Paris.

Commaille, J. (1997), *Les Nouveaux Enjeux de la question sociale*, Hachette, Paris.

Donzelot, J. (1986), 'La Fin des porteurs de pancartes', *Esprit*, March.

Donzelot, J. and Estebe, P. (1994), *L'État animateur. Essai sur la politique de la ville*, Éditions Esprit, Paris.

Dubar, C. (1991), *La Socialisation. Construction des identités sociales et professionnelles*, Armand Colin, Paris.

Dubet, F. (1994), *Sociologie de l'expérience*, Seuil, Paris.

Elbaum, M. (1994), 'Pour une autre politique de traitement du chômage', *Esprit*, August-September.

Eme, B. (1990), 'Développement local et pratiques d'insertion', *Économie et humanisme*, no. 315, October-December.

Eme, B. (Collab. De Gardin, L. and Gounouf, M.F.) (1995), 'Le Travail, creuset de lien civil', in *Les Régies de quartier. Expérience et développements, regards de chercheurs*, Plan urbain, diff. La Documentation Française, Paris.

Eme, B. (1996a), *Les Constructions sociales de l'insertion par l'insertion par l'économique*, CRIDA-LSCI/CGP, ronéo IRESCO-CNRS.

Eme, B. (1996b), 'Politiques publiques, société civilçe et associations d'insertion par l'economique', in B. Roudet (ed.), *Des jeunes et des associations*, L'Harmattan, Paris.

Eme, B. (1996c), 'De quelques interrogations sur la création d'un troisième secteur d'activités', in B. Eme, L. Favreau, J.-L. Laville and Y. Vaillancourt (eds), *Société civile, état et économie plurielle*, CRIDA-LSCI/CRISES, Ronéo IRESCO-CNRS.

Eme, B. and Laville, J.-L. (1988), *Les Petits Boulots en question*, Syros, Paris.

---

[54] Commaille (1997), p. 133.

Eme, B. and Laville, J.-L. (1994), *Cohésion social et emploi*, Desclée de Brouwer, Paris.

Eme, B., Favreau, L., Laville, J.-L. and Vaillancourt, Y. (1996), *Société civile, état et économie plurielle*, CRIDA-LSCI/CRISES, ronéo IRESCO-CNRS.

Fourquet, F. (1989), *Richesse et puissance*, La Découverte, Paris.

Gautié, J. (1993), *Les Politiques de l'emploi. Les Marges étroites de la lutte contre le chômage*, Vuibert, Paris.

Gauthier, A. (1997), *Aux frontières du social. L'exclu*, L'Harmattan, Paris.

Giddens, A. (1987), *La Constitution de la société. Élements de la théorie de la structuration*, PUF, Paris.

Habermas, J. (1987), *Théorie de l'agir communicationnel*, vols I and II, Fayard, Paris.

Habermas, J. (1988), *Le Discours philosophique de la modernité*, Gallimard, Paris.

Ion, J. (1990), *Le Travail social à l'épreuve du territoire*, Privat, Toulouse.

Jellab, A. (1997), 'La Mission locale face aux jeunes. Quelle socialisation pour quelle insertion?', *Cahiers internationaux de sociologie*, vol. 102, January-July.

Juan, S. (1997), 'Les segmentations symboliques instituées et vécues', in A. Gauthier (ed.), *Aux frontières du social. L'Exclu*, Paris, L'Harmattan, 1997.

Madec, A. and Murard, N. (1995), 'Citoyenneté et politiques sociales', Flammarion, Paris.

Malglaive, G. (ed.) (1985), *Observation et évaluation du dispositif de formation des jeunes de seize à dix-huit ans*, vol. III, rapport national, Noisy-le-Grand, C2F-CNAM, ADEP.

Mollet, A. (n.d.), *Quand les habitants prennent la parole*, Plan construction, Paris.

Monaco, A. (1993), *L'Alternance école-production*, PUF, Paris.

Paugam, S. (1993), *La Société Française et ses pauvres*, PUF, Paris.

Perret, B. and Roustang, G. (1993), *L'Économie contre la société*, Seuil, Paris.

Pharo, P. (1985), *Le Civisme ordinaire*, Librairie des Méridiens, Paris.

Quéré, L. (1985), 'L'Expérience bretonne des pays en trois leçons', *Autogestions*, no 19.

Revue *Esprit* (1972), 'Pourquoi le travail social', no. 4-5, April-May.

Rosanvallon, P. (1993), 'L'État et les régulations sociales', *CFDT-Aujourd'hui*, no. 110, September.

Rosanvallon, P. (1995), *La Nouvelle Question sociale. Repenser l'état-providence*, Seuil, Paris.

Roudet, B. (1996), *Des jeunes et des associations*, L'Harmattan, Paris.

Sainsaulieu, R. (1996), *À propos du changement des institutions*, ronéo LSCI-IRESCO, Paris, June.

Sainsaulieu, R. (1998), *L'Identité au travail* (3rd ed.), Presses de la Fondation nationale des sciences politiques, Paris.

Sauvage, P. (1988), *Insertion des jeunes et modernisation*, Economica, Paris.

Schmid, G. (1995), 'Le Plein-emploi est-il encore possible? Les Marchés due travail transitionnels comme nouvelle stratégie dans les politiques d'emploi', *Travail et emploi*, no. 65, Paris.

Schnapper, D. (1989), 'Rapport à l'emploi, protection sociale et statuts sociaux', *Revue Française de sociologie*, XXX.

Schwartz, B. (1981), *L'Insertion professionnelle et sociale des jeunes*, La Documentation Française, Paris.

Supiot, A. (1994), *Critique du droit du travail*, PUF, Paris.

Tanguy, L. (1986), *L'Introuvable Relation formation-emploi*, La Documentation Française, Paris.

Touraine, A. (1991), 'Face à l'exclusion', *Esprit*, February.

Touraine, A. (1993), *Production de la société*, Seuil, Librairie générale Française (*livre de poche*), Paris (1st edn 1973).

Touraine, A. (1997), *Pourrons-nous vivre ensemble? Égaux et différents*, Fayard, Paris.

Weber, M. (1971), *Wirtschaft und Gesellschaft*, published as *Économie et société*, Plon, Paris (1st edn 1921; Pocket, 1995).

CONCLUSION

15 New Directions in a Plural Economy

JACQUES DEFOURNY, LOUIS FAVREAU
AND JEAN-LOUIS LAVILLE

Insertion through economic activity has no fixed model. It emerges from the interaction between local initiatives and more or less appropriate, experimental and innovative public policies, against the background of a decade, the 1990s, which saw a deterioration in the employment situation marked by persistent mass unemployment, poverty and loss of security for part of the working population. In simple terms, society is increasingly split into three large groups: employees in permanent legally regulated employment; a supply of labour moving in and out of employment, unemployment and training; and those out of work, some of whom face long-term unemployment. This major feature of the developed economies determines the extent of the challenge confronted by schemes for insertion through economic means, which arose mainly during the 1970s and 1980s against a very different background. Given that the crisis no longer appears to be a passing aberration, this requires the examination of the possibilities; taking the trends at work as a starting point, three approaches are apparent each proposing a different role for insertion through economic activity and the new social economy.

As indicated in the preceding chapter 'Third Sector and Social Economy Re-examined in the Light of Initiatives Promoting Insertion', the socio-economic regulations for insertion through economic activity have not yet stabilised, either in terms of internal operation or in relation to the environment. However, insertion through economic activity has passed the experimental stage and a number of patterns can be distinguished in the approaches adopted. This is not a matter of classifying national practices, but of underlining certain of their features in order to set out the terms of the debate regarding future developments. There are three possible directions:[1] forming an intermediate economy, setting up a socially useful sector, and building new relationships between solidarity and locality.

---

[1] All three of which may be present at the same time in the same country.

1. Forming an Intermediate Economy

In this approach, the aim of organisations for insertion is to prepare people for permanent work by providing work and training opportunities for a limited period. The intermediate economy option derives from the rationale of schemes for insertion through economic activity during the 1970s and 1980s. Although in the years before the recent crisis many of these insertion initiatives saw themselves as part of an alternative economy,[2] for the public authorities only recognised them when unemployment had become a persistent problem. At this point people began to question an approach to social work that rejected all forms of intervention in employment and that was restricted to individual support. Comments to the effect that this training too often led to nebulous qualifications[3] reached the institutions concerned. As a reaction against this traditional approach to training and social work, insertion through economic activity appeared as a way of getting people into work, whilst adding socialising and training values in an enterprise that was subject like others to market constraints. If it provided a real job and real training, as opposed to subsidised work and a trainee-ship divorced from the conditions of production within a company, an insertion post could prove to be a valuable springboard from which to find a normal job. Access to work for a transitional period is regarded as the best approach to social integration by way of occupational insertion.

However, official recognition of such initiatives proved difficult, because of the separation of policies for the different branches of the economy; this characteristic of the Fordist period was emphasised in the previous chapter: the market economy was regarded as of central importance and the major engine of job creation; the non-market or public economy had a corrective role and, through public service intervention, fulfilled those needs which the market did not supply, thereby providing a supplementary source of job creation. And the non-monetary economy based on reciprocity and mutual aid that sought to preserve or strengthen social bonds, was regarded as of residual importance and identified with invisible or subordinate economic forms such as the domestic or informal economies. From this perspective the emerging experiences of insertion through economic activity were reluctantly accepted only with regard to their non-market, non-monetary character.

This negative discriminatory approach to the new social economy was evident in several countries, e.g. in Great Britain, where the Conservative

---

[2] As Eme noted in his contribution.
[3] In the phrase used by Brinkmann, quoted in the case study on Germany.

government demonstrated an ideological preference for the capitalist enterprise, and in Sweden where worker co-operatives were regarded as ambiguous organisations. In Germany, too, there was no place for such organisations in traditional social partnership. As a result, some countries initially restricted the scope for action of bodies operating in the social economy. In Sweden, for example, the first insertion initiatives received no support from employment public policies for activities that could be performed by commercial organisations. In Germany, meeting the criteria of public utility in order to gain access to tax advantages restricted the development of economic activities. In Belgium, public service contracts imposed conditions that could not be met by non-profit associations[4] and in France voluntary organisations were historically only able to undertake economic activities if they submitted to public supervision.[5]

Though insertion organisations remain marginalised in countries such as Spain, they have made great strides in legitimacy given their original disadvantages. The popularisation of such initiatives, as indicated by their gradual recognition, has been helped by local pressure, and in several countries has led to the founding not only of co-operatives but also of limited companies in Spain or independent enterprises in Austria. This has also been assisted by wider social movements such as the alternative and environmental movements in Germany. Policies have thus moved on from protecting employment to creating jobs for the unemployed, particularly through re-orienting social work and training towards economic activities. In the end, public authorities were forced to pay attention to the increasing numbers of new organisations; legislative and regulatory measures began to appear, but not without some hesitations. In Germany, the general term BQG refers to a variety of different companies for employment and qualifications in different regions, but all had the common aim of reintegrating the unemployed into paid work: this included companies for the promotion of work, employment and structural development in former East Germany (*ABS*), social enterprises in Lower Saxony, and enterprises for job creation in Berlin. In France insertion enterprises and intermediate voluntary organisations were recognised, whilst in Belgium regional authorities recognised various forms of organisation, in particular enterprises for on-the-job training. New legal statutes were even adopted to help the spread of such experiments in Italy: the social co-operatives, like

---

[4] Defourny (1994).
[5] See the part of the conclusion regarding the legitimacy of the associative sector in France by Laville and Sainsaulieu (1997).

the new 'company with a social purpose' in Belgium, are commercial companies that do not aim to generate profit for their members, since the influence of capital in decision making is limited and the distribution of profits is restricted by a ban on distributing reserves. These measures establish a coherent body of regulations relating to the social economy, including for those initiatives where the aims are broader, as in the case of social co-operatives that serve the interests of the whole community as well as their members.

These initiatives have had no real influence on the unemployment statistics, but they have demonstrated their usefulness in helping hard-to-place[6] unemployed people back onto the road to work and in providing opportunities for them to access work outside the sheltered employment sector.[7] Their credibility is strengthened thanks to a civic and social entrepreneurial approach that introduced both private and public sources of finance, contributing to eliminating the fatal division between efficient enterprises and the solidarity-based realm of the welfare state.[8] Often, however, self-financing through commercial income can only be achieved at the cost of lowering wage levels to an extent that can be self-defeating. This was the fate of *Fergulsie Park Community Holdings Ltd*,[9] a Glasgow community enterprise that had to close because the wages it paid were lower than the income available to local people on the black market. To avoid this poor outcome, experiments have been initiated with a dual form of production – market, through goods and services traded in the market, and non-market, through provision of integration and training services, where payment for non-market services is from the public authorities. This can be seen in German regional employment programmes where companies for job creation and training received partial subsidies for their wage costs, in Belgium (Flanders) and in France through the public financing of insertion posts, and in Italy and Belgium through social charge exemptions for disadvantaged workers. According to the available data, public contributions come in various forms (60% of total charges for socio-economic employment schemes in Austria; 8.4% in subsidies and 53.6% in contracts with local authorities for social co-operatives in Italy) and are at supportable levels, as shown by studies carried out in the province of

---

[6] In the term used by Erhel *et al.* (1996) quoted in the Introduction.

[7] Cf. Ballet (1997).

[8] Rosanvallon (1995), pp. 190–191.

[9] Laville and Gardin (1997).

Trento, in France and in Wallonie.[10] The cost is lower than for most public measures to aid employment and training; the windfall and substitution effects are lower in insertion enterprises than in others because their target group is the long-term unemployed; and they produce social and fiscal gains while avoiding social expenditure.[11]

In such an intermediate economy, for the purposes of internal regulation the beneficiaries – who are only temporary – are regarded as probationers who must adjust to the limitations of the enterprise. Even if, in some cases, they may become involved in higher level responsibilities in the organisation of production, the fact that they are not full members of the organisation can lead to problems of motivation.[12] The social networks promoting these organisations are perceived as providing support but over time the dominant support role is devolved to the manager-entrepreneur. These enterprises try to become more mainstream, moving closer to private for-profit companies and entering the market economy. This can even lead to a suppression of all reference to the social economy, as can be seen in several texts issued by the *Comité national des entreprises d'insertion* (CNEI) in France during the 1980s, advocating the use of standard commercial, rather that associative, legal forms.

This approach has produced results. The fear of unfair competition, ever present in France and Germany during the early days of insertion through economic activity, has been followed by partnerships with local employers seeking to integrate insertion initiatives into inter-enterprise alliances stimulated by local industrial systems. Formalised relationships with local authorities and professional groups have established the rules of the game for price competition, and given priority to the recruitment of people in need of integration. Conversely, some large enterprises have been able to use insertion enterprises as subcontractors enabling them to support reintegration without becoming directly involved and without changing their approach to human resources management.

Despite these results, the development of an intermediate economy that remains focused on insertion objectives is proving difficult since transaction costs are high, even crippling. To begin with, insertion organisations have to apply for finance under various different policies

---

[10] Dughera (1996); *Agenzia del Lavoro della Provincia Autonoma di Trento*, 1997; Defourny (1994); Gaussin (1997). Although these different studies reach similar conclusions, all stress the methodological difficulties and call for more detailed research.

[11] Cost-benefit calculations do not, however, exhaust the question of evaluating insertion initiatives (see Lefevre, 1997).

[12] According the theory set out in the contribution on Germany.

(employment, social, urban, business creation, aid to SMEs, etc.); thus they tend to suffer the effects of bureaucratic inefficiencies. Next, overall public investment is less than the enterprises need, particularly since pressures on public finances leads to insertion through economic activity being often the first to be threatened, both because of their recent and innovative character and their low numbers. This is the case in Germany, when employment and training companies have seen responsibility for their work passed from federal to local authorities.[13] When these initiatives are not hit by reduced financial support, stagnation can have damaging effects, as in the example of work-based training enterprises in Belgium, whose numbers have not increased despite strong demand. Establishing an intermediate economy thus requires a much broader revamping of the institutional framework. The proposed 'transitional' labour markets model forms such a project, capable of bringing together different public funds and linking with existing measures so that transitions (between part-time work and full-time work, between employment and self-employment, between unemployment and work, between work and training, between work and retirement), which are usually experienced as times of insecurity, can benefit from public regulation.[14] This kind of reformulation of public policies as a whole is what intermediate labour market organisations such as the British *Wise Group* and *Glasgow Works* have been calling for: they have a well-developed system for providing the unemployed with short-term jobs at 'normal' pay levels that could be increased tenfold through a national strategy.

However, even if employment policy is to be rethought globally linking together transitional labour markets, there remains the problem of helping the intermediate economy cope with the tertiarisation of productive activities. Viewing insertion as an intermediate phase avoids the questions posed by changes that are under way, because it rests on two implicit assumptions: the market economy is capable of absorbing the great majority of excluded people if they are properly trained; and a return to full employment could result from political will, which combines public intervention with a greater awareness of the issues from corporate leaders. These two assumptions must be questioned in the light of ominous trends emerging in today's economy.

---

[13] The situation has not stabilised, the relevance of support for 'jobs through innovation' is being assessed at federal level, which could lead to new responsibilities for the national authorities.

[14] Schmid (1995), pp. 5–17. In French, some prefer to use *'transitionnels'* rather than *'transitoires'* to describe these markets (see Gazier, 1997).

The basis for economic growth has been through activities that are standardisable in industries and services.[15] Standardisable services are in market services, such as banking, insurance and telecommunications, and public services such as administration, where codifiable information can be processed, enabling them to follow an industrial type of development with significant increases in productivity. However, hardly any jobs are now created by standardisable industries and services. Most industrial sectors lost jobs during the 1980s, and standardisable services, such as in banking, faced with similar demands for competitiveness in more open national markets, are now forced to undergo similar changes or have already done so. The outsourcing of high-status services (advisory services, advertising, other professional services) and lower-status services (cleaning, security) only explains these changes in part. In actual fact, even though the industries with the greatest increases of productivity are losing fewest jobs, the formula according to which today's investments are tomorrow's jobs no longer holds true. This change in the nature of productive activities presents corporate leaders with conflicting obligations, and the awareness of the damage caused by unemployment runs up against the constraints of international competition.

In short, the insertion economy, viewed as an intermediate economy,[16] remains dependent on employment demand from enterprises. It cannot single-handedly overcome the difficulties arising from the tertiarisation of the economy. When these problems are considered in relation to persistent large-scale unemployment, it is legitimate to ask if it is realistic to hold fast to the principle of short-term insertion activities leading to real jobs[17] in the market economy.

This means that insertion through economic activities has to develop a strategy with regard to newly emerging activities if it is to avoid merely shuffling the dole queue. In other words, it must pay particular attention to areas such as personal and collective services (education, health, social services, other services to individuals, etc.). These services have stable productivity because they are based on a direct relationship between the producer and the consumer, and are therefore in a position to create the jobs that sectors with rapidly increasing productivity are unable to provide. If these sources of jobs are to fulfil their potential, it will be necessary to solve the problems of matching supply and demand, enabling potential

---

[15] Baumol (1987); Roustang (1987).

[16] Rosanvallon (1994).

[17] The question asked by Elbaum (1994).

users to afford these services and structuring the supply. Furthermore, there may be problems due to the profile of individuals in need of integration not necessarily matching the requirements of such services. An option, fully consistent with the idea of the intermediate economy, consists of waiting for the market economy to generate these personal service jobs so that they can then be offered to people needing integration. But this raises another major issue for society: to what extent is it possible to commercialise personal and collective services that have a special characteristic of a close social relationship with users, and how does this change the nature of every day life?[18]

2.   Setting up a Socially Useful Sector

Another option for future development may be defined. Given that a major upturn in job creation in the market economy seems to be unlikely or undesirable, one can attempt to develop a completely new role for the public-sector economy. Since some people are likely to be out of work in the long term, the approach aims to develop a new sector of activities specifically for them. The sector thus developed is socially useful in a double sense: the goods and services produced, even though they may be for individual consumers, are of community interest, and the jobs created support the integration of particularly disadvantaged people.

One response, from social players and public authorities alike, to the difficulties raised by integrating certain types of people into work is to extend the scope of sheltered employment. This has happened in Belgium (particularly in Flanders), Spain, Italy, the United Kingdom and Sweden, where solutions have been found for people with no hope of work due to rising unemployment, who in some cases are regarded as unemployable: single mothers, ethnic minorities, people without literacy skills or with a criminal record, young people from difficult family backgrounds, alcoholics, drug addicts, etc. The capacity for popular innovation is illustrated by the growth in the United Kingdom of little co-operatives with an average of five workers; these co-operatives are set up in services or trade and are assisted in their development by relatively independent support structures, the success of which led Sweden to adopt this model when establishing their own co-operative development agencies (LKU). In

---

[18] These questions cannot be discussed here. For personal services provided locally, see Laville (1993, 1998) and Giddens (1994).

1992 the LKU had supported the creation of 300 co-operatives providing 1300 jobs, at a cost per job of a third of the average.

Compared to the first option of forming an intermediate economy, this approach represents a greater attempt at democratisation, since most of the promoters are themselves experiencing great difficulties. However, the problems encountered in the process can lead to demands for special status for disadvantaged people rather than economic insertion. A 'social disability' category for disadvantaged people may emerge alongside the recognised categories of physically and mentally disabled people. This trend can be seen in the demands by the Spanish Association of Rehabilitation Groups in the Social Economy, for the recognition of 'incapacity for work' as a social disability. Certainly a legal definition of the people to be helped means that people would not be selected on the basis of their past experiences, but the risk is that this would produce a labour market rigidly serving excluded people, with stigma as an inescapable consequence.

The socially useful sector could be initiated by deliberately targeting specific groups, but it could also result from reintegration difficulties in enterprises. Instead of being in itself an objective, it could be the unintended consequences of misapplied public measures. Thus in Germany the 'second labour market', which was originally conceived as a bridge towards the first market has instead become a closed sector. This echoes what has happened in the quasi-public insertion sector in France,[19] formed on the basis of intermediate jobs that have become long-term, as in Belgium. In Austria, measures against this were taken relating to pay and the nature of the work in the '*Aktion 8000*' programme for the long-term unemployed; at the end of it, two-thirds of the people taken on were still employed by the host organisation. In some instances, as in Spain, in order to find work for people unable to get jobs in other enterprises, schemes that were intended as transitional moved towards job creation, and became indistinguishable from schemes aimed at providing permanent employment for certain groups.

The status of the job seems to be the critical factor in establishing whether these strategies for permanent job creation involve accepting an erosion of employment conditions or provide access to the labour market for people who would otherwise remain excluded. And if we are to assess the risks of substitution, it is important to know whether new or existing activities are involved. These are the two aspects stressed by analysts who

---

[19] Eme (1994).

conceptualise a socially and environmentally useful third sector in which employing bodies/agencies could benefit from double subsidies:[20] grants and tax exemptions (on social security contributions or taxes). These independent social agencies would act as providers of community or social services and pay unemployed people to carry out these tasks.[21]

The internal regulation of these organisations is determined by their desire to establish a right to work, since work is seen as the vehicle of an enriching social identity. Their internal arrangements are thus designed to effect a fresh approach to social policy. They try to give practical effect to this right to work, which would remain a non-starter without entrepreneurial intervention; but because of this social concern, they risk becoming too closely allied to the social sector, and isolated from other enterprises. Rather than orienting towards the market economy, they look for their main partners in the non-market economy, with public authorities who are requested to subsidise the low productivity inherent in their operation. As has happened in Italy, negotiations may lead to legislation defining disadvantaged people and give them rights to exemptions from social charges when employed. Reality is likely to run ahead of such administrative definitions, and the socially useful sector can also lead to confusion between new activities and insertion. If financial support for insertion becomes necessary in order to balance the books, the investment needed for viable activities in new economic fields may be displaced in favour of a strategy 'on the cheap'; and this could soon run into trouble, especially in services to individuals, where users' trust is of paramount importance.

Focusing on target groups may also lead to a sector for keeping excluded people occupied, which occurs in countries that have broadly closed the gaps with the wage earning classes thanks to the social treatment of unemployment. Whilst, as noted in the Introduction, insertion through economic activity and the social treatment of unemployment are distinct approaches (one being bottom-up, the other top-down), political and administrative pressures have encouraged them to come closer together. Organisations for insertion through economic activities have often been urged, by local authorities among others, to increase their capacity even if this has meant adopting employment contracts deviating from conventional

---

[20] Lipietz (1997), pp. 265–279.
[21] Rosanvallon (1995), p. 193; Pierre Rosanvallon refers in this connection to an intermediate economy, but he appears to have in mind the institutionalisation of a socially useful sector through these agencies.

requirements. This has led to a partial overlap between schemes for insertion through economic means and the treatment of unemployment, particularly through the increasing adoption of an intermediate status between benefit and work. Although the starting point was different for each type of scheme, it is now sometimes difficult to distinguish the two. Developing a special sector for the unemployed can dissolve the specific features of insertion through economic activity if it becomes a quasi-public sector of long-term insecure jobs. And it raises the question: what kind of progress or future plans can people make in a sector designed to give work to unemployed people, but with no chance of reintegrating into normal employment?

Basically, what we are beginning to see in the socially useful sector is perhaps not so much a reorganisation of social policies as a redefinition of them. The ideology of 'workfare' is emerging in plans for the reform of social programmes in several developed countries, guaranteeing income in return for work or training; this is seen as a way of activating the passive expenditure of social assistance and unemployment benefit,[22] for instance in the United Kingdom. This option has fed the debate on local employment agencies (ALE) in Belgium and the sanctions at one time envisaged for people refusing a job offered through these agencies. Insertion has many meanings, but to some public authorities it is almost regarded as obligatory work. However, it cannot really be seen as such, for it rests on commitments and obligations between the individual and society, or on a dual principle: the right to an income and the right to integration.[23] Integration tries to replace the feelings of guilt experienced by people on social security by establishing a new link between rights and duties in which active citizens have a right to participation and a right to be socially useful. Individuals thus have 'positive duties'[24] that are quite different from the *quid pro quo* implied by 'workfare'. But although the underlying principle is certainly different, in practice it may be hard to distinguish if the insertion contract is individual, if it is concluded between parties the disparity of whose positions is obvious, and if it appears that belonging to society, which comes naturally to some citizens, is regarded as a contractual procedure for others.[25] To conclude, changes in social policy can greatly influence insertion initiatives: these organisations have so far

---

[22] Normand (1996), pp. 86–89 and pp. 109–135.
[23] Morel (1996).
[24] Rosanvallon (1995), p. 179.
[25] Eme and Laville (1996).

relied on voluntary participation of disadvantaged people, but this feature of their operations is being called into question, because of the way in which a socially useful sector is established, and how the duties of the beneficiaries are defined.

3.   Building New Relationships between Solidarity and Locality

A third voluntarist approach has emerged, to avoid over-reliance on social policy, drawing on the original spirit of the social economy, in its attempt to establish new relations between economic and social forces.

With regard to internal regulation, emphasis is placed on involvement in civic life.[26] Employment is one, but not the only, expression of citizenship. And active citizenship is as eagerly sought as job creation. It is a matter of addressing both together – increasing opportunities for democratic socialisation as well as the supply of labour, tackling the crisis in social integration through work and the crises in civil and civic bonds. The insertion schemes aim to bring democracy to life in the everyday world, enabling everyone to express their views directly regardless of status (employee, voluntary worker, user, etc.), as for example in the social co-operatives of Italy. This means regarding the beneficiaries of insertion as active members of the enterprise, whose goal is thus understood as a common good that members provide for themselves and others. The outcomes go further than employment; they include developing new activities, influencing both the psycho-social and the socio-economic dynamic through measures that are based on making the best possible use of existing abilities rather than exposing the inadequacies and failings of groups and individuals. This nevertheless presents difficulties of evaluation.

With regard to external regulation, the economic practices associated with insertion initiatives, because of their social, cultural and political embeddedness, have links with not only with the market and the non-market economy, but also with the non-monetary economy. In other words they mobilise resources of voluntary work to contribute not just to their start-up but to their long-term operations. Voluntary work and job creation are not incompatible but complementary, and this aspect is reinforced through the local or territorial basis of insertion initiatives and the actions of local people helping develop it. Neighbourhood management

---

[26] 'Civic urbanism', in Eme's phrase.

associations, '*Régies de quartier*', for instance, cannot be seen purely in terms of their job-creation capacity; their work also involves developing citizenship, and the presence of voluntary workers helps them to maintain civic linkages.[27] The creation of temporary jobs, leading to permanent jobs, can be achieved by measures based on the dynamics of socialisation and through support for local enterprises in difficulty. The community economic development corporations (CDEC) in Canada (Québec) and North America operate in this way; they are springboards for co-ordination, collaboration and solidarity for insertion in the context of local development.[28] Their structures attempt to provide occupational integration without neglecting support for community activities based on unpaid work, such as community kitchens.[29]

Such schemes demonstrate a desire to combine initiative and solidarity, and so prompt a political rethink of the economy. Thus they echo the multiple forms of associationism that have led to the social economy, and they demand a power to act in the economy that is independent of capital. These schemes revive the perspective of a solidarity-based economy[30] that was blurred historically in the social economy by the ascendancy of the economic over the political.[31] However, building on citizens' voice and restructuring the various elements of the economy to develop original solutions is often seen as a threat by the existing powers.[32]

The dual political dimension of a solidarity-based economic perspective, which is based on the direct involvement of stakeholders and rethinking the economy, attracts such resistance that it cannot make progress without establishing a balance of power through links with social movements. This is the advantage enjoyed by the Canadian (Québec) initiatives that can draw support from civil society initiatives such as the *Forum for Jobs* run since 1989 by representatives of employers, trade unions and the voluntary sector and supported by organisations from the women's movement. The influence of social movements can also be seen in the National Trade Union Confederation's support for developing a solidarity-based economy.[33] Their weight and significance was such that at the *Summit on the Economy and Employment* called by the Québec

---

[27] Eme (1994).
[28] Favreau (1994), pp. 166–175.
[29] Noraz (1996).
[30] For a historical approach, see Laville (1994).
[31] Laville (1999a,b).
[32] See the views of A. Berger (1997).
[33] Aubry and Charest (1995).

government in March 1992, women's groups and the community movement were invited alongside the traditional partners (politicians, employers and trade unionists). A decision was taken to set up a working group on the social economy that stimulated a broad nationwide debate on the issue.[34] With a similar concern to protect the autonomy and promote the recognition of these organisations, the financial institutions set up by civil society can help projects achieve success through their credit activities. Examples such as *Fondaction*, created by one of the two major trade unions, and the community funds that achieve a balance between maximising profitability and the need for local and regional development[35] in Québec, *Credal and Hefboom* in Belgium, the *Caisse régionale solidaire* in Nord-Pas-de-Calais in France show that local savings are available for such investments.

Once micro-economic structures have been set up, it is important to organise them both around a locally constructed development model and at a broader more global level. Taking account of the different stakeholders involved and the necessary mix of market, non-market and non-monetary resources requires new structures for representation and negotiation. It is no longer just a matter of making jobs accessible, but of defining an institutional context for establishing new socio-economic organisations through second level organisations together with appropriate forms of local governance. In the United Kingdom such organisations have helped to promote co-operative enterprises in an unfavourable environment; they have provided support and financial assistance for start-ups and have acted as mediators in relationships with the many public partners. In Sweden, support organisations have also coordinated wage negotiations, like in Italy where the national *consorzi* (support organisation) negotiated an appropriate collective agreement with trade unions. Italian national and regional *consorzi* play key roles in providing technical assistance (training, advisory services, etc.) as well as representing their member organisation interests; this is also the case in France, where the national committee of neighbourhood management associations (*Régies de quartier*) provides these same services for its member associations. Without aiming for an alternative socio-economic system, these insertion initiatives accept that their development requires multiple negotiations to influence the conditions imposed on them. The outcome of these negotiations is undoubtedly always uncertain, but the further development of these initiatives requires

---

[34] Levesque and Ninacs (1996).
[35] Levesque *et al.* (1997).

collaboration between networks of stakeholders and the public authorities for the progressive development of medium-term solutions.

From declining public finance, and failed partnerships, to competition between new social economy and public authority insertion initiatives: there is no shortage of risks. However, an emphasis on support structures like the Canadian CDEC or French *Régies de quartier* that bring together various interests avoids a narrow management strategy, where each element is separated from its territorial and social base. From the perspective of a solidarity-based economy, this type of intermediary organisation evolves through its inter-dependence with the whole changing socio-economic framework. This can produce, as in Québec, local bodies for co-ordination and localised social negotiation. Within these organisations, the requisite types of co-operation may be developed to encourage the integration of finance for economic activities, training and employment within a geographical area, and to establish a democratic framework for the distribution of public funds amongst the structures. This can produce, as in Québec, local bodies for co-ordination and localised social negotiation, notably the community economic development corporations that bring together representatives of trade unions, enterprises, and groups of voluntary organisations, and which manage development funds for disadvantaged communities.

Because of their local base and their plural composition, these kinds of local development institutions have governance capabilities that allow new forms of collective negotiations outside enterprises. This can bypass two problems with public finance: on the one hand the rejection of initiatives caused by the inflexible application of standardised funding criteria by public administrations, and on the other the development of clientelism when the allocation of funds is entirely devolved to local authorities. It is hoped that these support organisations with local governance capabilities can make allocation more appropriate to the particular features of local projects.

Regarding the groups targeted, there must be an open local debate that can genuinely take account of the different contexts, in order to avoid the undesired side-effects of *a priori* controls or tendencies for selection where controls are lacking.

With regard to employment, public support has diverse aims, i.e. some is directed towards creating insertion posts that are seen as temporary or *ad hoc* jobs, whilst others include permanent jobs. Since both may be relevant, public intervention should adopt an approach that respects the varied nature of projects and apply support procedures appropriate to both types of insertion schemes, i.e. for temporary and permanent employment.

The intersectoral co-ordination and the networking of local schemes make it easier to finance investment in the early phases of development. These features also make it easier to secure the long-term objective of permanent jobs with high professional standards under ordinary legislation, rather than an intermediate status between employment and unemployment. The link with the voluntary sector in this case is more likely to demonstrate proof of local commitment rather than recourse to voluntary work due to a lack of resources. If the balance between jobs and voluntary work is to remain flexible, it is important to stress the validity of these two approaches to social action (intersectoral co-ordination and networking of local schemes), rather than reduce them to a mass of 'meaningless jobs' or 'under-employment'. The more the needs of the economic activities are taken into account, the more it becomes possible to avoid confusion with addressing only the social aspects of unemployment. Respecting the differences between activities is also a critical factor: some initiatives may be very labour intensive, while others have little impact in terms of jobs but are crucial in terms of social linkages; and these differences may be complementary within a particular community.

According to this approach, for insertion by economic activities to achieve an acknowledged status, and the social economy to fulfil its potential, it is necessary to replace a target-based based approach with a transversal approach where the initiatives of the new social economy become one element in the development of local potential. Therefore, the form this takes varies widely from place to place. However, there is limited experience of this approach, building new relations between solidarity and locality, and several difficulties may be mentioned:

(a) Difficulties in the dynamics of participation: treating the beneficiaries as active members is far from easy with some people, either because they do not themselves wish it, or because their brief time within the enterprise does not provide a basis for such participation.

(b) Difficulties developing an entrepreneurial approach that is at least partly market-oriented in its focus, in a sector that has inherited a public financing culture based on lobbying and negotiation with the public authorities. It is hard to learn to live by market forces when still relying on subsidies. This is the painful lesson of a number of pilot insertion enterprises in Belgium.

(c) Difficulties in operating between two institutions (the market and the state), since they have developed their own distinctive practices and rules, and they tend to reject or crush unusual bodies. Accusations of unfair competition or rampant privatisation of public services by voluntary organisations are clear examples of this.

(d) Difficulties in finding appropriate legal structures for activities that are readily seen as too commercial to qualify for traditional voluntary organisation status but that are not sufficiently self-financing to risk commercial company status. The new form, 'company with a social purpose', recently introduced in Belgium but so far little used, demonstrates the problems of finding a balance between these two extremes.[36]

(e) Difficulties in persuading public policy to take a transversal approach when powers and budgets are compartmentalised, thereby favouring only a sectoral approach and the targeting of specific groups of people or power struggles between public officials.

4. Democratisation and a Plural Economy

Each of the three approaches discussed above raises concerns that both lend legitimacy and reduce their scope.

The intermediate economy perspective relies on legislative measures and it is particularly sensitive to the need to avoid stigmatising the beneficiaries of insertion. However, in confusing the importance of legislation and the market economy it fails to acknowledge the structural changes in productive activities in today's economies that are strongly internationalised with rapidly expanding service sectors. It suggests that the goal for everyone, after a period of insertion, should be recruitment in a private enterprise, without realising that many such enterprises are caught in a mesh of constraints that prevent them, for the foreseeable future, from returning to the recruitment levels of the post-war boom years.

The vision of a socially useful sector draws its strength from its desire not to abandon the most disadvantaged people but to enable them to play a part in the economic sphere, seen as essential to their social integration. Consequently it focuses on setting up a new form of public or non-market economy only accessible to certain people; thus it faces the problems of

---

[36] Defourny *et al.* (1996).

identifying this target group in a rapidly changing society, and the risks of isolation in a sector of the economy that is generally regarded as merely palliative and thereby constantly undermined.

The vision of building new relationships between solidarity and locality seeks to extend the range of possible measures by combining the three economic dimensions: market, public, and non-monetary. But this use of approaches and resources that are normally kept separate constantly comes up against institutional structures from the past. For this reason it remains hampered by limitations such as the risk of parochialism, activism, and a compartmentalised approach to experimentation, all exacerbated by separation from the organisations of the traditional social economy.

These three approaches have evolved from different perspectives, but it is important not to set them against each other in an unreasonable fashion. The target groups for insertion initiatives are too varied, and the challenges too complex to ignore the value of a range of diverse approaches. However, instead of recognising their complementarity and acknowledging their limitations, one could regard these approaches as clashing, leading to conflict between actors and partners. Rather than popularising measures for integration through economic activities, such attitudes are likely to undermine and restrict it. Furthermore, the institutional partners may choose to focus on certain aspects of insertion through economic activity to the detriment of others. This has indeed already happened; in some countries, the public authorities' response to these initiatives has greatly restricted the range of possibilities and, because of the technical nature of criteria used by financial sponsors, has often made this an area reserved for specialists. Every country, for its own historical reasons, has chosen to focus on certain aspects of insertion through economic activity. In France, for example, self-organised initiatives and those aiming to provide permanent employment have no access to the finance for insertion posts that other initiatives have been able to obtain from employment and social affairs ministries. Insertion through economic activity seems therefore likely to fragment into a number of areas following different paths. This will only make it more difficult to open up a broad debate in society and it is reminiscent of the centrifugal forces that characterised the social economy in the 19th century.

However, despite the variety of perspectives and a degree of fragmentation in the world of integration initiatives, these approaches are all against reducing the economy simply to the market. They share an awareness that the market is not enough to ensure that everyone can be socially integrated through work. Whilst recognising the importance of belonging to the market economy, they retain one foot in the public-sector economy. They cannot provide a regular integration service unless the public authorities reward them for this service, or else they are prepared to cope with severe financial problems. This dichotomy may be reconciled through an appeal to solidarities that normally take the form of locally based non-monetary economy. In contrast to the slide towards a market society, i.e. a society solely regulated by market forces, these practices invoke a plural economy[37] in which the market, though it plays a central role, is not the only force at work. It is within this plural economy, taking into account the various elements (market, non-market and non-monetary) of the real economy, that they can fight against large-scale exclusion that is incompatible with democracy.

This implicit or explicit reference to a plural economy, however, produces more conflicts than consensus. Discussions within the European Union on tax exemptions for companies with a social purpose or the inclusion of integration clauses in public service contracts show that the choice between a market society and a plural economy is one of current concern; this raises the possibility of positive discrimination for structures that internalise the social costs externalised by most enterprises. And reconciling participative democracy in the operation of initiatives with a plural approach to the economy is not easy: there is a paradox between maintaining access to internal discussion, and the use of expertise that is required to manage these initiatives in their relations with the outside world.

Despite all this, it is through this underlying conception of a plural economy and the response it produces that the importance of insertion initiatives far exceeds their impact in terms of turnover and employment. Despite being heavily influenced by trends outside their control, and repeatedly encountering resistance, they are playing their part in refashioning the social state. As their presence, which remains modest, increases with time, it is possible to conclude by suggesting that these initiatives, while remaining at once independent and rooted in partnership, may contribute to new solutions to the crises of exclusion, unemployment and the welfare state. They are not an isolated phenomenon. They stand at the crossroads of the state and civil society, of economic and social interests, of local and national levels, without losing sight of the need for increasing their visibility internationally. In doing so they represent a sort

---

[37] Territorial Development Service (1996).

of springboard for the transformation of the economy and social affairs throughout society, and for extending social and economic democracy.

References

Agenzia del Lavoro della Provincia Autonoma di Trento (1997), 'Monitorragio en valutazione dell'attivita el Progitto II dell Agenzia del Lavoro della Provincia di Trento', Trento, mimeo.

Aubry, F. and Charest, F. (1995) *Développer l'économie solidaire - élements d'orientation*, Confédération des syndicats nationaux (CSN).

Ballet, J. (1997), *Les Entreprises d'insertion*, PUF, Paris.

Baumol, W.-J. (1987), 'Microeconomics of unbalanced growth: the anatomy of the urban crisis', *American Economic Review*, June.

Berger, A. (1997), 'Qui doit définir les activités à développer?', in G. Aznar, A. Caillé, J.-L. Laville, J. Robin and R. Sue (eds), *Travail, activité, revenus pourtous? Vers l'économie plurielle*, Syros, Paris.

Defourny, J. (ed.) (1994), *Développer l'entreprise sociale*, Fondation Roi-Baudouin, Brussels.

Defourny, J., Simon, M. and Van Pachterbeke, I. (1996), *L'Entreprise d'insertion en Wallonie. Premières leçons de sept projets-pilotes*, Fondation Roi-Baudouin, Brussels.

Dughera, J. (1996), 'Coût et avantages de l'insertion par l'économique', Rapport à l'instance d'évaluation de l'insertion par l'économique, Commissariat Général du Plan.

Eme, B. (1994a), *Entre économie et territoire: des régies de quartier, creuset de lien civil*, CRIDA-LSCI, CNRS-IRESCO, Paris.

Eme, B. (1994b), 'Insertion et économie solidaire', in B. Eme and J.-L. Laville (eds), *Cohésion sociale et emploi*, Desclée de Brouwer, Paris.

Eme, B. and Laville, J.-L. (1996), 'L'Intégration sociale entre conditionnalité et inconditionnalité', *Revue des affaires sociales*, no. 3/96.

Elbaum, M. (1994), 'Les Activités intermédiaries: une sphère d'insertion autonome et un mode de partage du travail par défaut', *Travail et emploi*, October.

Erhel, C., Gautier, J., Gazier, B. and Morel, S. (1996), 'Job opportunities for the hard to place', in G. Schmid *et al.* (ed.), *International Handbook of Labour Market Policy and Evaluation*, Edward Elgar, Cheltenham.

Favreau, L. (1994), 'L'Approche du développement économique communautaire au Québec et aux états-unis', *Revue des études coopératives, mutualistes et associatives (RECMA)*, no. 253–254 (51–52), Paris.

Favreau, L. and Levesque, B. (1997), *Développement économique communautaire: économie sociale et intervention*, Presses de l'Université du Québec, Sainte-Foy.

Gaussin, C. (1997), 'Analyse multidimensionnelle du coût des entreprises de formation par le travail en Wallonie', *Les Cahiers du CERISIS*, 97/3a, Université Catholique de Louvain – Centre de recherche interdisciplinaire pour la Soldarité et l'Innovation Sociale, Charleroi.

Gazier, B. (1997), *Plein-emploi, régimes d'emploi et marchés transitionnels: une approche comparative*, Colloque de l'Association d'économie politique, Montréal, 24–25 October.

Giddens, A. (1994), *Beyond Left and Right. The Future of Radical Politics*, Polity Press, Cambridge.

Laville, J.-L. (1993), *Les Services de proximité en Europe*, Syros, Paris.

Laville, J.-L. (1994), 'Économie et solidarité: esquisse d'une problématique', In J.-L. Laville (ed.), *L'Économie solidaire, une perspective internationale*, Desclée de Brouwer, Paris.

Laville, J.-L. (1998), *Services de proximité: la construction sociale d'un champ d'activités économiques*, CRIDA-LSCI, CNRS-IRESCO, Paris.

Laville, J.-L. (1999a), 'The future of work', *The Welfare Society in the 21st Century*, 39, Institute for Applied Social Research, Fafo, Norway.

Laville, J.-L. (1999b), *Une troisième voie pour le travail*, Desclée de Brouwer, Paris.

Laville, J.-L. and Sainsaulieu, R. (1997), *Sociologie de l'association*, Desclée de Brouwer, Paris.

Laville, J.-L. and Gardin, L. (eds) (1997), *Les Initiatives locales en Europe. Bilan économique et social*, CRIDA-LSCI, CNRS, Paris.

Lefevre, C. (1997), 'Un modèle multidimenstionnel de la qualité de vie', *Les Cahiers du CERISIS*, 97/3b, Université Catholique de Louvain – Centre de recherche interdisciplinaire pour la Solidarité et l'Innovation Sociale, Charleroi.

Levesque, B. and Ninacs, W.-A. (1996), *L'Économie sociale au Canada: l'expérience québecoise*, Document de réflexion pour le colloque: stratégies locales pour l'emploi et l'économie sociale, OCDE, Montréal, 17–18 June.

Levesque, B., Mendell, M. and Van Kemenade, S. (1997), *Profil socio-économique des fonds de développement local et régional au Québec*, Étude réalisée pour le Bureau fédéral de développement régional, Ottawa, Ministére des approvisionnements et services, Canada.

Lipietz, A. (1997), *La Société en sablier. Le Partage du travail contre la déchirure sociale*, La Découverte, Paris.

Morel, S. (1996), 'France et états-unis: les politiques d'"insertion" et de "work-fare" en matière d'assistance sociale', *Les Cahiers du SET-METIS*, no. 96-01, CNRS-Université Paris I Sorbonne.

Noraz, C.A. (1996), 'Les Cuisines collectives, émergence d'une nouvelle pratique de développement économique communautaire', *Économie et solidarités*, vol. 28, no. 1, Presses HEC, Montréal.

Normand, B. (1994), 'Le Projet Québecois de l'employabilité et les organismes sans but lucratif: enjeux et interpellations', in L. Lamarche (ed.), *Emploi précaire et non-emploi: droits recherchés*, Éditions Yvon-Blais inc., Montréal.

Normand, B. (1996), 'Mesures d'insertion en emploi: deux visions opposées', *Relations*, April.

Rosanvallon, P. (1995), *La Nouvelle Question sociale. Repenser l'état-providence*, Le Seuil, Paris.

Roustang, G. (1987), *L'Emploi: un choix de société*, Syros, Paris.

Schmid, G. (1995), 'Le Plein-emploi est-il encore possible? Les Marchés du travail 'transitoires' en tant que nouvelles stratégies dans les politiques d'emploi', *Travail et emploi*, no. 65 (French translation).

Territorial Development Service (1996), *Reconciling Economy and Society. Towards a Plural Economy*, Organisation for Economic Co-operation and Development (OECD), Paris.

Index

For Product Safety Concerns and Information please contact our EU
representative GPSR@taylorandfrancis.com Taylor & Francis Verlag GmbH,
Kaufingerstraße 24, 80331 München, Germany

Printed and bound by CPI Group (UK) Ltd, Croydon, CR0 4YY
01/05/2025
01858351-0007